JOSHUA
JUDGES

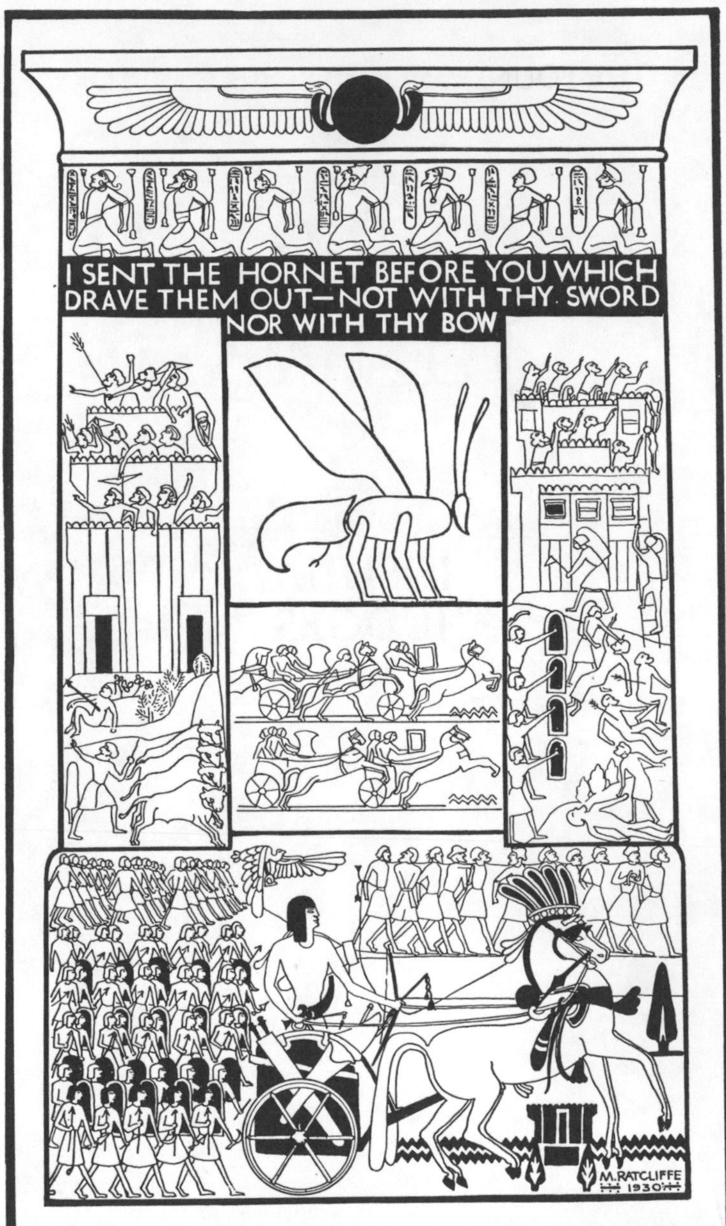

THE HORNET: Joshua xxiv. 12.

A Symbolic grouping of scenes from the Egyptian monuments of successive Pharaohs who pillaged Canaan and dismantled many of its fortresses.

See pp. 112, 259.

THE FOUNDATIONS OF BIBLE HISTORY

JOSHUA JUDGES

by

John Garstang

KREGEL PUBLICATIONS
Grand Rapids, Michigan 49501

Joshua-Judges by John Garstang

Library of Congress Cataloging in Publication Data

Garstang, John, 1876-1956.
Joshua-Judges

Reprint of the 1931 ed. published by Constable, London, under title: The foundations of Bible history: Joshua, Judges.
Includes index.
1. Bible. O.T. Joshua—Criticism, interpretation, etc. 2. Bible. O.T. Judges—Criticism, interpretation, etc. 3. Jews — History — To 953 B.C. 4. Palestine—Historical geography. I. Title.
BS1295.G35 1978 222.2'07 78-9518
ISBN 0-8254-2719-3

Printed in the United States of America

CONTENTS

THE SETTLEMENT OF THE TRIBES

THE TRIBES UNDER THE JUDGES

CONTENTS

PUBLISHER'S PREFACE

A trip to the Holy Land is out of reach for most Christians, even with the advent of jet travel and the package tourism. However, no Christian's knowledge of the geographical and archeological facts of the Holy Land need be found wanting now. There is no peer to this book and the treatment of the subject matter it covers.

The Books of Joshua and Judges have come under the critics' knife and the doubters' easel for centuries. With the coming of the archeological dig in the eighteenth century, the facts of these two books, with many others, have been confirmed and illuminated by the unearthed evidences.

The findings of archeology by men such as Garstang have given a new welling of faith in the Word of God. Also there is hope for even further finds that will continue to prove that God knew, and recorded, facts as they were, even though modern science may at sometime seem to disagree.

Mr. Garstang's chronolizing of the facts he discovered and his proof of the validity of the historical record of Joshua-Judges will be a faith-booster to many a weary Christian. Too long have we heard the doubters broadcast their information and left their statements unanswered. Now, here is the book of ammunition that will silence those doubters.

For the serious Bible student, this book is a must. With its sectioned format and the wealth of maps and charts, there is no stone left unturned on the subject dealt with. The book is well indexed and the subject matter is easily found.

The average Christian will find here a treasure of well-mined gems, the study of which will root his faith ever deeper and cause a well of greater faith to spring up in his heart.

THE PUBLISHERS

PREFACE

Of recent years Palestine has been the scene of an unparalleled activity in archaeological investigation, and the results throw light in particular upon the Books of Joshua and Judges. The Bible text contains, as all know, perplexing discrepancies. None the less, the historic sites and walled cities which the writer had the privilege of visiting repeatedly while excavation was in progress, during the seven years that he directed the British School of Archaeology in Jerusalem and the Department of Antiquities in Palestine, impressed him deeply with a sense of material reality underlying the historical narrative. The impression, however, eluded definition, until at last he decided to examine separately the archaeology of those passages which are now generally recognised by scholars as the oldest elements. The result was so full of promise that he returned to Palestine in 1928 to examine the problem further in this light. Every identified site mentioned in the oldest sources (J, E and JE) of the Books of Joshua and Judges was revisited; while three selected cities, Jericho, Ai and Hazor, were examined more thoroughly with the spade. The impression now became positive. No radical flaw was found at all in the topography and archaeology of these documents. Moreover, a study of the subject-matter shows that these old portions of the Books contain after all the core of the historical narrative, and are relatively free from discrepancies, giving a straightforward and fairly continuous account of the sequence of events. The difficulties of chronology also, which have long perplexed students, are eliminated, as they arise only with the inclusion of the later elements. On the other hand, the chronological outline will be seen to fit into the known history of the period as derived from the records of Egypt, which ruled the country as an essential part of its empire in Syria almost throughout the whole time covered by the narrative.

The present volume aims at elucidating the history in the Books upon these lines. Happily it is now possible to replace the fanciful pictures of other days by photographs and other scientific materials. The results of piecing together the threads of evidence in this way will probably astonish many readers; and it has convinced the writer, after years of study, that not only were these records in general founded upon fact, but they must have been derived from earlier writings, almost contemporary with the events described, so detailed and reliable is their information.

In regard to the structure of this volume, each Section has been made as far as possible self-contained. This has involved a certain amount of reduplication, which it is hoped will be more than compensated by the increased convenience of reference. On the other hand, it is not the purpose of the book to cover again ground already made familiar by abler pens, such as Sir George Adam Smith's in *The Historical Geography of the Holy Land*; nor has it been deemed necessary to re-argue old questions such as the date of the Exodus: the reader will find this point fully treated in Prof. Peet's *Egypt and the Old Testament*, and the whole field of discussion surveyed in Mr. Jack's work, *The Date of the Exodus*.

The literature of the subject being inexhaustible, our references are confined for the most part to current books and journals. But it is not possible to overlook the earlier contributions in the *Memoirs* and *Quarterly Statements of the Palestine Exploration Fund*, the *Revue Biblique*, the *Palästina-Jahrbuch*, and the *Zeitschrift des Deutschen Palästina-Vereins*; nor such masterpieces of pioneer study as the T.R. Père Vincent's *Canaan d'après l'Exploration Récente*, and Prof. Macalister's *Excavations at Gezer*. The writer greatly regrets that he could not get sight of that valuable and now rare book, *Le Livre des Juges*, par Le P. Marie-Joseph Lagrange, in time to make adequate reference to it in the notes.

In the hope that this volume may prove helpful to

teachers and students, standard text-books have been selected for current reference, such as the editions of the Cambridge Bible for Schools and Colleges, by the Rev. G. A. Cooke, D.D.; and Dr. S. A. Cook's articles in the *Cambridge Ancient History*. With two exceptions the Biblical spelling of place names has been retained; in the case only of Ashkelon and Taanach the forms Askalon and Taanak have been adopted from their Egyptian and Arabic equivalents for convenience of pronunciation. The text of the Books, as translated in the Revised Version, according to the sources J and E, is quoted fully, so far as useful for the reader's purpose, in the Introductory Section; and this privilege is due to the courtesy of the University Presses of Oxford and Cambridge. Grateful acknowledgment is made also to the Palestine Exploration Fund and to the British School of Archaeology in Jerusalem, for permission to make use of the plans of excavated sites described in the Appendix, and to the publishers of the late Canon Burney's *Book of Judges*, Messrs. Rivington, for permission to reprint a good part of that scholar's translation of the Song of Deborah.

Among other helpers whom the author desires to thank in particular are his sister, Mrs. Robert Gurney, and his friend the Rev. Phythian-Adams, who from start to finish have given unsparingly their time and help to the criticism and construction of this book and to the reading of the proofs. Miss Gertrude Levy and Miss Mabel Ratcliffe have furnished the drawings; and Miss D. Vaughan has assisted in the preparation of the Appendix and the Index. The photographs reproduced in this volume have all been taken personally by the writer. That of Tell el Harbaj on Pl. LXIII has already appeared in *Bulletin II* of the British School in Jerusalem, which body, through its chairman, Professor J. L. Myres, kindly authorises its reproduction. The writer takes this opportunity of expressing his appreciation of the cordial spirit of collaboration on the part of the French and

American Schools in Jerusalem, in the persons particularly of the Very Rev. Pères Abel, Dhorme, and Vincent, and of Dr. Albright, which so greatly heartened his own work during the memorable years he spent with them in Palestine. The formal acknowledgment of their publications in the footnotes is but a sparse recognition of the help and inspiration he received from them in person.

The identification of the Egyptian Yenoam with Tell Abeidiyeh proposed by Mr. Phythian-Adams, and that of Lachish with Tell el Duweir proposed by Dr. Albright, seem to the writer on examination of the sites so completely to suit the various contexts to these names that he has adopted them without further question.

Finally and chiefly, to Sir Charles Marston, to whom this volume is dedicated, are due both gratitude and esteem, not only because of his generous co-operation, which has provided the means of carrying out many of the investigations described in these pages, both those superintended by the writer and the work of others, but also because of the unfailing interest with which he has followed the progress of this book, giving the writer with equal generosity the help of his criticism and ripe experience.

JOHN GARSTANG

Institute of Archaeology,
University of Liverpool.

PLATES

APPENDIX

MAPS

FIGURES IN THE TEXT

PLANS IN THE APPENDIX

BOOKS OF REFERENCE AND ABBREVIATIONS

ABBREVIATIONS

Adam-Smith, *H.G.*	SIR GEORGE ADAM SMITH: The Historical Geography of the Holy Land. London 1896.
Kn. (No....)	KNUDTZON, J. A.: Die El Amarna-Tafeln. Leipzig 1915.
B, *AR*. or Breasted, *Anct. Rec.*	BREASTED, J. H.: Ancient Records of Egypt. Chicago 1927.
Breasted, *Hist.*	BREASTED, J. H.: A History of Egypt. New York 1910.
Burchardt, *Fremdw.*	BURCHARDT: Altkanaan. Fremdworte. Leipzig 1902.
Burney, *Judges.*	BURNEY, C. F.: The Book of Judges. London 1918.
C.A.H.	Cambridge Ancient History (1924-5).
Charles, *Bk. of Jubilees.*	CHARLES, R. H.: Apocrypha and Pseudepigraphia of the O.T., vol. ii. Oxford 1913.
Cooke, *Jos.*	Cambridge Bible, Joshua. Ed. by Rev. G. A. COOKE, D.D. 1918.
Cooke, *Jud.*	Cambridge Bible, Judges. Ed. by Rev. G. A. COOKE, D.D. 1918.
G. 1928, etc.	Year of the writer's investigations.
Gardiner, *Pap. Anast.* I	GARDINER, A. H.: The Papyrus Anastasi I and the Papyrus Koller (Egyptian Hieratic Texts, I). Leipzig 1911.
G., *H.E.*	GARSTANG, J.: The Hittite Empire. London 1929.
Lepsius, *Denk.*	LEPSIUS, C. R.: Denkmäler. Ägypten und Äthiopien. Berlin.
Müller, *Asien.*	MÜLLER, W. M.: Asien und Europa nach Altägyptischen Denkmälern. Leipzig 1893.
P., *L.I.A.*	Pottery specimens at the Liverpool Institute of Archaeology.
Saarisalo, Bound. Issach. and Naph.	SAARISALO, A.: The Boundary between Issachar and Naphtali. Helsinki 1927.
Sethe, *Urkunden.*	SETHE, K.: Urkunden der 18 Dynastie, iii. Leipzig 1907.
Weber, *Anmerk.*	WEBER, O.: Notes in Knudtzon Amarna Letters (*q.v.*), vol. ii.
Winckler, *T.A.L.*	WINCKLER, G.: Tell el Amarna Letters. Berlin 1896.
LXX.	Septuagint.

ARABIC WORDS IN FAMILIAR USE

Ain, Spring; *El*, the; *Khurbeh*, ruin; *Nahr*, river; *Tell*, mound; *Wady*, valley, or watercourse usually dry.

In pronunciation the final letter of *el* is often assimilated to the following consonant, and that of *Khurbeh* becomes *t* before a vowel. Thus El Deir is pronounced *Ed-Deir*, and Kh. el Kefireh *Khurbet e'Kefireh.*

JOURNALS

Ann. Am. S.O.R.	Annual of the American Schools of Oriental Research.
Bull. Am. S.O.R.	Bulletin of the American Schools of Oriental Research, 1922 *sqq*.
Bull. B.S.A.J.	Bulletin of the British School of Archaeology, Jerusalem 1922 *sqq*.
J.E.A. or *Journ. Eg. Arch.*	Journal of Egyptian Archaeology (Egypt. Expl. Soc.). London.
J.P.O.S.	The Journal of the Palestine Oriental Society, Jerusalem, 1921 *sqq*.
Liv. AA.	Liverpool Annals of Archaeology: Institute of Archaeology, University of Liverpool.
Mus. Journ. Phil.	The Museum Journal (Quarterly), Philadelphia, Pa.
P.E.F., Q.S.	Palestine Exploration Fund, Quarterly Statement.
P. J-B.	Palästina-Jahrbuch.
Rev. Assyr.	Revue d'Assyriologie et d'Archéologie Orientale, Paris 1904 *sqq*.
R.B. or *Rev. Bibl.*	Revue Biblique. Journal of the École Biblique de St. Étienne. Jerusalem, N.S. 1904 *sqq*.
Z.A.T.W.	Zeitschrift für die alttestamentliche Wissenschaft und die Kunde des Nachbiblischen Judentums. Giessen 1929.
Z.D.M.G.	Zeitschrift der Deutschen Morgenländischen Gesellschaft.
Z.D.P.V. or *Zeits. Deut. Pal. Ver.*	Zeitschrift des Deutschen Palästina-Vereins. Leipzig.
Zeits. f. Assyr.	Zeitschrift für Assyriologie. Berlin and Leipzig, N.S. 1924 *sqq*.

INTRODUCTION

THE BOOKS OF JOSHUA AND JUDGES

ANALYSIS OF THE TEXT

It will be the purpose of this work to test the Foundations of Bible History by comparing the oldest portions of the Bible narrative with the archaeology and known history of the Land.

The selection of the passages to be examined is not arbitrary, but conforms with the accepted results of Textual Analysis, about which the following brief explanation is offered to those not familiar with this field of study.

The received text of the Bible contains numerous discrepancies, of which examples can be found in the opening chapters of the Book of Judges. Thus the first verse makes it appear that the events subsequently narrated came to pass after the death of Joshua; but the death and burial of Joshua are described in the second Chapter (vv. 8, 9), as occurring after those events. Another illustration appears in the allusion to the capture of Jerusalem (i. 8) which is in disagreement with verse 21 and contradicts the statement of Joshua xv 63. Thus:

Joshua xv 63.	Judges i 8.
63 As for the Jebusites the inhabitants of Jerusalem, the children of Judah could not drive them out. [J]	8 And the children of Judah fought against Jerusalem and took it and smote it with the edge of the sword. [P]

Discrepancies of this kind and other textual difficulties have led scholars to examine closely the literary and grammatical structure of the text, which is found to be a composite production and the growth of centuries. The original nucleus of the Book is found to comprise two independent strains of tradition, which are believed to have been set down in writing during the ninth and eighth centuries B.C., and in part welded together during the seventh century B.C. The symbols used to denote these elements in the text are J, E, and JE respectively. These old documents were grouped, amplified and explained from a national and religious standpoint in the sixth century by the Deuteronomic School (D) under which the Bible began to take connected form. Then ensued the Exile, during and after which the Book was further supplemented and edited from the point of view of the organised priesthood, [P] in the light of more recent political developments. Thus the O.T. did not gain its final form until about the second century B.C. Even so, no surviving Hebrew version of the text can be attributed to an earlier date than the end of the first millenium A.D. Earlier copies exist of the Greek rendering, known from the circumstances of its translation as the Septuagint (abbreviated as LXX) which was begun at Alexandria about the middle of the third century B.C., and may thus preserve the original form or meaning of various passages better than the Massoretic or standard Hebrew text.

In this volume we consider only the recognisably early elements of the Book, namely J, E and JE, as these refer most nearly to contemporary events and seem to have survived the subsequent redactions without radical modification. It must not be supposed that we reject the later elements D and P as unhistorical; on the contrary, each is found to enfold information derived from earlier sources; but their precise historical value and relevance is a more complex question, involving also a wide and searching archaeological investigation. We simply lay them aside for the time being, and deal with those which may be rightly claimed as the foundation of the Bible narrative. Nor do we find it necessary to draw a fine distinction between the early elements of the text, and we adopt accordingly a simpler set of symbols than are usually employed by the Critics.[1] Thus as regards the early Documentary Sources:

J denotes that part of the narrative, distinguished by the use of the divine name YAHWEH, which preserves chiefly the traditions of Judah and took written form during the ninth century, possibly about 850 B.C. E denotes that part of the narrative in which the divine name is rendered Elohîm (God): this took form apparently about 750 B.C. and seems to embody more particularly the traditions of Ephraim. E2 is used especially to denote the somewhat later origin of most of the Book of Judges, which took form about 700 B.C. JE denotes the narrative in which portions of J and E were combined, probably in the first half of the seventh century B.C. between 700 and 650 B.C.

[1] Cf. Burney : *Israel's Settlement in Canaan* (1918). p. xi.

All later additions and redactions are covered in this book by two symbols, D and P. D represents the sixth century redaction of the existing earlier text (J, E, JE and E2) by the school which prepared the Book of the Law, the nucleus of Deuteronomy, promulgated about 620 B.C. P denotes the late editorial work and additions of the legalistic priestly school during and after the exile, the process not being completed until about 200 B.C. Other annotations and additions of unknown origin are known as Glosses and indicated as such by the initial letters Gl.

The narrative in the Book of Joshua may be divided into two chief parts,[1] namely the accounts of campaigns led by Joshua, which are largely based upon the early sources J and E, amplified in some obvious instances by D, and the partition of the land, in which the early elements J and E are almost hidden among the amplifications of D and by the later explanatory but largely anachronistic details introduced by P.

Chapters i and ii deal with Joshua's appointment and preparations. In chapter 1 v. 1-2 are attributed to E; vv. 3-9 to D; vv. 10-11 to E; vv. 12-18 to D. In Chapter ii vv. 1-9^a are ascribed variously to J and E (as detailed in our quotations below);[2] vv. 9^b-11 to D; vv. 12-24^a variously to J and E, and v. 24^b to D.

Chapters iii and iv describe the moving of the camp of the Israelites across the Jordan from East to West. In Chap. iii v. 1 is ascribed to JE, vv. 2-4 to D; 5 to JE; vv 6-9 to D; v. 10^a to JE; v. 10^b to D; vv. 11-17 to JE. In Chap. iv, vv. 1-8 are attributable to J and E; vv. 9-10 to D; v. 11 to E; v. 12 to D; v. 13 to P; v. 14 to D; vv. 15-17 to P; v. 18 to JE; v. 19 to P; v. 20 to JE; vv. 21-24 to D.

Chapters v and vi describe the sacrifice of Jericho to Jehovah. In Chap. v, v. 1 is ascribed to D; vv. 2-3 to J; vv. 4-8^a to D; vv. 8^b-9 to J; vv. 10-12 to P; vv. 13-15 to J; In Chapter vi, vv. 1-2 are ascribed to JE; vv. 3-17 to J and E; v. 18 to D; v. 19 to P; vv. 20-24^a to J and E, 24^b to P; 25-26 to J; v. 27 to D.

Chapters vii and viii describe the destruction of Ai. In Chap. vii, v. 1 is ascribed to P; vv. 2-5^a to J; 5^b to D; vv. 6-7^a to J; v. 7^b to D; vv. 8-10 to J; vv. 11-12 variously to J and D; vv. 13-15^a to J; v. 15^b to D; vv. 16-18^a to J; v. 18^b to P; vv. 19-23 to J; v. 24 to D and P; v. 25 to J, D and P; v. 26 to

[1] Cf. Cooke, *Joshua* (*Camb. Bible* 1918), pp. xii-xxxii.

[2] Suffixes ^{a} and ^{b} attached to verse number in these schedules of analytical details indicate the first and second portions of the verse in question: a third part would be indicated in like manner by a suffix ^{c}.

J. In Chap. viii, vv. 1-2 are ascribed variously to J and D; vv. 3-26. to J and E; vv. 27-28 to D; v. 29 to J; vv. 30-35 to D.

Chapters ix and x describe the Relief of Gibeon. In Chap ix, vv. 1-2 are ascribed to D; vv. $3\text{-}9^a$ to J and E; vv. 9^b-10 to D; vv. 11-16 to J and E, 15^b to P; vv. 17-21 to P; v. 22 to E; v. 23 to J; vv. 24-25 to D; v. 26 to J; v. 27 jointly to P, J and D;. In Chap. x, v. 1-7 are ascribed to J and E, 1^b to D; v. 8 to D; vv. $9\text{-}12^a$ to J and E; v. 12^b to D; vv. $13\text{-}14^a$ to J; 14^b-15 to D; vv. $16\text{-}19^a$ to J; 19^b-20 to D; vv. 21-24 to J; v. 25 to D; vv. $26\text{-}27^a$ to J; v. 27^b to P; vv. 28-43 to D.

Chapter xi describes the Fall of Hazor; v. 1 is ascribed to J; vv. 2-3 to D; vv. 4-7 to J; v. 8 to J and D jointly; v. 9 to J; vv. 10-23 to D.

Chapter xii is devoted to a summary of Joshua's victories and is ascribed entirely to D; vv. 1-6 may usefully be compared with the older account in Judg. ii, vv. 16-26 (E2).

Chapter xiii describes the Division of the Land: v. 1 is ascribed to J; vv. 2-6 to D; v. 7^a to J; vv. 7^b-12 to D; v. 13 to J; v. 14 to D; vv. 15-33 to P.

Chapter xiv is devoted chiefly to the claim of Caleb for an inheritance with the Israelites, vv. 1-5 are ascribed to P; vv. 6-15 to D.

Chapter xv describes the tribal movement of Judah and Simeon with Caleb in the South. Vv. 1-13 are ascribed to P; vv. 14-19 to J; vv. 20-62 to P; v. 63 to J.

Chapters xvi and xvii deal with the settling of Ephraim and Manasseh in the Centre. In Chap. xvi, vv. 1-3 are ascribed to J; vv. 4-9 to P; v. 10 to J. In Chap. xvii, vv. 1-10 are ascribed to P; vv. 11-18 to J.

Chapters xviii and xix deal with the other tribal portions chiefly in the north. In Chap. xviii v. 1 is ascribed to P; vv. 2-6 to JE; v. 7 to D; vv. $8\text{-}10^a$ to JE; v. 10^b to D; vv. 11-28 to P. In Chap. xix vv. 1-46 are ascribed to P; v. 47 to J; vv. 48-51 to P.

Chapters xx and xxi, dealing with the Cities of Refuge and the Levitical cities, are ascribed to P (xxi vv. 43-45 D).

Chapter xxii describes the dismissal of the Eastern tribes to their inheritance across Jordan and the dispute which arose out of their construction of an altar in their land, vv. 1-8 are ascribed to D; vv. 9-34 to P.

Chapter xxiii contains Joshua's (first) farewell and is ascribed to D.

Chapter xxiv contains Joshua's farewell. V. 1 is ascribed to E and D; vv. $2\text{-}7^a$ to E; v. 7^b to D; vv. $8\text{-}11^a$ to E; v. 11^b to

D; vv. 11^c-12^a to E; v. 12^b to D; v. 13 to D; vv. 14-17^a to E; v. 17^b to D; vv. 17^c-22^a to E; v. 22^b to D; vv. 23-30 to E.; v. 31 to D; vv. 32-33 to E.

The text of all the early passages (J, E and JE) from the Book of Joshua, as translated in the Revised Version, is quoted below in full, by permission of the University Presses of Oxford and Cambridge. The Sources are indicated as assigned by Professor S. A. Cooke in the Cambridge Bible for Schools and Colleges.

The Book of Judges is found to be more homogeneous in structure, though on the whole less ancient in composition.[1] The opening chapters, however, are composite and reduplicate to some extent passages scattered through the latter part of the Book of Joshua.[2] The last five Chapters are more complex in structure, and their subject matter, unlike the rest of the Book, claims no specified place in the history of The Judges.

Chapter i deals with the separate efforts of the tribes to settle. V. 1^a, which is at variance with ii 8, is ascribed to P; vv. 1^b-3 to J; v. 4 to P; vv. 5-7 to J; vv. 8-10^a to P; vv. 10^b-17 to J; v. 18 to P; vv. 19-36 to J.

Chapter ii is chiefly concerned with the death of Joshua and the subsequent backslidings of the Israelites. V. 1^a is attributed to J; vv. 1^b-5^a to P; 5^b to J; vv. 6-11 to E; v. 12 to D; vv. 13-14^a to E; vv. 14^b-15 to D; vv. 16-17 to E; vv. 18-19 to D; vv. 20-21 to E; v. 22 to D; v. 23 to J.

Chapter iii introduces the first Judges Othniel and Ehud, and also Shamgar Ben Anath who saved Israel from the Philistines. V. 1^a is ascribed to D; 1^b to P; v. 2^a to J; 2^b to P; v. 3 to D; v. 4 to E; v. 5^a to J; v. 5^b to JE; v. 6 to J; vv. 7-8 to E2; v. 9 to E2 and P; vv. 10-15^a to E2; vv. 15^b-29 to JE; v. 30 to E2; v. 31 to an editorial or copyist's gloss.

Chapter iv describes the oppression of Israel by Sisera and the deliverance by Barak inspired by Deborah. With the exception of short glosses, *e.g.* vv. 5 and 11^b, the whole of the narrative as far as v. 22 is ascribed to E, and the two concluding verses, 23-24, to E2.

Chapter v, Deborah's triumph song, describing the political significance of the victory, is based on very old tradition and is

[1] Cf. particularly Burney, *Judges*, pp. xxxvii-xlix; also Cooke, *Judges* (*Cambr. Bible*), pp. xiii-xxiv.

[2] See especially Sects. 10-12, pp. 201-237.

attributable in its present form to E. The first verse may be due to JE, and last line of v. 31 to E2.

Chapter vi describes the Midianite oppression and the call of Gideon. Vv. 1-6 are ascribed to JE; vv. 7-10 to E2; vv. 11-24 to J; vv. 25-32 to E2; v. 33 to E; v. 34 to J; v. 35 to E, JE E2 jointly; vv. 36-40 to E.

Chapter vii describes the rout of the Midianites by Gideon. V. 1 is ascribed to JE and E jointly; vv. 2-7 to E2; v. 8^a to JE; v. 8^b to E2; vv. 9-15 to E; v. 16 to J and JE; v. 17^a to J; v. 17^b-18^a to E; v. 18^b to JE; v. 19^a to E; v. 19^b to JE; vv. 20-21 jointly to J and JE; v. 22 to E; v. 23 to E (with a gloss) and to J; v. 24 to J; v. 25 jointly to J and JE.

Chapter viii describes the pursuit of the Midianites in Transjordania. Vv. 1-3 are attributed to J; vv. 4-21 to E; vv. 22-23 to E2; vv. 24-27^a to E; 27^b to E2; v. 28 to E2; v. 29-32 to P and E; vv. 33-35 to E2.

Chapter ix narrates the relations of Abimelech with the men of Shechem. Vv. 1-16^a are ascribed to E; vv. 16^b-19^a to JE; vv. 19^b-21 to E; v. 22 to E and JE jointly; vv. 23-25 to E; vv. 26-41 to J; v. 42 to JE; vv. 43-56 to E.

Chapter x introduces two minor Judges followed by the Ammonite oppression. Vv. 1-2, referring to Tola, and vv. 3-5, relating to Jair, are ascribed to P; v. 6 to E2 with an insertion by P; v. 7^a to E2; v. 7^b to JE; v. 8^a to E2; 8^b to JE; v. 9^a to JE; v. 9^b to E2; vv. 10-11^a to E2; v. 11^b to P; v. 12^a to P; vv. 12^b-16 to E2; v. 17^a to JE; v. 17^b to E; v. 18 to JE.

Chapter xi is concerned with Jephthah, including a reminiscence of the Israelites' earlier passage through Trans-Jordania. V. 1^a is ascribed to J; vv. 1^b-2 to P; vv. 3-4 to J; v. 5^a to a gloss; vv. 5^b-11 to J; vv. 12-13 to E and JE; v. 14^a to E; v. 14^b to JE; v. 15^a to E; v. 15^b to JE; vv. 16-25 to E; v. 26 to E and JE[1]; v. 27^a to E; v. 27^b to JE; v. 28 to E and JE; v. 29 to J; v. 30 to E and JE; v. 31 to E and JE; v. 32^a to JE; v. 32^b to J; v. 33^a to J and E; v. 33^b to E2; vv. 34-36^a to E; v. 36^b to JE; vv. 37-40 to E.

Chapter xii concludes in vv. 1-7 the narrative of Jephthah, ascribed to J; v. 7^a to JE and 7^b to P. Thereafter references are introduced by P to three minor Judges, namely Ibzan, vv. 8-10; Elon, vv. 11-12; and Abdon, vv. 13-15.

Chapters xiii-xvi are mostly based on old legends of Samson's adventures among the Philistines. In Chap. xiii v. 1 is ascribed to E2; vv. 2-3^a to J; v. 3^b to a gloss; vv. 4-5^a to J; v. 5^b to JE;

[1] See p. 58 on the reference to 300 years in v. 26.

vv. 6-25 to J with two brief glosses. In Chap. xiv vv. 1-15 are all attributable to J but for short glosses; vv. 16-18 to J; v. 19^a to a gloss; v. 19^b to J; v. 20 to J. Chap. xv vv. 1-19 is ascribed to J; v. 20 to E2. Chap. xvi vv. 1-31^a to J; v. 31^b to JE.

Chapters xvii-xxi constitute a sort of Appendix to the narrative of the Book; they embody two groups of tribal traditions without indication of their historical setting. The origins of their present form and even the sources of their different elements have formed the subject of much discussion; but the critics are mostly agreed in recognizing numerous glosses and retouches by late hands.[1] Chapters xvii-xviii describe the migration of the tribe of Dan to the north. In Chap. xvii vv. 1-4 are ascribed to E with glosses by P; v. 5 to J; v. 6 to P; v. 7 to E and J; v. 8 to J and JE; vv. 9-11^a to J; vv. 11^b-12^a to E; vv. 12^b-13 to J. In Chap. xviii v. 1 is ascribed to P and J; vv. 2-12^a to J and E; v. 12^b to P; v. 13 to J; v. 14 to E and JE and P; v. 15 to E and JE; vv. 16-17^a to E (glossed ?); v. 17^b to JE and P (glossed ?); v. 18 to J, JE and P; v. 19 to J; v. 20 to JE and J; vv. 21-28^a to J; v. 28^b to P and J; v. 29 to J and P; v. 30 to E (glossed ?); v. 31 to E.

Chapters xix-xxi describe an outrage at Gibeah and the punishment of Benjamin by the other tribes of Israel. In Chap. xix v. 1 is ascribed to P, J and E; v. 2 to J and E; v. 3 to J; v. 4 to E and J; v. 5 to E, J and JE; vv. 6-7 to J and E; v. 8 to JE and J; v. 9 to J and E; v. 10 to E, P and J; vv. 11-12 to J; vv. 13-14 to E; vv. 15-30 to J. Chapters xx-xxi are more complex, embodying the elements of two differing traditions, some of which are undoubtedly very ancient, with the traces of an unknown hand [X], apparently of post-exilic date.[2] Chap. xx v. 1 is ascribed to X and P; v. 2 to P; v. 3^a to X; v. 3^b to P; vv. 4-10 to P; v. 11 to J; vv. 12-13 to P; v. 14 to X; vv. 15-18 to P; v. 19 to X; v. 20 to J; v. 21 to X; v. 22 to J and P; vv. 23-24 to X; v. 25 to J, X and P; vv. 26-28 to X and P; v. 29 to J; v. 30 to X; v. 31 to P and X; v. 32 to X; vv. 33-34 to J and X; v. 35 to X and P; v. 36 to X and J; vv. 37-44^a to J; v. 44^b to P; v. 45^a to X; v. 45^b to P; v. 46 to P; v. 47 to P, X and J; v. 48 to J. In Chap. xxi v. 1 is ascribed to J; vv. 2-5 to P; v. 6 to X; v. 7 to J and P; v. 8^a to J; v. 8^b to P; v. 9 to P; v. 10 to J and P; v. 11^a to P; v. 11^b to J; vv. 12-13 to J and P;

[1] See Driver, *Introd. to the Lit. of the O. T.* (1913), pp. 168 ff.

[2] See especially Burney, *Judges*, pp. 445 ff., who made an exhaustive analysis of text and subject matter. These schedules are based upon his conclusions.

v. 14^a to J; vv. 14^b-16 to P ; vv. 17-19^a to X; v. 19^b to P; vv. 20-24^a to X; v. 24^b to J; v. 25 to P.

Selected passages from the early sources of the Book of Judges having a national aspect or a special topographical interest are quoted below. The foregoing schedule will enable the reader to satisfy himself that the omissions do not involve important topographical or archaeological questions. Exception must be made of the last three chapters of the Book of Judges, which do not fit into the historical sequence of the narrative, and reflect a more advanced stage of national organisation than is disclosed by the earlier chapters: they can be more usefully examined in their proper setting. The Sources for the Book of Judges, as shown in the margins, are taken for the most part from the late Canon Burney's *Book of Judges* (1918).

THE TEXT OF JOSHUA AND JUDGES

According to the Earliest Sources J, E and JE as translated in the Revised Version.

THE CAMPAIGNS LED BY JOSHUA

(JOSHUA I.-XI.)

JOSHUA'S APPOINTMENT AND PREPARATIONS

JOSHUA i. *Joshua appointed leader*

1 Now it came to pass after the death of Moses the servant E
of the Lord, that the Lord spake unto Joshua the son of
2 Nun, Moses' minister, saying Moses my servant is dead;
now therefore arise, go over this Jordan, thou, and all this
people, unto the land which I do give to them, even to the
children of Israel.

Preparations to strike camp

10 Then Joshua commanded the officers of the people saying, E
11 Pass through the midst of the camp, and command the
people, saying, Prepare you victuals; for within three days
ye are to pass over this Jordan, to go in to possess the land,
which the Lord your God giveth you to possess it.

JOSHUA ii. *Spies visit Jericho*

1 And Joshua the son of Nun sent out of Shittim two men J
as spies secretly, saying, Go view the land, and Jericho.
And they went, and came into the house of an harlot
2 whose name was Rahab, and lay there. And it was told
the king of Jericho, saying, Behold there came men in
hither to-night of the children of Israel to search out the
3 land. And the king of Jericho sent unto Rahab, saying,
Bring forth the men that are come to thee, which are E
entered into thine house: for they be come to search out J
4 all the land. And the woman took the two men, and hid E
them; and she said, Yea, the men came unto me, but I J
5 wist not whence they were: and it came to pass about the
time of the shutting of the gate, when it was dark, that the
men went out: whither the men went I wot not: pursue

6 after them quickly; for ye shall overtake them. But she E
had brought them up to the roof and hid them with the J
stalks of flax, which she had laid in order upon the roof.
7 And the men pursued after them the way to Jordan unto E
the fords: and as soon as they which pursued after them
8 were gone out, they shut the gate. And before they were J
9 laid down, she came up unto them upon the roof; and she
said unto the men, I know that the Lord hath given you
12 the land, and that your terror is fallen upon us. . . . Now
therefore, I pray you, swear unto me by the Lord, since
I have dealt kindly with you, that ye also will deal kindly
13 with my father's house, and give me a true token: and that
ye will save alive my father, and my mother, and my E
brethren, and my sisters, and all that they have, and will
14 deliver our lives from death. And the men said unto her, J
Our life for yours, if ye utter not this our business; and it
shall be, when the Lord giveth us the land, that we will
15 deal kindly and truly with thee. Then she let them down E
by a cord through the window: for her house was upon the ?
16 town wall, and she dwelt upon the wall. And she said E
unto them, Get you to the mountain, lest the pursuers
light upon you; and hide yourselves there three days,
until the pursuers be returned: and afterward may ye go
17 your way. And the men said unto her, We will be guilt- ?
less of this thine oath which thou hast made us to swear.
18 Behold, when we come into the land, thou shalt bind this J
line of scarlet thread in the window which thou didst let
us down by: and thou shalt gather unto thee into the
house thy father, and thy mother, and thy brethren, and E
19 all thy father's household. And it shall be, that whosoever J
shall go out of the doors of thy house into the street, his
blood shall be upon his head, and we will be guiltless: and
whosoever shall be with thee in the house, his blood shall
20 be on our head, if any hand be upon him. But if thou
utter this our business, then we will be guiltless of thine
21 oath which thou hast made us to swear. And she said,
According unto your words, so be it. And she sent them
away, and they departed: and she bound the scarlet line
22 in the window. And they went, and came unto the E
mountain, and abode there three days, until the pursuers
were returned: and the pursuers sought them throughout
23 all the way, but found them not. Then the two men
returned, and descended from the mountain, and passed
over, and came to Joshua the son of Nun; and they told

24 him all that had befallen them. And they said unto E
Joshua, Truly the Lord hath delivered into our hands all
the land. . . .

THE ADVANCE ACROSS JORDAN

JOSHUA iii. *The camp moved*

1 And Joshua rose up early in the morning, and they JE
removed from Shittim, and came to Jordan, he and all the
children of Israel; and they lodged there before they
passed over.

The Crossing of the Jordan

5 And Joshua said unto the people, Sanctify yourselves for JE
10 to-morrow the Lord will do wonders among you. And
Joshua said, Hereby ye shall know that the living God is
11 among you. Behold, the ark of the covenant of the Lord
12 of all the earth passeth over before you into Jordan. Now E
therefore take you twelve men out of the tribes of Israel,
13 for every tribe a man. And it shall come to pass, when JE
the soles of the feet of the priests that bear the ark of the
Lord, the Lord of all the earth, shall rest in the waters of
Jordan, that the waters of Jordan shall be cut off, even the
waters that come down from above; and they shall stand
14 in one heap. And it came to pass, when the people
removed from their tents, to pass over Jordan, the priests
that bare the ark of the covenant being before the people;
15 and when they that bare the ark were come unto Jordan,
and the feet of the priests that bare the ark were dipped in
the brink of the water, (for Jordan overfloweth all its banks
16 all the time of harvest), that the waters which came down
from above stood, and rose up in one heap, a great way off,
at Adam, the city that is beside Zarethan: and those that
went down toward the sea of the Arabah, even the Salt Sea,
were wholly cut off: and the people passed over right
17 against Jericho. And the priests that bare the ark of the
covenant of the Lord stood firm on dry ground in the
midst of Jordan, and all Israel passed over on dry ground,
until all the nation were passed clean over Jordan.

JOSHUA iv

1 And it came to pass, when all the nation were clean passed JE
over Jordan, that the Lord spake unto Joshua, saying,
2 Take you twelve men out of the people, out of every tribe

3 a man, and command ye them saying, Take you hence out JE
of the midst of Jordan, out of the place where the priests'
feet stood firm, twelve stones, and carry them over with
you, and lay them down in the lodging place, where ye
4 shall lodge this night. Then Joshua called the twelve E
men, whom he had prepared of the children of Israel, out
5 of every tribe a man: and Joshua said unto them, Pass over
before the ark of the Lord your God into the midst of
Jordan, and take you up every man of you a stone upon
his shoulder, according unto the number of the tribes of
6 the children of Israel: that this may be a sign among you, ?J
that when your children ask in time to come, saying,
What mean ye by these stones? then ye shall say unto
7 them, Because the waters of Jordan were cut off before the
ark of the covenant of the Lord; when it passed over
Jordan, the waters of Jordan were cut off: and these stones
shall be for a memorial unto the children of Israel for ever.
8 And the children of Israel did so as Joshua commanded, and J
took up twelve stones out of the midst of Jordan, as the
Lord spake unto Joshua, according to the number of the
tribes of the children of Israel; and they carried them over
with them unto the place where they lodged, and laid them
11 down there. And it came to pass, when all the people E
were clean passed over, that the ark of the Lord passed over,
18 and the priests, in the presence of the people. And it came JE
to pass, when the priests that bare the ark of the covenant
of the Lord were come up out of the midst of Jordan, and
the soles of the priests' feet were lifted up unto the dry
ground, that the waters of Jordan returned unto their
place, and went over all its banks, as aforetime.

Camp pitched at Gilgal

20 And those twelve stones, which they took out of Jordan, JE
did Joshua set up in Gilgal.

Joshua v

2 At that time the Lord said unto Joshua, Make thee knives J
of flint, and circumcise again the children of Israel the
3 second time. And Joshua made him knives of flint, and
circumcised the children of Israel at the hill of the fore-
9 skins. And the Lord said unto Joshua, This day have I
rolled away the reproach of Egypt from off you. Wherefore the name of that place was called Gilgal, unto this
day.

THE SACRIFICE OF JERICHO TO JEHOVAH

Joshua receives Orders

13 And it came to pass, when Joshua was by Jericho, that he J
lifted up his eyes and looked, and behold, there stood a man
over against him with his sword drawn in his hand: and
Joshua went unto him, and said unto him, Art thou for us,
14 or for our adversaries? And he said, Nay; but as captain
of the host of the Lord am I now come. And Joshua fell
on his face to the earth, and did worship, and said unto him,
15 What saith my Lord unto his servant? And the captain
of the Lord's host said unto Joshua, Put off thy shoe from
off thy foot; for the place whereon thou standest is holy.
And Joshua did so.

JOSHUA vi

1 (Now Jericho was straitly shut up because of the children JE
2 of Israel: none went out, and none came in.) And the
Lord said unto Joshua, See, I have given unto thine hand
Jericho, and the king thereof, and the mighty men of
3 valour. And ye shall compass the city, all the men of J
war, going about the city once. Thus shalt thou do six
4 days. And seven priests shall bear seven trumpets of E
rams' horns before the ark; and the seventh day ye shall
compass the city seven times, and the priests shall blow
5 with the trumpets. And it shall be, that when they make
a long blast with the ram's horn, and when ye shall hear
the sound of the trumpet, all the people shall shout with a
great shout; and the wall of the city shall fall down flat,
and the people shall go up every man straight before him.

The Ceremonial

6 And Joshua the son of Nun called the priests, and said E
unto them, Take up the ark of the covenant, and let seven
priests bear seven trumpets of rams' horns before the ark
7 of the Lord. And they said unto the people, Pass on, and J
compass the city, and let the armed men pass on before the E
8 ark of the Lord. And it was so, that when Joshua had
spoken unto the people, the seven priests bearing the seven
trumpets of rams' horns before the Lord passed on, and the
9 ark of the covenant of the Lord followed them. And the J
armed men went before the priests that blew the trumpets,
10 and the rearward went after the ark. And Joshua commanded the people saying. Ye shall not shout, nor let

your voice be heard, neither shall any word proceed out of J
your mouth, until the day I bid you shout ; then shall ye
11 shout. So he caused the ark of the Lord to compass the
city, going about it once; and they came into the camp,
and lodged in the camp.

Annihilation of the city

12 And Joshua rose early in the morning, and the priests took J
13 up the ark of the Lord. And the seven priests bearing the E
seven trumpets of rams' horns before the ark of the Lord
went on continually, and blew with the trumpets: and the ?
armed men went before them; and the rearward came after E
the ark of the Lord, the priests blowing with the trumpets ?
14 as they went. And the second day they compassed the J
city once, and returned into the camp: so they did six
15 days. And it came to pass on the seventh day, that they
rose early at the dawning of the day, and compassed the
city after the same manner seven times: only on that day ?
16 they compassed the city seven times. And it came to pass E
at the seventh time, when the priests blew with the trumpets, Joshua said unto the people, Shout; for the Lord hath J
20 given you the city. . . . So the people shouted, and the ?
priests blew with the trumpets: and it came to pass, when E
the people heard the sound of the trumpet, that the people
shouted with a great shout, and the wall fell down flat, so
that the people went up into the city, every man straight J
21 before him, and they took the city. And they utterly
destroyed all that was in the city, both man and woman,
both young and old, and ox, and sheep, and ass, with the
22 edge of the sword. And Joshua said unto the two men E
that had spied out the land, Go into the harlot's house, and
bring out thence the woman, and all that she hath, as ye
23 sware unto her. And the young men the spies went in,
and brought out Rahab, and her father, and her mother,
and her brethren and all that she had, all her kindred also
they brought out; and they set them without the camp of
24 Israel. And they burnt the city with fire, and all that was
25 therein. But Rahab the harlot, and her father's house- J
hold, and all that she had, did Joshua save alive; and she
dwelt in the midst of Israel, unto this day; because she hid
the messengers, which Joshua sent to spy out Jericho.

The ruins laid under a curse

26 And Joshua charged them with an oath at that time, J
saying, Cursed be the man before the Lord, that riseth up

and buildeth this city Jericho : with the loss of his first- J
born shall he lay the foundation thereof, and with the loss
of his youngest son shall he set up the gates of it.

THE DESTRUCTION OF AI

JOSHUA vii. *Spies visit Ai*

2 And Joshua sent men from Jericho to Ai, which is beside J
Bethaven, on the east side of Beth-el, and spake unto them,
saying, Go up and spy out the land. And the men went
3 up and spied out Ai. And they returned to Joshua, and
said unto him, Let not all the people go up; but let about
two or three thousand men go up and smite Ai; make not
all the people toil thither; for they are but few.

A reverse

4 So there went up thither of the people about three thousand J
5 men: and they fled before the men of Ai. And the men
of Ai smote of them about thirty and six men: and they
chased them from before the gate even unto Shebarim, and
6 smote them at the going down: And Joshua rent his
clothes, and fell to the earth upon his face before the ark
of the Lord until the evening, he and the elders of Israel;
7 and they put dust upon their heads. And Joshua said,
Alas, O Lord God, wherefore hast thou at all brought this
8 people over Jordan. Would that we had been content and
dwelt beyond Jordan! Oh Lord, what shall I say, after
that Israel hath turned their backs before their enemies!
9 For the Canaanites and all the inhabitants of the land shall
hear of it, and shall compass us round, and cut off our name
from the earth: and what wilt thou do for thy great
name ?

Sacrilege the Cause

10 And the Lord said unto Joshua, Get thee up; wherefore J
11 art thou thus fallen upon thy face ? Israel hath sinned;
yea, they have even taken of the devoted thing, and they
12 have even put it among their own stuff. Therefore the
children of Israel cannot stand before their enemies, they
turn their backs before their enemies, because they are
13 become accursed: Up, sanctify the people, and say,
Sanctify yourselves against to-morrow: for thus saith the
Lord, the God of Israel. There is a devoted thing in the
midst of thee, O Israel: thou canst not stand before thine

enemies, until ye take away the devoted thing from among J
14 you. In the morning therefore ye shall be brought near
by your tribes: and it shall be, that the tribe which the
Lord taketh shall come near by families; and the family
which the Lord shall take shall come near by households:
and the household which the Lord shall take shall come
15 near man by man. And it shall be, that he that is taken
with the devoted thing shall be burnt with fire, he and all
16 that he hath. So Joshua rose up early in the morning, and
brought Israel near by their tribes; and the tribe of Judah
17 was taken: and he brought near the family of Judah; and
he took the family of the Zerahites : and he brought near
the family of the Zerahites man by man: and Zabdi was
18 taken: and he brought near his household man by man:
19 and Achan was taken. And Joshua said unto Achan,
My son, give, I pray thee, glory to the Lord, the God of
Israel, and make confession unto him; and tell me now
20 what thou hast done; hide it not from me. And Achan
answered Joshua, and said, Of a truth I have sinned against
the Lord, the God of Israel, and thus and thus have I done:
21 when I saw among the spoil a goodly Babylonish mantle
and two hundred shekels of silver, and a wedge of gold of
fifty shekels weight, then I coveted them, and took them,
and, behold, they are hid in the earth in the midst of my
tent, and the silver under it.

The Expiation

22 So Joshua sent messengers, and they ran unto the tent; J
and, behold, it was hid in his tent, and the silver under it.
23 And they took them from the midst of the tent, and brought
them unto Joshua, and unto all the children of Israel; and
24 they laid them down before the Lord. And Joshua took
Achan the son of Zerah and all that he had, and they
25 brought them up unto the valley of Achor. And Joshua
said, Why hast thou troubled us ? the Lord shall trouble
26 thee this day. . . . And they raised over him a great heap
of stones, unto this day; and the Lord turned from the
fierceness of his anger. Wherefore the name of that
place was called, The valley of Achor, unto this day.

JOSHUA viii. *An Ambush set*

1 And the Lord said unto Joshua, take all the people of war J
2 with thee, and arise, go up to Ai. . . . set thee an ambush
3 for the city behind it. So Joshua arose, and all the people

of war, to go up to Ai: and Joshua chose out thirty thousand J
men, the mighty men of valour, and sent them forth by
4 night. And he commanded them, saying, Behold, ye
shall lie in ambush against the city, behind the city: go
not very far from the city, but be ye all ready; and
5 I, and all the people that are with me, will approach
unto the city: and it shall come to pass, when they come
out against us, as at the first, that we will flee before them;
6 and they will come out after us, till we have drawn them
away from the city; for they will say, They flee before us,
7 as at the first; so we will flee before them. And ye shall
rise up from the ambush, and take possession of the city:
8 for the Lord your God will deliver it into your hand. And
it shall be, when ye have seized upon the city, that ye shall
set the city on fire; according to the word of the Lord
9 shall ye do: see I have commanded you. And Joshua
sent them forth: and they went to the ambushment, and
abode between Beth-el and Ai, on the west side of Ai: but
Joshua lodged that night among the people.

The main attack

10 And Joshua rose up early in the morning, and mustered J
the people, and went up, he and the elders of Israel, before
11 the people to Ai. And all the people, even the men of
war that were with him, went up, and drew nigh, and came
before the city, and pitched on the north side of Ai: now
12 there was a valley between him and Ai. And he took E
about five thousand men, and set them in ambush between
13 Beth-el and Ai, on the west side of the city. So they set JE
the people, even all the host that was on the north of the
city, and their liers in wait that were on the west of the
city, and Joshua went that night into the midst of the vale.
14 And it came to pass, when the king of Ai saw it, that they J
hasted and rose up early, and the men of the city went out
against Israel to battle, he and all his people, at the time
appointed, before the Arabah; but he wist not that there
15 was an ambush against him behind the city. And Joshua E
and all Israel made as if they were beaten before them, and
16 fled by the way of the wilderness. And all the people that J
were in the city were called together to pursue after them:
and they pursued after Joshua, and were drawn away from
17 the city. And there was not a man left in Ai or Beth-el,
that went not out after Israel: and they left the city open
18 and pursued after Israel. And the Lord said unto Joshua, E

Stretch out the javelin that is in thy hand toward Ai; for E
I will give it into thine hand. And Joshua stretched out J
the javelin that was in his hand toward the city.

Destruction of Ai

19 And the ambush arose quickly out of their place and they J
ran as soon as he had stretched out his hand, and entered
into the city, and took it; and they hasted and set the city
20 on fire. And when the men of Ai looked behind them,
they saw, and, behold, the smoke of the city ascended up to
heaven, and they had no power to flee this way or that way:
21 And when Joshua and all Israel saw that the ambush had
taken the city, and that the smoke of the city ascended, then
22 they turned again, and slew the men of Ai. And the other
came forth out of the city against them, so they were in the
midst of Israel, some on this side, and some on that side:
and they smote them, so that they let none of them remain
23 or escape. And the king of Ai they took alive, and brought
24 him to Joshua. And it came to pass, when Israel had made E
an end of slaying all the inhabitants of Ai in the field, and
they were all fallen by the edge of the sword, until they
were consumed, that all Israel returned unto Ai, and
25 smote it with the edge of the sword. And all that fell that J
day, both of men and women, were twelve thousand, even
26 all the men of Ai. For Joshua drew not back his hand, E
wherewith he stretched out the javelin, until he had utterly
destroyed all the inhabitants of Ai.

29 And the king of Ai he hanged on a tree until the eventide: J
and at the going down of the sun Joshua commanded, and
they took his carcase down from the tree, and cast it at the
entering of the gate of the city, and raised thereon a great
heap of stones, unto this day.

THE RELIEF OF GIBEON

JOSHUA ix. *The Hivite Alliance*

3 But when the inhabitants of Gibeon heard what Joshua E
4 had done unto Jericho and to Ai, They also did work J
wilily, and went and made as if they had been ambassadors,
and took old sacks upon their asses, and wine-skins, old and
5 rent and bound up; and old shoes and clouted upon their
feet, and old garments upon them; and all the bread of
6 their provision was dry and was become mouldy. And E
they went to Joshua unto the camp at Gilgal, and said unto J

him, and to the men of Israel, We are come from a far J
7 country: now therefore make ye a covenant with us. And
the men of Israel said unto the Hivites, Peradventure ye
dwell among us; and how shall we make a covenant with
8 you? And they said unto Joshua, We are thy servants. E
And Joshua said unto them, Who are ye? and from
9 whence come ye? And they said unto him, From a very
far country thy servants are come because of the name of
11 the Lord thy God. And our elders and all the inhabitants
of our country spake to us, saying, Take provision in your
hand for the journey, and go to meet them, and say unto
them, We are your servants: and now make ye a covenant E
12 with us. This our bread we took hot for our provision
out of our houses on the day we came forth to go unto you;
13 but now, behold, it is dry, and is become mouldy: And
these wine-skins, which we filled, were new; and, behold,
they be rent: and these our garments and our shoes are
14 become old by reason of the very long journey. And the
men took of their provision, and asked not counsel at the
15 mouth of the Lord. And Joshua made peace with them, E
16 and made a covenant with them, to let them live: And it J
came to pass at the end of three days after they had made a
covenant with them, that they heard that they were their
22 neighbours, and that they dwelt among them. And Joshua E
called for them, and he spake unto them, saying, Wherefore
have ye beguiled us, saying, We are very far from you;
23 when ye dwell among us? Now therefore ye are cursed, J
and there shall never fail to be of you bondmen, both hewers
of wood and drawers of water for the house of my God.
26 And so did he unto them, and delivered them out of the
hand of the children of Israel, that they slew them not.

JOSHUA X. *Defeat of a Southern League*

1 Now it came to pass, when Adoni-zedek king of Jerusalem J
heard how Joshua had taken Ai, and had utterly destroyed
it; and how the inhabitants of Gibeon had made peace E
2 with Israel, and were among them; that they feared greatly J
because Gibeon was a great city, as one of the royal cities,
and because it was greater than Ai, and all the men thereof
3 were mighty. Wherefore Adoni-zedek king of Jerusalem
sent unto Hoham king of Hebron, and unto Piram king
of Jarmuth, and unto Japhia king of Lachish, and unto
4 Debir king of Eglon, saying, Come up unto me, and E
help me, and let us smite Gibeon: for it hath made peace

5 with Joshua and with the children of Israel. Therefore E
the five kings of the Amorites, the king of Jerusalem, the J
king of Hebron, the king of Jarmuth, the king of Lachish,
the king of Eglon, gathered themselves together, and went
up, they and all their hosts, and encamped against Gibeon,
6 and made war against it. And the men of Gibeon sent
unto Joshua to the camp to Gilgal, saying, Slack not thy
hand from thy servants; come up to us quickly, and save us, E
and help us: for all the kings of the Amorites that dwell in
7 the hill country are gathered together against us. So J
Joshua went up from Gilgal, he, and all the people of war
9 with him. Joshua therefore came upon them suddenly;
10 for he went up from Gilgal all the night. And the Lord
discomfited them before Israel, and he slew them with a
great slaughter at Gibeon, and chased them by the way of
the ascent of Beth-horon, and smote them to Azekah, and
11 unto Makkedah. And it came to pass, as they fled from E
before Israel, while they were in the going down of Beth-
horon, that the Lord cast down great stones from heaven
upon them unto Azekah, and they died: they were more
which died with the hailstones than they whom the children
12 of Israel slew with the sword. Then spake Joshua to the J
Lord; Sun, stand thou still upon Gibeon; And thou,
13 Moon, in the valley of Aijalon. And the sun stood still,
and the moon stayed, Until the nation had avenged themselves of their enemies. Is not this written in the book of
Jashar? And the sun stayed in the midst of heaven, and
14 hasted not to go down about a whole day. And there was
no day like that before it or after it, that the Lord hearkened
16 unto the voice of a man: And these five kings fled, and hid
17 themselves in the cave at Makkedah. And it was told
Joshua, saying, The five kings are found hidden in the cave
18 at Makkedah. And Joshua said, Roll great stones unto
the mouth of the cave, and set men by it for to keep them:
19 But stay not ye; pursue after your enemies, and smite the
21 hindmost of them. . . . that all the people returned to the
camp to Joshua at Makkedah in peace: none moved his
22 tongue against any of the children of Israel. Then said
Joshua, Open the mouth of the cave, and bring forth those
23 five kings unto me out of the cave. And they did so, and
brought forth those five kings unto him out of the cave,
the king of Jerusalem, the king of Hebron, the king of
24 Jarmuth, the king of Lachish, the king of Eglon. And it
came to pass, when they brought forth those kings unto

Joshua, that Joshua called for all the men of Israel, and J
said unto the chiefs of the men of war which went with
him, Come near, put your feet upon the necks of these
kings. And they came near and put their feet upon the
26 necks of them. And afterward Joshua smote them, and
put them to death, and hanged them on five trees: and they
27 were hanging upon the trees until the evening. And it
came to pass at the time of the going down of the sun, that
Joshua commanded, and they took them down off the trees,
and cast them into the cave wherein they had hidden themselves, and laid great stones on the mouth of the cave.

THE FALL OF HAZOR

JOSHUA xi. *The Northern League*

1 And it came to pass, when Jabin, king of Hazor heard J
thereof, that he sent to Jobab king of Madon, and to the
4 king of Shimron, and to the king of Achshaph. And they
went out, they and all their hosts with them, much people,
even as the sand that is upon the seashore in multitude, with
5 horses and chariots very many. And all these kings met
together; and they came and pitched together at the waters
of Merom, to fight with Israel.

By the Waters of Merom

6 And the Lord said unto Joshua, Be not afraid because of J
them: for to-morrow at this time will I deliver them up
all slain, before Israel: thou shalt hough their horses, and
7 burn their chariots with fire. So Joshua came, and all the
people of war with him, against them by the waters of
8 Merom suddenly, and fell upon them. And they smote
them, and chased them unto great Zidon, and unto
Misrephoth-maim, and unto the valley of Mizpeh east-
9 ward. And Joshua did unto them as the Lord bade him:
he houghed their horses, and burnt their chariots with fire.

THE TEXT OF JOSHUA AND JUDGES

THE SETTLEMENT OF THE TRIBES

(*Josh. XIII-XXIII aud Judg. I-II,* 10)

JOSHUA xiii. *Allotment of Tribal Areas*

1 Now Joshua was old and well stricken in years; and the J
Lord said unto him, Thou art old and well stricken in
years, and there remaineth yet very much land to be
possessed.

7 Now therefore divide this land for an inheritance. J

Areas beyond Jordan not conquered

13 Nevertheless the children of Israel drave not out the J
Geshurites, nor the Maacathites: but Geshur and Maacath
dwelt in the midst of Israel unto this day.

JUDAH AND SIMEON WITH CALEB IN THE SOUTH

JUDGES i. *Bezek*

1 . . . the children of Israel asked of the Lord, saying, Who J
shall go up for us first against the Canaanites, to fight
2 against them? And the Lord said, Judah shall go up:
3 behold, I have delivered the land into his hand. And
Judah said unto Simeon his brother, Come up with me
into my lot, that we may fight against the Canaanites: and
I likewise will go with thee into thy lot. So Simeon went
5 with him. And they found Adoni-bezek in Bezek: and
they fought against him, and they smote the Canaanites
6 and the Perizzites. But Adoni-bezek fled; and they
pursued after him, and caught him, and cut off his
7 thumbs and his great toes. And Adoni-bezek said,
Threescore and ten kings, having their thumbs and their
great toes cut off, gathered their meat under my table: as
I have done, so God hath requited me. And they brought
him to Jerusalem, and he died there.

Hebron and Debir

JOSHUA xv

13 And unto Caleb the son of
Jephunneh he gave a portion among the children of

JUDGES i

20 And they gave Hebron unto
Caleb as Moses had spoken
and he drave out thence

Judah, according to the commandment of the Lord to Joshua, even Kiriath-arba,[a] which Arba was the father of Anak (the same is Hebron).

14 And Caleb drove out thence the three sons of Anak, Sheshai, and Ahiman and Talmai, the children of Anak.[b] [J]

15 And he went up thence against the inhabitants of Debir: now the name of Debir beforetime was Kiriath-sepher. [J]

16 And Caleb said, He that smiteth Kiriath-sepher, and taketh it, to him will I give Achsah my daughter to wife. [J]

17 And Othniel the son of Kenaz, the brother of Caleb, took it: and he gave him Achsah his daughter to wife. [J]

18 And it came to pass when she came unto him, that she moved him to ask of her father a field: and she lighted down from off her ass: and Caleb said unto her, What wouldest thou ? [J]

19 And she said, Give me a blessing[c]: for that thou hast set me in the land of the South, give me also springs of water. And he gave her the upper springs and the nether springs.[d] [J]

the three sons of Anak. . . . [J]

10 Sheshai, and Ahiman, and Talmai. [J]

11 And from thence he went against the inhabitants of Debir (Now the name of Debir beforetime was Kiriath-sepher). [J]

12 And Caleb said, He that smiteth Kiriath-sepher, and taketh it, to him will I give Achsah my daughter to wife. [J]

13 And Othniel the son of Kenaz Caleb's [younger] brother took it, and he gave him Achsah his daughter to wife. [J]

14 And it came to pass when she came unto him, that she moved him to ask of her father a field: and she lighted down from off her ass: and Caleb said unto her What wouldest thou ? [J]

15 And she said unto him, Give me a blessing: for that thou hast set me in the land of the South, give me also springs of water. And Caleb gave her the upper springs and the nether springs. [J]

[a] That is, the city of Arba. [b] Not in the LXX. [c] Or, present. [d] Or, Pools.

JUDGES i. *Arad and Hormah*

16 And the children of the Kenite, Moses' brother in law, J
went up out of the city of palm trees with the children of
Judah into the wilderness of Judah, which is in the south
17 of Arad: and they went and dwelt with the people And
Judah went with Simeon his brother, and they smote the
Canaanites that inhabited Zephath, and utterly destroyed
it And the name of the city was called Hormah.
19 And the Lord was with Judah; and he drave out the
inhabitants of the hill country; for he could not drive out
the inhabitants of the valley, because they had chariots of
iron.

Jerusalem not captured

JOSHUA XV

63 And as for the Jebusites, the inhabitants of Jerusalem, the children of Judah could not drive them out: but the Jebusites dwelt with the children of Judah at Jerusalem unto this day. [J]

JUDGES i

21 And the children of Benjamin did not drive out the Jebusites that inhabited Jerusalem: but the Jebusites dwelt with the children of Benjamin in Jerusalem, unto this day. [J]

THE HOUSE OF JOSEPH, EPHRAIM AND MANASSEH, IN THE CENTRE

JOSHUA xvi. *Southern Boundary*

1 And the lot for the children of Joseph went out from the J
Jordan at Jericho, at the waters of Jericho on the east, even
the wilderness, going up from Jericho through the hill
2 country to Beth-el: and it went out from Beth-el to Luz,
and passed along unto the border of the Archites to
3 Ataroth: and it went down westward to the border of the
Japhletites, unto the border of Beth-horon the nether, even
unto Gezer: and the goings out thereof were at the sea.

JUDGES i. *Bethel*

22 And the house of Joseph, they also went up against Beth-el: J
23 and the Lord was with them. And the house of Joseph
sent to spy out Beth-el (Now the name of the city before-
24 time was Luz). And the watchers saw a man come forth
out of the city, and they said unto him, Shew us, we pray
thee, the entrance into the city, and we will deal kindly with
25 thee. And he shewed them the entrance into the city, and

they smote the city with the edge of the sword; but they J
26 let the man go and all his family. And the man went into
the land of the Hittites and built a city, and called the name
thereof Luz; which is the name thereof unto this day.

Gezer not captured

JOSHUA xvi

10 And they drave not out the Canaanites that dwelt in Gezer: but the Canaanites dwelt in the midst of Ephraim, unto this day, and became servants to do taskwork. [J]

JUDGES i

29 And Ephraim drave not out the Canaanites that dwelt in Gezer; but the Canaanites dwelt in Gezer among them. [J]

The Canaanite frontier in the north

JOSHUA xvii

11 And Manasseh had in Issachar and in Asher Beth-shean and her towns, and Ibleam and her towns, and the inhabitants of Dor and her towns, and the inhabitants of En-dor and her towns, and the inhabitants of Taanach and her towns, and the inhabitants of Megiddo and her towns, even the three heights. [J]

12 Yet the children of Manasseh could not drive out the inhabitants of those cities; but the Canaanites would dwell in that land. [J]

JUDGES i

27 And Manasseh did not drive out the inhabitants of Beth-shean and her towns, nor of Taanach and her towns, nor the inhabitants of Dor and her towns, nor the inhabitants of Ibleam and her towns, nor the inhabitants of Megiddo and her towns; but the Canaanites would dwell in that land. [J]

28 And it came to pass, when Israel was waxen strong, that they put the Canaanites to taskwork, and did not utterly drive them out. [?]

JOSHUA xvii. *Eastward extension authorised*

14 And the children of Joseph spake unto Joshua saying, Why J
hast thou given me but one lot and one part for an inheritance, seeing I am a great people, forasmuch as hitherto the
15 Lord hath blessed me? And Joshua said unto them, If
thou be a great people get thee up to the forest, and cut
down for thyself there in the land of the Perizzites and of ?
the Rephaim: since the hill country of Ephraim is too
16 narrow for thee. And the children of Joseph said, The J

hill country is not enough for us: and all the Canaanites J
that dwell in the land of the valley have chariots of iron,
both they who are in Beth-shean and her towns, and they
17 who are in the valley of Jezreel. And Joshua spake unto
the house of Joseph, even to Ephraim and to Manasseh, ?
saying, Thou art a great people, and hast great power: J
18 thou shalt not have one lot only: but the hill country shall
be thine: for though it is a forest, thou shalt cut it down,
and the goings out thereof shall be thine: for thou shalt
drive out the Canaanites, though they have chariots of
iron, and though they be strong.

TRIBAL PORTIONS IN THE NORTH
ISSACHAR, ZEBULUN, ASHER, NAPHTALI AND DAN

JOSHUA xviii. *The Land Surveyed*

2 And there remained among the children of Israel seven JE
3 tribes, which had not yet divided their inheritance. And
Joshua said unto the children of Israel, How long are ye
slack to go in to possess the land, which the Lord, the God
4 of your fathers, hath given you ? Appoint for you three
men for each tribe: and I will send them, and they shall
arise, and walk through the land, and describe it according
5 to their inheritance: and they shall come unto me. And JE
they shall divide it into seven portions; Judah shall abide
in his border on the south, and the house of Joseph shall
6 abide in their border on the north. And ye shall describe
the land into seven portions, and bring the description
hither to me: and I will cast lots for you here before the
8 Lord our God. And the men arose, and went: and
Joshua charged them that went to describe the land, saying
Go and walk through the land, and describe it, and come
again to me, and I will cast lots for you here before the
9 Lord in Shiloh. And the men went and passed through
the land, and described it by cities into seven portions in a
book, and they came to Joshua unto the camp at Shiloh.

Lots cast in Shiloh

10 And Joshua cast lots for them in Shiloh before the Lord.... JE

JUDGES i. *Difficulties of Zebulun*

30 Zebulun drave not out the inhabitants of Kitron, nor the J
inhabitants of Nahalol; but the Canaanites dwelt among
them, and became tributary.

Difficulties of Asher

31 Asher drave not out the inhabitants of Acco, nor the J
inhabitants of Zidon, nor of Ahlab, nor of Achzib, nor of
32 Helbah, nor of Aphik, nor of Rehob: but the Asherites
dwelt among the Canaanites, the inhabitants of the land:
for they did not drive them out.

Difficulties of Naphtali

33 Naphtali drave not out the inhabitants of Beth-shemesh J
nor the inhabitants of Beth-anath; but he dwelt among
the Canaanites, the inhabitants of the land; nevertheless
the inhabitants of Beth-shemesh and of Beth-anath became
tributary unto them.

Difficulties of Dan in the South

34 And the Amorites forced the children of Dan into the hill J
country: for they would not suffer them to come down to
35 the valley: but the Amorites would dwell in mount Heres,
in Aijalon and in Shaalbim: yet the hand of the house of
Joseph prevailed, so that they became tributary.

Dan forced to migrate towards the North

JOSHUA xix

47 And the border of the children of Dan went out beyond them: for the children of Dan went up and fought against Leshem, and took it, and smote it with the edge of the sword, and possessed it, and dwelt therein, and called Leshem Dan, after the name of Dan their father. [J]

JUDGES xviii

27 And they . . . came unto
Laish, unto a people quiet
and secure, and smote them
with the edge of the sword;
and they burnt the city
28 with fire. . . . and they
built the city, and dwelt
29 therein. And they called
the name of the city Dan,
after the name of Dan their
father. . . . [J]

JUDGES i. *The Amorite Border*

36 And the border of the Amorites was from the ascent of
Akrabbim, from the rock, and upward. [J]

JUDGES ii. *Bochim*

1 And the angel of the Lord came up from Gilgal to Bochim. J
5 and they sacrificed there unto the Lord.

JOSHUA'S FAREWELL

JOSHUA xxiv. *Shechem*

1 And Joshua gathered all the tribes of Israel to Shechem E
and they presented themselves before God.

The Covenant Renewed

2 And Joshua said unto all the people, Thus saith the Lord
the God of Israel, Your fathers dwelt of old time beyond
the River, even Terah, the father of Abraham, and the ?
3 father of Nahor: and they served other gods. And I took
your father Abraham from beyond the River, and led him
throughout all the land of Canaan, and multiplied his seed
4 and gave him Isaac. And I gave unto Isaac Jacob and E
Esau: and I gave unto Esau mount Seir to possess it; and
5 Jacob and his children went down into Egypt. And I sent
Moses and Aaron, and I plagued Egypt, according to that
which I did in the midst thereof: and afterward I brought
6 you out. And I brought your fathers out of Egypt: and ?
ye came unto the sea; and the Egyptians pursued after your E
fathers with chariots and with horsemen unto the Red Sea.
7 And when they cried out unto the Lord, he put darkness
between you and the Egyptians, and brought the sea upon
them, and covered them; and ye dwelt in the wilderness
8 many days. And I brought you into the land of the
Amorites, which dwelt beyond Jordan; and they fought
with you: and I gave them into your hand, and ye possessed
9 their land; and I destroyed them from before you. Then
Balak the son of Zippor, king of Moab, arose and fought
against Israel; and he sent and called Balaam the son of
Beor to curse you: but I would not hearken unto Balaam;
10 therefore he blessed you still: so I delivered you out of his
11 hand. And ye went over Jordan, and came unto Jericho;
and the men of Jericho fought against you: and I delivered
12 them into your hand. And I sent the hornet before
14 you, which drave them out from before you, . . . Now
therefore fear the Lord, and serve him in sincerity and in
truth: and put away the gods which your fathers served
15 beyond the River, and in Egypt: and serve ye the Lord.
And if it seem evil unto you to serve the Lord, choose you
this day whom ye will serve; whether the gods which your
fathers served that were beyond the River, or the gods of the
Amorites, in whose land ye dwell: but as for me and my
16 house, we will serve the Lord. And the people answered

and said, God forbid that we should forsake the Lord, to E
17 serve other gods; for the Lord our God, he it is that
brought us and our fathers up out of the land of Egypt, and
preserved us in all the way wherein we went, and among
18 all the peoples through the midst of whom we passed: and
the Lord drave out from before us all the peoples, even the
Amorites which dwelt in the land; therefore we also will
19 serve the Lord; for he is our God. And Joshua said unto
the people, Ye cannot serve the Lord; for he is an holy
God; he is a jealous God; he will not forgive your trans-
20 gression nor your sins. If ye forsake the Lord and serve
strange gods, then he will turn and do you evil, and consume
21 you, after that he hath done you good. And the people
22 said unto Joshua, Nay; but we will serve the Lord. And
Joshua said unto the people, Ye are witnesses against yourselves that ye have chosen you the Lord, to serve him.
23 Now therefore put away, said he, the strange gods which
are among you, and incline your heart unto the Lord, the
24 God of Israel. And the people said unto Joshua, The
Lord our God will we serve, and unto his voice will we
25 hearken. So Joshua made a covenant with the people
that day, and set them a statute and an ordinance in
26 Shechem. And Joshua wrote these words in the book of ?
the law of God; and he took a great stone, and set it up E
there under the oak that was by the sanctuary of the Lord.
27 And Joshua said unto all the people, Behold, this stone
shall be a witness against us; for it hath heard all the words
of the Lord which he spake unto us; it shall be therefore
28 a witness against you, lest ye deny your God. So Joshua
sent the people away, every man unto his inheritance.

Death of Joshua

JOSHUA xxiv

29 And it came to pass after
these things, that Joshua
the son of Nun, the servant
of the Lord, died, being an
hundred and ten years old.
30 And they buried him in
the border of his inheritance
Timnath-serah, which is in
the hill country of Ephraim,
on the north of the moun-
tain of Gaash. [E]

JUDGES ii

8 And Joshua the son of Nun,
the servant of the Lord, died,
being an hundred and ten
9 years old. And they buried
him in the border of his
inheritance in Timnath-
heres, in the hill country
of Ephraim on the north
of the mountain of Gaash.
[E]

JOSHUA xxiv. *The Tomb of Joseph*

32 And the bones of Joseph, which the children of Israel E
brought up out of Egypt, buried they in Shechem, in the
parcel of ground which Jacob bought of the sons of Hamor
the father of Shechem for an hundred pieces of money: and
they became the inheritance of the children of Joseph. [E]

JOSHUA xxiv. *Death of Eleazar*

33 And Eleazar the son of Aaron died, and they buried him
in the hill of Phinehas his son, which was given him in the
hill country of Ephraim. [E]

JUDGES ii. *Passing of Joshua's Generation*

6 Now when Joshua had sent the people away, the children
of Israel went every man unto his inheritance to possess
7 the land. And the people served the Lord all the days of
Joshua, and all the days of the elders that outlived Joshua,
who had seen all the great work of the Lord, that he had
10 wrought for Israel. And also all that generation were
gathered to their fathers; and there arose another generation
after them which knew not the Lord, nor yet the work
which he had wrought for Israel. [E]

THE TEXT OF JOSHUA AND JUDGES

PERIOD OF THE JUDGES

(*Book of Judges II-XVIII*)

Selected Passages

JUDGES ii. *Prologue*

11 And the children of Israel did that which was evil in the E
14 sight of the Lord, and served the Baalim: . . . And the
anger of the Lord was kindled against Israel, and he
delivered them into the hands of spoilers that spoiled them,
and he sold them into the hands of their enemies round
16 about, . . . And the Lord raised up judges, which saved
17 them out of the hand of those that spoiled them. And yet
they hearkened not unto their judges, for they went a
whoring after other gods, and bowed themselves down unto
them: they turned aside quickly out of the way wherein
their fathers walked, obeying the commandments of the
Lord: but they did not do so.

[vv. 17-19.—*Israel worships other Gods.*]

20 And the anger of the Lord was kindled against Israel; and E
he said, Because this nation have transgressed my covenant
which I commanded their fathers, and have not hearkened
21 unto my voice; I also will not henceforth drive out any
from before them of the nations which Joshua left when he
23 died: So the Lord left those nations, without driving them JE
out hastily; neither delivered he them into the hand of
Joshua.

JUDGES iii

2 Only that the generations of the children of Israel might J
5 know, to teach them war . . . And the children of Israel
dwelt among the Canaanites; the Hittite, and the Amorite,
6 and the Perizzite, and the Hivite, and the Jebusite. And
they took their daughters to be their wives, and gave their
7 own daughters to their sons, and served their gods. And E2
the children of Israel did that which was evil in the sight
of the Lord, and forgat the Lord their God, and served
Baalim and the Asheroth.

EARLY OPPRESSIONS

Oppression of Cushan.

8 Therefore the anger of the Lord was kindled against E2
Israel, and he sold them into the hand of Cushan-rishathaim
king of Mesopotamia: and the children of Israel served
Cushan-rishathaim eight years.

Deliverance by Othniel

9 And when the children of Israel cried unto the Lord the E2
Lord raised up a saviour to the children of Israel who saved
them, even Othniel the son of Kenaz, Caleb's younger
10 brother . . . And he judged Israel . . .

Period of Peace

11 And the land had rest forty years. And Othniel the son E2
of Kenaz died.

Oppression by Eglon of Moab

12 And the children of Israel again did that which was evil in E2
the sight of the Lord, and the Lord strengthened Eglon
the king of Moab against Israel, because they had done that
13 which was evil in the sight of the Lord. And he gathered
unto him the children of Ammon and Amalek. And he
went and smote Israel and they possessed the city of palm
14 trees. And the children of Israel served Eglon the king
of Moab eighteen years.

Deliverance by Ehud of Benjamin

15 But when the children of Israel cried unto the Lord, the E2
Lord raised them up a saviour, Ehud the son of Gera, the
Benjamite, a man left-handed: and the children of Israel JE
sent a present by him unto Eglon the king of Moab.
16 And Ehud made him a sword which had two edges, of a
cubit length; and he girded it under his raiment upon his
17 right thigh. And he offered the present unto Eglon king
18 of Moab: now Eglon was a very fat man. And when he
had made an end of offering the present, he sent away the
19 people that bare the present. But he himself turned back
from the quarries that were by Gilgal, and said, I have a
secret errand unto thee, O king. And he said, Keep
silence. And all that stood by him went out from him.
20 And Ehud came unto him; and he was sitting by himself
alone in his summer parlour. And Ehud said, I have a

message from God unto thee. And he arose out of his JE
21 seat. And Ehud put forth his left hand, and took the
sword from his right thigh, and thrust it into his belly.
22, 23 And the haft also went in after the blade. . . . Then
Ehud went forth into the porch, and shut the doors of the
26 parlour upon him, and locked them. . . . And Ehud
escaped while they tarried, and passed beyond the quarries,
27 and escaped unto Seirah. And it came to pass, when he
was come, that he blew a trumpet in the hill country of
Ephraim, and the children of Israel went down with him
28 from the hill country, and he before them. And he said
unto them. Follow after me: for the Lord hath delivered
your enemies the Moabites into your hand. And they
went down after him, and took the fords of Jordan against
29 the Moabites, and suffered not a man to pass over. And
they smote of Moab at that time about ten thousand men,
every lusty man, and every man of valour; and there
30 escaped not a man. So Moab was subdued that day under E2
the hand of Israel.

Prolonged Period of Peace

30 the land had rest fourscore years. E2

Shamgar Ben-Anath smites the Philistines

31 And after him was Shamgar the son of Anath which smote Gl
of the Philistines six hundred men with an ox goad; and
he also saved Israel.

JUDGES iv. *Oppression by Sisera*

1 And the children of Israel again did that which was evil in E2
2 the sight of the Lord, when Ehud was dead. And the
Lord sold them into the hand of Jabin king of Canaan, that
reigned in Hazor; the captain of whose host was Sisera,
3 which dwelt in Harosheth of the Gentiles. And the
children of Israel cried unto the Lord, for he had nine
hundred chariots of iron; and twenty years he mightily
oppressed the children of Israel.

REUNION OF THE TRIBES BY DEBORAH

Defeat of Sisera

4 Now Deborah, a prophetess, the wife of Lappidoth, she
5 judged Israel at that time. And she dwelt under the palm Gl
tree of Deborah between Ramah and Beth-el in the hill

6 country of Ephraim. . . . And she sent and called Barak E
the son of Abinoam out of Kedesh-Naphtali, and said unto
him, hath not the Lord, the God of Israel, commanded
saying, Go and draw unto Mount Tabor, and take with
thee ten thousand men of the children of Naphtali and of
7 the children of Zebulun ? And I will draw unto thee to
the river Kishon Sisera, the captain of Jabin's army, with
his chariots and his multitude; and I will deliver him unto
8 thine hand. And Barak said unto her, If thou wilt go
with me, then I will go: but if thou wilt not go with me,
9 I will not go. And she said, I will surely go with thee:
notwithstanding the journey that thou takest shall not be
for thine honour; for the Lord shall sell Sisera into the
hand of a woman. And Deborah arose, and went with
10 Barak to Kedesh. And Barak called Zebulun and
Naphtali together to Kedesh, and there went up ten
thousand men at his feet, and Deborah went up with him.
11 Now Heber the Kenite had severed himself from the
Kenites, and had pitched his tent as far as the oak in
12 Zaanannim, which is by Kedesh. And they told Sisera
that Barak the son of Abinoam was gone up to mount
13 Tabor. And Sisera gathered together all his chariots,
even nine hundred chariots of iron, and all the people that
were with him from Harosheth of the Gentiles, unto the
14 river Kishon. And Deborah said unto Barak, Up; for
this is the day in which the Lord hath delivered Sisera into
thine hand; is not the Lord gone out before thee ? So
Barak went down from mount Tabor and ten thousand
15 men after him. And the Lord discomfited Sisera, and all
his chariots, and all his host, with the edge of the sword
before Barak; and Sisera lighted down from his chariot and
16 fled away on his feet. But Barak pursued after the
chariots, and after the host, unto Harosheth of the Gentiles
and all the host of Sisera fell by the edge of the sword;
17 there was not a man left. Howbeit Sisera fled away on
his feet to the tent of Jael the wife of Heber the Kenite;
for there was peace between Jabin the king of Hazor and
18 the house of Heber the Kenite. And Jael went out to
meet Sisera, and said unto him, Turn in, my lord, turn in
to me; fear not. And he turned in unto her into the
19 tent, and she covered him with a rug. And he said unto
her, Give me, I pray thee, a little water to drink; for I am
thirsty. And she opened a bottle of milk, and gave him
20 drink, and covered him. And he said unto her, Stand in

the door of the tent, and it shall be, when any man doth E
come and inquire of thee, and say, Is there any man here?
21 that thou shalt say, No. Then Jael Heber's wife took a
tent-pin, and took an hammer in her hand, and went
softly unto him, and smote the pin into his temples, and it
pierced through into the ground; for he was in a deep sleep;
22 so he swooned and died. And, behold, as Barak pursued
Sisera, Jael came out to meet him, and said unto him,
Come, and I will shew thee the man whom thou seekest.
And he came unto her; and behold, Sisera lay dead, and
23 the tent-pin was in his temples. So God subdued on that E2
day Jabin the king of Canaan before the children of Israel.
24 And the hand of the children of Israel prevailed more and
more against Jabin the king of Canaan, until they had
destroyed Jabin king of Canaan.

JUDGES V. *From the Song of Deborah*

6 In the days of Shamgar the son of Anath
In the days of Jael, the high ways were unoccupied, E
And the travellers walked through byways.
7 The rulers ceased in Israel, they ceased,
Until that I Deborah arose,
That I arose a mother in Israel
8 They chose new gods;
Then was war in the gates:
Was there a shield or spear seen
Among forty thousand in Israel?
9 My heart is toward the governors of Israel,
That offered themselves willingly among the people:
Bless ye the Lord.
10 Tell of it, ye that ride on white asses,
Ye that sit on rich carpets,
And ye that walk by the way.
11 Far from the noise of archers, in the places of drawing water.
There shall they rehearse the righteous acts of the Lord.
Even the righteous acts of his rule in Israel.
Then the people of the Lord went down to the gates.
12 Awake, awake, Deborah;
Awake, awake, utter a song:
Arise, Barak, and lead thy captivity captive, thou son of Abinoam.
13 Then came down a remnant of the nobles and the people;
The Lord came down for me against the mighty.

14 Out of Ephraim came down they whose root is in Amalek;
After thee, Benjamin, among thy peoples;
Out of Machir came down governors,
And out of Zebulun they that handle the marshal's staff.
15 And the princes of Issachar were with Deborah;
As was Issachar, so was Barak;
Into the valley they rushed forth at his feet.
By the watercourses of Reuben
There were great resolves of heart.
16 Why satest thou among the sheepfolds.
To hear the pipings for the flocks?
At the watercourses of Reuben
There were great searchings of heart.
17 Gilead abode beyond Jordan:
And Dan, why did he remain in ships?
Asher sat still at the haven of the sea,
And abode by his creeks.
18 Zebulun was a people that jeoparded their lives unto the death,
And Naphtali, upon the high places of the field.
19 The kings came and fought;
Then fought the kings of Canaan,
In Taanach by the waters of Megiddo:
They took no gain of money.
20 They fought from heaven,
The stars in their courses fought against Sisera.
21 The river Kishon swept them away,
That ancient river, the river Kishon.

Period of Peace

31 And the land had rest forty years. E2

THE QUEST FOR A LEADER

JUDGES vi. *Oppression by the Midianites*

1 And the children of Israel did that which was evil in the E2
sight of the Lord: and the Lord delivered them into the JE
2 hand of Midian seven years. And the hand of Midian
prevailed against Israel: and because of Midian the children
of Israel made them the dens which are in the mountains,
3 and the caves, and the strongholds. And so it was, when
Israel had sown, that the Midianites came up, and the
Amalekites, and the children of the east; and they came
4 up against them; and they encamped against them and

destroyed the increase of the earth, till thou come unto JE
Gaza, and left no sustenance in Israel, neither sheep, nor
5 ox, nor ass. For they came up with their cattle and their
tents, they came in as locusts for multitude; both they and
their camels were without number: and they came into the
6 land to destroy it. And Israel was brought very low
because of Midian; and the children of Israel cried unto
the Lord.

[vv. 7-10.—*A prophet is sent to denounce Israel.*]

Deliverance by Gideon

11 And the angel of the Lord came, and sat under the oak J
which is in Ophrah, that pertained unto Joash the Abiez-
rite: and his son Gideon was beating out wheat in the
12 winepress, to hide it from the Midianites. And the angel
of the Lord appeared unto him, and said unto him, The
13 Lord is with thee, thou mighty man of valour. And
Gideon said unto him, Oh my lord, if the Lord be with us,
why then is all this befallen us? and where be all his
wondrous works which our fathers told us of, saying,
Did not the Lord bring us up from Egypt? but now the
Lord hath cast us off, and delivered us into the hand of
14 Midian. And the Lord looked upon him, and said, Go
in this thy might, and save Israel from the hand of Midian:
15 have not I sent thee? And he said unto him, Oh Lord,
wherewith shall I save Israel? behold, my family is the
poorest in Manasseh, and I am the least in my father's house.
16 And the Lord said unto him, Surely I will be with thee,
and thou shalt smite the Midianites as one man.

[vv. 17-32.—*Gideon destroys the altar of Baal and is called Jerubbaal.*]

33 Then all the Midianites and the Amalekites and the E
children of the east assembled themselves together: and
they passed over, and pitched in the valley of Jezreel.
34 But the spirit of the Lord came upon Gideon; and he J
blew a trumpet; and Abiezer was gathered together after
35 him. And he sent messengers throughout all Manasseh; E
and they (also) were gathered together after him: and he JE
sent messengers unto Asher, and unto Zebulun, and unto E2
Naphtali; and they came up to meet them.

[vv. 36-40.—*Gideon proves the divine call by two miracles on a fleece.*]

Judges vii. *Rout of the Midianites*

1 Then Jerubbaal (who is Gideon) and all the people who JE/E
were with him, rose up early, and pitched beside the spring
of Harod: and the camp of Midian was on the north side
of them, by the hill of Moreh, in the valley.

[vv. 2-11 E2.—*Gideon reduces his army to 300 men.*]

12 And the Midianites and the Amalekites and all the children E
of the east lay along in the valley like locusts for multitude;
and their camels were without number, as the sand which
is upon the sea shore for multitude.

[vv. 13-15.—*Gideon overhears the panic of the enemy in their camp.*]

16 And he divided the three hundred men into three companies, J
and he put into the hands of all of them (trumpets and) JE/J
empty pitchers, with torches within the pitchers.

[vv. 17-19.—*Gideon issues his commands.*]

20 And the three companies blew the trumpets, and brake the JE
pitchers, and held the torches in their left hands, and the J
trumpets in their right hands to blow withal; and they J/JE
22 cried, The sword of the Lord and of Gideon. . . . And J
they blew the three hundred trumpets, and the Lord set E
every man's sword against his fellow, and against all the
host: and the host fled as far as Beth-shittah toward
Zererah, as far as the border of Abel-meholah, by Tabbath.
23 And the men of Israel were gathered together out of
Naphtali, and out of Asher, and out of all Manasseh, and Gl
24 pursued after Midian. And Gideon sent messengers J
throughout all the hill country of Ephraim saying, Come
down against Midian, and take before them the waters, as
far as Beth-barah, even Jordan. So all the men of
Ephraim were gathered together and took the waters as far
25 as Beth-barah, even Jordan. And they took the two
princes of Midian, Oreb and Zeeb; and they slew Oreb J
at the rock of Oreb, and Zeeb they slew at the winepress of
Zeeb, and pursued Midian: and they brought the heads of JE/J
Oreb and Zeeb to Gideon beyond Jordan. JE

Judges viii. *Pursuit of the Midianites*

1 And the men of Ephraim said unto him, Why hast thou J
served us thus, that thou calledst us not, when thou wentest
to fight with Midian? And they did chide with him
2 sharply. And he said unto them, What have I now done

in comparison of you? Is not the gleaning of the grapes J
3 of Ephraim better than the vintage of Abiezer? God
hath delivered into your hand the princes of Midian, Oreb
and Zeeb: and what was I able to do in comparison of you?
Then their anger was abated toward him, when he had
4 said that. And Gideon came to Jordan, and passed over, E
he, and the three hundred men that were with him, faint,
5 yet pursuing. And he said unto the men of Succoth, Give,
I pray you, loaves of bread unto the people that follow me;
for they be faint, and I am pursuing after Zebah and
6 Zalmunna, the kings of Midian. And the princes of
Succoth said, Are the hands of Zebah and Zalmunna now
in thine hand, that we should give bread unto thine army?
7 And Gideon said, Therefore when the Lord hath delivered
Zebah and Zalmunna into mine hand, then I will tear
your flesh with the thorns of the wilderness and with briers.
8 And he went up thence to Penuel, and spake unto them in
like manner: and the men of Penuel answered him as the
9 men of Succoth had answered. And he spake also unto
the men of Penuel, saying, When I come again in peace,
10 I will break down this tower. Now Zebah and Zalmunna were in Karkor, and their hosts with them, about
fifteen thousand men, all that were left of all the host of the
children of the east: for there fell an hundred and twenty
11 thousand men that drew sword. And Gideon went up by
the way of them that dwelt in tents on the east of Nobah
and Jogbehah, and smote the host; for the host was secure.
12 And Zebah and Zalmunna fled; and he pursued after
them; and he took the two kings of Midian, Zebah and
13 Zalmunna, and discomfited all the host. And Gideon the
son of Joash returned from the battle from the ascent of
14 Heres. And he caught a young man of the men of
Succoth, and inquired of him: and he described for him
the princes of Succoth, and the elders thereof, seventy and
15 seven men. And he came unto the men of Succoth, and
said, Behold Zebah and Zalmunna, concerning whom ye did
taunt me, saying, Are the hands of Zebah and Zalmunna,
now in thine hand, that we should give bread unto thy men
16 that are weary? And he took the elders of the city, and
thorns of the wilderness and briers, and with them he
17 taught the men of Succoth. And he brake down the
18 tower of Penuel, and slew the men of the city. Then he
said unto Zebah and Zalmunna, What manner of men
were they whom ye slew at Tabor? And they answered,

As thou art so were they; each one resembled the children E
19 of a king. And he said, They were my brethren, the sons
of my mother: as the Lord liveth, if ye had saved them
20 alive, I would not slay you. And he said unto Jether his
firstborn, Up, and slay them. But the youth drew not his
21 sword: for he feared because he was yet a youth. Then
Zebah and Zalmunna said, Rise thou, and fall upon us:
for as the man is, so is his strength. And Gideon arose,
and slew Zebah and Zalmunna, and took the crescents that
were on their camels' necks.

FIRST MOVEMENTS TOWARDS A KINGSHIP

22 Then the men of Israel said unto Gideon, Rule thou over E2
us, both thou, and thy son, and thy son's son also: for thou
23 hast saved us out of the hand of Midian. And Gideon
said unto them, I will not rule over you, neither shall my
son rule over you: the Lord shall rule over you.

[vv. 24-27.—*Gideon makes an 'ephod' out of the golden ornaments of the spoil.*]

28 So Midian was subdued before the children of Israel, and E2
they lifted up their heads no more. And the land had rest
forty years in the days of Gideon.

[vv. 29-31.—*Gideon has 70 sons—a concubine from Shechem bears him Abimelech.*]

32 And Gideon the son of Joash died in a good old age, and E
was buried in the sepulchre of Joash his father, in Ophrah
of the Abiezrites.

JUDGES ix. *Abimelech made local king at Shechem*

1 And Abimelech the son of Jerubbaal went to Shechem E
unto his mother's brethren, and spake with them, and with
all the family of the house of his mother's father, saying.
2 Speak, I pray you, in the ears of all the men of Shechem,
Whether is better for you, that all the sons of Jerubbaal,
which are threescore and ten persons, rule over you, or
that one rule over you? remember also that I am your
3 bone and your flesh. And his mother's brethren spake of
him in the ears of all the men of Shechem all these words:
and their hearts inclined to follow Abimelech; for they
4 said, He is our brother. And they gave to him threescore
and ten pieces of silver out of the house of Baal-berith,
wherewith Abimelech hired vain and light fellows, which

5 followed him. And he went unto his father's house at E
Ophrah, and slew his brethren the sons of Jerubbaal,
being threescore and ten persons, upon one stone; but
Jotham the youngest son of Jerubbaal was left; for he hid
6 himself. And all the men of Shechem assembled themselves together, and all the house of Millo, and went and
made Abimelech king, by the oak of the pillar that was in
Shechem.

[vv. 7-21.—*Jotham denounces the men of Shechem in a parable.*]

22 And Abimelech was prince over Israel three years. JE/E

Abimelech not accepted by a section of the Shechemites

23 And God sent an evil spirit between Abimelech and the E
men of Shechem, and the men of Shechem dealt treacher-
25 ously with Abimelech: . . . And the men of Shechem
set liers in wait for him on the tops of the mountains, and
they robbed all that came along that way by them: and it
26 was told Abimelech. And Gaal the son of Ebed came J
with his brethren, and went over to Shechem: and the men
27 of Shechem put their trust in him. And they went out
into the field, and gathered their vineyards, and trode the
grapes, and held festival, and went into the house of their
28 god, and did eat and drink, and cursed Abimelech. And
Gaal the son of Ebed said, Who is Abimelech, and who is
Shechem, that we should serve him ? is not he the son of
Jerubbaal ? and Zebul his officer ? serve ye the men of
Hamor the father of Shechem: but why should we serve
him ?

[vv. 29-33.—*Zebul, in wrath, counsels Abimelech to ensnare Gaal.*]

34 And Abimelech rose up, and all the people that were with J
him, by night, and they laid wait against Shechem in four
companies.

[vv. 35-40.—*Gaal is attacked and pursued by Abimelech.*]

41 And Abimelech dwelt at Arumah: and Zebul drave out J
Gaal and his brethren, that they should not dwell in
42 Shechem. And it came to pass on the morrow, that the JE
people went out into the field; and they told Abimelech. . . .
44 And Abimelech, and the companies that were with him, E
rushed forward, and stood in the entering of the gate of
the city: and the two companies rushed upon all that were

45 in the field, and smote them. And Abimelech fought E
against the city all that day; and he took the city, and slew
the people that was therein: and he beat down the city,
46 and sowed it with salt. And when all the men of the
tower of Shechem heard thereof, they entered into the
48 hold of the house of El-berith. . . . And Abimelech gat
him up to mount Zalmon, he and all the people that were
with him; and Abimelech took an axe in his hand, and cut
down a bough from the trees and took it up, and laid it on
his shoulder: and he said unto the people that were with
him, What ye have seen me do, make haste, and do as I
49 have done. And all the people likewise cut down every
man his bough, and followed Abimelech, and put them to
the hold, and set the hold on fire upon them; so that all
the men of the tower of Shechem died also, about a
thousand men and women.

Death of Abimelech at Thebez

50 Then went Abimelech to Thebez, and encamped against E
51 Thebez, and took it. But there was a strong tower within
the city and thither fled all the men and women, and all
they of the city, and shut themselves in, and gat them up to
52 the roof of the tower. And Abimelech came unto the
tower, and fought against it, and went hard unto the door
53 of the tower to burn it with fire. And a certain woman
cast an upper millstone upon Abimelech's head, and brake
his skull.

LATER OPPRESSIONS

JUDGES X. *Oppression by Ammon*

7 And the anger of the Lord was kindled against Israel and E2/JE
he sold them into the hand of the Philistines, and into the
8 hand of the children of Ammon. And they vexed and E2
oppressed the children of Israel that year: eighteen years JE
oppressed they all the children of Israel that were beyond
Jordan in the land of the Amorites, which is in Gilead.
9 And the children of Ammon passed over Jordan to fight
also against Judah, and against Benjamin, and against the
house of Ephraim; so that Israel was sore distressed. E2

[vv. 10-15.—*The Repentance of Israel for past idolatry.*]

17 Then the children of Ammon were gathered together, and JE/E
encamped in Gilead. And the children of Israel assembled
themselves together, and encamped in Mizpah.

JUDGES xi. *Jephthah made Leader*

1[a] Now Jephthah the Gileadite was a mighty man of valour. J
4 And it came to pass after a while, that the children of
5 Ammon made war against Israel. And it was so, that Gl
when the children of Ammon made war against Israel, the
elders of Gilead went to fetch Jephthah out of the land of J
6 Tob: and they said unto Jephthah, Come and be our
chief, that we may fight with the children of Ammon.

[vv. 7-10.—*Jephthah reproaches the Gileadites but consents to join them.*]

11 Then Jephthah went with the elders of Gilead, and the J
people made him head and chief over them: and Jephthah
spake all his words before the Lord in Mizpah.

Reminiscences of conquests in Trans-Jordania under Moses

12 And Jephthah sent messengers unto the king of the E
children of Ammon, saying, What hast thou to do with me, JE/E
that thou art come unto me to fight against my land?
13 And the king of the children of Ammon answered unto JE
the messengers of Jephthah, Because Israel took away my E
land, when he came up out of Egypt, from Arnon even
unto Jabbok, and unto Jordan: now therefore restore
14 those lands again peaceably. And Jephthah sent messengers
15 again unto the king of the children of Ammon: and he JE/E
said unto him, Thus saith Jephthah, Israel took not away
the land of Moab, nor the land of the children of Ammon: JE
16 but when they came up from Egypt, and Israel walked E
through the wilderness unto the Red Sea, and came to
17 Kadesh; then Israel sent messengers unto the king of
Edom, saying, Let me, I pray thee, pass through thy land:
but the king of Edom hearkened not. And in like manner
he sent unto the king of Moab: but he would not: and
18 Israel abode in Kadesh. Then he walked through the
wilderness, and compassed the land of Edom, and the land
of Moab, and came by the east side of the land of Moab,
and they pitched on the other side of Arnon; but they came
not within the border of Moab, for Arnon was the border
19 of Moab. And Israel sent messengers unto Sihon king
of the Amorites, the king of Heshbon; and Israel said
unto him, Let us pass, we pray thee, through thy land unto
my place. But Sihon trusted not Israel to pass through
20 his border; but Sihon gathered all his people together, and
21 pitched in Jahaz, and fought against Israel. And the Lord,

the God of Israel, delivered Sihon and all his people into E
the hand of Israel, and they smote them: so Israel possessed all the land of the Amorites, the inhabitants of that
22 country. And they possessed all the border of the
Amorites, from Arnon even unto Jabbok, and from the
23 wilderness even unto Jordan. So now the Lord, the God
of Israel, hath dispossessed the Amorites from before his
24 people Israel, and shouldest thou possess them? Wilt not
thou possess that which Chemosh thy god giveth thee to
possess? So whomsoever the Lord our God hath dis-
25 possessed from before us, them will we possess. And now
art thou any thing better than Balak the son of Zippor
king of Moab? did he ever strive against Israel, or did he
26 ever fight against them? While Israel dwelt in Heshbon
and her towns, and in Aroer and her towns, and in all the
cities that are along by the side of Arnon, three hundred ?JE
years; wherefore did ye not recover them within that E
27 time? I therefore have not sinned against thee, but thou
doest me wrong to war against me: the Lord, the Judge,
be judge this day between the children of Israel and the
children of Ammon.

Deliverance from the Ammonites

29 Then the spirit of the Lord came upon Jephthah and he J
passed over Gilead and Manasseh, and passed over Mizpeh
of Gilead, and from Mizpeh of Gilead he passed over unto
the children of Ammon.

[vv. 30-31.—*Jephthah's vow.*]

32 So Jephthah passed over unto the children of Ammon to JE
fight against them, and the Lord delivered them into his
33 hand. And he smote them from Aroer until thou come J
to Minnith, even twenty cities, and unto Abel-cheramim, E?
with a very great slaughter. So the children of Ammon J
were subdued before the children of Israel. E2

[vv. 34-40.—*Jephthah offers his daughter in fulfilment of his vow.*]

JUDGES xii. *Strife with Ephraim*

1[a] And the men of Ephraim were gathered together, and J
passed northward; and they said unto Jephthah, Wherefore
passedst thou over to fight against the children of Ammon,
and didst not call us to go with thee? we will burn thine
2 house upon thee with fire. And Jephthah said unto them,

I and my people were at great strife with the children of J
Ammon; and when I called you ye saved me not out of
3 their hand. And when I saw that ye saved me not, I put
my life in my hand, and passed over against the children of
Ammon, and the Lord delivered them into my hand:
wherefore then are ye come up unto me this day, to fight
4 against me? Then Jephthah gathered together all the
men of Gilead, and fought with Ephraim: and the men of
Gilead smote Ephraim, because they said, Ye are fugitives
of Ephraim, ye Gileadites, in the midst of Ephraim and
5 in the midst of Manasseh. And the Gileadites took the
fords of Jordan against the Ephraimites; and it was so
that when any of the fugitives of Ephraim said, Let me go
over, the men of Gilead said unto him, Art thou an
6 Ephraimite? If he said, Nay: then said they unto him,
Say now Shibboleth; and he said Sibboleth; for he could
not frame to pronounce it right; then they laid hold on
him, and slew him at the fords of Jordan: and there fell
at that time of Ephraim forty and two thousand.

Judgeship of Jephthah

7 And Jephthah judged Israel six years. . . . JE

JUDGES xiii. *Oppression by the Philistines*

1 And the children of Israel again did that which was evil E2
in the sight of the Lord; and the Lord delivered them into
the hand of the Philistines forty years.

Birth of Samson.

2 And there was a certain man of Zorah, of the family of J
the Danites, whose name was Manoah; and his wife was
3 barren, and bare not. And the angel of the Lord appeared
5 unto the woman and said unto her. . . . Lo thou shalt J
conceive and bear a son; and no razor shall come upon
his head: for the child shall be a Nazirite unto God . . .
and he shall begin to save Israel out of the hand of the JE
Philistines.

[vv. 6-23.]

24 And the woman bare a son; and called his name Samson; J
25 and the child grew, and the Lord blessed him. And the
spirit of the Lord began to move him in Mahaneh-dan,
between Zorah and Eshtaol.

[Ch. xiv and xv, vv. 1-19. xvi.—*Exploits of Samson.*]

JUDGES xv. *Judgeship of Samson* E2
20 And he judged Israel in the days of the Philistines twenty
years.

[Ch. xvii.—*Micah of Mt. Ephraim and his Levite.*]

THE MIGRATION OF DAN

JUDGES xviii. *Capture of Laish*

1 In those days the tribe of the Danites sought them an J
inheritance to dwell in; for unto that day their inheritance
2 had not fallen unto them among the tribes of Israel. And JE
the children of Dan sent of their family five men from
their whole number, men of valour, from Zorah, and from
Eshtaol, to spy out the land, and to search it; and they said
7 unto them. Go, search the land. . . . Then the five J
men departed and came to Laish, and saw the people that
were therein, how they dwelt in security, after the manner E
of the Zidonians, quiet and secure; for there was none in J
the land, possessing authority, that might put them to
shame in anything, and they were far from the Zidonians,
8 and had no dealings with any man. And they came unto JE
11 their brethren to Zorah and Eshtaol: . . . And there set
forth from thence of the family of the Danites, out of
Zorah and out of Eshtaol, six hundred men girt with
12 weapons of war. And they went up, and encamped in
Kiriath-jearim, in Judah: wherefore they called that
13 place Mahaneh-dan, unto this day. And they passed thence J
unto the hill country of Ephraim, and came unto the house
27 of Micah. . . . And they took that which Micah had made,
and the priest which he had, and came unto Laish, unto a
people quiet and secure, and smote them with the edge of
28 the sword; and they burnt the city with fire. And there
was no deliverer, because it was far from Zidon, and they
had no dealings with any man.

Re-building of Dan, the City

29 And they built the city, and dwelt therein. And they J
called the name of the city Dan, after the name of Dan
their father: howbeit the name of the city was Laish at
the first.

THE HISTORICAL BACKGROUND

SECTION 1

CHRONOLOGY AND DATES

Israel and Egypt

THE passages quoted in the foregoing Introductory Section make it clear to the reader that the core of the narrative embodied in the Books of Joshua and The Judges is based essentially on the old sources (J and E), the historical value of which forms the main subject of our present enquiry. These documents are seen to relate in an intelligible though not complete sequence the events of Joshua's active leadership over united Israel, embodied in Chapters i-xi, but to become fragmentary in the later chapters which record the separation of the tribes to take up their allotted territory.

A comparison of these two portions of the Book of Joshua shows that while the effort of the Israelites to secure a footing on the highlands by force of arms was not attended by permanent success, inasmuch as the sequel to Joshua's campaigns finds them back in their base-camp at Gilgal; yet the settlement of the tribes, so far as it could be effected in accordance with the dictates of the Lot, seems to have been accomplished for the most part without fighting. This abandonment of military methods in favour of a policy of peaceful penetration suggests a corresponding change in political conditions which in the latter end would seem to have favoured the Israelites' endeavour. It must be regarded, then, as singular, that the Book contains no suggestion of any organised administrative system or political authority, with which the Israelites would necessarily be brought into contact, but pictures the various local centres like Jerusalem and Hazor as acting on their own initiative. Yet it is a fact not to be overlooked that, under any chronological system which can reasonably be advanced, the date of Israel's invasion and settlement falls within the period (1500-1100 B.C.) when the country was ruled by Egypt as an essential portion of its Syrian Empire.

The Book of Judges in the opening chapters, as far as ii 10, is seen to cover much the same ground as the second half of the Book of Joshua. Thereafter the records become less fragmentary, but at the same time less connected, reflecting in this respect the political disunity of the tribes during the succeeding centuries. Stories of local episodes have survived in some cases with considerable detail; but only occasionally is the national consciousness disclosed in the account of some united effort, such as the great rally of Deborah. Lastly it must be noticed that the longest periods, namely those of Rest, are dismissed in single lines, without any allusion to the political conditions which assured, thus intermittently, the peace of Israel. Here then once more, as in the Book of Joshua, we realize the need of an historical background. Not merely these periods of Rest, but the entire series of alternating Oppressions and Respites may be likened to the separate studies for a picture, inchoate and hardly intelligible until viewed in a common perspective. It is only when set into the background of contemporary Egyptian history that they find their place and recover their true meaning. Egyptian chronology can equally supply the frame which lends definition to the completed picture. One other thing only is needed, the *point d'appui*, and this too will be forthcoming, if we can fix the starting point, the date of Joshua's invasion, in strict relation to contemporary events.

At the outset it should be observed that all the cities mentioned in the early documents of Joshua and of Judges, i-v, which can be identified, such as Gezer, Megiddo, Bethshean and Hazor, flourished during the Bronze Age,[1] and occupied for the most part the great,

[1] Archaeologists working in Palestine to-day mostly adopt the following general scheme of classification and round dates: Early Bronze Age, 2500 B.C. Middle Bronze Age, 2000 B.C. Late Bronze Age, 1600 B.C. Rise of the Iron

old, strategic positions of the land. This is apparently not the case with the places first mentioned in the later chapters of the Book of Judges, such as Eshtaol, Timnah and Thebez, which occupy positions of secondary importance and seem to have developed chiefly with the rise of the Iron Age, after 1200 B.C.

Moreover, numerous cities of the Canaanites in the age of Joshua are identical in name and strategic importance with those mentioned in the annals of the Pharaohs of the XVIIIth Dynasty, more particularly in the records covering the hundred years between the conquests of Thutmose III and the decline of the Empire under Akhenaton, 1475-1375.[1] Twenty-four Canaanite cities may be recognised as common to both lists, which include practically all the familiar names, and may still be supplemented from the Egyptian side.[2] This suggestive accordance attains real significance from the fact that a number of the cities which the Israelites were unable to subdue, including Bethshean, Megiddo, Acco, Gezer, Jerusalem, and Gaza, are found to have been organised centres of Egyptian authority.[3] It would seem then, at first glance, that the background to the exploits of Joshua

Age, 1200 B.C. Excavations tend to show that the latter part of the Middle Bronze Age marks the culmination of Canaanite civilisation and prosperity. A summary of the archaeological data is given in the Appendix, pp. 348 ff. For the history of the place-names, see Burchardt, *Altkanaan. Fremdworte*, Leipzig, 1902.

[1] The Egyptian sources are chiefly the Name-Lists of Thutmose III, Sethe, *Urkunden*, III; iv, pp. 781 ff. Annals of Thutmose III (Breasted, *Anc. Rec. of Egypt*, ii, 408-539), and the Tell el Amarna Letters (Knudtzon, *Die El Amarna-Tafeln*, Leipzig, 1915).

[2] Names which can be recognised include: Acco—Achshaph—Aijalon—Askalon — Beth Anath — Bethshean — (Dothan) — Eglon — Gaza — Gezer — Hazor — Ibleam — Jerusalem — Kadesh — (Kinnereth) — Lachish — Libnah — Luz — Madon — Makkedah — Megiddo — Merom — Rehob — Shechem—Taanach—Sidon (26). Of these all but three (Madon, Merom and Rehob) can be identified with Bronze Age Sites. Four (Askalon, Gaza, Dothan and Kinnereth) are not mentioned by name until later in the Bk. of Judges, but the two former are doubtless to be included in the 'inhabitants of the valley' (Judg. i 19, J). For other identifications and further details see below, Sect. 2, p. 111.

[3] *T.A. Letters*, Knudtzon, Nos. 243-290, also Louvre Mus. AO. 7096. Rev., ll. 20, 22. *Rev. d'Assyriologie*, xix. 1922, p. 99.

in the land of Canaan was that which is disclosed by the Egyptian archives of the fifteenth century B.C.

In an effort to secure some more tangible evidence on this point, preliminary excavations were undertaken by the writer in 1928 on the three sites which Joshua is stated to have destroyed, namely Jericho, Ai, and Hazor. A month's work at Hazor and brief soundings on the other sites disclosed in each case the evident traces of destruction at an undetermined date near the middle of the Late Bronze Age, at the close of the fifteenth century B.C.[1] A more complete investigation of the ruined fortifications and site of Jericho in the spring of 1930 has contributed archaeological evidence in support of this conclusion.[2] The city of Ai and the camp-enclosure of Hazor were apparently abandoned from that time, while Jericho was not rebuilt, nor more than partially reoccupied, for some centuries. Moreover, soundings made by the American School of Oriental Research on the site of Bethel (Beitîn), said to have been taken by the Josephites, disclosed there also a layer of destruction attributable to the same period.[3] Details of these investigations are given in the Appendix to this volume.[4]

The fact that the three important cities which Joshua is said to have overwhelmed in the course of his campaigns, and one other subsequently captured, seem on archaeological grounds one and all to have suffered destruction at about the same time, is of itself sufficiently striking to merit consideration; it becomes of first importance when the approximate date, at the close of the fifteenth century, or in round figures 1400 B.C., is found to tally closely with the one clear indication in Biblical tradition. This is embodied in the statement that the Exodus occurred 480 years before Solomon began to

[1] See pp. 146, 151, 198. [2] Cf. *P.E.F., Q.S.* July 1930, p. 132.

[3] See p. 225; also cf. Albright in *Zeits. f. d. Alttest. Wiss.* (Giessen, 1929), p. 11, who tentatively dates this event to the fifteenth century B.C., the layer of occupation ranging between 1700 and 1400 B.C.

[4] See the Appendix, pp. 350 ff., under the several place-names.

build his temple,[a] that is about 1447 B.C.,[1] so that the date of Joshua's invasion of Canaan would fall about 1407 B.C. This tradition, it is true, has generally been assigned by critics to a late source and treated with mistrust, as the round figure of 480 years is found not to agree with the summary of details recorded in the received text of the Book of Judges.[2] None the less it will be found on re-examination in fresh light to be based exclusively on the oldest sources, while the elements of disagreement will be seen to have been introduced by the later insertions. It will evidently be helpful at this stage of our enquiry to reconsider the internal evidence of the Books themselves.

The Book of Joshua does not contain direct evidence as to the period of time covered by the narrative. The death of Joshua is recorded both in the Book of Joshua[b] and in that of Judges,[c] but in neither book is there to be found a precise statement as to the duration of his leadership or that of the Elders[d] who outlived him. From Judges ii 8, we learn that Joshua was one hundred and ten years old when he died; and if we admit the force of tradition which was at least pre-exilic, he must have been considerably over eighty-five after the fall of Hazor and before the taking of Hebron, since according to the narrative[e] that age was ascribed to Caleb, a man still full of vigour when Joshua himself was considered an old man.[f] The period of Joshua's leadership may then be estimated at twenty-five to thirty years. It is worthy of note that this estimate depends not directly on the figures of Joshua's age, which may appear to some unnaturally high, but on the relative ages of Joshua and Caleb, about which there is apparent consistency in the recorded

[a] I Kings vi 1.
[b] Joshua xxiv 29 [E].
[c] Judges ii 8 [E2].
[d] Joshua xxiv 31 and Judges ii 7 [E].
[e] Joshua xiv 7, 10 [D].
[f] Joshua xiii 1 [JE].

[1] Cf. *Camb. Anct. Hist.* I, p. 160, when the fourth year of Solomon is shown to fall about 967 B.C. by calculation from the fixed date of the battle of Karkor.

[2] Cf. Burney, *Judges*. Introd., pp. li ff. Cooke, *Judges* (*Camb. Bib.*), pp. xxvi ff.

traditions. Again in Judges ii 10, Joshua and the Elders who outlived him seem to be grouped together as one generation distinct from that which followed, while the gap itself is bridged by the career of Othniel,[a] Caleb's (younger) brother, who became the first Judge, so that the familiar round estimate of forty years to cover the periods of Joshua and of the Elders satisfies the indications of the texts.

Looking forward through the Book of Judges in the standard version (including therefore all the sources, and not only J and E), we find the following chronological data to be embodied in the text.

		Years	Source
iii 8	Israel serves Cushan-rishathaim - -	8	E2
iii 11	Deliverance by Othniel: the land rests -	40	E2
iii 14	Israel serves Eglon - - - -	18	E2
iii 30	Deliverance by Ehud: the land rests -	80	E2
iv 3	Oppression by Jabin - - - -	20	E2
v 31	Deliverance by Deborah: the land rests -	40	E2
vi 1	Oppression by the Midianites - -	7	E2
viii 28	Deliverance by Gideon: the land rests -	40	E2
ix 22	Abimelech reigns over Israel - -	3	JE, E
x 2	Tola judges Israel - - - -	23	P
x 3	Jair judges Israel - - - -	22	P
x 8	Ammonite oppression in Trans-Jordania	18	JE
	Ammonite oppression of Israel - -	1	E2
xii 7	Jephthah judges Israel - - -	6	JE
xii 9	Ibzan judges Israel - - - -	7	P
xii 11	Elon judges Israel - - - -	10	P
xii 14	Abdon judges Israel - - - -	8	P
xiii 1	Oppression by the Philistines - -	40	E2
xv 20	(xvi 31, JE) Samson judges Israel - -	20	E2
		411	

The round figures of forty years described as periods of Rest are in all probability approximations, but the fact that the figures 20 and 80 also are used shows that there is an underlying scheme limiting the error in each case to

[a] Joshua xv 17 [J]; Judges i 13 [J]; Judges iii 9 [E].

ten years and aiming at a general average of accuracy. It is to be noticed also that these round figures apply to periods vaguely defined, without any hint as to the nature of the government or political conditions which it will be our purpose to discover.

In the foregoing schedule the total number of years amounts to 411; but if we subtract from that the 91 years following after the accession of Jephthah and add to it the 40 years estimated for the leadership of Joshua and the Elders, we get 360 as the number of years from the accession of Joshua to that of Jephthah. But the accession of Joshua to the leadership followed closely (not more than two years) after the sojourn in Heshbon, so that this result is in disagreement with the statement by Jephthah in Judg. xi 26, that 300 years had elapsed since the sojourn in Heshbon. Further examination of the text, however, shows that the passages regarding the 45 years under Tola and Jair, as also those under Ibzan, Elon and Abdon, are unanimously deemed by critics to be priestly insertions of post-exilic date, and indeed their difference in style is obvious to the careful reader. All the other figures and years are derived from the old documents J and E. Moreover, it will be seen from an examination of the contexts that 18 years of the Ammonite oppression applied only to those Israelites who lived beyond Jordan in the land of the Amorites.[a] It was only at the end of that period that the Ammonites passed over Jordan to fight against all Israel. The period of national oppression therefore lasted only one year, being brought to an end apparently in the second year of Jephthah's leadership.[b] Further, the oppression of the Philistines recorded[c] as lasting 40 years is not altogether independent of the period of Samson's resistance, as may be gathered from the statement[d] that 'he judged Israel in the days of the Philistines 20 years.' The narrative of chap. xiii seems to confirm this view, the first twenty

[a] Judges x 8 [JE].
[b] Judges x 8, xi 4, xi 9, xi 32, 33.
[c] Judges xiii 1 [E2].
[d] Judges xv 20 [E2].

years of the Philistine oppression being covered by the birth, youth and preparation of Samson, and the second period by his term of opposition and judgeship. To sum up these conclusions, the narrative of the Books of Joshua and Judges, as derived from the oldest sources only, covers in round figures a period of about 343 years made up as follows:

Joshua and the Elders	Estimated	40	years
Cushan-rishathaim	Oppression	8	"
Othniel	Period of Rest	40	"
Eglon	Oppression	18	"
Ehud	Period of Rest	80	"
Sisera	Oppression	20	"
Deborah	Period of Rest	40	"
Midianites	Oppression	7	"
Gideon	Judgeship	40	"
Abimelech	Judgeship	3	"
Ammonites	Oppression	1	"
Jephthah	Judgeship	6	"
Philistines and Samson	Oppression and Judgeship	40	"
	Total	343	"

By subtracting 45, namely the 40 years of the Philistine oppression and 5 of the 6 years of Jephthah's judgeship, from this total of 343, we find that the lapse of time between the appointment of Joshua and the second year of Jephthah approximates to 298 years. Reference to the relevant passages in the Book of Numbers [a] will show that the sojourn at Heshbon preceded Joshua's appointment by a year or two at the most, bringing the total approximately to 300 years. This result is in absolute conformity with the tradition embodied in Judges xi 26.

> **While Israel dwelt in Heshbon and her towns, and in Aroer and her towns and in all the cities that are along by the side of Arnon, three hundred years ; wherefore did ye not recover them within that time ? [E]**

[a] Numbers xxi 20, 25, 26 [JE].

It is true that certain critics regard this passage as unreliable and ascribe the words 'three hundred years' to the post-exilic priestly hand, though the body of the text belongs to the early source E.[1] The words are admittedly an insertion, being ungrammatical in the Hebrew text; but the reason usually given for their rejection is itself fallacious.[2] It is based on the assumption that the figure 300 was mistakenly obtained by adding together the preceding chronological data in the Book of Judges (as set out in the schedule on p. 56), down to but not including the Ammonite oppression, which happen to amount to 301 years. But it is clearly stated that the period of 300 years is to be reckoned from the sojourn in Heshbon, and therefore must include the period of Joshua's leadership and that of the Elders, which we have seen may be estimated at about forty years, down to a time under Jephthah when the oppression of Israel west of Jordan had lasted a year. Moreover we have seen that the figure is exact when computed from the early sources. Nor can it be attributed to a late priestly insertion, because it disagrees with the total of years as increased by the added passages from that source [P]. On the other hand, as we have seen, by omitting these priestly passages, all discrepancy disappears.

We conclude, then, that inasmuch as this figure of three hundred years tallies with the details recorded exclusively in the old documents (mostly derived from E) it must have been based on the earliest traditions, and have been inserted not later than the pre-exilic (or Deuteronomic) redaction, if not as early as the seventh century B.C., when the two old documents, J and E, were blended into one.

This conclusion enables us to test in a general way the value of the other tradition mentioned, namely, that embodied in the first Book of Kings,[a] to the effect that the fourth year of King Solomon's reign, in which he

[a] I Kings vi 1.

[1] Burney, *Judges*, p. 317. [2] *Ibid.* p. 304.

began to build the temple, fell 480 years after the Exodus. Now 480 is a round figure conforming with the practice of estimating the lapse of time by periods of 40 years; presumably the exact figure would lie between 489 and 471, but in all probability not outside those limits, because in that case the nearest round figure would have become 500 or 460. The familiar critical view that the figure may be a mere computation based upon the idea of twelve judgeships or twelve high-priesthoods of precisely 40 years each, does not stand examination.[1]

However that may be, we proceed to examine the figure independently. We have already seen that the records account for 300 years down to Jephthah's second year, leaving five years to be attributed to that Judge, while 40 years covers both the oppression of the Philistines and the 20 years of Samson's judgeship. Details concerning the rest of the period down to King David are lacking in precision, but may be estimated as follows:

Remainder of Jephthah's judgeship - - - -	5	years
Samson and the Philistines (Judg. xiii 1, xv 20) - -	40	,,
Judgeship of Eli (1 Sam. iv 18), 40 years, but modified to 20 years in the LXX, the difference of 20 years being generally attributed to the period of the Philistine domination - - - - -	20	,,
Samuel (1 Sam. vii 2 and 3) not less than - - -	20	,,
Saul (C.A.H. ii, p. 701) estimated - - - -	15	,,
David (1 Kings ii 11) - - - - - -	40	,,
Solomon (1 Kings vi 1) - - - - - -	4	,,
	144	,,

These figures approximate to 144 years, leading to the following general summary:

Exodus to Heshbon - - -	38	years
Heshbon to Jephthah - - -	300	,,
Jephthah to Solomon - - -	144	,,

giving a total of 482 years, as against the 480 years of tradition.

[1] Burney, *Judges*, p. liv; cf. Jack, *Date Exod.* pp. 206, 207.

Summing up these considerations we find that the chronological scheme embodied in the original sources of the Book of Judges is consistent in itself, while the outline figures are adequately filled by the details of the narrative. Without discussing the matter further we turn to see whether the results satisfy the tenets of history as derived from Egyptian sources. Happily the reference to Solomon enables us to adopt a fixed standpoint, for the fourth year of his reign is determined by calculation as the year 967 B.C.,[1] and from this starting point, as already indicated, we arrive at 1407 B.C. for the beginning of the history of Israel in Canaan under Joshua. Upon this basis we may establish a sequence of dates and examine the political conditions prevailing in Egypt at the times indicated. We have to remember that we are still dealing with round figures, those of the Bible admitting a possible error of plus or minus nine, and those of the Egyptian chronology as between the estimates of Dr. Breasted and Dr. Hall[2] of about six years. Professor Breasted's dates, which we quote, adopt the lower scale. It should then be borne in mind that the average liability to error in making this comparison is eight years, plus or minus. Examining now the records of Egypt[3] we glean the following details as to the political status of Canaan at the approximate dates of the successive periods of Rest and Unrest.

1407-1367. *Joshua* (30 years) *and the Elders* (10 years). The Israelite invasion, with the sack of Jericho and Ai, the defeat of the Jerusalem League and the burning of Hazor, corresponds with a period of apathy under Amenhotep III, when, satisfied with his diplomatic relations and growing old, he was content to leave Syrian affairs in the hands of his vassals. The second half of the period, covering the settlement of the tribes, falls at a time when the advance from the north of invading Hittites was spreading defection rapidly; and the entry

[1] C.A.H. i, p. 160. [2] *Ibid.* ii, p. 702.
[3] Breasted, *Anct. Records of Egypt*, vols. ii-iv.

of the Ḥabiru into Shechem synchronises with the last years of Joshua, who there delivered his farewell address. The last part of the period under the Elders who succeeded Joshua[a] falls in the first part of the reign of Amenhotep IV, Akhenaton (1375 B.C.), under whom the Egyptian Empire in Canaan was temporarily lost and the country fell away to the Ḥabiru.

1367-1359. *Oppression by Cushan* (8 years). This falls in the latter part of the reign of Akhenaton when a Hittite conqueror, having annexed Mesopotamia (the land of Mitanni), had penetrated southward and entered Palestine, leaving traces at Bethshean and elsewhere.

1359-1319. *Period of Rest after Othniel* (40 years). This covers the reign of Tutenkhamon, 1356-50, during which Egyptian authority was re-established, probably through his chief general Harmhab, 1350-1314, who subsequently mounted the throne, reorganised the government and effectively maintained Egyptian supremacy.

1319-1301. *Oppression by Eglon* (18 years). This falls mostly in the first half of the reign of Seti I, 1314-1292, and synchronises closely with a coalition among the Bedouin, who were reported in that Pharaoh's first year to be gaining a footing in Palestine, and to be 'disregarding the laws of the Palace.' Following these disturbances punitive expeditions visited Acco, Bethshean, Yenoam and Hamath, and even penetrated east of the Jordan to Pahel (Fahil), restoring order; and finally left monuments recording the Pharaoh's achievements in the Hauran on the road to Damascus as well as at Bethshean.

1301-1221. *Period of Rest after Ehud* (80 years). This comprises the latter half of the reign of Seti (1314-1292), who had re-established order in Trans-Jordania and Palestine; and it covers entirely the long reign of Ramses II (1292-1225), who maintained his authority in southern

[a] Judges ii 7 [E].

Syria by treaty with the Hittites and by effective administration. It closes with disturbance early in the reign of Merneptah (1223 B.C.), with which Israel was associated. (See p. 291.) About this time Shamgar Ben Anath saved Israel by smiting the Philistines on their first appearance: Ben Anath was the name of a Syrian sea-captain signally rewarded by Ramses II.

1221-1201. *Oppression of Jabin and Sisera* (20 years). This period commences with the invasion of Northerners (Achaeans) in the reign of Merneptah, who, however, after quelling the great rebellion in Canaan (1223) showed no further sign of activity in Syria: it closes with anarchy in Egypt under a Syrian usurper named Yarsu (1205-1200).

1201-1161. *Period of Rest after Deborah* (40 years). This commences with the reign of Set-Nekht (1200-1198) who set the entire land in order; it covers the reign of Ramses III (1198-1167) who re-established Egyptian authority by defeating the great coalition of tribes in migration with the Philistines, and for some time maintained order. At the end of the period Egyptian power was weakening; and soon afterwards even the working of the mines of Sinai was abandoned.

1161-1154. *Oppression by the Midianites* (7 years). This falls in the period of Egyptian decline under the weak Ramessides.

1154-1114. *Rest under Gideon* (40 years). The growing need for a kingship, with the decline of Egyptian protection, now begins to find definite expression.

The cogency of the synchronisms apparent in the foregoing summary lends emphasis to the main fact, that throughout all the time covered by these records Canaan was administered as a part of the Egyptian Empire in Syria. Fluctuations in the efficiency of the Egyptian rule are reflected plainly in the history of Israel. The attempts under Joshua to seize the lands and cities of the Canaanites by force fall at the close of the fifteenth century B.C., previous to the complete breakdown of Egyptian authority as a sequel to the Hittite-Habiru disturbances. These in their turn opened the door, almost suddenly, to the penetration of the central highlands, and admitted soon afterwards the first Oppressor. The restoration of Egyptian control under Tutenkhamon brought with it peace for Israel, and thereafter the periods of Rest recorded in the Book of Judges correspond severally and without discrepancy to the epochs of effective Egyptian rule. In particular the one long period of 80 years' Rest covers precisely the exceptionally long reign of Ramses the Great. The periods of Oppression also synchronize in general with times when the archives express mutely Egyptian inactivity or actually tell of disturbance. It is true, on the other hand, that the Oppressions arise mostly from beyond Jordan and affect little, if at all, the seaboard and the north, wherein lay Egypt's chief interest and sphere of control. In some cases, however, the parallelism of records or events suggests direct relation. The state of disturbance under Seti I, which called for an expedition beyond the Jordan, corresponds to the oppression of Eglon; while the period of anarchy and Syrian usurpation in Egypt, following the Achaean invasions in the reign of Merneptah, coincides with the moment when Sisera and his Canaanite overlord established their independent tyranny. Similarly the mention of Ben Anath as a noted leader in Egypt at about the time when Shamgar Ben Anath saved Israel suggests a direct contact in the records of both peoples.

Such points of agreement and difference establish an inductive probability that the chronological system in general is founded on a historical basis: the possible margin of error as to the precise dates must, however, restrain us from placing full reliance on the apparent synchronism of details, which otherwise would constitute a definite proof. Further suggestive parallelisms between the records of Egypt and those of Israel will be discussed with the relevant Bible passages later in this volume. Omitting details, the outline and chief divisions of this chronological scheme may be arranged in schedule form as follows:

	B.C.			Political Situation.
Books of Exodus and Numbers	1447	40	Wandering	Domination of Egypt
Book of Joshua				
Joshua and the Elders	1407	40	(*a*) Invasion	(*a*) Apathy of Egypt in Canaan, followed by
			(*b*) Penetration	(*b*) Ḥabiru revolt and general disorder
Book of Judges				
Cushan	1367	8	Oppression	Hittite supremacy
Othniel	1359	40	Rest	Domination of Egypt
Eglon	1319	18	Oppression	Rebellion of chieftains
Ehud	1301	80	Rest	Domination of Egypt
Sisera	1221	20	Oppression	Anarchy and Syrian Usurpation in Egypt
Deborah	1201	40	Rest	Domination of Egypt
Midianites	1161	7	Oppression	Weakening of Egypt
Gideon	1154	40	Rest	Withdrawal of Egypt
Abimelech	1114	3		Withdrawal of Egypt
Ammonites	1111	1	Oppression	Withdrawal of Egypt
Jephthah	1110	6		Withdrawal of Egypt
Philistines / Samson 20	1105	40	Oppression	Philistine domination
End of the Book of Judges				
Eli	1065	20	”	Philistine domination
Samuel	1045	20	Rise of the Monarchy	
Saul	1025	15	Rise of the Monarchy	
David	1010	40	Monarchy:	Relations with Amenenopet (1020-970)
Solomon	967	4	”	Siamon (970-950)
		482		

Viewed in this tabular form the parallelisms derived from the records of Israel and of Egypt appear to be too consistent and too complete to be founded on mere coincidence. Even if the schedule were only a working theory, it would comprise at least a striking series of synchronisms. But the fact that it is derived directly from an examination of the original documents imbues it with a scientific value. Moreover, it satisfies the three fundamental conditions of the problem. In the first place, its basic date, the year of Joshua's invasion, is deduced from the only extant tradition preserved in the Biblical records; secondly, it fulfils, as we saw at the outset, the existing archaeological requirements; and thirdly, the chronological outline which depends upon it is found to agree closely with the data embodied in the earliest sources of the Book of Judges. It is therefore possible to accept with confidence the date in question, 1407 B.C., as the nearest available approximation to the opening year of the Book of Joshua, and as a basis for the chronology of the Book of Judges.

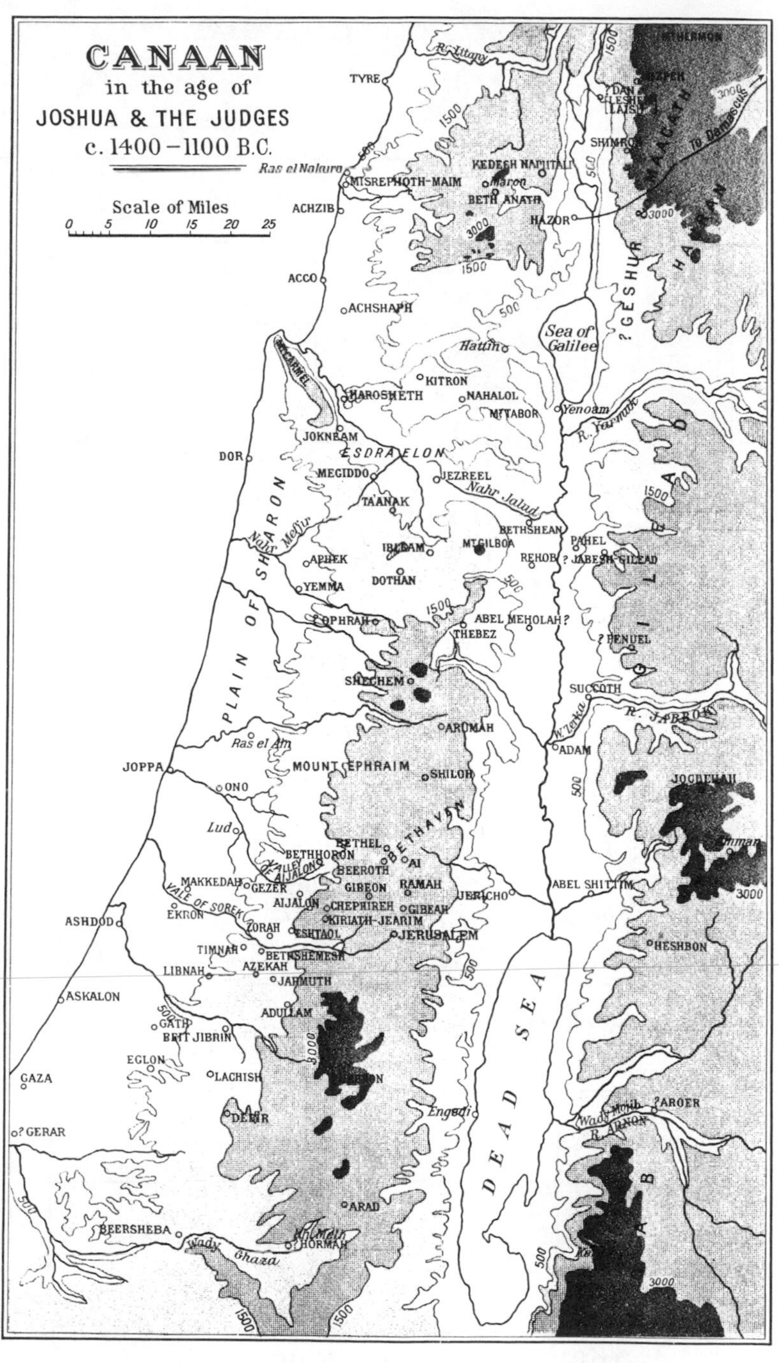
CANAAN
in the age of
JOSHUA & THE JUDGES
c. 1400 – 1100 B.C.
Scale of Miles
0 5 10 15 20 25
TYRE
R. Litany
Ras el Nakura
MISREPHOTH-MAIM
ACHZIB
KEDESH NAPHTALI
Maron
BETH ANATH
HAZOR
DAN
LESHEM
LAISH
SHIMRON
MAACATH
To Damascus
GESHUR
HAURAN
ACCO
ACHSHAPH
Sea of Galilee
Hattin
KITRON
HAROSHETH
NAHALOL
Mt. TABOR
Yenoam
R. Yarmuk
JOKNEAM
ESDRAELON
DOR
MEGIDDO
JEZREEL
Nahr Jalud
TAANAK
BETHSHEAN
PLAIN OF SHARON
Nahr Mefjir
IBLEAM
Mt. GILBOA
PAHEL
REHOB
? JABESH-GILEAD
GILEAD
APHEK
DOTHAN
YEMMA
? OPHRAH
ABEL MEHOLAH ?
THEBEZ
? PENUEL
SHECHEM
SUCCOTH
W. Zerka
R. JABBOK
ARUMAH
Ras el Ain
ADAM
JOPPA
MOUNT EPHRAIM
SHILOH
ONO
JOGBEHAH
Lud
BETHAVEN
BETHEL
BETHHORON
AI
VALLEY OF AIJALON
BEEROTH
MAKKEDAH
GEZER
GIBEON
RAMAH
JERICHO
ABEL SHITTIM
Amman
VALE OF SOREK
AIJALON
CHEPHIREH
GIBEAH
EKRON
KIRIATH-JEARIM
ASHDOD
ZORAH
ESHTAOL
JERUSALEM
HESHBON
TIMNAH
BETHSHEMESH
LIBNAH
AZEKAH
JARMUTH
ASKALON
ADULLAM
DEAD SEA
GATH
BEIT JIBRIN
EGLON
GAZA
LACHISH
HEBRON
Engedi
Wady Mojib
? AROER
R. ARNON
? GERAR
DEBIR
MOAB
ARAD
BEERSHEBA
Khurmeh
HORMAH
Wady Ghaza
Kir
500
1500
3000

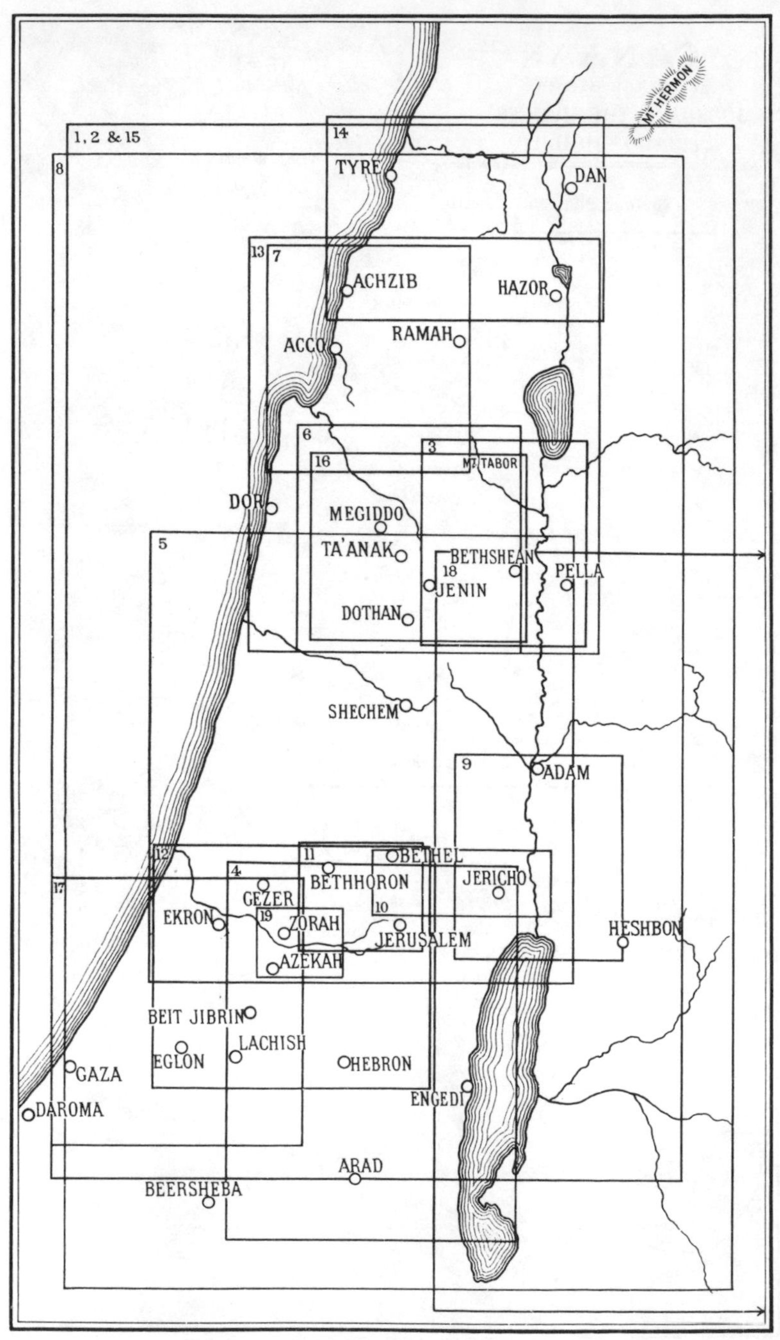

Key to Sectional Maps 2 – 19

SECTION 2

CANAAN AT THE COMING OF ISRAEL

The Rôle of Egypt

PALESTINE occupies little more than one-third of the Syrian seaboard. In length, from Dan in the north to Beersheba in the south, it measures as the crow flies less than 150 miles; while its average width, from the Mediterranean coast to the Jordan valley, is only 45 miles. Its importance lies rather in its situation as the meeting place of the old civilisations, and its character in the intense variety of its physical features. The plains that skirt the seashore, and here and there trend eastward, present indeed some uniformity of appearance; but they were for the most part too strongly held for Israel to seize, while the central highlands, on which Joshua and his followers first secured a footing, are reft in every direction by deep rock-strewn valleys. The valour of the military exploits recorded in the Books of Joshua and Judges is to be gauged by their difficulty rather than their magnitude. An appreciation of the physical character of the land is indeed essential to a proper understanding of its history.

Palestine is a land of contrasts. It may be regarded as bounded on the north by Mt. Hermon and the lower reach of the Litany River where this breaks westward around the foot of Lebanon towards the sea; and on the south by the partially desert plains of North Arabia. In broad outline its chief features are three, namely the valley of the Jordan, the coastal plains, and, between these, the central highlands. None of these features is altogether uniform in itself: each is interrupted at about one-third of its course from north to south, the river by the sea of Galilee, the ridge of mountains by the Plain of Esdraelon, and the coastlands by the bold headland of Mt. Carmel.

THE JORDAN VALLEY

The River Jordan rises in the western slopes of Mt. Hermon, but only when passing the southern extremity that mountain does it enter Palestine. Thereafter it winds in a southerly course down the northern extension of the Great Rift, falling steadily below sea level, until in the Dead Sea it finds the bottom of this extraordinary fault, which then rises gradually as far as Akabah. In its upper reaches for some twelve miles the Jordan collects from the surrounding hills and marshes the waters of Lake Huleh, which is almost at sea-level. Flowing then through a rocky bed a further ten miles it enters the Sea of Galilee or Gennesaret.

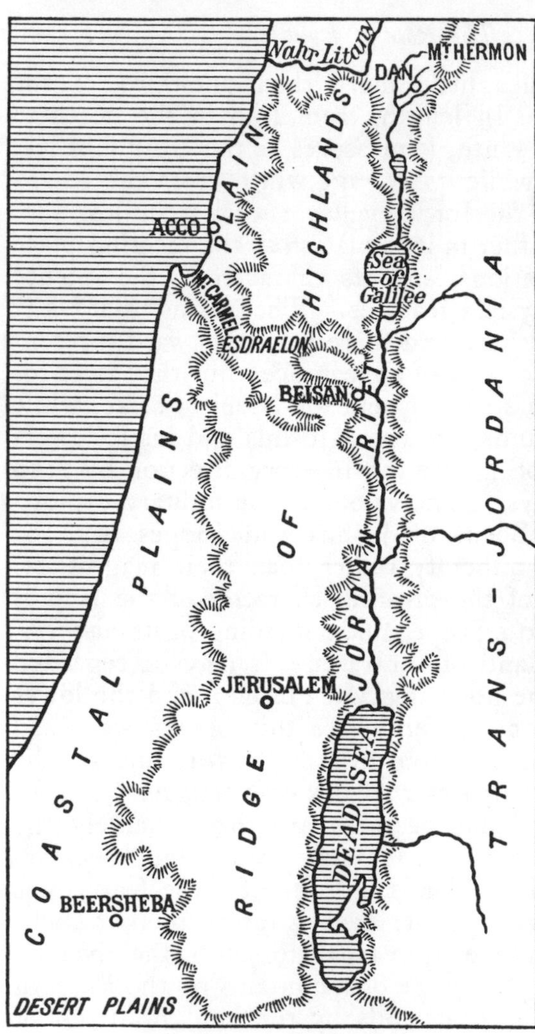

Map 2. Chief physical features of Palestine.

THE SEA OF GALILEE, NORTHERN END.

Viewed from below the site of Chinnereth, to the S.W.

THE SEA OF GALILEE, SOUTHERN END.

Where the Jordan flows out.

See pp. 68, 101.

This lake is thirteen miles long and about seven miles across, and its waters are nearly 700 feet below sea-level. Thereafter the river pursues a sinuous southerly course through marl beds and alluvium for a further sixty-five miles, falling steadily the while, but more gently, so that where it enters the Dead Sea its greatest depth is found to be 1300 feet below the level of the Mediterranean. The Dead Sea being completely enclosed, its waters are too saturated with salts to support life. The Rift-valley also, apart from the actual banks of the river, is not generally fertile. The rainfall is not sufficient to cleanse the soil of its mineral deposits, so that the land remains sour, and agriculture is only possible in those few places where some perennial spring or tributary permits a constant irrigation of the soil. But for the most part the Rift, both north and south of the Dead Sea, presents to the eye a forbidding panorama of desolation, intensified here and there by fantastical formations into which the age-long erosion of wind and rain has cut out its surface of alternating marl and limestone.[1]

The watercourses that flow to the Jordan from the western side are steep. From the middle of the ridge at Shechem the horizontal distance to the river is only eighteen miles,[2] while the fall is 3000 feet, and this is an average situation. Consequently, these watercourses are mostly dry except in the early spring when they are scoured bare by the abundant albeit intermittent rains. One or two streams like the Jalud which flows from the Plain of Esdraelon, and the Farah below Shechem, are fed by relatively copious springs; but little of their water reaches the Jordan itself, being absorbed by irrigation and village requirements on its course.

On the eastern side the basin of the river has no definite boundary.[3] Great tributaries like the Yarmuk, the Zerka (Jabbok) and, on a smaller scale, the Wady Mojib (Arnon) drain a relatively wide area of the eastern plateau, which in turn reaches away, and is only bounded

[1] See Pl. III. [2] Cf. Map 1, p. 67. [3] Cf. Map 13, p. 188.

by the indefinite edges of the great plains beyond; so that the lands east of Jordan, though perhaps not claiming so rich a soil, are more extensive and more habitable, being more readily cultivated than on the west. Not much is known about the ancient topography of Trans-Jordania, since on that side no excavation has been carried out on Bronze Age sites. But the nature of the mounds and the pottery to be found upon their surface indicate a development collateral with the early civilisations of the Jordan valley. While some sites such as Heshbon (Hesban),[1] and Rabbath-Ammon (Amman) can be identified with a degree of certainty, others such as Ramoth-Gilead and Jabesh-Gilead can only be located in a general way from superficial indications. Kir of Moab, if rightly placed at Kerak,[2] and Petra, have been examined to some extent, but little if anything older than the third century B.C. has been recovered. Both, however, are naturally habitable sites; and there is little reason to doubt but that excavation will trace them, like the cities of Palestine, to a much earlier origin.

On the west bank of the river modern Jericho stands near the ancient city of that name, and not far from the north-west shore of the Dead Sea; but no other town or ancient site of moment is to be found upon the western bank for twenty miles.[3] The sun-heat in this enclosed valley is hard to bear, and this fact coupled with the lack of water and the poorness of its soil, renders it unsuitable for settlement, especially on the western bank. Jericho owes its life to the copious springs of Ain el Sultan and Ain el Duk,[4] and its position marks the meeting point of routes descending from the plateau upon the fords of Jordan leading to the land of Moab. Twenty-five miles higher up the valley, the mouth of the Wady Farah

[1] See the Appx. p. 384, and Pl. LXVIII. [2] See Pl. LVIII.

[3] Cf. Map of the Lower Jordan Valley, p. 126.

[4] Pronounced euphoniously Es-Sultan and Ed-Duk, and so in general. *El*, the definite article in Arabic, does not change its spelling, but is assimilated in pronunciation to the following consonant.

THE JORDAN VALLEY AT EL DAMIEH.

The River flows below the cliff in the foreground, the view being from the west with the hills of Moab in the background.

TELL EL DAMIEH, THE SITE OF ADAM: Joshua iii, 16.

To be seen in the upper photograph on the left of the plain at the foot of the eroded ridge.

See pp. 71. 136.

provides another link with the plateau; but the amount of the water that escapes the village life by the stream's upper course is small, so that no important city has arisen at the junction, notwithstanding that this route descends directly upon one of the best fords of the Jordan, the Jisr el Damieh. The small city of El Damieh (Adam) that watched this ford stood upon the opposite bank in a tiny plain, just below the last bend and the junction of the Jabbok.

Above this ford, the western bank narrows to a strip of foothills [1] now traversed by a road, for some fifteen miles, after which the hills begin to recede behind a habitable plain of increasing fertility, until at the foot of Gilboa, fifty miles above Jericho, the whole aspect changes. Here the valley of Jezreel links the Plain of Esdraelon by a broad opening with the valley of the Jordan, providing at the same time a channel for a small stream called the Nahr Jalud, and the traces of ancient settlement are plentiful. The strategic spot where these two valleys merge into one has been dominated through all time by the city of Bethshean, now Beisan.[2] It stood at the focus of important routes connecting Damascus and the cities of Gilead with the cities of Esdraelon and the port of Acco. Excavations, which have been proceeding for some years on this site, have shown that it shared to the full in the life history of the country, at any rate back to the fifteenth century B.C. At that time a dominating element in local culture was still derived from Babylonia [3]; but after that date it figures in the records of Egypt as an important military outpost, and the monuments of successive Pharaohs, Seti I, Ramses II and III, no less than the annals of their reigns, attest the fact that, but for occasional interruptions, it maintained this rôle until the twelfth century B.C.

Other mounds in the vicinity indicate a contemporary

[1] Cf. Map, p. 72, and Pl. LIX. [2] Pl. LIII.

[3] Cf. Rowe, *Mus. Journ.* Philadelphia, March 1924. Pl. J, p. 48; also G., *H.E.*, p. 331.

and even earlier development. Some forty sites of the Bronze Age may be counted in the immediate neighbour-

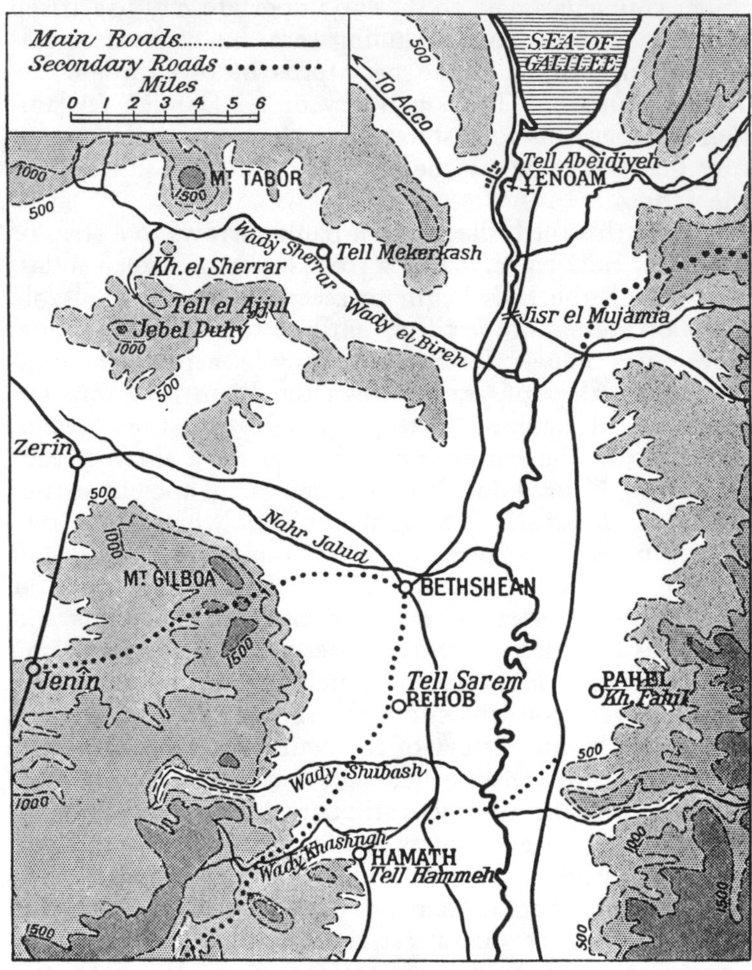

Map 3. The Middle Jordan Valley.

hood to the south and east, extending to the far side of the Jordan, and others are to be seen in the valley northwards as far as the foot of the Sea of Galilee. To judge by the superficial indications, some of these were the homes of communities whose greatest activity belonged to the earliest days of the Bronze Age, before 2000 B.C., after which they seem to have been deserted, while other sites came into prominence. This change, no doubt, was the result of the Hyksos invasion and occupation, the close of which must have brought about a corresponding reaction, though not necessarily the reoccupation of the original sites.

Several of the ancient cities in the vicinity of Bethshean are known to us only from the Egyptian records. Two of these, Rehob and Pahel,[1] were connected with the road system of which Beisan is the centre, Rehob at Tell el Sarem four miles to the south, and Pahel, clearly the classical Pella, at Kh. Fahil seven miles south-eastward, across a convenient ford. Further south, on the west bank, some fifteen miles below Beisan, the imposing mound of Tell Hammeh[2] also marks a Bronze Age settlement, and may prove to be the site of Hamath, which is associated with Pahel and Rehob in an inscription discovered at Beisan.[3] It is placed at the foot of the hills, where the valley widens, not far from the outlet of the Wady Khasneh, and so commands the route which descends in a north-easterly direction from the highlands by way of Tubas. Above Beisan the most important position strategically is that of Tell Abeidiyeh, which is found on the west bank of the Jordan about fifteen miles higher up, in a loop of the river, where it dominated the best ancient ford connecting with the Hauran. In this position it stands two miles below the Sea of Galilee, and some five miles above the point where the waters of the Yarmuk join the main stream, with the fords of Jisr el Mujamia just below. Its appearance and strategic importance correspond well with the *Yenoam* of Egyptian texts,[4] so often the objective of the Pharaoh's expeditions.

[1] Cf. Rowe, *The Mus. Journ.*, March 1929, p. 93; Albright, *Bull. Am. S.O.R.*, October 1925, p. 18; Saarisalo, *Bound. Issach. and Naph.*, 1927, p. 111; Abel, *Rev. Bibl.*, N.S. 10, 1913, p. 218.

[2] See Pl. LIX. [3] Rowe, *loc. cit.* ll. 15, 19. [4] See Pl. IV and fig. 1.

The four sites, Bethshean, Rehob, Pahel, and Yenoam, are associated, one with another, in more than one

Fig. 1. *Yenoam*, retaken by Seti I.

record, notably the inscription found at Beisan which describes the measures taken by Seti I to restore order in the locality.[1]

THE CENTRAL HIGHLANDS

Leaving for the time being further consideration of the north country, we return to take a nearer view of the central and southern highlands. These, we have seen, are so torn by the sharp watercourses descending on either side, for the most part through bare rock, that the habitable areas are determined and at the same time restricted by the local features. Along the whole ridge direct communication between north and south is only practicable by the tortuous line of the main watershed,

[1] Rowe, *loc. cit.* p. 93, l. 21. See further, p. 271.

TELL ABEIDIYEH, POSSIBLY THE EGYPTIAN YENOAM, VIEWED FROM THE SOUTH.

See pp. 73, 271 and cf. fig 1.

whereas in the other direction, east to west, numerous valleys provide ready means of communication with the coastal plains and with the Jordan valley.

These highlands find their culmination in the vicinity of Hebron, without, however, breaking into mountains, for the highest point attains only 3700 feet. The formations none the less are bold, and cultivation is restricted to the small stony plains and terraced hills in the immediate neighbourhood. The ancient city, the precise position of which is not defined, stood in all probability above the modern town and hence upon the main road from north to south which, in the latter direction, led by Beersheba (25 miles) to the plains of the southern Negeb, and so towards Egypt. It is also possible to descend from Hebron to the shores of the Dead Sea at Engedi,[1] though the road is rough and steep, the fall being more than 4000 feet in a distance of fifteen miles. A good track descends westwards by the Wady el Afranj, and crossing the foothills of the Shephelah in the vicinity of Beit Jibrîn, leads over the plain to Askalon and to Gaza.

Jerusalem, twenty miles to the north, stands also upon the central spine, though inclining towards the east, and so overlooking the Jordan valley opposite the head of the Dead Sea. The ground in the vicinity is stony, but small plains are found immediately to the north and to the south-west. The ancient city stood in the south-east of the modern site upon a sharp ridge at the head of the Wady el Nar.[2] In this position it commanded the main route by Jericho towards the east, which communicated westward by the Wady Surar (the Vale of Sorek) with the plains, crossing the Shephelah near Bethshemesh.

Northward again stood Bethel at a distance of ten miles, the approach to it from the Jordan Valley being covered by the strong position of Ai.[3] West of the line from Jerusalem to Bethel, six miles from each, almost on the present site of El Jib, stood Gibeon, rising above

[1] See Map, p. 76. [2] Pl. XXXVIII. [3] Pl. XXVIII.

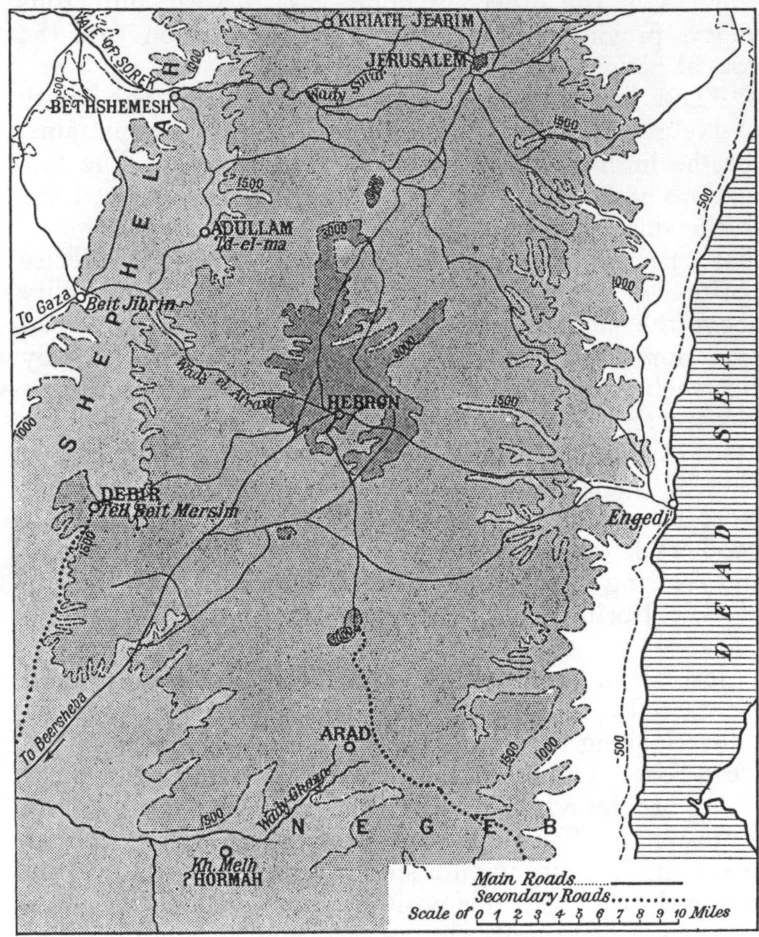

Map 4. The Southern Highlands and Negeb.

the eastern border of a small plain,[1] and the political centre, according to tradition,[a] of a number of dependent cities.[2]

[a] Joshua ix 17 [P].

[1] Plates XXXIV, XLI.

[2] Though the passage naming these cities is ascribed by critics to P, it would seem to be derived from earlier sources as the sites prove on examination to have been in active occupation in the late Bronze Age. See also p. 163 and Map No. 11.

THE PLAIN OF LUBBAN IN MT. EPHRAIM, FROM THE SOUTH.

Now traversed by the main road from Jerusalem to Nablus.

THE CITY OF NABLUS, WHICH REPLACES ANCIENT SHECHEM.

Viewed from above its chief spring on Mt. Gerizim, with Mt. Ebal in the background.

See pp. 78, 248.

These within their restricted territory formed a strategic group: Beeroth at Tell Nasbeh near Bireh guarded the approaches from the east, while Chephirah (to-day Kh. Kefireh) and Kiriath Jearim (Kiryat el Enab) respectively covered those from the coastal plains by way of the Wady Kotneh and by the now familiar route from Jerusalem to Jaffa through the Bab el Wad. A more direct way to Jaffa from Gibeon would pass, however, north-west down the Wady Selman or down the adjoining ridge past Beth-horon, and both these were used in Roman times as main roads from Jerusalem. The first stage involved a slight detour, as a low ridge crowned by Nebi Samwîl separates Jerusalem from the position of El Jib. It is not known at what date direct communication was established between Jerusalem and Jaffa. In the time of Joshua the tetrapolis of Gibeon seems to have formed a group apart, inhabited by an alien element, the Hivites [1]; while Beth-horon, though linked with Gibeon by an open road, seems to have nurtured a distinct population with its own policy and relations. None the less in the opening of the fourteenth century B.C., to which period we assign the settlement of the tribes, the valley road leading down past Gibeon and below Beth-horon into the Vale of Aijalon,[2] between the Shephelah and the hills, is known to have been used for caravans plying between Jerusalem and Egypt.[3] It is worthy of recollection that amid the disturbances of that time this road was evidently considered safer for some reason than those by Hebron or Beit Jîbrîn or the Wady Surar, all of which are more direct: it is true that even on this route one caravan was robbed, and it is the report of Jerusalem's ruler to the Pharaoh on the subject that provides the information.

[1] There is doubt about this name. In the LXX [Josh. ix 7] it is rendered 'Horite,' which may refer to an aboriginal population; cf. the Egyptian *Ḥaru*, applied to the southern highlands. Another easy emendation would read 'Achæan,' which, however, seems historically improbable in the present state of information: see below, p. 314.

[2] Pronounced 'Aiyalon,' and so written in contemporary documents. The name survives as 'Yalo.' Cf. Pl. LII.

[3] *T.A. Letters*, Kn. No. 287.

This relatively open and fertile area of Gibeon and Bethel gives place towards the north in turn to a series of bolder highlands forming part of the system known as the Mountains of Ephraim, a region of broken limestone hills, freely bedecked with oak scrub and varied by an occasional wooded valley. Herein few Bronze Age sites have been examined, though Seilun, the site of Shiloh,[a] lying just off the track towards the east, at the head of the Wady Kub, dates its origin from that period, while other places of later Biblical interest have been tentatively located.[1] From here northwards past Nablus the mountains become less rugged, and the watercourses less precipitous. The small plains, which form so marked a feature of the plateau-ridge,[2] become more expansive, and generally more fertile, as the average level of the mountain mass falls gradually towards the Plain of Esdraelon. Thus Shechem, the most historic position of this area, though occupying like Nablus, its successor, the narrow valley between Mts. Ebal and Gerizim, with the tower of Shechem [b] at its mouth, marks at the same time the north end of a relatively extensive plain, drained by the uppermost sources of the Wady Kanah. The watershed itself hereabouts lies eastward, along a narrow and well marked ridge, whereon reposes the strong place of El Ormë, possibly the site of Arumah.[c] The ridge is broken by the Wady Farah which, though at the outset steep, provides direct communication with the Jordan valley, across which it leads to the ford of the Jisr el Damieh. At first the descent by this valley clings to the abrupt face of a ravine, recalling the words used by the Egyptian courier of the thirteenth century B.C., trying to terrify a friend by his description of the roads through Canaan—'a ravine is on one side of thee, the mountain rises on the other. On thou goest jolting. . . . thy chariot on its side.'[3]

[a] Cf. Judges xxi 19 [P]. [b] Judges ix 46, 47, 49 [E].
[c] Judges ix 41. [J].

[1] Cf. Albright: *Bull A.S.O.R.*, No. 35, 1929, p. 6. [2] See Pl. V.

[3] Gardiner: *Pap. Anast.* I, p. 26. Cf. our Pl. XI.

MAP Nº 5

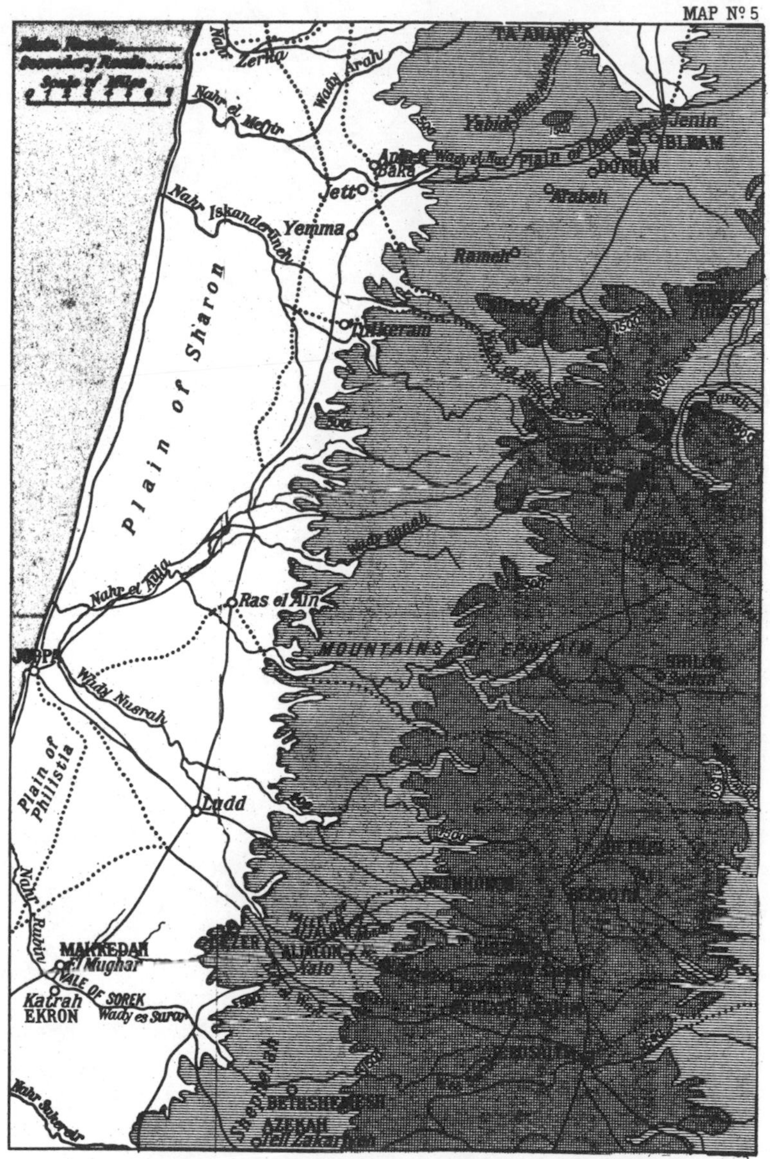

THE CENTRAL HIGHLANDS AROUND SHECHEM

The best of all roads leading from Shechem to the coastal plain is provided by the Wady Shaîr, which has a gradual descent and an open course. It leads, however, north-westwards, and its importance could hardly have been developed to its full until the Roman administration established headquarters upon the sea-coast at Caesarea, towards which it points. Nevertheless, Shechem throughout the whole Bronze Age constituted the political centre of a wide area. As early as the XIIth Dynasty of Egypt the chance record of an Egyptian general [1] shows that it shared with *Retenu* a special position in the organisation of southern Palestine. Its prominence in Egyptian literature of that time is fully accordant with the importance attributed to it in the narratives of the Patriarchs,[a] which find an echo also in later legend.[2] It may indeed at that time have been the chief city of the territory known to the Egyptians as Upper Retenu, in distinction to Lower Retenu, the centre of which seems to have been near Ludd. It is open to conjecture that the whole country was divided at that early period (*c.* 2200 B.C.) into principalities of much wider range than the city states of a later age [3]; even so Shechem was numbered among the few ruling centres, of which the most important were Jerusalem in the south, Ludd upon the Plain, and Hazor in the far north. However that may be, in the Amarna age (*c.* 1380-1360 B.C.) Shechem still occupied a unique place in the political organisation of the area; indeed neither in the Egyptian records nor in the Book of Joshua is there trace of any rival city between Bethel and Dothan.[3] Villages like Arrabeh, Sileh, and Ramah, between Shechem and Dothan, may mark the sites of fairly ancient communities; but their origins and

[a] Genesis xxxiii 18, etc.

[1] Cf. Peet: *The Stela of Sebek-Khu*, ll. 1, 2. Manchester Museum, 1914. P. 4; also Newberry in G., *El Arabah*, Ch. V., p. 33.

[2] Cf. *Bk. of Jubilees*, xxxiv, and *Testament of Levi* in the Apocrypha. Ed. Charles, vol. ii, pp. 64, 316, 364.

[3] Cf. Alt: *Landnahme der Israeliten*, pp. 5 f. Very few sites in the central highlands have been traced to Bronze Age origins.

their relation to Dothan have not been determined, and it remains doubtful whether their history goes back beyond the rise of the Iron Age (1200 B.C.).

Dothan is found some twenty miles farther towards the north, in the south-east corner of an extensive plain, at a point where the main north-south road is crossed by a caravan route which connects Beisan by the lower slopes of Gilboa with the coastal plains [a] near Jett. Presumably it stood upon the mound which still bears its ancient name and is well watered by a perennial spring.[1] Though no excavation has yet been made within the Tell, the antiquity of the site is indicated by the potsherds to be found upon its slopes. Curiously enough, though mentioned in the Bible at the time of the Patriarchs, as well as in the records of Egypt [2] under Thutmose III (*c.* 1480 B.C.) and possibly also as *Tatna* in the *Tell el Amarna Letters* [3] (*c.* 1375 B.C.), Dothan escapes mention in the Books of Joshua and Judges. None the less it would appear from its size and position to have been the centre of an important and prosperous area, too great and too far from the nearest Canaanite cities of Esdraelon, Ibleam, Taanak,[4] and Megiddo, to have been counted amongst their dependent cities.

Neither Egyptian nor Biblical tradition suggests that any one of these greater cities was ever sufficiently powerful of itself to dominate the rest. Rather it seems probable that at the time of the Egyptian conquest the land became broken up politically into numerous small principalities of an extent determined ultimately by their physical surroundings. In this system the walled city of the local chief (called king) would doubtless still be looked upon in certain areas as a refuge and trade centre by a number of surrounding towns and village communities.

[a] Cf. Genesis xxxvii 25 [J].

[1] See Plate VI.

[2] Sethe: *Urkunden*, iv, 781, No. 9.

[3] *Amarna Letters*, Kn. No. 233, and Weber, *Anmerk.* p. 1302.

[4] *Bibl.* Taanach: the final letter 'k' is adopted on phonetic grounds from the Egyptian and Arabic spellings: modern Tell Ta'anuk.

THE TELL OR CITY MOUND OF DOTHAN.

The place still bears its ancient name, and was known to the Egyptians as Tatna (c. 1375 B.C.)

THE SPRINGS OF DOTHAN FROM THE SOUTH.

To be seen in the upper picture on the right foreground.

See pp. 80, 89.

Thus Gibeon, the chief Hivite city, is regarded as the centre and head of three others; and though the record in the received text is not all attributed to the old sources,[a] in this case the sites themselves can be ascribed without hesitation to the period of the narrative.[1] The organisation of the great Canaanite centres of Esdraelon and Jezreel is, however, clearly indicated in the oldest elements of both Books,[b] wherein reference is made to 'Beth-shean and her towns, . . . Dor and her towns, . . . Taanach and her towns and . . . Megiddo and her towns.' This passage gives at the same time a good indication of the normal size of these small states, the three last named places being only about eight miles apart. On the other hand Hazor, according to Biblical tradition, seems to have controlled a wide zone: 'for Hazor beforetime was the head of all those kingdoms,'[c] and though this passage is attributed for textual reasons to the pre-exilic redactor D, the statement seems to be confirmed by the Tell el Amarna letters, for the king of Hazor writes assuring the Pharaoh that he was guarding Hazor and its cities for his lord, the King,[2] and other contemporary records indicate a wide range of influence.[3] However, in this respect the position of Hazor appears to have been altogether exceptional. Jerusalem itself was obviously the administrative centre of an important district; but though Abd-Khipa its king reported to the Pharaoh the taking of one of his towns by the Ḥabiru,[4] and, as we know, zealously kept his suzerain informed about the development of events in general, he never intervened in the affairs of the other great cities. The zone of each vassal prince was circumscribed by nature. The physical features and configuration of the central plateau seem to dictate one general conclusion: that these highlands, while supporting life to a limited extent and determining

[a] Joshua ix 3 [E], 17 [P]. [b] Joshua xvii 11 [J], Judges i 27 [J]. [c] Joshua xi 10 [D].

[1] See pp. 164 ff.

[2] *Amarna Letters*, Kn. No. 228.

[3] See below, p. 183.

[4] *Amarna Letters*, Kn. No. 290.

the places for settlement, did not foster communication between the different habitable areas, except along a single line of road which required some controlling power such as Egypt to put it to full advantage.

THE SOUTHERN NEGEB

We have considered two of the leading features in the south country, namely the lower Jordan and the southern highlands. Before proceeding northwards it remains to examine the coastal plains, and as these merge towards the south with the plains of the Negeb, we may usefully take a passing glance at this area. A single description covers the whole region from the Great Rift westward to the sea,—a land of rolling plains with a not ungrateful soil, but dependent in the main upon a capricious rainfall, and hence never able to retain a settled population. At the approach of harvest the land becomes dotted with tents of Bedawi; but these disappear as the year draws on and the soil becomes parched under the relentless sun. Some of the tribes by immemorial right make for the coastlands where they glean, and graze their famishing flocks; some few even pass on into Esdraelon.[1] For the rest, the desert tracks wind away in all directions and disappear into the distant haze.

In antiquity Arad,[2] still recognisable from its vast Tell bearing the same name, occupied an important position at the centre of numerous desert routes. It stood on the foothills below Hebron, at the very head of the longest watercourse of the area, the Wady Ghaza, along which are found several of the best known sites. Among these may be noted Kh. Melh (possibly Hormah),[3] Tell el Saba (Beersheba), where to-day meet all roads and tracks from hills and plains, lower down Tell Fara, and, six miles from the sea, Tell Jemmeh, the reputed site of Gerar. The Wady Ghaza may be regarded for our

[1] Cf. below, p. 301. [2] Pl. VII., see also below, p. 215.

[3] Cf. below, p. 216; also the Map No. 4, p. 76.

THE SOUTHERN NEGEB, VIEWED FROM TELL ARAD.
The Wilderness of Judah: Judges i, 16.

TELL ARAD, THE SITE OF ARAD: Judges i, 16.
Traces of ancient defensive works are visible around this deserted site.

See pp. 82, 215.

present purpose as the southern boundary of Palestine, as it rises only fifteen miles from the Dead Sea, and with a broad sweep southward enters the Mediterranean to the south of Gaza. The regions of partial desert further to the south concern chiefly the story of the Exodus and the desert wandering: they hardly enter at all into the history of Joshua and The Judges.

THE COASTAL PLAINS

The coastlands of Palestine present throughout their whole length from the Negeb northwards to Mt. Carmel a similarity of general appearance, though varying in width, fertility and political importance. The immediate vicinity of the shore, particularly towards the south between Gaza and Jaffa, is continually menaced by encroaching sand-drifts, which have indeed already almost obliterated the ancient site of Ashdod. Further inland, the plains, though level compared with the open spaces upon the hills and correspondingly easy to plough, are by no means flat, but undulate like the swell of a calm sea: so that while even a small height commands an extensive view, for the most part the immediate horizon is circumscribed. The land is further divided into irregular areas by the courses of numerous winter streams which, following the low ground, have scoured out deep channels in the alluvial soil. Some of these watercourses are permanent and by their size affect appreciably the communications of the area.[1] Such are, from south to north, the Wady Ghaza, already mentioned, being the longest of all, with a course of not less than sixty miles, the Wady el Sharîa and the Wady el Hesy, which drain the south-western slopes of the plateau, the Nahr Sukereir which as the Wady Afranj comes down from near Hebron by Beit Jibrin, the Nahr Rubin, better known in its upper reaches as the Vale of Sorek, the Wady Nusrah, which is fed from the Vale of Aijalon and the hills of Ephraim,

[1] Cf. Map No. 5, facing p. 79.

and is joined near the sea by the Wady Kanah from the heights south and east of Shechem, the Nahr Iskandaruneh which rises also near Shechem but flows north-east, the Nahr el Mefjir, which by the Wady el Nar drains the plain of Dothan and descends to the northern plain by Jett, and the Nahr el Zerka or Crocodile River, which has a shorter course from the hills that lie between the Plain of Esdraelon and the sea. These river beds with their numerous affluents not only divide up the plains in a manner which in antiquity cannot but have influenced local development and political conditions, but they have determined the main lines of communication throughout the country. Most of these watercourses for some geological reason trend north-westward, a feature which facilitated in its day the road service between Jerusalem and Jaffa, as between Samaria and Caesarea, but lay across the line of the earlier trunk road from Egypt.

The route of the Egyptians through the coastal plains from Gaza can be followed with some certitude. Its course is determined by considerations of a permanent character, the crossings of torrent beds, the supply of water, and the suitability of camping grounds, so that in the Middle Ages the Mamelukes moving northward once again disclosed the most favourable line.[1] Its main stages ran from Gaza to Katra and thence to Ras el Ain; these places are twenty-five to thirty miles apart, a good day's journey for a mounted courier with pack animals. The armies moved of necessity much slower. Near Katra in particular, between the ancient city, which is found in the north of that site, and Moghar, lies a suitable camp ground and good water. At Ras el Ain water is abundant, and just above the springs a broad flat mound, ten or twelve acres in extent, partly covered by the mediaeval

[1] Cf. Gaudefroy-Demombynes: *La Syrie à L'Epoque des Mamelouks* (1923), pp. 242 ff, where we find that the posts from Gaza to Damascus pursued the following line: Ghaza—El Jetîn—Bet Daras formerly Tadâris, where was a Ḥan, or alternatively Yasour—Qatra—Ludd—El Auja (Ras El Ain)—El Tira (Ḥan)—Qaqoun—Fahma—Jenîn—Dar'in (Zerîn)—'Ain Jaloud—Beisan—Jisr El Majami'. Cf. Map No. 8, p. 110.

RAS EL 'AIN, 'THE SPRING HEAD,' FROM THE NORTH-WEST.

A stage on the route of the Egyptian armies towards the north.

THE MOUND AND HEADLAND OF DORA JUST NORTHWARD OF TANTURAH.

Possibly the site of Dor which marked the western extremity of the old Canaanite frontier : Joshua xvii. 2. *See pp. 84, 232.*

Ḥan,[1] shows traces of actual occupation in the Late Bronze Age. A similar stage northwards brings us to the neighbourhood of Yemma, Jett and Baka, from each of which tracks turn inwards towards Esdraelon,[2] by way of a defile well known in the locality and called the Bab el Ebweib, 'the Door of the Doors.'

Baka lies nearest to this pass, but seems to be exclusively an Iron Age site, and rather far from Ras el Ain for a one-day stage. It corresponds well, however, to 'Aphek,' where the Philistines concentrated previous to their attack upon the Israelites under Saul.[a] Jett is a Bronze-age city, strongly placed upon a knoll which dominates its surroundings. Good camping ground with a water-supply is found upon the plain to the north, between Jett and Baka, but it is unprotected, and as we have said rather too far north for a regular halting-place on the Egyptian military road. The starting-off point for Thutmose III previous to his attack on the enemy near Megiddo was called Yehem, and the modern Yemma while recalling this name provides an appropriate position at the requisite distance, twenty-five miles northwards from Ras el Ain. At this place a wide low platform some fifteen to twenty acres in extent provides a suitable camp ground, and seems to have been further defended in the Bronze Age by a surround of megalithic blocks. Traces of a well and storage cisterns, though filled up, are visible within the enclosure. The march of the Egyptian armies from Gaza took eleven days,[3] the distance being about eighty miles, an average performance.

For the safe accomplishment of such marches, this coastal road must have been prepared and maintained, for the difficulty of travel on horseback across the plains in

[a] I Samuel xxix 1.

[1] Arabic *Khan,* a wayside hostelry. See Pl. VIII.

[2] See below, p. 89, also Map No. 6, p. 90, and Pl. IX. The village of Baka is divided into two detached portions: it is the western part, Baka el Gharbiyeh, that marks the ancient site.

[3] Breasted: *Anct. Rec.* ii, p. 177.

wet weather is increased to danger by the numerous slippery gullies that lie across the track. For this reason its course has probably remained in constant use, so that any traces of Egyptian roadmaking would be lost under the work of later centuries. This route was of radical importance to the Egyptian Empire, and indeed it is evident that the plains and seaboard of Canaan interested the Pharaoh chiefly because they provided this pathway for his troops, and at the same time supplied his soldiery and horses with food and fodder. A study of the campaigns of Thutmose III,[1] who finally annexed the land to Egyptian suzerainty, displays a deliberate policy directed to securing this essential line of communication against disturbance and disaffection. Thus, the first campaign which he led in his 22nd or 23rd year, *c.* 1480 B.C., primarily against Megiddo, and subsequently against *Yenoam*, as well as the unknown *Nuges* and *Herenkeru*, possibly *Hor Nakura*,[2] clearly aimed at reopening the ways towards Damascus and the north. The second and third campaigns brought back spoils of *Retenu*, *i.e.* the coastal plains. The expeditions of the next three successive years, directed farther afield as far as Kadesh and Naharîn, did not hesitate to extort more tribute from the land of Retenu in passing, and on the last occasion even to reap its harvest (1469). Thereafter for some years the sea route was more used; but evidently the latent opposition along the land-route revived and called for repressive measures, so that in the 16th Campaign the unhappy coastland of Retenu was ravaged once again. It was the destiny of Palestine's situation that its most fertile acres should be trampled down or reaped by the passing armies of foreign conquerors.

The coastlands south of Carmel, hitherto considered as a whole, in reality comprise two portions, whereof the southern is known as the Plain of Philistia and the

[1] Ereasted: *Anct. Rec.* ii, 406. See also below, pp. 109 ff.

[2] The headland of Ras el Nakura, more familiar as the Ladder of Tyre Cf. Petrie: *Hist. Egypt*, ii, p. 110.

BAKA EL GHARBIYEH, OR WESTERN BAKA, POSSIBLY APHEK OF THE PHILISTINES: I Samuel xxix, 1.

Roads to Dothan and Ta'anach lead from this point eastward by the Bab el Ebweib.

YEMMA, THE SITE OF YEHEM, A STAGE ON THE NORTH ROAD.

Where the Egyptians under Thutmose III concentrated before their attack upon Megiddo.

See pp. 85, 90.

northern as the Plain of Sharon. The Wady el Nusrah, which rises above Bethhoron and enters the sea just north of Jaffa, may be regarded as the line of separation. The distinction while more apparent politically has a physical basis. The southern portion, ranging from Lydda to Tell Sharî'eh (*Sharuhen*), and containing numerous ancient cities like Gezer, Makkedah, Ekron, Lachish [1] and others, as far as Gerar, in addition to the historic cities mentioned upon the coast, though linked by the numerous natural routes already indicated with the hill country around Jerusalem and Hebron, was bordered and at the same time separated by a barrier of foothills called the Shephelah. This low ridge, which lies generally parallel to the highlands with a pronounced lateral valley in between, has through all time played a leading part in local history. Its strategic potency is evident from the map,[2] where all the avenues of approach are seen to have been guarded anciently by strong cities, Bethhoron, Aijalon (Yalo), Gezer itself, Bethshemesh, Azekah (Tell Zakariya), Adullam ('Id-el-Ma), and Debîr (Tell Beit Mersîm). The long strife of Israel with the Philistines centred largely around its possession. The struggle was in vain. The people of Israel never entered into their ' inheritance ' upon the Plain. These fortress cities with their Canaanite-Amorite populations had submitted early to the suzerainty of Egypt; Thutmose III mentions a number of them by name, among which may be recognised Gerar, Gaza, Makkedah, Ekron, Joppa, Lud, Ono, Yehem and Carmel; and the terrible policy exercised by successive Pharaohs was calculated to ensure the continuance of their servitude. The irruption of the Israelites under Joshua by the Valley of Aijalon [a] disclosed only a temporary weakness in the Egyptian organisation; the breach was closed, and the Israelites returned again to their camp in the Jordan valley. Gezer, which lay across their path remained in possession of the

[a] Joshua x 10 [J].

[1] Cf. Plates XXXIX, XL. [2] Map No. 5, to face p. 79.

Canaanites,[1] and the later efforts of Judah with Caleb were confined to Hebron and Debir: 'he could not drive out the inhabitants of the valley because they had chariots of iron.'[2]

The letters subsequently addressed to the Pharaoh at Tell el Amarna by the chiefs of Gezer, Askalon, Lachish and other centres,[3] at a time when the spreading revolution offered great temptation, not only recognise the suzerainty of the Pharaoh in loyal terms, but show that these vassals had come to rely upon the imperial organisation for their very safety. Later, when Ramses II undertook to re-establish the dominion of Egypt in the land, the people of Askalon, which he took by storm, are seen to be of the same stock as of old.[4] And when finally the rise of the Iron Age brought a radical change in the population of the coastlands, the southern area was repeopled by Philistines, the northern portion by their comrade Thekels, both from across the seas: the Israelites had no share in the events on the Plain. It is as though the Shephelah, during the long period of the Judges, formed a screen as well as a barrier, as though the passing of the Pharaoh's armies remained unseen, the coming and going of his messengers unnoticed. The fact is that the southern highlands lay off the beaten track. So long as the Israelites attracted no attention to themselves, they remained unmolested in their tents among the hills, as oblivious of the affairs of government as are the tent-dwellers of to-day. It was only in the north that the aspirations of Israel crossed the pathway of the Pharaohs, where the main road, after leaving the Plain of Sharon, traversed the territory allotted to Issachar and Naphtali.[5]

[1] Cf. Joshua xvi 10, Judges i 29. It is noteworthy that D's additions to Joshua x 31, 33 lay no claim to the capture of Gezer. There is also archaeological evidence of relations between Gezer and Egypt during the reigns of Amenhotep III and IV. (*Vid. P.E.F., Fifty Years' Work*, p. 133).

[2] Judges i 19. Cf. also i 33 which by some critics is thought to indicate an early effort of Naphtali to establish themselves in the Vale of Sorek. But see pp. 243 ff.

[3] Notably Kn. 297-300; 320-321; 328-329.

[4] See p. 287 and fig. 10.

[5] See p. 291.

THE BAB EL EBWEIB, A VIEW OF THE PASS FROM THE NORTH-WEST.

This pass through the ridge between Baka and Dothan marked an ancient line of route from Yehem to Ta'anak, and is still in use.

THE DESCENT TO TA'ANAK BY THE WADY ABDALLAH.

Tell Ta'anuk which marks the site of Ta'anak, Bibl. Taanach, is just visible in the sunlight at the foot of this pass.

See pp. 85, 90, 282.

In the northern plain of Sharon the border ridge of the Shephelah disappears; the plain itself is narrower, and areas of marshland as well as sand-drifts line the coast. Its history is still largely a closed book, for though some sites can be recognised as pertaining to the Bronze Age, or perhaps identified with their Egyptian names, few of them are mentioned in the Bible text. It was not conquered by Joshua, nor did it belong to Israel during the era of the Judges. Dan was forced out of it into the hill country by the Amorite population around Aijalon[a]; Aphek, possibly at Baka,[1] a road centre for Dothan and Esdraelon, is mentioned only as a point of concentration for the Philistines; and further north, upon the coast, Dor, before it was peopled by the Thekels from over the sea,[2] was counted among the strong cities of the Canaanites, in league and strategic union with Megiddo, Taanach and Ibleam.[b] This row of fortresses [3] reached from the sea across the ridge of Carmel and along the plain of Esdraelon, presenting a strategic frontier between the coastlands and the Canaanite territory of the north.

PASSES FROM SHARON

The passes through this ridge had thus a special importance, particularly to the Egyptians. It is on record that previous to the advance of Thutmose III on Megiddo their relative advantages were debated by the Pharaoh's generals.[4] Three routes were known to converge upon Yehem and these may readily be traced from Yemma.[5] The one leads, as we have seen, by the Bab el Ebweib eastward towards Dothan, whence Esdraelon may be gained at Jenin by way of Ibleam and the Wady Bilameh, the 'ascent of Gur.'[c] From the pass a bifurcation leads over the hills by Yabid, or alternatively around

[a] Judges i 34 [J]. [b] Joshua xvii 11 [J]. [c] II Kings ix 27.

[1] Cf. above, p. 85. [2] See below, p. 88, and Pl. VIII.

[3] See also pp. 232 ff. and Plates XX, LXVI.

[4] Breasted: *Anct. Rec.* ii 421. [5] See the Map, p. 90, also Pl. IX.

their base past Kefreireh, and over a low divide into the Wady Abdallah, down which a track descends directly upon Tell Ta'anuk, already visible at the mouth of the valley below.[1] This route recalls the words of the Egyptian text : ' Why should we go by this road [the Wady Arah] which threatens to be narrow ? . . . There are yet two (other)

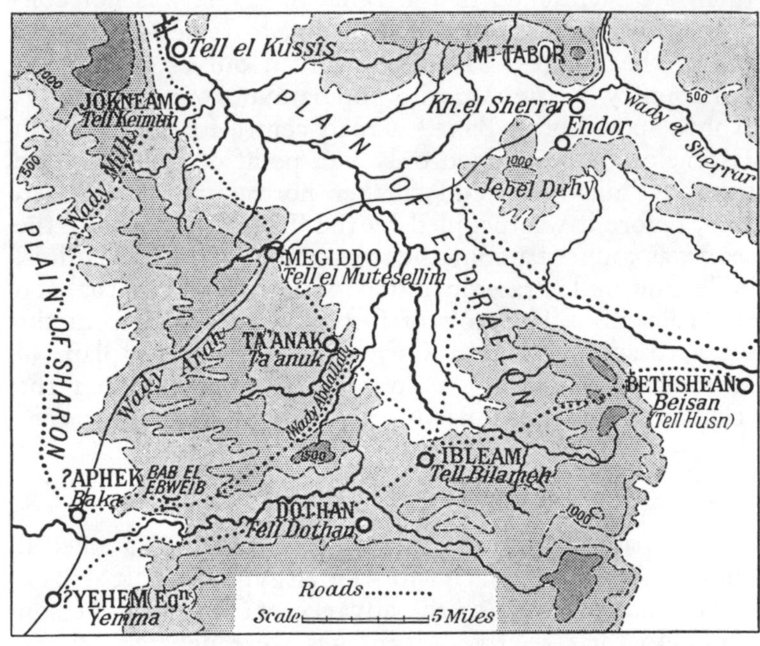

Map 6. Passes from Sharon into Esdraelon.

roads: the one . . . comes forth at Taanak, the other . . . will (bring us upon) the way north of Zefti, so that we shall come out to the north of Megiddo.'[2] The second or middle road is well known, and during the world-war it was employed with success by British cavalry for a rapid flanking movement, a tactical operation similar to that for which it was adopted by the Pharaoh. It enters the hills behind Khurbet el Sumrah by an easy valley, in which the village and Tell of Arah[3] are passed about

[1] See Pl. X. [2] Breasted : *Anct. Rec. loc. cit.* [3] See Plate XI.

THE WADY ARAH, A CHIEF PASS FROM SHARON INTO ESDRAELON.

Egyptian armies marched this way from Yehem to Megiddo on the highroad to the North

THE WADY FARAH, LEADING FROM SHECHEM DOWN TO THE FORDS OF EL DAMIEH.

'A ravine is on one side of thee, the mountain rises on the other.'

See pp. 78, 90.

midway. The latter part is narrower and somewhat rocky, but it can be traversed by a motor-car and cannot have presented much difficulty to chariots, the ruts of which are still visible here and there in the rocks. The third and most northerly route led through the Wady Milh around the foot of Carmel, debouching at Jokneam (Tell Keimun) seven miles from Megiddo: it is an open way, and was preferred by Napoleon for his advance on Acre, and under the Turks was constituted the main road to the north. If the intention of Thutmose's generals was to enter the plain nearer to Megiddo it would in fact be possible to take a right-hand track by Kefrein, down past Abu Shusheh, an ancient site which in that case might be Zefti; but the track is less favourable and the defile more enclosed than the Wady Arah.

Evidently the strategical merits of the various crossings from the coast into the plain of Esdraelon occupied the due attention of the Egyptian staff, to whom their difficulties and possibilities were known by repute but not altogether familiar. This general knowledge of the road towards Hazor and Damascus is reflected in the later document describing the conversation of the Maher to which we have referred. Though to some extent the descriptions in this document are confused, one passage in particular refers apparently to 'the way of crossing over to Megiddo.'[1] This reads when translated 'The narrow defile is infested with Shasu concealed beneath the bushes, the pathway is strewn with boulders and pebbles, overgrown with reeds and brambles,' and may well be derived from personal recollections of a journey through the Wady Arah or more aptly the defiles below the Bab el Ebweib. This familiarity with the main route through the land is in marked contrast with the absence of all reference to the central highlands in the record of campaigns. With the exception of the possible allusion to the descent by the Wady Farah from Shechem to the Jordan in the same papyrus,[2] it is hardly possible to

[1] *Pap. Anast.* I, *op. cit.* xix, 23, 2, p. 24.

[2] Above, p. 78.

find a single name or campaign in any Egyptian document that clearly refers to the hill country of Judaea and Ephraim.[1] The eyes of Egypt were turned towards the fairer territory of the Lebanon and the valley of the Orontes in the north, towards which led the well-beaten road by way of the coast, the Wady Arah, and the plain of Esdraelon.

THE PLAIN OF ESDRAELON

Esdraelon, the heart of Palestine, is a roughly triangular area of partly arable land lying wholly in the upper basin of the Kishon. It is bounded on the north by the hills of Lower Galilee, on the south-west by a spur from the central plateau which terminates in Mount Carmel, and on the east, partially, by outliers of Mt. Gilboa and the Jebel Duhy.[2] Numerous tributaries of the Kishon trace their sources from these surrounding hills; some indeed rise as far as Mount Gilboa in the east. But though coming from afar these rivulets attain little depth, filling only after rain and lying dry during the summer and autumn months. Such streams as are fed by springs continue to flow, but these, too, dwindle as the year passes, and are gradually absorbed by the thirsty land around; so that the main stream of the Kishon is practically dry by midsummer, and so shallow is its bed that it is noticed only when its muddy bottom here and there checks free passage across the plain. Its course at all times is gentle, for the low watershed dividing Esdraelon from the Jordan system is only 170 feet above the level of the sea, while the distance from there to the mouth of the Kishon, as the crow flies, is fully twenty-five miles.

Esdraelon has three outlets, openings, that is, by which water can escape.[3] Two of these are familiar. The one

[1] This does not apply with the same force to the Tell el Amarna Letters, which were written to the Pharaoh by resident chieftains, and mention Shechem, Jerusalem, Hebron and other chief towns.

[2] See the Map, p. 72, and Plates XIII, LXII, LXIV.

[3] See the Map, p. 299.

THE WADY MILH, A VIEW FROM THE NORTH-EAST.

This pass, which skirts the eastern foot of Carmel, was used by Napoleon, and under the Turks was maintained as a high road towards Acre and the north.

JOKNEAM, TELL KEIMUN, FROM THE EAST.

The city which guarded the entrance of the Wady Milh into the plain of Esdraelon.

See pp. 91, 94, 299.

is the narrow valley less than a mile in width in its north-western angle between Carmel and the Galilean hills, by which the Kishon finds its way past Tell Kussîs into the plain of Acre. The other is found in the middle of the eastern side, about midway between Jenin and Tabor, where the valley of Jezreel breaks insensibly away and falls towards the Jordan, carrying with it the waters of the Nahr Jalud. This valley separates Mount Gilboa from the Jebel Duhy, the latter a pointed hill which, as seen from the plain, seems to stand isolated in the middle of its eastern side, but in reality marks the western culmination of the ridge that bounds the valley of Jezreel to the north. The Jebel Duhy and Mount Tabor thus stand opposite to one another in the north-east angle of the plain, and between them a second valley, that of the Sherrar, also falls away towards the Jordan. This valley is less known than the others and indeed for long remained almost deserted; but in antiquity it attracted a number of settlements, including the Bronze Age sites of Kh. el Sherrar, not marked upon the maps, and Tell Mekurkash. The former is to be found near the head of the valley, between Endor and Tabor, but the site appears to have been already deserted by the Late Bronze Age. Tell Mekurkash rises conspicuously from a loop in its course some four miles farther east, from which point it commanded the defile leading by the river gorge towards the Jordan valley. It claimed accordingly a measure of strategic importance, albeit its name, 'the dried up,' is reminiscent of the fate that at length overwhelmed this outlying corner of the plain. This outlet of Esdraelon was thus practically blocked in the Late Bronze Age by at least one powerful city. It was also overlooked from a spur of the Jebel Duhy by another strong place which covered the Tell now called El Ajjul to the west of the village of Endor, marking possibly the ancient city of that name.

The valley of Jezreel, by contrast, lay relatively open, although barred strategically at its lower end, where it debouches upon the Jordan valley, by the Tell and fortress of Bethshean.[1] This valley follows for the twelve miles of its course the northern foot of Mt. Gilboa, varying little in width and appearance the while, a feature in which it contrasts sharply with its northern neighbour, and has led in consequence to its being preferred at all classical epochs as the main channel of communication with the East. It is, moreover, relatively fertile and populous; for the Jalud, which follows its course towards the Jordan, though little more than a stream, is fed by several perennial springs which maintain a constant supply of water for cultivation, the most plentiful being the historic "'Ain Harûd' at the foot of the village of Zerin (Jezreel).

While there are but three outlets from Esdraelon, its entrances are numerous. From the plain of Sharon it may be approached, as we have seen, by three routes. The most northerly of these comes down the Wady Milh at the foot of Mt. Carmel, and its entrance is guarded by Tell Keimun,[2] or Jokneam. The central pass leads through the Wady Arah directly upon Megiddo; while a third less frequented but known to the Egyptian soldiers of the day, came through from Yehem by the Bab el Ebweib and descended upon Taanak by the Wady Abdallah.[3] The main road from Dothan and the south, following still the central watershed of the country, descended the easy slopes of the Wady Bilameh past Ibleam (or Bileam) now Bilameh, and entered the plain at Jenin, a green spot which marks as of old the bounteous springs of En-gannim.[4] The row of fortresses from Jokneam to Ibleam, which includes not only the strong places of Megiddo and Taanak, but others of less account like Tell Abu Shusheh, thus formed by their positions a barrier against access to the plain from the south-west and south, closing every entrance from that side.

To the north by contrast, the approaches to the plain lie relatively exposed. The main road from Megiddo to

[1] Cf. Plates LIII, LXIV. [2] Pl. XII. [3] Above, p. 90. [4] Pl. XIII.

JENÎN, EN-GANNÎM, FROM THE SOUTH.

A well watered spot below Ibleam where the central highroad towards the North enters the S.E. corner of the Plain of Esdraelon.

MT. GILBOA, FROM THE NORTH-WEST.

The view is taken in the evening, at a point about midway between Beisan, (Bethshean) and Zer'in (Jezreel).

See p. 94.

Hattîn might pass freely on either side of Tabor, whereon no fortified position has been detected; and further west, save for the old city of Semuniyeh[1] at the foot and Malul upon the hill, numerous routes connecting with the north lie quite unguarded. The fortresses of the south-west, then, clearly define the frontier of an organised area which included Esdraelon. The centre of this organisation was found in the Bronze Age at Hazor; and when this old Canaanitish city fell, the inefficiency of Egyptian protection and the recurring unsteadiness of the political barometer in other ways, made it the more important for these cities to maintain their own strength and alliances. The wide acres lying before Megiddo and Taanak comprised some of the most valuable corn land and pastures in the whole country, much coveted and ever liable to be preyed upon.[2] Caravans bound for Acco from the south and east passed by their gates, dependent upon their protection and control; while the highroad from Egypt towards Damascus crossed the plain north-eastward, in full view, from Megiddo to Tabor, whence it found its way by Tell 'Oreimeh (Chinnereth), on the Sea of Galilee, and so over to Hazor in the Huleh Basin.

NORTHERN PALESTINE

In a general way the north of Palestine resembles the south, in that it comprises the three main features of coastal plain, central highlands, and river valley, but with a marked difference of detail which distinguishes its appearance. The Jordan valley, which in its lower reaches seems like an unnatural abyss, though still deep, here loses its forbidding aspect, while the vicinity of the lakes is pleasant to the eye. The highlands are not so rugged: the hills are softer in contour, the slopes are gentler, and the open spaces less confined. Even on the high plateau of Upper Galilee the landscapes are more

[1] Pl. XLV. [2] See below, pp. 112, 319, and Pl. LXII.

expansive; and the soil, though stony, does not convey the same impression of bareness and inhospitality. The coastal plain is more compact, its borders are visible and defined, it is attractive because self-contained and comparatively fertile, though long neglect has resulted in its swamps overtaking the cultivation.

THE PLAIN OF ACRE

These northern coastlands take the form of a capital B with Acre opposite the central projection. Maps showing only contours of 500 feet do not convey the same impression as a journey through the country, in which minor elevations sometimes loom big as local obstacles. Acre (Acco) is the natural centre of this area, and though modern shipping goes to Haifa and elsewhere, the roads which descend from the interior or pass along the coast are still focussed upon that ancient port. The modern town stands upon a beak of land which turning southward encloses a tiny bay;[1] indeed this promontory may at one time have been almost an island. The ancient Acco apparently stood back upon the mound now called Tell el Fokhar, the 'mound of pots,' and with a larger harbour than now, it readily accommodated the shipping of the period.

The northern portion of the plain has a sea-board of some thirteen miles, reaching as far as the rocky headland of Ras el Nakura, which effectively separated it in antiquity from the coastlands of Tyre, though engineers have now established communication. The coast road passed by Tell el Semiriyeh, El Zib (Achzib), and Kh. el Misherifeh (Mishrephoth-maim), all Bronze Age sites.[2] The tracks from Upper Galilee, the eastern boundary of this area, are necessarily steep and difficult, and under the changed conditions of to-day little used except for local intercourse, the central attraction of which is the weekly market at Bint Um el Jebeil. The most northerly comes

[1] Pl. LV. [2] See also below, p. 190, and Pl. XLVII.

down through Dibl almost to the point of Nakura, communicating in that way with Mesherefeh, and a second from Rumeish descends by the Wady Kurn upon El Zib.[1]

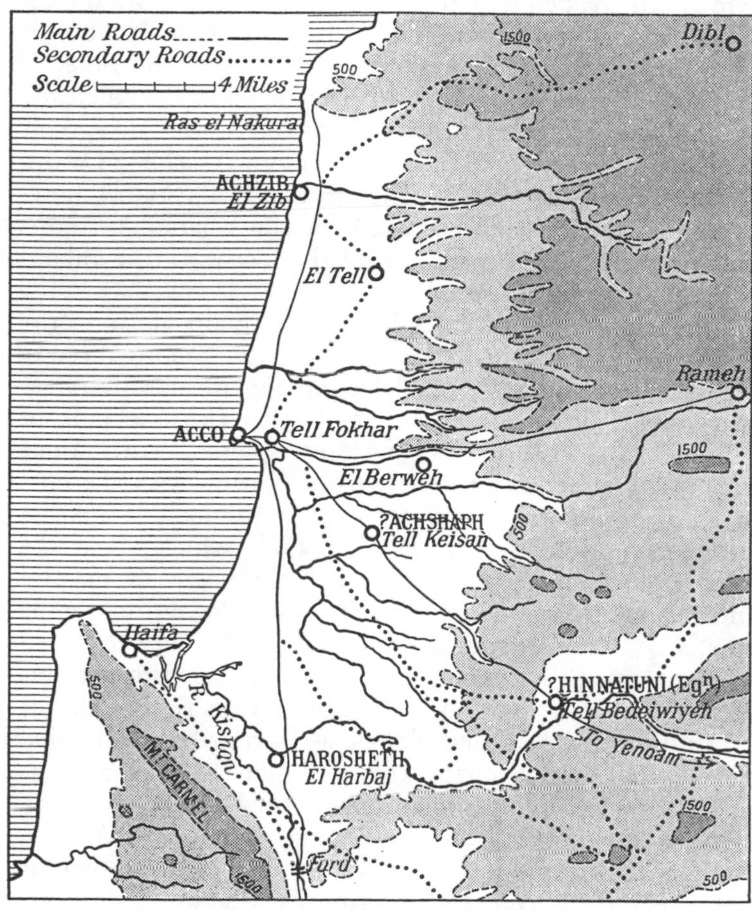

Map 7. Acco (Acre) and its communications.

Another from Rumeish leads more directly to Acre by Kefr Yesif, but the latter site is not ancient. A local track from near Kabry preserves an ancient line of communication, for near this village there rises a nameless

[1] See also the Map, p. 195.

Tell, the site of a Bronze Age city which some students would identify with Achshaph. Other less important sites of the Late Bronze Age may be found at Kh. el Amri, Kh. Abdeh and Kh. Suweijireh,[1] which we do not place upon our map of the locality as their identity is doubtful alike in the Egyptian records as in the Book of Joshua. None the less the district in general, which fell to the lot of Asher, became known to the Egyptians under Seti (*c.* 1310 B.C.) by the name 'Asaru.[2] Owing to the difficulty of crossing the headland of Nakura, however, it lay off the direct route of the Pharaoh's troops and representatives, who travelled mostly by the inland route or at times by sea.

The southern and larger half of the plain of Acre (the lower portion of our imaginary B) enters more directly into the active history of Palestine, by its close contact with the Plain of Esdraelon and with the lowlands of Galilee. Its broad well watered plains, with their potential fertility and ready communication with the port of Acco, must early have attracted settlement, indeed its surface is dotted with numerous Tells which attest the fact, though since Roman times the ravages of malaria and changed economic conditions have driven its people mostly to the surrounding hills. Tell Berweh, Tell Keisan, and Tell Harbaj[3] are among some fifteen abandoned sites that may be recognised, from the potsherds protruding through their slopes, as having been occupied during the Late Bronze Age.[4] Their copious springs still supply the local flocks and herds and travelling caravans with water. All three occupy strategic positions. El Berweh, nestling at the foot of the hills, commands the direct road from the interior by the wooded valley called El Shaghur, which descends past Rama from near Safed. Keisan stands boldly out in the northern part of

[1] Cf. *inter alia,* Saarisalo; *Topogr. Res. in Galilee,* pp. 38 ff. in *J.P.O.S.* ix. 1929.

[2] *'A-sh-r*: cf. Müller: *Asien,* pp. 236 ff.; Burney: *Israel's Settlement,* p. 82.

[3] See Plates XIV, XLV, LXIII.

[4] Cf. *B.S.A.J. Bul.* No. 2, pp. 10 f.

THE SPRINGS AND WELL OF TELL BERWEH, IN THE PLAIN OF ACRE.

TELL BERWEH, POSSIBLY REHOB. Judges i, 31.

A deserted Bronze Age Site in the plain of Acre.

See pp. 98, 241.

the plain at the junction of two or three routes, one of which descends from the hills by Kabul, and another still follows the historic pass from the inland plains of Lower Galilee by the Wady Abellîn which formed in antiquity and in Roman times one of the most familiar ways of access to the sea.[a] Neither of these sites can be identified with any certainty; but it is possible to surmise that El Berweh may represent the Rehob of Joshua xix 28 and xxi 31, while Tell Keisan from the importance of its position and its relation to Acco only six miles away, may lay claim to be the real site of Achshaph.

El Harbaj lies near the southern limit of the plain, twelve miles from Acco, on a small branch of the Kishon, at a point which looks directly through the opening at the foot of Carmel into the plain of Esdraelon.[1] It stood beside the main road from Egypt towards Acco, which, to avoid the marshes of the Kishon-mouth and the difficulties of the shore, followed the inland route around Carmel, by the Wady Milh and the Kishon gap, the line used by the Turks for their posts and telegraphs. Harbaj communicated also by a natural passage along the Wady Melik with the inland plain of Lower Galilee, the Sahel el Buttauf, and at Tell Bedeiwiyeh met the road through the Wady Abellîn. Its position and communications alike suggest that it must have filled some special rôle, and excavation leaves it open to identification with Harôsheth of the Gentiles.[2]

Looking again at the Plain of Acre as a whole, with its system of roads still radiating on the single port long shorn of its importance, we realise that its history and outlook must have been at all times linked with the sea. To-day Acre is only a picturesque village on the highroad between Haifa and Beyrouth, where travellers sometimes halt but no longer trade. The plain itself is indefensible, with an exposed seaboard of sand dunes, and dominated from within by the half-circle of hills. Here

[a] Cf. Isaiah ix 1.

[1] See the Map, p. 97.

[2] Cf. *B.S.A.J. Bul.* No. 2, 1922, pp. 12 f.

there is no Shephelah to serve as barrier between hill and plain. For the most part its history was that of Galilee, for both were Canaanite; but there arose periods when raiders and strangers settled on its borders, and as such we must deem the Goyyim who for a time peopled Harôsheth and parts of Galilee.[a] Under such conditions Acco must have found itself at times in danger of isolation. Consequently, it is natural to find this city-port, though not prone to intervene actively in the affairs of the interior, where its life-trade depended on good relations, nevertheless maintaining an armed force and chariots sufficient for its needs,[1] and looking across the sea to Egypt for support and assistance in necessity. And the destiny of Asher was interlocked with the fate of Acco.

GALILEE

The most striking feature of Lower Galilee is the central plain, El Buttauf, which with its outliers and ramifications provides a ready means of communication between the shores of the sea of Galilee and the coast. The 'Way of the Sea' from the Hauran took this route. Leaving the Jordan at the ford of Abeidiyeh,[2] it followed up the Wady Feyjars into and across the plain of Ahma to the west of the lake of Galilee, then over the low divide to the Wady Rummaneh which leads into the Buttauf, and so by the Wady Abellîn to Acco. In this plain are two Bronze-age sites, the names and history of which are alike unknown, Tell Bedeiwiyeh[3] and Tell el Wawiyat. Ten other such sites are to be seen in Lower Galilee,[4] but without systematic excavation it is impossible to assign their names or appreciate their importance.

[a] Judges iv 2-13 [E].

[1] T.A. Letters, Louvre, A.O. 7096.

[2] Possibly the Egyptian Yenoam: cf. pp. 73-4, and Pl. IV.

[3] Possibly Ḥinnatuni in Kinakhi of the T.A., Kn. No. 8. Cf. Weber's *Notes*, pp. 1027, 1299; cf. also Alt, *P.J.-B.* No. 22, p. 63 f.

[4] Cf. Saarisalo: *Bound. of Issach. and Naph.*, pp. 26 ff.

THE WADY ABELLÎN, BETWEEN BEDEIWIYEH AND KEISAN.

A sector on the Way of the Sea from Acco by Yenoam to the East.

TELL BEDEIWIYEH, POSSIBLY THE EGYPTIAN ḤINNATUNI.

In the plain of Lower Galilee called Sahel el Buttauf, viewed from the East.

See p. 99.

The whole region of Lower Galilee is dominated by the great fortress of Hattîn,[1] which sits athwart the north road of antiquity from Egypt towards Damascus. Protected by great ramparts of stone, some parts of which suggest Hittite handiwork, and commanding a wide view of roads and lake, it must have played a leading part in the early history of the country, though at some time in the Bronze Age the Pharaohs seem to have demolished its fortifications. The Egyptian highroad led through it from Megiddo directly upon Tell Oreimeh,[2] which rises above the north-west corner of the Lake, the places being plainly visible from one another and only six or seven miles apart. At the latter Thutmose III left trace of his passage in an inscription which chance has recently brought to light,[3] and in this he tells of his victories over the Mitannian-Hittites, almost suggesting an early penetration of his northern rivals thus far to the south.

Upper Galilee may be regarded as the high plateau lying between the Wady Shaghur on the south and the westerly reach of the Litany river in the north. Though generally higher, it is not so rugged as the southern highlands around Hebron. Its boldest promontory, the Jebel Jermuk, rises west of Safed to a height of 3900 feet. But though the highest mountain in the land, its contours are rounded, and the country that lies away northwards, though broken ever and again by stony valleys, suggests rather the slopes of Lebanon. Archaeologically this district is little known, and in antiquity parts of it were given over to primeval forest; but it claims a number of ancient sites, some of which may date back to the Bronze Age. One such has recently been recognised. Though without a distinctive name, being called simply Tell el Khurbeh, the Mound of Ruins, it occupies the most strategic position of the plateau at the southern foot of Jebel Marun, overlooking and partly defended by the upper course of the Wady Farah.[4] Potsherds attest that its great days,

[1] See Pl. XVI and the Map, p. 188.
[2] See Pl. XIX.
[3] Cf. *Jour. Egn. Arch.*, 1928, p. 281.
[4] See Pl. LXI and Map, p. 195.

probably its last, date from the Late Bronze Age. Locally the name El Khurbeh seems to refer particularly to an adjoining area of broken columns and sarcophagi, the ruins of some Roman or Byzantine buildings; but the Tell is separate from these, and in the Late Bronze Age the city which stood upon it was without a rival in this part of Galilee.[1] It may, therefore, mark the site of Beth-Anath,[2] one of the two Canaanite cities that long barred the progress of Naphtali.[a] Presumably at that time it stood at the centre of the road system of the area, which is now found two or three miles to the north, where in modern times the village of Bint Um el Jebeil has become the acknowledged market-place of all the region. Between the ancient and modern centres there rises the prominent ridge called the Jebel Marun, a name which seems to preserve the Biblical form Maron, and reappears further north in one or two places, notably Kalat Marun. Somewhere in this northern area it may be anticipated that further research may bring to light another important Bronze Age site, Madon of the Massoretic text, Egyptian Mazon, which in the Septuagint is replaced, like Merom, by the local name Maron in the account of Joshua's victory over the King of Hazor and his allies.[b] Another Bronze Age site long known is that of Kedesh Naphtali, now Kades,[3] seven miles north-east as the crow flies from El Khurbeh. The position is marked by a characteristic Tell standing at one end of a small but very fertile plain, which reaches out eastwards almost to the edge of the plateau. The road which connects the coast near Nakura

[a] Judges i 33 [J]. [b] Joshua xi 1 [J].

[1] Yarun, which seems to mark the site of Iron, stands a mile towards the west, but seems from its remains and history to date back only to the Early Iron Age. See Pl. XLVIII.

[2] See fig. 5. In an inscription of Rameses II the 'mount of Beth Anath' is associated with a place-name Kerpe(t) (Breasted, *Anct. Rec.* iii 356), which may conceivably have survived and become assimilated to the Arabic form Khurbeh (*ruin*). The modern name is in fact rendered 'Kurbeh' in Sir G. Adam-Smith's *Atlas*, pp. 16 and 20.

[3] See Pl. LXI, also fig. 4, p. 243, and the Map, p. 195.

Pl. XVI.

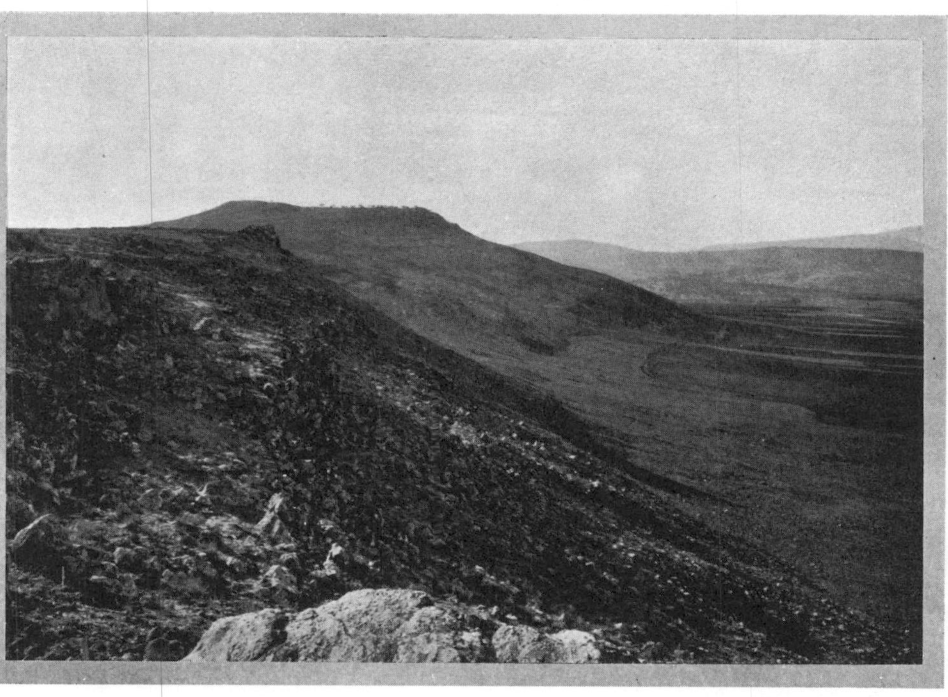

HATTÌN, A BRONZE AGE CITY WHICH DOMINATED THE HIGHROAD THROUGH LOWER GALILEE.

See pp. 101, 189.

and Mesherefeh with Dibl, continuing eastward by Bint Um el Jebeil, passes through Kades, descending thence to the Huleh Basin.

THE HULEH BASIN

The low-lying area of marshland which collects at its northern end the numerous sources of the Jordan, and in the south the waters of Lake Huleh, claims an importance altogether disproportioned to its area and economic potentiality. Hardly more than sixteen miles in length and six in width, it is to-day given over mostly to marshes abounding in papyrus and wild duck. The small lake near the exit is only three miles by two, and below this the Jordan flows through a rocky bed. The lake and surrounding basin are practically at sea level, while the enclosing circuit of hills rises somewhat abruptly about three thousand feet. In this depression, as may be imagined, the sun heat produces over the swamps a haze which from early morning till afternoon obscures the view, and lends to the area an atmosphere of mystery and desolation.[1] Yet this hollow marks the place of a geographical hub where all the chariot roads of antiquity, the motor roads of to-day, meet and cross, radiating like spokes of a wheel northwards to Damascus, Hamath and Sidon, southwards towards Bethshean and Megiddo, while east and west other pack roads climbing the hills complete the circuit of communications. To Damascus there are two ways;[2] the one, most used, crosses the Jordan just below Lake Huleh and climbs north-eastward past Kuneitrah. The other leads from the north-east corner of the plain past Banias (the site of Caesarea Philippi) up a steep gorge, overlooked by the towering fortress of the crusaders at Kalat Subeibeh,[3] and so past Mejdel el Shems, the 'watch-tower of the Sun.' The entry of this road to the plain is guarded by the Bronze Age site of Tell el Kadi,[4] usually identified with Laish, later Dan.

[1] Cf. Pl. XVII. [2] See the Map, p. 188. [3] Pl. XLVI. [4] Pl. LVI.

The road due north leads from the extreme end of the plain up towards the farthest sources of the Jordan, here called the Nahr Hashbany, between the foot of Hermon in the east and the watershed of the Litany on the west. This passage, which might very appropriately be called the 'Entering in of Hamath,' is guarded where it leaves the plain by the prominent hill and Tell of Abl (Abel-Maim), and just north where the valley narrows, it is almost closed by the unidentified mound called Tell El Dubbîn. Towards the north-west from Abl, leads the road to Sidon, which descends the steep gorge of the Litany and may be seen from afar winding its way across and up the farther slopes, some four or five miles above the bend, at a spot dominated since the Crusades by the imposing fortress of Beaufort (Kalat el Shukf). West of Abl a steep track climbs the ridge, leading past the Byzantine ruins of Kh. Iksaf and Kalat Marun due westwards down towards Tyre. Further south the lake is fed by some sweet waters of which the 'Ain el Mallahah is best known; and hereabouts another track climbs up the rocky ridge to Kades (Kedesh Naphtali) and so westward towards the coast by way of Bint Um el Jebeil and Dibl. Opposite the foot of the lake, some four miles to the west, stood Hazor, camp and fortress, at the junction of all the roads.[1] Placed upon a low defensive platform giving ready access for its chariotry to the plains, this place dominated the situation, and early became the head of all the Canaanite city kingdoms of the area.

The location of Hazor and a study of the strategic organisation of which it was the natural centre, enables us to realise something of the Canaanites' position. These people reached at one time from Sidon to Gaza, along the coastal plain; but the centre of their military and commercial organisation lay inland at this point, where all the trade routes converged. Westward the valley of the Shaghur led directly upon the port of Acco, which the heavier caravans could reach without undue fatigue by

[1] Pls. XVIII, XLIII, and Map, p. 188.

Pl. XVII.

THE HULEH BASIN: ON THE NEAR SIDE OF THE LAKE THE SITE OF HAZOR.

In the background: the hills of Bashan and Mt. Hermon.

See p. 103.

way of the Buttauf and the Wady Abellîn, or by the longer detour of Beisan and Esdraelon. It is worthy of note that Acco is the only port for Damascus and the Hauran which does not involve the crossing of at least one mountain range. Trade with Egypt again might follow the direct route by Oreimeh, Hattîn, Megiddo and the Wady Arah to Yehem and so to Gaza, the road traversed time and again by the Pharaoh's armies in their Syrian campaigns. In peace even when the great power of Hazor was broken, it still remained the focus and objective of all journeys north. The ebb and flow of political and military ascendancy as between the Pharaoh and the Canaanites in southern Syria had set up a frontier between these rivals along the natural barrier, where the ridge of Carmel connects with the central plateau along the south-west frontier of Esdraelon. There, as we have seen, the line of fortresses, Jokneam, Megiddo, Taanak, Ibleam, guarded the several passes that connected with the coastal plain. These belonged by nature to the dominion of the Canaanites centred upon Hazor, and apparently delimited the original boundary of Canaan or *Kinakhi* on that side. This would seem primarily to have comprised, geographically and politically, all the plateau of Galilee together with the plains of Acco and of Esdraelon, and thence to have spread southward down the coasts as far as Gaza, strengthened by maritime relations, and down the Jordan valley as far as this is habitable below Bethshean. The range of Canaanite supremacy was dominated by one factor, the chariot roads.

CIVILISATION

'Amalek dwelleth in the land of the south; and the Hittite and the Jebusite and the Amorite dwell in the mountains; and the Canaanite dwelleth by the sea and along by the side of Jordan.' This informative reference from the early sources[a] (JE) indicates at any rate a

[a] Numbers xiii 29.

broad geographical separation between Amorite and Canaanite. Whether these leading elements in the population of the land could claim an original racial difference is not readily determined, for the two names became almost synonymous in familiar usage. It may be that both should be regarded as Aramaean, and that it was their separate geographical relations which gave rise gradually to a distinctive culture, the Canaanite by his ready contact with the Mediterranean coasts, and the Amorite by his proximity to his original centre Amurru in central Syria. On the one hand the coastal trade between the Aegean world and Egypt during the Late Bronze Age produced a marked influence upon the local arts, introducing in particular during the earlier part of that period the peculiar wares of Cyprus, and later, from 1400 B.C., the products of Mykenae. Inland, on the other hand, out of the earliest traditions of Israel there emerges the memory of a powerful Amorite Kingdom in Bashan [a]; while traces of Hittite art at the foot of Hermon [1] not only conform also with one strain of Israelite tradition,[b] but recall the now established fact of intimate political relations in historic times between Amorite and northern Hittite, dating no doubt from that pre-Hyksos epoch when the Hittite Kings claimed empire over 'Damasḫunas.' [2]

However potent these diverging tendencies between the Canaanite and Amorite inhabitants of Palestine, the foundation of their civilisation seems traceable to a common source in Babylonia. This relation is particularly noticeable in religion and religious art. The prevailing Astarte cult with its attendant rites, a form of nature worship, is hardly to be distinguished from that of Istar. So too the earliest dated piece of temple sculpture found in the country with its striking design of fighting lion and dog, is Babylonian both in motive and execution: it was excavated in a deposit of the fifteenth century B.C.

[a] Cf. Joshua ii 10, ix 10 [D]. Judges xi 19 [E].

[b] Joshua xi 3 [LXX]. Judges i 26 [J]. Judges iii 3 [LXX].

[1] G., *H.E.* p. 327 and Pl. LIII.

[2] G., *Index H.N.*, p. 12.

Pl. XVIII.

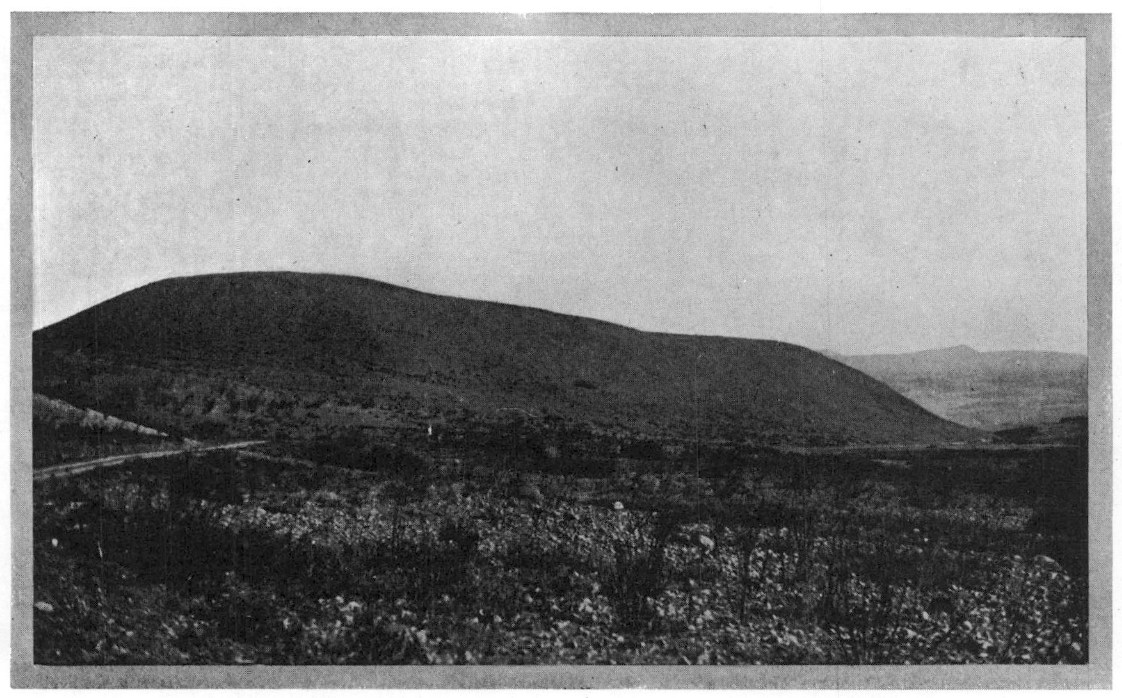

TELL EL KEDAH, FROM THE SOUTH: THE SITE OF HAZOR, CHIEF CITY OF CANAAN. Joshua xi, 1.

See pp. 104, 183.

at Beisan.[1] Derceto of Askalon again was identical with the Syrian goddess Atargatis, the centre of whose worship lay in the far north at Mumbij near the Euphrates.[2] Further, the cuneiform script and Semitic language employed for all correspondence on state affairs, not only with the officials in Egypt but even between neighbouring cities, is attributable likewise to a Babylonian origin and permeated all Western Asia.[3]

At the time when the Egyptian and Biblical records begin to throw light upon the state of society in the country, the predominating political influence is found, in fact, to have been Mesopotamian, that of the Mitannian-Hittites; and it is remarkable that the earliest Egyptian inscription found hitherto in Palestine, alludes to the first contest of Thutmose III with these rivals. This monument was found, as already stated, at Tell 'Oreimeh; and on the other side of the Sea of Galilee, upon the plateau of Bashan, there have been observed a sculptured lion and other monuments of early Hittite style.[4] Subsequently, in the Amarna period, as is well known, it was the Hittites of Asia Minor who pushed down from their bases at the foot of Taurus and established their suzerainty over the whole land, to the discomfiture of Egypt. Traces of their penetration and occupation are found here and there in Palestine, and are particularly clear at Beisan where alone excavation has scientifically examined the levels of this early period[5] (*c.* 1370 B.C.). There Hittite weapons of war and other unmistakable objects were uncovered in the local sanctuary which lay in ruins[6] between

[1] Rowe: *Mus. Journ.* (Phil.), March 1929, p. 49; also G., *H.E.*, p. 331.

[2] Lucian: *De Dea Syria.* Cf. G., *H.E.*, pp. 303 ff., with figs. 42, 44.

[3] The further development of script and language in the West is well illustrated by two recent discoveries in Central Syria. Cf. Dussaud, *Syria*, V, 1924, pp. 133 ff.: *Les Inscr. Phénic. du tombeau d'Ahiram*, also: Virolleaud, *Syria*, X, 1929, pp. 304 ff. *Les Inscr. Cunéif. de Ras Shamra*, the latter disclosing an alphabetic system.

[4] Cf. Sir G. Adam-Smith, *Hist. Geog.*, p. 549, and G., *H.E.*, p. 327.

[5] Rowe: *Mus. Journ.* (Phil.) 1927 (March), p. 17.

[6] *Ibid.* June, 1928, p. 160, etc. Cf. G., *H.E.*, p. 331 and Pl. XIX.

the well-defined strata of Thutmose III below and of Seti I above. But though Egypt and the Hittites contested the political supremacy in the land at this time, and thereafter Egypt regained its ascendancy and administered the country for still two centuries, neither power made any appreciable impression upon the local civilisation. The objects which tell of their presence—and those of Egypt are found in numerous sites, particularly upon the coastal plains [1]—remained to the last 'foreign' and easily distinguished: Egyptian art was never assimilated into the culture of the Canaanite. By contrast the many beautiful objects of metal-work pictured among the spoils taken by Thutmose III at Megiddo,[2] include a number which in form and motive have long been regarded as distinctive of the Middle Bronze Age culture of Syria and Palestine, but are now traced by recent discovery to a much earlier origin in Ur of the Chaldees.[3] In like manner, it will be remembered, the spoils of Jericho, captured later in the same century by Joshua, contained 'a goodly Babylonian garment.'[a] These indications are slight it is true, but they consistently point towards Babylonia as the original home of the civilisation enjoyed by the people of Canaan, though modified by the local conditions, and upon the coast revivified by contact with the Mediterranean world. How advanced was this civilisation and how prosperous its people before it was overwhelmed by the ambitions of the Pharaohs, is now beginning to be revealed by excavations, substantiating in that respect the contemporary writings and scenic records of Egypt. By contrast, Biblical literature in general is not informative about the social conditions of the age, but the Book of Judges, which

[a] Joshua vii 21 [J].

[1] *E.g.* at Askalon, Tell el Hesy, Tell el Safi, Tell Zakariya, Bethshemesh, and Gezer; as well as at Megiddo and Beisan. For details and bibliography cf. the Appendix to this volume.

[2] Cf. below, p. 113.

[3] Woolley: 'The Royal Tombs of Ur,' *Mus. Jour.*, 1928, figs. pp. 18, 27.

TELL 'OREIMEH, THE SITE OF CHINNERETH *Egn.* KINNERET.

A strong city of Canaan on the highroad from Megiddo to Hazor and the north, captured by Thutmose III.

THE PLAIN OF CHINNERETH, FROM THE NORTH.

Viewed from Tell 'Oreimeh, on the north west shore of the Sea of Galilee which was later called the Lake of Gennessaret.

See pp. 107, 1:1.

covers the period of the Canaanite decline, contains suggestive passages: one in particular is set like a charming vignette in the triumph song of Deborah.[a]

28 Through the window she looked forth and cried,
The mother of Sisera cried through the lattice,
Why is his chariot so long in coming ?
Why tarry the wheels of his chariots ?
29 Her wise ladies answered her,
Yea, she returned answer to herself,
30 Have they not found, have they not divided the spoil ?
A damsel, two damsels to every man ;
To Sisera a spoil of divers colours,
A spoil of divers colours of embroidery,
Of divers colours of embroidery on both sides, on the necks of the spoil ? [E]

EGYPTIAN POLICY

This picture belongs to the closing years of the Bronze Age; and though the final storm which brought the Canaanite regime to a close may be attributable to movements on a wider scale, it is easy to see that the activities of Egypt during the three preceding centuries had been calculated to accelerate the end. From the time when the Pharaohs first aspired to empire in Syria, following indeed on the heels of the retreating Hyksos (1600 B.C.), the subjugation of Canaan became a first consideration in the accomplishment of their ambitions. Through Galilee ran the one road by which they might attain their goal; the siege and sack of Megiddo in 1479 B.C. by Thutmose III was of vital importance to Egypt, not specially because of the value of the spoils, but because its fall reopened the road which had passed into the control of his northern rivals of Kadesh. And though thereafter the Pharaohs pursued a consistent policy of terrorisation, this, as we have indicated, was based on the necessity of maintaining safety of communication along this line, no less across Esdraelon and through Galilee than upon the

[a] Judges v 28-30 [E].

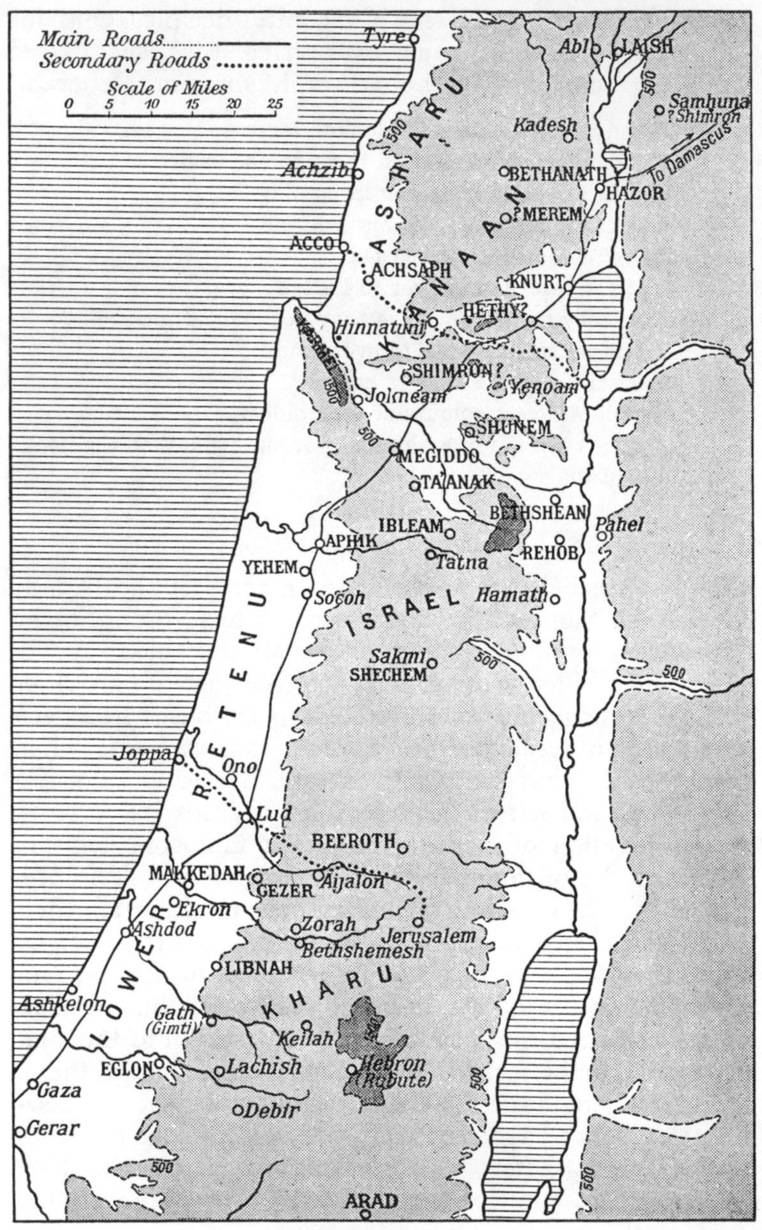

Map 8. Canaan under Egypt in the 15th and 14th centuries B.C.

coast.[1] Thutmose III has left record of 119 cities which he claimed to have captured and presumably bespoiled or held to tribute.[2] Many names are garbled, but a number, as many as thirty-five, can be recognised, though not without hesitation, and of these some twenty-seven figure in the Book of Joshua. They include:

In the coastal plain: (No. 21) Sharon, (30) ? Makkedah, (62) Joppa, (64) Lud (Rtn.), (65) Ono, (66) Aphek, (67) Socoh, (68) Yehem, (80) Gerar, (87) Rehob, (89) Eglon or Ekron, (96) Karmel, (104) Gezer.
In and near Esdraelon: (113) ? Jokneam, (2) Megiddo, (9) Dothan, (38) Shunem, (42) Taanak, (43) Ibleam, (110) Bethshan.
In the plain of Acre: (40) Aksaph, (47) Acco.
In Galilee: (3) Ḥethy, (12) Merem, (20) Mazon.
By Jordan: (90) Abl, (16) Hamath, (31) Luz (Laish), (32) Hazor, (33) Pahel (Pella), (34) Knnrt (Kinnereth)

Arad also is mentioned (Nr. 100) and Aruna (Nr. 27); also the much discussed Joseph-El (No. 78) and Yacob-El (No. 102). The line of the main highroad from Egypt via Megiddo and Hazor towards the north[3] is well marked by the names : Gerar, Makkedah, Gezer, Lud, Sharon, Yehem, Aruna, Megiddo, Ḥethy (? Hattîn), Kinnereth, Hazor, Abl; and though the identifications are in some cases merely tentative, the noticeable preponderance of names aligning the main route points again to the conclusion that the chief interest of the Pharaoh was centred on his communications with the North.

It is also significant that in this list no name can be related to the central or southern highlands, which clearly lay off the customary line of march. This fact was of the highest consequence to the tribes of Israel in their attempt at settlement. The first intimation of their

[1] Cf. p. 86.

[2] Breasted : *Anct. Rec.* ii 402. Cf. *inter alia* Alt, *Landnahme der Israeliten*, pp. 13, 14, etc.

[3] See the Map 8, p. 110.

effective penetration appears in fact in the mention by Seti I (*c.* 1310 B.C.) of Asher, which, as we have seen, lay in close contact with Achshaph and Acco, vassal cities of the Pharaoh, in the plain of Acre. In further illustration may be noted the one reference to Israel in Egyptian history, on the well-known stele of Merneptah (1223 B.C.) in which the record of victories assumes the following sequence: Kheta, Kanaan, Askalon, Gezer, Yenoam, Israel, and lastly Kharu or Southern Palestine.[1] Israel is thus named between Yenoam upon the Upper Jordan and Kharu. Now though the headquarters of united Israel had been fixed by Joshua at Shechem, the location of which would suit the context, it is to be gathered from the Book of Judges that, notwithstanding the repeated claims of Ephraim,[a] the predominance of this centre was hardly maintained after the dispersal of the tribes. On the other hand it is known from the Song of Deborah (Judges v) that at this time Issachar and Naphtali were becoming established within their allotted areas in Esdraelon and Galilee, where their presence across the Pharaoh's pathway may account for this unique reference in the Egyptian annals.

THE 'HORNET'

'Plundered is Kanaan, with every evil,' reads the inscription.[1] Let us grasp the full significance of these words as affecting the destiny of Israel. The event falls two and a half centuries after the sack of Megiddo by the armies of Thutmose III, in 1479 B.C., and during the intervening time most of the campaigns in Syria had inflicted similar punishments with a regularity so persistent as to suggest a deliberate policy of devastation. On that first occasion the spoils of Megiddo not only included weapons of war, tents and chariots of special workmanship, but numbered 2041 mares and 6 stallions, 1929 large cattle, 2000 sheep and 20,500 goats, in

[a] Judges viii 1 [J], xii 1 [J].

[1] Breasted: *Anct. Rec.* iii 617: for the full text see below, p. 290.

TELL EL MUTESELLIM, THE SITE OF MEGIDDO, ON THE BORDER OF ESDRAELON. Joshua xvii, 2: Judges i, 27.
See p. 232.

addition to the harvest from the fields of Megiddo, which was counted by 208,200 fourfold measures of grain.[1] Yenoam, Nuges and Herenkeru were revisited and surrendered with their chiefs and lords together with a number of refugees, the total prisoners from these cities totalling 2503 souls.[2]

Fig. 2. Gold and silver vessels from among the spoils of Megiddo taken by Thutmose III, c. 1479 B.C.

The tribute from the Chiefs of *Retenu* in the second campaign included[3] a chief's daughter and 30 of her slaves, 65 male and female slaves, 103 horses, 749 bulls, 5703 sheep, together with dishes of precious metals, 1718 jars of honeyed wine and many objects of luxury. The successive expeditions continued to drain the country of its resources, including almost yearly supplies of slaves, gold and silver objects, cattle and sheep, together with all the produce and all the fine fragrant woods of this country.[4] The harvest carried away included much clean grain, barley, incense, oil, wine, and fruit.[5] On the ninth campaign the levy was even heavier, after a year or two's respite, including again a large consignment of slaves, cattle, wine and wood. If the spoliation was in fact anything like that depicted in the records, the triumphs of Egypt meant in effect the ruin of the country and account in large measure for the decay of the old Canaanite power and civilisation.

[1] Breasted: *Anct. Rec.* ii, 435. [2] *Ibid.* 436. [3] *Ibid.* 447.
[4] *Ibid.* 471. [5] *Ibid.* 473.

The lists are long and are repeated in successive reigns. The next Pharaoh, Amenhotep II, in his second year, conducted a campaign towards N. Syria to quell rebellion, passing through northern Palestine,[1] and returned to Egypt bearing the plunder which he had taken in the country of Retenu. This included more than 350 nobles and 240 of their wives, 6800 'deben' of golden vessels and half a million deben of copper, together with 240 horses and 300 chariots.[2] He subsequently sacrificed with his own hand seven captured princes.[3] We do not dwell upon his conquests farther afield in the realm of Mitanni, nor those of his successor Thutmose IV (1420-1411 B.C.) who maintained the empire at its former northern limits.[4] It may be assumed from inscriptions making mention of Retenu that the same methods were continued: it was only with the accession of Amenhotep III in 1411 B.C. that the persecutions temporarily ceased. Thereafter for fifty years no army was led by the Pharaoh into Syria.[5] This interlude proved fateful.

So long as the reign of terror continued and Egyptian troops passed to and fro the situation of the inhabitants was not helpless; but on the day when the soldiers should be withdrawn, with the land bespoiled, its fortresses dismantled, its population diminished, what would be its fate? British people know that when the Roman legions were withdrawn from this island, even though the land had prospered and the people thrived, the 'wails of the Britons' went up in vain. Those who were waiting an opportunity upon its frontiers broke through its enfeebled ramparts and established themselves in the land. In Syria the sequel was much the same.

The reaction to the Pharaoh's continuous apathy was profound, and coupled with the menace of the Hittites from the north (*c.* 1385 B.C.) it rapidly proved fatal to Egyptian prestige and authority. Unrest led to disorder. The

[1] Breasted: *Anct. Rec.* ii. 285. [2] *Ibid.* 790. [3] *Ibid.* 797.
[4] *Ibid.* 816. [5] Breasted, *Hist.*, p. 410; cf. *T.A. Letters*, Kn. No. 96.

resident Governor, the inspectors, and loyal chieftains, were alike powerless without troops to stem the growing revolution, much less protect the frontiers of Canaan. It was at the opening of this period, according to Biblical chronology about 1406 B.C. and therefore in the earlier years of Amenhotep's reign, that Joshua and the Israelites appeared from the east before the walls of Jericho.

I sent the hornet before you which drave them out.

THE CAMPAIGNS LED BY JOSHUA

Joshua I-XII

SECTION 3

JOSHUA'S APPOINTMENT AND PREPARATIONS

JOSHUA i. *Joshua appointed Leader*

1 Now it came to pass after the death of Moses the servant of
the Lord, that the Lord spake unto Joshua, the son of
2 Nun, Moses' minister, saying, Moses my servant is dead;
now therefore arise, go over this Jordan, thou, and all this
people, unto the land which I do give them, even to the
children of Israel. [E]

To realise the setting of these introductory sentences to the Book of Joshua, it is necessary to look back briefly into earlier pages of the Bible. The Israelites were dwelling at the time in the Plains of Moab on the east side of the Jordan[a] opposite to Jericho. Moses, who had led them to this point from Egypt, and held them together through the long years of desert wandering, had died within sight of the Promised Land.[b] The succession of Joshua to the leadership was indicated in various ways. He may have been already eighty years of age,[c] and could claim seniority of status: indeed later tradition declares that he and Caleb alone survived[d] of all the adult males whom Moses and Aaron had numbered[e] nearly forty years before in the Desert of Sinai. Moreover, the strength of his character and his powers of leadership had been tested. From the beginning of the desert life he had been placed at the head of the fighting men[f]; and later as Moses' minister he had gained experience also in religious affairs,[g] and learnt to understand the temper of his people. Throughout these years,

[a] Numbers xxxiii 49 and xxv 1 [JE].
[b] Deuteronomy xxxiv 5.
[c] Joshua xiii 1.
[d] Numbers xxvi 65.
[e] Numbers i 44.
[f] Exodus xvii 9.
[g] Numbers xi 28 [JE], xxvii 22.

despite all difficulties and disappointments, he had never wavered in his loyalty to his chief nor in his ardent faith in Jehovah and the destiny of Israel. A man of action and moral force, he was a leader divinely chosen, and his call to fill that office provoked no question.

The Israelites were still nomadic.[a] Their contact with the town-life of Moab had led to religious back-sliding[b]; in tents it was more possible to maintain the unity of their faith and their purity of race. Their Government was theocratic: the leader received his commands direct from Jehovah,[c] and his powers in the execution of the divine law were absolute.

The numbers of the Israelites at this time are not stated: they must be inferred (if need be) from one or two indirect but suggestive passages in other Books, and the result may be checked by considerations of common-sense. It is necessary at the outset to disabuse one's mind of the familiar figures of the priestly tradition,[d] which have been incorrectly handed down, partly no doubt through errors of copying and partly maybe by a confusion at some stage in the interpretation of the word *Alif* which means both *thousand* and *family group*.[1] Half a million fighting men implies at least two million souls, a number which, without accounting for the animals, would have involved on the journey from Egypt a continuous column of four abreast extending over the whole length of the desert wandering between Succoth and Jericho at its maximum estimate of 400 miles. The whole Jordan valley could not have contained their camp. The armed men alone if formed up ten abreast when encompassing the walls of Jericho would have formed a column forty miles in length, requiring two whole days for their defiling. Such figures cannot be reconciled with the details of the old narrative,[e] and are quite incompatible

[a] Numbers xxxiii; Joshua i 11 [E]. [b] Numbers xxv 1 [JE].
[c] Joshua i 1 [E]. [d] Exodus xii 37, Numbers i 46 [P], xxvi 51 [P].
[e] Cf. Joshua iii 1 [JE].
[1] Cf. McNeile, *Numbers*, *C.B.*, p. 7. Petrie, *Res. in Sinai*, pp. 207-17.

with the historical picture of the age derived from independent sources. The strength of the Egyptian imperial army appears to have been normally about 5000 men.[1] The cities of Canaan which we are still to examine, with their areas varying from five to twelve acres,[2] cannot well have housed more than 1000 to 3000 souls apiece. The chief of Tyre asks the Pharaoh for 20 men, trained soldiers, to guard his cities[3]; another Syrian chieftain applies for a stronger force of 40 men,[4] 20 Egyptians and 20 Nubians. The King of Jerusalem, while pointing out the dire peril of the country before the invading Ḥabiru, appeals for 50 men as a garrison to protect the land.[5] These official figures reflect the realities of the age. Looking also at certain early passages in the Book of Judges, we find the tribe of Dan[a] to have comprised an effective strength of 600 fighting men at the time of their migration towards the north. Two hundred years later, it is true, six tribes together mustered in round figures forty thousand strong at the call of Deborah,[b] but this episode followed an exceptionally long period of Rest, and the coefficient of increase must be taken into account. Taking into consideration also the limited support for life in the deserts of Sinai and the Wady Arabah, the numbers of the Israelites when Joshua assumed command may be reasonably estimated at about six thousand souls, with a fighting strength of some 1200 to 1500 men.

There is no clear indication in the early part of the Book of Joshua of any organisation by tribes whether for social or religious purposes or for war; but as such is the custom of desert peoples, and the allocation of tribal areas for settlement follows, in the old sources, the narrative

[a] Judges xviii 11 [J]. [b] Judges v 8 [E].

[1] *Anastasi*, I xv 17, 5. Ed. Gardner, p. 19; cf. Amarna Letter No. 132. Kn. p. 563.

[2] See below, p. 167.

[3] *Amarna Letters*, Kn. No. 151, ll. 15, 16. Kn. p. 623.

[4] Ribaddi of Gebeil and Beyrout, *ibid*. Kn. No. 24, l. 67.

[5] Abd-Hipa to the Pharaoh. Kn. 289.

of the campaigns,[a] it may be safely assumed that the elements of such an organisation were already present.[1] For war purposes each tribe would contribute to the central force a contingent of fighting men. In later times all adult males, over twenty years of age, were liable for military service. They were grouped apparently by families, each contingent under the command of its clan-leader. But it may be presumed that on emerging from their long sojourn in the desert their methods of war and their arms would be behind the times. Though apparently familiar with the use of the sword and the bow, and possibly the sling stone, there is no mention of body armour or chariots; indeed, in all but the use of the horse, their mode of life, organisation, dress and arms, seem to have differed little from those of the Bedouin living in the same region to-day. The poorness of their military equipment it is true would hardly be felt in the first stages of the task before them. If the Jordan could be crossed, the plan would be to force an opening by way of Jericho, which was visible on the far side of the valley, at the foot of the western hills. And though Jericho stood upon the edge of a plain in a position favourable for chariotry, nothing suggests that the use of this superior arm was familiar to its defenders, any more than in the highland cities that looked down from above. In the one case the severe heat which prevails most of the year, and in the other the general rudeness of the country itself, were indeed unfavourable to the use of the horse and chariot, which in the plains, by contrast, proved an insuperable difficulty.[b] The weapons and organisation of the cities of Canaan in general, however, cannot fail to have been improved by their long contact with Egypt, and in this respect they would have an advantage. The Israelites relied largely on their numbers, and on the courage inspired by their faith.

[a] Joshua xiii 7 [J], xvi 1 [J], xvii 11 [J], xviii 2 [JE].
[b] Joshua xvii 16 [J], Judges i 19 [J].

[1] See below, pp. 207, 222, 236.

THE WADY KELT AND JEBEL KURUNTUL BY JERICHO.

OLD ROAD FROM JERICHO TO JERUSALEM BY THE WADY KELT.

See pp. 124, 133.

Looking at the military position as a whole, the present proposal would seem more practicable for the Israelites than the attack from the south previously contemplated and in part attempted with disastrous consequences.[a] At that time the Amalekites who occupied the country between the Israelites and their goal had been supported by other inhabitants in resisting the Israelites' first effort to gain a footing; while behind them the spies reported that the people who dwelt in the land were strong, their cities were fenced and very great.[b] Wherever excavation has been attempted in that zone, the results tend to confirm the spies' report. In the lower Jordan valley, however, conditions were more favourable. This is not naturally a corn-producing area like the Negeb and does not support large numbers. With difficulty, indeed, Roman engineers managed to give fertility to certain spots, while to-day few live upon its soil. The water supplies of Ain el Sultan and Ain el Duk gave permanent life to the vicinity; but the city of Jericho stood isolated, remote from help. Several tracks descending from the hills linked it with the cities upon the plateau; but these neighbours were invisible, too distant to rely upon in emergency and probably too different in race to share its fortunes.

Immediately above Jericho to the west, upon the plateau, Jerusalem was peopled by Jebusites, who, it would appear, were of Hittite-Amorite stock.[c] Farther south Hebron, for which later tradition claimed also a Hittite element,[d] stood upon the route towards Gaza, and, with other places in like case, was still loyal to the Egyptian cause. Immediately to the north the inhabitants of Gibeon and its dependent cities were 'Hivites,' of unknown race. Farther north again, in the neighbourhood of Shechem, the population seems to have been more nearly akin to the Israelites, descendants from the Abrahamic stock, who had gained their footing according

[a] Numbers xiii 30 [JE], xiv 45 [JE]. [b] Numbers xiii 28 [JE].
[c] Ezekiel xvi 3. [d] Genesis xxiii 10; xlix 29, 30 [P].

to one cycle of tradition in the age of Jacob,[1] or at any rate before the descent of the Patriarch into Egypt. It is to be realised, moreover, that except for the shadow of Egyptian authority, these various city states were independent, watchful and even jealous of one another as they differed to some extent in race and sympathies. Jerusalem, it is true, under the Egyptian organisation had been recognised as the seat of a responsible chieftain, who at a later stage did not fail to call together the still loyal allies to punish those who leagued themselves with Joshua.[2] But that event was local: Jericho lay in an abyss out of sight, and though under normal conditions its fate might have occasioned the Egyptian representative some concern, under the prevailing circumstances of growing disquietude, arising largely from Egyptian apathy, the sending of a relief force to Jericho was out of the question.

Politically, also, the time and circumstances were favourable to the Israelites' occupation of the land. According to the Bible reckoning it must have been in the last years of the fifteenth century B.C., the round date giving 1407 B.C., when Joshua was called to the leadership.[3] In the previous section we realised the tendency of this age. The hold which Egypt had established over the country under Thutmose III, seventy years before, was rapidly relaxing under Amenhotep III. The chief interest of the Pharaoḥs, in any case, lay in the control of the direct line of communication between Gaza and Damascus. In the course of the Egyptian conquest, as we have seen, all the great fortresses along that route between Egypt and Syria had been stormed or had opened their gates. Other strong places in the country had been similarly reduced. The records of Thutmose III alone mention 119 cities which had been subdued: many of them no doubt had been pillaged or destroyed. This was but the first of a series of incursions of like kind, all of which contributed to the rapid decay of the old civilisation of

[1] Charles, *Apocrypha*, ii, pp. 64, 316, 364. See above, p. 79.
[2] See below, p. 169. [3] See above, p. 65.

the Canaanites, and to the decline of their political power and organisation. At this time under Amenhotep III the situation was becoming critical. The increasing years of that monarch, the prosperity of his own country, internal religious and political problems, all contributed to discourage his interest in a land which had already been shorn of its riches, and was in a great measure depopulated. Disquietude was leading rapidly to discontent and disaffection, so that when the Israelites descended from the mountains of Moab into the valley of the Jordan, the country before them was already becoming broken and disunited.

JOSHUA i. *Preparations to strike camp*

10 Then Joshua commanded the officers of the people saying,
11 Pass through the midst of the camp, and command the
people saying, Prepare you victuals, for within three days
ye are to pass over this Jordan, to go in to possess the
land which the Lord your God giveth you to possess it. [E]

The Israelites had not moved camp for some time, not in fact since they had descended from the highlands of Moab to the valley in their last march under the leadership of Moses.[a] On that occasion, according to later tradition, they had 'pitched their camp by Jordan from Beth Jesimoth even unto Abel Shittim.'[b] Neither place is known with certainty, but the general position indicated is fairly clear. The name Abel-Shittim means the 'meadow of the acacias,' and it was thus probably given in the first instance to a district. The first part *Abel* reappears in the form *Abila*, which according to Josephus lay back some seven miles from the river.[1] This brings us to the edge of the plain below the foothills; and the site corresponds with the remains observable in the

[a] Numbers xxxiii 48 [P]. Cf. Numbers xxxiii 50 [D] and Joshua i 2 [E].
[b] Numbers xxxiii 49 [P].

[1] *Antiq.* iv 8 1, v 1 1. Cf. Buhl, *Geog.* p. 265.

vicinity of a modern village called Kufrein. Just to the south-west of this place there reaches out a low stony platform, covering an area of some thirty acres.[1] No

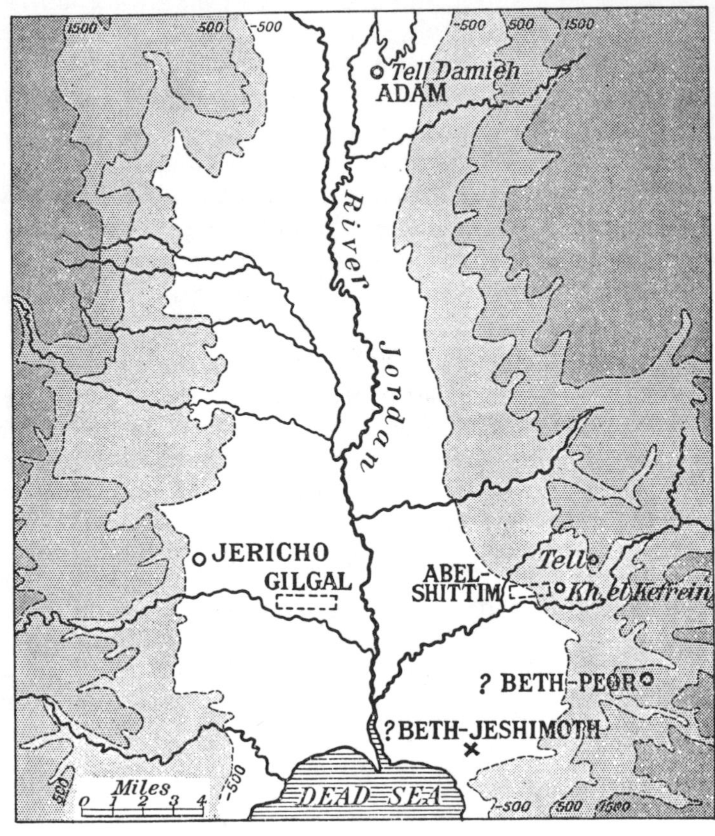

Map 9. The Lower Jordan Valley.

ruins are to be seen, but the surface is littered with potsherds among which predominate those of the Late Bronze Age (1600-1200 B.C.). The area is bounded on two sides by shallow watercourses which are green even in the summer with an exceptional amount of verdure, including mimosa scrub and scattered clumps of small

[1] See Pl. XXII.

acacia trees. Evidently water can be reached just below the surface. Here then was a favoured camping spot, and it seems to conform with the site of Shittim, which marked the north end of the camp of the Israelites and the actual site of Joshua's headquarters.[a]

Eastward, at the foot of the mountains, there rises a small mound called Tell el Kufrein, which identifies the spot. This stands upon rock, and though too small in itself for a village site, it is large enough to have supported a small cluster of houses or a watch tower; and the walls or foundations of small buildings of various ages may be traced in its steep slopes.[1] As a look-out position, it had indeed great advantages. Not only did it control the immediate vicinity of the camp, but it commanded a wide view of the valley as far as the highlands in the west; and from this standpoint the task in front of Joshua can be appreciated. In the early morning or after rain the range of visibility attains forty miles, but usually the heat-haze narrows down the view. To the north indeed the valley leads away beyond range of sight, closed on either hand by the broken ridges that form its boundaries. To the south it is filled by the waters of the Dead Sea which in their turn reach away into the distant haze. On the opposite side of the valley, which is here about fifteen miles across, the horizon is bounded, as far as the eye can reach in either direction, by the broken ridge which forms the edge of the western highlands. Seen from this standpoint towards midday, with the sun working round by the left, this ridge is thrown up in high relief. Above the lake, where the shadows lie in great blue patches, it appears to rise from the very waters, and to present a massive and unscaleable barrier along that shore. In front, however, above Jericho, it is seen to be furrowed by numerous dry gorges sharply delineated in the rose-coloured rock as they descend steeply to the plain, lending to the whole ridge at this distance a savage and

[a] Joshua ii 1 [J], iii 1 [JE].
[1] See Pl. XXII.

mysterious aspect. This view of the Promised Land shows clearly how great a part would be played by the primary physical features of mountain and ravine in the development of the now imminent invasion and later history. Many of these gorges mark in reality lines of roads giving access to the plateau; and on the heights there can be discerned on clear days the towers which now rise upon the summit of the ridge above Jerusalem, at a distance as the crow flies of thirty miles.[1] At the foot of this glowing wall of mountains, 4000 feet down and rather to the right, can be distinguished the palm groves and other trees that now mark, as of old, the site of Jericho; even the deserted mound just to the north upon which stood the historic city, may just be discerned, though thirteen miles away, showing grey against the rosier tint beyond of sand and rock.

The intervening valley, though speckled freely with green-grey scrub, with here and there a patch of irrigated garden, is for the most part arid and deserted. Nor does it show signs of much ancient cultivation except for occasional traces of Roman aqueducts and water channels. Agriculture must indeed at all times have been arduous. The sun heat on the low-lying plains is hardly tolerable. Human life is soon sapped of its activity. Except in winter travelling is done at night, while the goats and flocks glean a bare ration from the scrub, standing during the heat of the day with their heads hung low in the shadow of their own bodies.

Down the middle of the valley the course of the riverbed can be traced as a sinuous line of dark green in a broader band of white, descending very gently from the north until it merges with the lake. The water itself is not visible, being lost among the clustering hummocks eroded by time in the soft limestones and marl through which it flows.[2] This ground is sterile, but the actual banks of

[1] At night-time the writer has seen the lights of Jerusalem from Kerak, distant sixty-five miles.

[2] Cf. Pl. III.

VIEW OF THE JORDAN VALLEY AT NOONDAY FROM TELL EL KUFRĒN

The site of Abel Shittim lies in the left foreground.

TELL EL KUFRĒN AT THE FOOT OF THE HILLS OF MOAB.

The mound which marks the site of Abel Shittim.

See p. 126.

the river are mostly alluvial and freely covered with growth. The fords in the last ten miles of the river's course are three in number; but they are hardly ever passable during the rains or in the spring, when the melting snows of Hermon maintain the upper lakes at a high level.

It was the season of floods when Joshua disclosed his immediate purpose of crossing the Jordan, and it is to be realised that the difficulties in the way of accomplishing this intention and of attaining the goal would have been sufficient to deter anyone who lacked his ardour and inspiration. Yet his direct instructions were of the simplest; to prepare portable foodstuffs, to be ready to strike camp, and within three days to cross the river. His commands involved not only the fighting men but the women and children of nearly all the tribes, together with their animals, tents, and baggage. There is no suggestion as yet of military precautions. The fact that the near side of the river was already being grazed by his people's flocks undisturbed explains the situation thus far. But the Israelites, with their families, cattle, and baggage, once across the Jordan would enter enemy country.

Promptitude of decision and of action is characteristic of Joshua's leadership, but in this case it would appear that the issuing of his general instructions to prepare for the crossing of the river actually preceded the elaboration of his further plans. This fact, coupled with the specified time limit of three days, suggests that he had reason to anticipate within that time some stupendous development which would materially facilitate the accomplishment of his task. It was necessary only to seize the moment. In the meanwhile, according to the sequence of events as described in the narrative, his next thought seems to have been devoted to the military outlook.

JOSHUA ii. *Spies visit Jericho*

1 And Joshua the son of Nun sent out of Shittim two men as spies secretly, saying, go view the land and Jericho. . . . [J]

Jericho stood at the foot of the western hills, upon a low mound, about a mile to the north-west of the modern village, and overlooking the most abundant water supply of the vicinity. The identity of the site is not in doubt; no other Canaanite city is to be found in the neighbourhood, nor indeed for miles around; and excavation in the mound itself has not only attested its early origins, but has disclosed the remains of a walled city, corresponding in general with the indications of the narrative.

All the great cities of the Canaanites were surrounded by defensive walls, and here there was especial need of protection against man and beast. For though Jericho occupied a strategic point, it stood isolated, remote alike from any centre of authority and order as from the possible support of local alliances. It had accordingly been enclosed by protective ramparts from a remote age.[1] In the latter half of the Middle Bronze Age, 1800-1600 B.C., in common with other Canaanite cities of the country, it had attained the zenith of its prosperity. At that time its buildings covered the whole of the mound, the foot of which was revetted from below ground level to a height of twenty feet, all round its circuit of 800 yards, with a formidable stone glacis. Upon this rose a defensive parapet of brick,[2] the whole being further protected by an outer fosse.

However, at the time of the spies' visit those great days of Jericho were already past. About 1600 B.C. some catastrophe had overwhelmed the city, which when rebuilt was confined to the top of the mound. The old wall at the foot of the slope was largely demolished, and

[1] The earliest brick walls excavated as yet pertain to the first half of the Middle Bronze Age, *c.* 2000 B.C., but there are traces of earlier defensive works. See further in the Appendix.

[2] See *P.E.F.Q.S.*, July, 1930, with Pl. IV, VI.

KÔM EL SULTAN: SITE OF ANCIENT JERICHO, FROM S.E.

Around the bottom, almost buried, the stone ramparts: around the upper contour the brick walls of the city destroyed about 1400 B.C. On the right, the spring called 'Ain el Sultan.

See pp. 70, 130.

the fosse filled with debris. The new ramparts followed the shorter contour around the top of the slope. The city was accordingly much smaller, being rather less than 230 yards in length and about 130 yards in width, so that its whole circumference was not more than 650 yards.[1] Its area was thus less than six acres, and the population it contained could hardly have numbered more than 1500 people. The defences at this time consisted of two parallel walls built of brick: the outer one was about six feet thick, while the inner one varied from eleven to twelve feet, the space between the two being from four to five yards across. Though so massive, these walls were faulty in construction. The bricks were sun-dried, contained no binding straw, and varied greatly in size, though their thickness was fairly uniform and averaged about four inches. The foundations consisted generally of two or three layers of field stones, which lacked uniformity of size and were unevenly laid. On such a basis it was difficult to maintain regularity in the courses of the brick wall, in which accordingly gaps and differences of level were made good with mud mortar, though adjoining bricks were freely left by negligence without bond. All along the western side the inner wall is found to have followed the line of a similar but much more ancient fortification,[2] upon which it rested in those places where the older ruins had protruded through the surface at the time of building; but the perished lower work had not been made good, so that much of the wall, in particular its outer face, was founded upon debris. On foundations so unequal in strength, a certain amount of irregular subsidence was inevitable, as may now be seen, especially in view of the great weight and size of the wall itself, which, being twelve feet wide, probably rose to a height of twenty-five or thirty feet.[3] Here and there defects in

[1] See the plan, No. 8 in the Appendix, p. 387.

[2] Part of the defences of the first half of the Middle Bronze Age, *c.* 2000 B.C.

[3] The greatest preserved height is eighteen feet, where it abuts upon the tower in the north-western angle. See Pl. XXVI.

this wall seem to have been recognised and strengthened at the time, and signs of breaching and repair may be seen along the western side at a number of places.

The outer wall was built wholly upon debris, and, as is now found, on the very brink of the mound, which must have been levelled out for the purpose. It seems to have been designed as an additional security, possibly somewhat later than that within, though both had been in common use at the time of the spies' visit more than a century. In the meantime the pressure upon the limited building-space within the original enclosure seems to have become so great that houses had arisen upon the walls themselves, the intervening space being bridged with timber, traces of which are clear among the excavated remains. On the north side a firmer foundation for such houses was provided by a number of narrow transverse walls of brick, which bonded the inner and outer rampart walls together. In the north-west corner these main walls abutted upon and enclosed the foundations of a tower or migdol, which seems to have originally contained a chamber at ground level; but by this date it had already been filled in solidly with brick to the level of the walls themselves, above which, however, it doubtless rose much higher, after the fashion of the age familiar from Egyptian representations. Within the city proper not many houses of this period have yet been excavated; but it may be seen that they tended to be small in size, and clustered together in Oriental fashion. A number of houses leaned against the inner face of the main city wall, which they must have tended not only to obscure from within, but together with those upon it, actually to encumber, to the extent of hampering its defence.

The water supply of the city lay at the foot of its eastern slope. No gateway has been found in the length of wall uncovered around the north, west and south sides: it would seem then that the city at this time had but one gate which would face directly towards the water and the east. This conclusion is accordant with the indications of the narrative, which in two passages speaks only of 'the gate.'[a] A gate-tower in the position suggested, giving access to the spring, has in fact been located by the most recent excavations,[1] and as it proves to have been adapted to several changes in the city's fortifications, it probably marks also the site of the gateway of this period.

It is to be inferred that the spies entered the city without attracting special attention. They probably spoke an Aramaean dialect which was intelligible to the inhabitants, who, on their side, were accustomed to the passing to and fro in peace time of Bedouin and other peoples from beyond the Jordan. But the presence of the host of the Israelites on the opposite bank and the known tendency of nomads to push into the country when opportunity afforded, coupled with the supine attitude of Egypt at this juncture, must have filled the king and people of Jericho with misgiving and perplexity. It may be believed that the words put into the mouth of Rahab, who received the spies in her home and aided their escape, did not misrepresent the feelings of her fellow townsmen when she said to the men,[b] 'I know that the Lord hath given you the land, and that your terror is fallen upon us.'

15 Then she let them down by a cord through the window, for her house was upon the town wall.

22 And they went and came into the mountain and abode there three days. [E]

The west side of the city looked towards the edge of the high plateau, where the bold ridge now called the Jebel Kuruntul[2] overlooked the city at a distance of about a mile, so near and so high that its shadow enfolds the site in the early afternoon. It may be gained either by a

[a] Joshua ii 5, 7 [J]. [b] Joshua ii 9 [J].

[1] See the Plan in the Appendix, No. 8, Square K. 7.

[2] Pl. XXIV. Cf. also Pl. XXI.

direct zig-zag trail up the face of the cliff, which rises some 1500 feet above the plain; or from Ain Duk in the north by an easier ascent which climbs gradually up the face as it proceeds southward, attaining the summit, as in the other case, immediately to the west of Jericho. The whole ridge with its deep dry river beds is rough and desolate: the Jebel Kuruntul, in particular, evidently 'the mountain' of the context, is without verdure or life of any kind. The rock itself is soft and friable and the face of the cliff, cracked by successive heat and cold and weathered by the storms of centuries, presents numerous hiding-places, in more recent time the resort of hermits and the site of monasteries of the silent. The spies, once they had gained this mountain under cover of twilight, ran little risk of detection, even though all the roads that converged on Jericho were kept under observation.

23 Then the two men returned, and descended from the
mountains and passed over and came to Joshua, the son
of Nun, and they told him all that had befallen them.
24 And they said unto Joshua, Truly the Lord hath delivered
into our hands all the land. [E]

'AIN EL DUK, A PERENNIAL SPRING TO THE N.W. OF JERICHO.

On the right, the valley up which climbs the route to Rummon and Bethel.

THE JEBEL KURUNTUL: WHICH RISES TO THE W. OF JERICHO.

In the foreground: a small plain watered from Ain el Duk.

See pp. 70, 133.

SECTION 4

THE ADVANCE ACROSS JORDAN

Joshua III-IV

JOSHUA iii. *The camp moved*

1 And Joshua rose up early in the morning, and they removed from Shittim, and came to Jordan, he and all the children of Israel; and they lodged there before they passed over.

[JE]

FROM the site of Shittim to the fords of the Jordan, the distance is about eight miles. The route lies through a sandy plain broken by shallow dry watercourses and sparse scrub. Experience of centuries has taught desert peoples how to move their camp. Evidently this cannot be done in close order, for their animals must feed and drink, and rest during the heat of the day, but at the same time the method must ensure safety for their households and non-combatants. The formation usually adopted is like a closed V. The flocks come first over an extended front, followed in open order by the herds and behind these the gunmen. Then come the women and families with the baggage, and last of all the elders and the chief. A clan of five thousand souls, complete with animals, moves on a seven-mile front, and seven miles is a good day's journey. In camp the formation is closer and by groups of families, the space required being in round figures about a square half-mile per 1000 persons.[1] Such a day's movement gives a good impression of what was involved in the removal of the Israelites from Shittim to the Jordan. We are not told, however, that they pitched a regular camp upon the bank, though they set up tents.[a]

[a] Joshua iii 14 [JE].

[1] The area occupied by a stationary Bedouin camp is commonly in the proportion of about twelve tents per acre.

Once by the ford Joshua and the people seem to have waited deliberately for the anticipated development. We gather that the river was high; the fords would be deep; it would be difficult for the grown men to cross, and impossible under such conditions for the women and children, sheep and goats, baggage and animals. It seems as though little short of some miraculous event could make the crossing possible. The fact that Joshua lived in lively anticipation of some providential intervention is visible, not only in his actions, but in the spirit of prophecy disclosed in several passages, thus:

iii. 5 Joshua said unto the people, Sanctify yourselves for
to-morrow the Lord will do wonders among you. . . .
10 Hereby ye shall know that the living God is among you. . . .
11 Behold, the ark of the covenant of the Lord of all the earth
13 passeth over before you into Jordan. . . . And it shall
come to pass that the waters of Jordan shall be cut off,
even the waters that come down from above. [JE]

THE CROSSING OF THE JORDAN

People trained to scientific thought to-day are not disposed to believe in the possibility of any phenomenon which defies the laws of human experience. Nor in this case is it necessary to do so. Joshua was in possession of the east bank of the Jordan as far north as the river Jabbok,[a] thus including the site of Damieh. This is doubtless the same as 'Adam' or 'Adamah' of the narrative[1]; it is found about sixteen miles up the river from Jericho or Shittim; and its position is marked by a small Bronze Age tell raised upon a terrace just above the general level of the low-lying plain by which it is surrounded, about half a mile eastward from the best ford of the middle Jordan, the Jisr el Damieh. It so happens that the river near this ford is liable to be blocked at intervals by great landslides. Several of these are on record. The earliest occurrence dates from A.D. 1266 when the

[a] Judges xi 22 [E]. [1] Cf. Cooke, *Joshua*, p. 23.

Sultan Bibars ordered a bridge to be built across the Jordan in the neighbourhood of Damieh. The task was found to be difficult owing to the rise of the waters. But in the night preceding the 8th December, 1267, a lofty mound, which overlooked the river on the west, fell into it and dammed it up, so that the water of the river ceased to flow and none remained in its bed. The waters spread over the valley above the dam and none flowed down the bed for some sixteen hours.[1] There was another similar occurrence about the year 1906, and the most recent during the earthquakes of 1927.[2] On this last occasion the high west bank immediately below the ford collapsed, carrying with it the roadway, as seen in our photographs;[3] and just below, a section of the cliff, which here rises to a height of 150 feet, fell bodily across the river and completely dammed it, so that no water flowed down the river bed for twenty-one and a half hours. Meanwhile the waters gradually filled up the plain around Tell el Damieh, and found their way eventually back to the river bed when the temporary barrage was in turn destroyed, and normal conditions were gradually resumed. During this time, it is asserted by several living witnesses that they crossed and recrossed the bed of the river freely on foot. An exactly similar occurrence appears to be described in iii 16:

16 The waters which came down from above stood, and rose up in one heap, a great way off, at Adam, the city that is beside Zarethan: and those that went down toward the sea of the Arabah, even the salt sea, were wholly cut off: and the people passed over right against Jericho. [JE]

[1] *P.E.F. Q.S.* 1895, 253 ff.

[2] The greatest shock occurred on Monday, July 11th, 1927, at 3.50 p.m., followed by milder shocks on Wednesday, July 13th, at 11.30 a.m.; on Sunday, July 17th, at 10 a.m.; a week later on July 24th at 12 noon; and again on Tuesday, August 2nd, at 10 a.m. Early in the next year, 1928, on Wednesday, January 28th, at 7.53 p.m. a great shock was felt in Trans-Jordania, particularly at Jerash where it was recorded as the worst of the series by the Director of Antiquities who supplies this information.

[3] Pl. XXV and cf. Pl. III.

The Israelites had been camped for some time at Shittim. Their flocks must have been grazing along the eastern banks of the river, and any unusual happening at Damieh could have been reported to Joshua the same day. The condition of the fords was a subject of immediate concern, and if a great part of the cliff was found at that time to be overhanging and in imminent danger of falling, as in A.D. 1267, this fact alone would be sufficient to account for the acceleration of his plan. But if, in addition, it was a period of earthquake,[1] as in A.D. 1927, there would be all the more cause for watchful anticipation. And though the narrative of Joshua is silent on the point, this possibility is suggested by the opening lines of Deborah's Song in Judges v, a passage derived from very ancient legend:

4 Lord, when thou wentest forth out of Seir,
When thou marchedst out of the fields of Edom,
The earth trembled. [E]

CAMP PITCHED AT GILGAL

Joshua iv

20 And those twelve stones, which they took out of Jordan, did Joshua set up in Gilgal. [JE]

The Israelites lodged that night at Gilgal; and there eventually they proceeded to establish the camp which was to remain their headquarters throughout the subsequent campaigns. Though no trace has been found of the twelve stones, the general position of Gilgal is well known.[2] The name Jiljulieh in which the ancient form

[1] No records are available before the Middle Ages: In May of 1202 an earthquake affected Syria and Egypt, and two years later (in 1204) a strong shock was felt throughout western Asia. In 1302 severe shocks were observed through a period of twenty days, both in Syria and Egypt; and again in 1303 Damascus and Acre were both shaken. In the year 1698 some eight or nine shocks were recorded at Rosetta and Alexandria. It is noticeable how the tremors have a tendency to recur within the space of one or two years, and then to quieten for a while.

[2] See further under this name in the Appendix.

THE WEST BANK OF THE JORDAN, OPPOSITE EL DAMIEH, 1928.

Where falls of this high bank destroyed the roadway during the earthquakes of 1927, and further subsidences were imminent.

THE RIVER JORDAN, BELOW THE FORD OF EL DAMIEH, LOOKING W.

Where the flow of water was stopped in 1927 by the fall of a cliff to the south of the view point.

See p. 137.

is preserved, is still attached to an area lying between Jericho and the Jordan, some two miles from the former, and this position agrees with the later tradition [a] which located Gilgal on the east border of Jericho. The site itself is inconspicuous, and differs only from other portions of the sterile plain by the presence of a number of low mounds of doubtful antiquity. But the area as a whole, particularly that which lies immediately to the south, is suitable for an encampment, and in many respects resembles that of Abel Shittim which the Israelites had just left. To the south it is bounded by a deepening valley, worn through the plain by the flood waters of the Wady Kelt, the 'Valley of Achor.' This valley, like that of Abel Shittim, is rich in verdure of varying kind; and the presence of water below the surface, already strongly suggested by this fact, is actually reported but not confirmed in our experience. Jiljulieh itself is two miles from Jericho and three miles from the Jordan, and would most appropriately mark the western extremity of the ancient camp, which, if a mile in length, would lie midway between Jericho and the river, two miles from each.

[a] Joshua iv 19 [P].

SECTION 5

JERICHO DEVOTED TO JEHOVAH

Joshua V-VI

Joshua v

13 **And it came to pass when Joshua was by Jericho that he**
lifted up his eyes and looked, and behold, there stood a
man over against him with his sword drawn in his hand:
and Joshua went unto him, and said unto him, Art thou
14 **for us, or for our adversaries? And he said, Nay, but as**
captain of the host of the Lord am I now come. [J]

This passage introduces the story of the annihilation of Jericho, which follows in Chapter vi. It is quoted here, though its subject matter is beyond our scope, for two reasons. Firstly, it reminds us appropriately at this stage of the essential fact that, although the earliest documents, quoted in our Introductory Section, contain a connected and reasonably coherent narrative of events, they, no less than the Bible as a whole, were conceived from first to last as the records of a religious movement, written down, arranged, and later annotated, by men who were inspired and guided by the very religion which it was their purpose to perpetuate. We should fail then to grasp the full meaning of the text, or to gauge the historical value even of those oldest documents, if we ignored altogether the spiritual element which pervades these writings. Secondly, it forms the prelude to an unparalleled episode, in which the sacrifice of Jericho with its living population is performed as a sacramental act; and so to some extent it prepares the reader to find the military incidents and material aspect of the occasion almost lost to view behind the details of the religious ceremonial that solemnised the event.

Certainly the capture of Jericho presented no great difficulty even to the inexperience of the Israelites. Its defences have been described[1]: though perhaps bold in appearance, being perched upon a mound and surrounded with high walls dominated by a solid corner tower, it was in fact a small affair when compared with some of the cities 'fenced and strong' which Joshua had seen in the interior.[a] Its chief weakness is apparent even now. The outer wall stood upon debris at the edge of the slope, and though six feet thick, its height and the weight of superincumbent houses made it a source of danger rather than an additional protection.

Joshua's subsequent commands, and indeed his Vision, show that as he stood by Jericho he was occupied with thoughts transcending the immediate problem. Jericho lay at the threshold of the Promised Land: the occasion was momentous and called for a unique rite. The narrative reflects this attitude clearly, leaving in obscurity all question of the imminent attack. None the less a scrutiny of the text and its separate elements discloses one or two passages derived from the oldest documentary source (J) in which there lurks a reminiscence of what may have been originally an instruction dealing with the military problem.

JOSHUA vi

> **3 And ye shall compass the city, all the men of war, going about the city once, this thou shalt do six days. [J]**

The word translated 'compass,' it should be noted, has nowhere in the historical books of the O.T. the sense of 'march round': the rendering 'surround' or 'encircle' would be more exact. This record, with its single issue, is in close accord with the version of the Septuagint:

> 'The Lord said unto Joshua, Behold I give Jericho into thy hand and her king which is in her, mighty men of valour, and do thou set

[a] Cf. Numbers xiii 28 [JE].

[1] Above, p. 130 f. See also Plates XXVI, XXVII.

> around about it (in a circle) the men of war,[1] and it shall be that when ye sound with the trumpet let all the people shout together, and when they shout the walls of the city will fall of their own accord, and all the people shall go in every one hastening before him into the city.' (LXX)

Both these passages point to a decision to surround the city with armed men. If this interpretation be correct, it becomes intelligible how the fact that the armed men 'went before' the ark might later give rise to the recorded tradition (mostly attributed to E) that they actually headed a procession. But the original meaning would seem to be that they went out to their allotted stations in advance of the procession and evidently for a special purpose. What that purpose was, or how it was effected, is not apparent. The introductory words to Chapter vi (attributed to JE) almost imply a state of siege: 'Now Jericho was straitly shut up because of the children of Israel: none went out and none came in,' but there is no suggestion of a deliberate investment. There is no record here of any fighting, nor indeed of any defensive measures at all on the part of the inhabitants of Jericho, who seem to have been reduced by fear to inactivity.[2]

JOSHUA vi

10 And Joshua commanded the people saying : Ye shall not
shout neither shall any word proceed out of your mouth,
11 until the day I bid you shout. . . . So he caused the ark
of the Lord to compass the city, going about it once : and
14 they came into the camp. . . . So they did six days. . . .
[J]

The ceremonial specially instituted for this occasion, the daily carrying of the Ark in solemn procession around

[1] *Or*, 'do thou surround it with the men of war round about'; cf. Cooke, *Joshua*, p. 41.

[2] The brief allusion of Joshua xxiv 11 hardly removes this impression: it follows the style of v. 9 and may be attributed with the rest of v. 11 to D. Cf. Cooke, *Joshua*, p. 217.

Pl. XXVI.

THE RUINED WALLS OF JERICHO, DESTROYED ABOUT 1400 B.C., VIEWED FROM THE N.E.

In the foreground, the double brick wall running back towards the right. In the middle, the remains of a tower. On the right, the Jebel Kuruntul.

See pp. 131, 141.

the walls, followed by the massed host of the Israelites in stern silence, must have presented indeed a grim and terrifying spectacle to the besieged inhabitants, to whom it foreshadowed their impending doom. History hardly bears witness to a design so frightful, accomplished with such deliberation. Ever and again the desert areas of the Near East have given violent birth to holy wars. The first flood of the Mohammedan invaders, the fiery Mahdists of two generations ago, the stern fanatical Wahabis of to-day, all stained their trails with blood in the name of their religion. But there is no record of a determination comparable with this, the solemn sacrifice of an entire town. The removal of Jericho from the path was no ordinary incident of raid, but the first step in the fulfilment of the Covenant. Nor was the slaying of its population a mere case of blood-lust: just as the firstborn of each family of Israel was dedicated to their God, and the firstlings of the flocks were sacrificed, so Jericho, as the first fruits of the Promised Land, was to be devoted in its entirety to Jehovah. There were to be no spoils and no captives. Only the woman who had helped the Israelites' cause was to be saved, with her family; all others were doomed to be sacrificed within the city in one awful holocaust.

JOSHUA vi

20 And it came to pass, when the people heard the sound of
the trumpet, that the people shouted with a great shout,
and the wall fell down flat,[a] so that the people went up into
the city every man straight before him, and they took the
21 city, And they utterly destroyed all that was in the city,
both man and woman, both young and old, and ox, and
24 sheep, and ass, with the edge of the sword. . . . And they
burnt the city with fire. [J]

The collapse of the walls of Jericho is not attributed by the Bible narrative to a physical agency. But we should not overlook in this connexion the possible effect of earth-

[a] *Or,* In its place.

quakes, which in themselves would doubtless have been regarded at the time as direct manifestations of Jehovah's powers. Walls of the period both at Ai and at Jerusalem, on excavation, showed signs of subsidence and dislocation [1] such as might be attributed to earth tremors; but there is no indication as to the date of these shocks, which may even have happened since the abandonment of the sites. We have already noted that earthquakes are said to have heralded the arrival of the Israelites,[2] and we have seen that in recent years an earthquake produced at El Damieh the very phenomenon which is said to have made possible the crossing of the Jordan.[3] Palestine is subject to earthquakes, some of which have wrought great damage. In 1837 four thousand people were killed in the district of Safed. The havoc caused by the earthquakes of 1927 amounted to a national disaster. Violent tremors were felt throughout the country on both sides of the river. At Nablus two whole streets of houses completely disappeared, and in all several hundred houses fell leaving thousands of people homeless. At Amman also the shocks caused much material damage; while at Jericho itself a hotel collapsed, with fatal consequences, and the ends of the Allenby bridge over the Jordan were displaced. Jericho lies particularly within the earthquake zone, and on that occasion violent shocks were recorded on four days out of seven.[4] Theoretically, then, the possibility of the walls of Jericho having been damaged or destroyed by earthquakes is to be admitted. But an examination of the remains of the walls themselves hardly substantiates the suggestion. Both lie in ruins, but the lowest courses are preserved to a height varying from one to three yards according to the depth of ground.[5] Neither shows much sign of transverse fracture. Dislocation of the bricks is noticeable in certain sections of

[1] Cf. p. 151. [2] P. 138. [3] P. 137.

[4] See above, p. 137, n. 2; cf. also *The Times* reports of July 12, 14, 1927; Jan. 14 and Feb. 22, 1928.

[5] Cf. Pl. XXVII.

the inner wall along the western side, but not to an extent that cannot be explained by normal subsidence arising from the unequal strength of its foundations.[1] Moreover, the collapse of a wall of this thickness, standing upon relatively level ground, would probably begin with a lateral splitting from the top; and in this case the process would involve not only the crumbling edges of the main wall itself, but the rooms or houses built thereon, and the debris might be expected to fall inwards almost as much as outwards. But in those few places where the inner face of the wall has been discovered undisturbed, this is not found to have been the case. Ruins and signs of burning are found against the wall in plenty, but they are apparently the last traces of houses that rested against the wall. Signs of damage and destruction are more apparent on the outer sides, in the space, that is, between the walls, and outside, down the slopes. Here several sections cut through both walls and into the ground below them tell plainly a consistent story which was summarised at the close of the excavations in the following memorandum.[2]

'The main defences of Jericho in the Late Bronze Age (*c.* 1600-1200 B.C.) followed the upper brink of the city mound, and comprised two parallel walls, the outer six feet and the inner twelve feet thick. Investigations along the west side show continuous signs of destruction and conflagration. The outer wall suffered most, its remains falling down the slope. The inner wall is preserved only where it abuts upon the citadel, or tower, to a height of eighteen feet; elsewhere it is found largely to have fallen, together with the remains of buildings upon it, into the space between the walls which was filled with ruins and debris. Traces of intense fire are plain to see, including reddened masses of brick, cracked stones, charred timbers

[1] See above, p. 131.

[2] Signed at Jericho on March 2, 1930, by the Very Rev. Père Vincent and the present writer; and endorsed as to its archaeological conclusions by Dr. Clarence Fisher.

and ashes. Houses alongside the wall are found burned to the ground, their roofs fallen upon the domestic pottery within.'

As to the main fact, then, there remains no doubt: the walls fell outwards so completely that the attackers would be able to clamber up and over their ruins into the city.

In one section the lower mass of the outer wall was found tilted forward, and apparently off its bed. It is possible that it had been dislodged by the weight and shock of the falling debris from behind; but an examination of the ground showed that it might have been undermined from the outside. The earth below it, as it lies, is not that of the one-time surface of the slope, but crushed earth without sign of preparation to serve as a foundation. Further investigation will be necessary in this and other spots before a general conclusion can be established; meanwhile the impression remains uppermost that the wall fell at that place because it had been partly undermined. (See however below, p. 404.)

The date of this destruction was not ascertained, but certain limits were established. Among the thousands of potsherds characteristic of the period, found among and below the ruins, not one piece of Mykenaean ware has been observed. This fact suggests that the fourteenth century had not begun at the time the walls fell.[1] A more precise indication was found outside the city, at the foot of its northern slope, in an undisturbed stratum that overlay the filled-up fosse of the Middle Bronze Age. The destruction of the Canaanite city is well marked by black layers of burnt matter running down from the ruined parapet of the outer wall.[2] In this area, uniquely, a few houses sprang up, outside and upon the disused fortifications, after the destruction of the upper city, in the second

[1] See above, p. 106. Cf. also Wace in *J.H.S.*, vol. xlvi, p. 116, and in *C.A.H.*, ii, pp. 459 f. An examination of the common pottery points to the same conclusion, which is endorsed after an independent study by Dr. Albright, Aug. 1930.

[2] Cf. *P.E.F., Q.S.* July 1930. Pl. VI.

SECTION OF THE INNER BRICK WALL OF JERICHO, DESTROYED ABOUT 1400 B.C.

The picture shows the ruins falling to the L. down the slope, amid layers of white ash and pockets of charcoal.

See p. 145.

half of the Late Bronze Age, to be destroyed in their turn, leaving a second layer of ashes as witness of the fact. Between the two layers of burnt matter, and underlying in particular the latter, there was found in the course of excavation a vase of Mykenaean style, the date of which may be assigned with some certainty to about 1300 B.C.[1] It pertains, as the evidence shows, to a partial reoccupation of the northern extremity of the site, outside the former limits of the upper city and above the debris that marks its fall. It follows that the upper city had already been reduced to ruins before that date. The evidence all points, then, towards the year 1400 B.C. for the fall of Jericho.

JOSHUA vi. *The ruins laid under a curse*

26 And Joshua charged them with an oath at that time,
saying, Cursed be the man before the Lord, that riseth up
and buildeth this city Jericho: with the loss of his first-
born shall he lay the foundation thereof, and with the loss
27 of his youngest son shall he set up the gates of it. So the
Lord was with Joshua; and his fame was in all the land. [J]

The charge was apparently observed. Excavations at Jericho have disclosed four chief periods in the occupation of the city. Three of these we have examined; they cover approximately three separate but fairly continuous periods of two hundred years each, from 2000 down to 1400 B.C. But after that date the city lay in ruins with no appreciable population for some five hundred years. The first part of the Early Iron Age (1200-900 B.C.) is not represented at all in the archaeology of the site: the stratifications representing the second phase of the Iron Age (900 B.C.) are found in general directly over the destruction layers of the Late Bronze Age.

Exception must be made of the traces of the several houses which sprang up independently of the fortifications upon the ruins of the city at its northern end, in the

[1] Cf. Hall *P.E.F., loc. cit.* p. 122.

fourteenth century B.C. The references in the Book of Judges (i 16, iii 13) to the ' City of Palm Trees ' may thus be applied to Jericho to that extent, but would be more properly descriptive of the cultivable area below the spring, to the east of the old city, and nearer the modern village. But the city itself was not rebuilt nor its fortifications restored until the ninth century B.C.

SECTION 6

THE DESTRUCTION OF AI

Joshua VII-VIII

JOSHUA vii. *The reverse before Ai*

2 And Joshua sent men from Jericho to Ai, which is beside Beth-aven, on the east side of Beth-el, and spake unto them saying, Go up and spy out the land. And the men went up and spied out Ai. [J]

THE fall and destruction of Jericho left Joshua in possession of a strategic centre, whence three main routes led up by separate valleys towards the highlands of the west.[1] The most southerly of these, entering the mountains by the Wady Kelt, gave access to Jerusalem, the city of Jebus, which, however, occupied a dominant position and was further protected at the time by formidable defences.[2] Joshua sought a more favourable opening by way of Ai, a city which could be approached by either of the other routes, being situated in fact at the point where they converged high up the ridge. Its position was a strong one befitting its importance as an advanced post of the dwellers upon the plateau. Perched on the summit of a low hill, overlooking the wilderness of tangled valleys that descend towards the Jordan, it commanded a wide view on all sides but the west, where rises a ridge that obscured the view of Bethel. Steep watercourses enclose the site on all sides but the south. Two of these are followed by the routes mentioned, and a third falls precipitously south-eastward, disgorging finally into the Wady Muheisin. These valleys descend very steeply towards the Jordan and pass at times through rocky gorges, so that though the two former indicate the

[1] See Map No. 10. Cf. Plate XXI.

[2] See below, p. 169, and Pl. XXXVIII.

general line of the roads, it must not be understood that these follow the actual watercourses. On the contrary they hold mostly to the high ground hugging the contours.

The position of Ai at the head of this valley, though now long abandoned, had evidently a certain strategic importance in its day, and from this point of view it was well chosen. On its northern side the valley is deep; and from the opposite slopes the city must have presented a bold and well-nigh impregnable appearance, crowning a detached hill which rises in a series of rocky terraces.[1] The disadvantage of the site would seem to have been its meagre water supply. The only source visible to-day is a tiny spring in the rock, almost at the foot of the hill, to the north-west. Here the water trickles down from the living rock, but in so slight amount that cup-holes have been hollowed out to collect it; and those who resort to this place in modern times must necessarily wait their turn, often for some hours. In antiquity a pathway led down to the spring from the western side of the city, where apparently was placed a gateway. The descent can be effected in about six minutes, but the return journey involves a considerable climb. About the middle of the knoll upon which the city stood, there may also be traced in our photograph a narrow footpath which falls steeply to the valley, issuing in like manner from the west side of the city, but turning north and east in its descent. The well-defined track seen in the picture leading down towards the spring from left to right is that which now serves the neighbouring village of Deir Diwan. The only other route to the valley descends directly from the south end of the knoll down the rocky scarps. This again does not seem to be connected with the ancient site, and it is used nowadays almost exclusively by goatherds.

Seen from the south the city is not so boldly placed;[2] but in compensation the indications of defensive walls are well defined on that side. The stout Canaanite masonry

[1] Pl. XXVIII. [2] Pl. XXX.

Pl. XXVIII.

EL TELL, THE SITE OF AI, FROM THE OPPOSITE SIDE OF THE VALLEY ON THE N. Cf. Joshua viii, 11.
See pp. 149, 150.

has been largely quarried out, leaving, however, traces of the foundations, while the course of the wall is clearly indicated by its debris. In this way the line of rampart has been traced from east to west for a distance of 180 yards, after which it bends north-westward around the contour of the hill, for a further fifty yards. At this point, in the western face of the city, the actual wall has been found on excavation to be still standing to a height of eight to ten feet,[1] though now entirely below the surface of the ground, and it was cleared in a northerly direction for a distance of about forty yards. Eight rough courses of characteristic Bronze Age masonry are preserved; and at one point, probably near the foundations, the thickness of this rampart proved to be thirteen feet. Here and there in the wall were noted conspicuous signs of dislocation as by subsidence or earthquake.

From the top of the mound hereabouts the remainder of the area may be seen to fall away towards the north and east in a series of descending terraces, any one of which would lend itself readily to a defensive system. The precise line of the ancient wall on those sides has not been determined, and it is doubtful whether it is preserved; but the contours of the hill, coupled with the suggestive traces of a return in the south-east corner, indicate a city about 230 yards long from north to south with a width of 200 yards. It thus tended to be square in outline, though rounded off at three corners conformably with the natural contours of the rock. It contained accordingly a superficial area of about nine acres, and on our basis of calculation could not have housed more than 2500 souls, 1500 being a more probable figure. None the less it was by comparison a city of considerable importance; larger than Jericho of the day, though not so large nor so strongly protected as Jerusalem. The spies did not properly appreciate the strength of Ai, and the small detachment sent to attack it, in accordance with their report, proved unequal to the task.

[1] Pl. XXIX.

JOSHUA vii

4 **So there went up thither of the people about three thousand**
5 **men; and they fled before the men of Ai. And the men of Ai smote of them about thirty and six men, and they chased them from before the gate even unto Shebarim[a] and smote them at the going down. [J]**

For reasons already given, the number of fighting men, being computed in round figures by 'thousands,' must be regarded with mistrust,[1] and obviously cannot in this case be exact. By contrast the definite figure of thirty-six seems proportioned to the circumstances, and may have come down unchanged from an original tradition.[2] The route taken in the retreat, and presumably in the attack, was apparently that which passes below Mukhmas,[3] as the only ancient quarries that have been observed are found to the south-west of Kh. Haiyan. Below this point the track commences its rapid descent towards the valley. As will be seen in the sequel, this route was not favourable for an attack on Ai, for nearing the city it crosses exposed and difficult ground, of which the defenders, forewarned, could take full advantage.

The effect of the reverse upon Joshua and the Elders is next described in a few powerful phrases derived from the oldest sources:

JOSHUA vii

7 **. . . would that we had been content and dwelt beyond**
8 **Jordan! Oh Lord, what shall I say after that Israel hath turned their backs before their enemies! For the Canaanites**
9 **and all the inhabitants of the land shall hear of it, and shall compass us round, and cut off our name from the earth: and what wilt thou do for thy great name? [J]**

[a] *Or*, the Quarries.

[1] See the discussion of this question on p. 120.

[2] The same figure is given in the LXX. Cf. the old reference to 600 men in the narrative of the migration of the tribe of Dan, Judges xviii 11. [J].

[3] Cf. p. 155, and Map No. 10.

SOUTHERN PROFILE OF EL TELL, THE SITE OF AI.
Showing the line of the stone wall which can be traced along this side of the western face.

BRONZE AGE WALLS OF THE CITY OF AI, AFTER CLEARANCE, ON THE WESTERN FACE.

See pp. 150, 151.

The narrative proceeds to describe how the cause of the disaster was traced to an act of sacrilege on the part of one Achan of the tribe of Judah, who at the sack of Jericho had taken some of the spoils, all of which we have seen had been devoted as first-fruits to Jehovah. Under the Israelite theocracy unswerving obedience to the divine will was a matter of vital principle affecting the unity of the people. Achan, having confessed his sin, was brought up with all he had unto the valley of Achor, where he was put to death, and buried under a great heap of stones. The valley indicated seems to be the lower course of the Wady Kelt, which has scoured a channel through the plain and passes to the south side of Jiljulieh. With the expiation of Achan's crime fulfilled

Jehovah turned from the fierceness of His anger.[a]

THE TAKING OF AI

The feelings of despair and bitter foreboding to which Joshua and his followers had given way were succeeded by plans for action. The immediate matter was to avenge the defeat, to lay hands upon the King of Ai and his people, to seize his city and his lands. Not only must the fresh attempt be crowned with victory, but the news of a terrible vengeance in its wake, like that inflicted upon the city and King of Jericho, would go far to stem the dangerous consequences of the previous reverse.

To attain this end all the resources of Joshua's command should be employed. A new genius for military organisation and tactics came into being. The capture of the city might still prove a relatively easy matter, but greater issues were involved, and this time the divine voice urged Joshua to greater circumspection.

[a] Joshua vii 26 [J].

JOSHUA viii

1 Take all the people of war with thee, and arise, go up to
2, 3 Ai. . . . Set thee an ambush for the city behind it. So
Joshua arose, and all the people of war, to go up to Ai, and Joshua chose out thirty[a] thousand men of valour, and sent them forth by night. [J]

Before starting he explained the new tactics to be employed.

JOSHUA viii

4 Behold ye shall lie in ambush against the city, behind the city; go not very far from the city, but be ye all ready:
5 And I, and all the people that are with me will approach unto the city: and it shall come to pass, when they come out against us, as at the first, that we shall flee before
7 them. . . . And ye shall rise up from the ambush and take
8 possession of the city: . . . And when ye have seized upon
the city, that ye shall set the city on fire. [J]

Their immediate task was clear: they were to take up a suitable position to the west of Ai, that is towards the side of Bethel, without being seen by the people of either city. Ai is in fact, as we have already found, invisible from Bethel, though distant little more than a mile. Between them rises a sharp spur of hill around which winds the road from Mukhmas. Immediately to the west of Ai the road itself is obscured by a ridge of broken rocks full of fissures, and separated from the village by a short declivity.[1] These rocks provided the hiding-place required for the ambush, and the tactical problem was to gain this valley-road unseen and unsuspected. This could be accomplished only under cover of darkness, and neither of the main routes from Old Jericho was favourable to the enterprise.

The easier and more open of these, heading northwestwards, skirts the Jebel Kuruntul as far as the green

[a] *Alternatively* five thousand: cf. v 12 [E].

[1] See Plates XXX, XXXII.

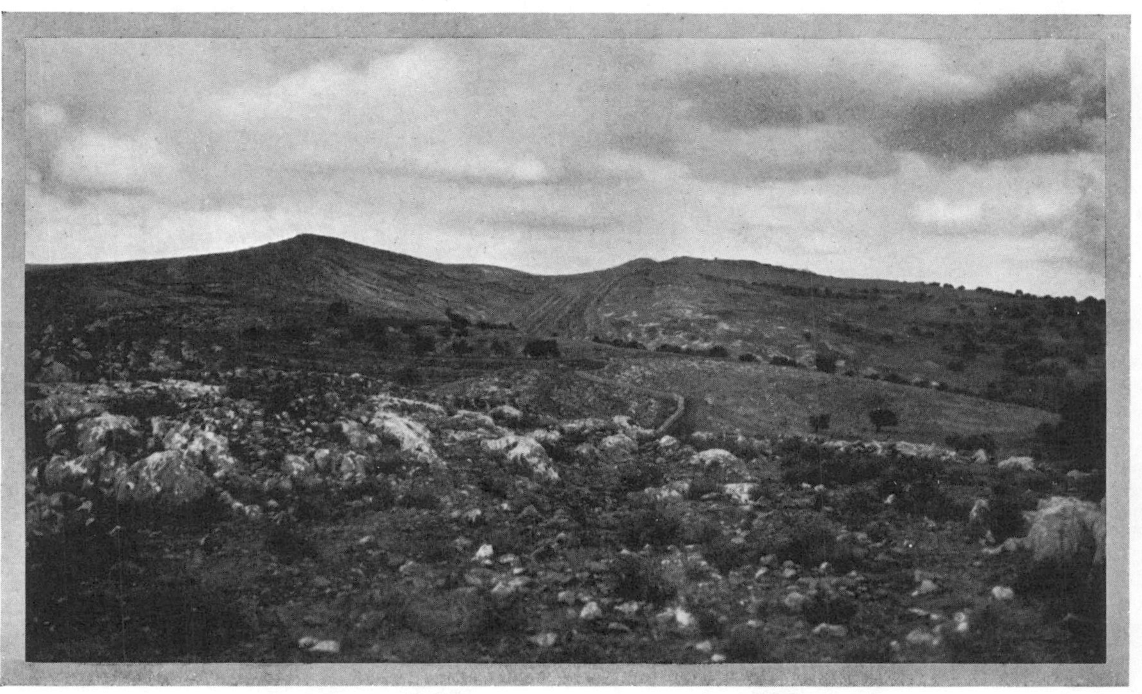

THE POSITION OF AI, VIEWED FROM THE SOUTH.

On the left, the hill of ambush: on the right, the site of the City.

See p. 154.

valley of Ain el Duk, and rounding the height of Um-Sirah begins the ascent by a short valley called the Wady Lereid.[1] Once the first steep climb of about fifteen hundred feet is surmounted, this road ascends by relatively easy grades, until near Rummon a smaller track branches westward towards Bethel, winding up the slopes and around the contours on the north of the Wady Muheisin, so passing the site of Ai on the opposite side of the valley. The total distance from Old Jericho to Ai

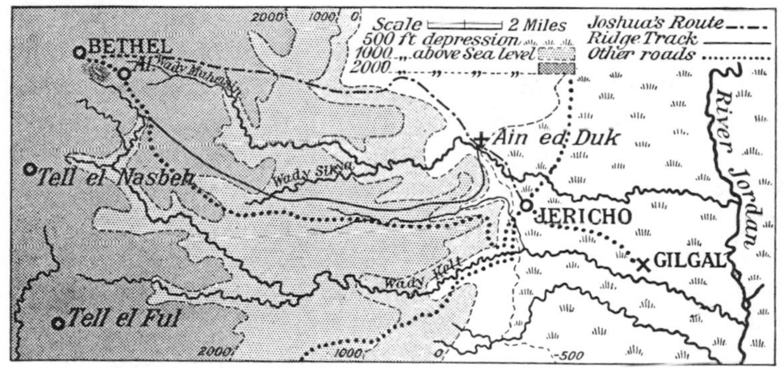

Map 10. Routes from Jericho to Ai.

is thirteen miles, and the total ascent 3200 feet. The other main route, though more direct, is rough and difficult. It enters the hills to the west of Jericho by the Wady Abu Retnah, and after a short detour to avoid the steep gorges at the foot it follows up that valley to its source, beyond which it bends northwards around the high ridge called Ras el Tawil, and passes by Khurbet el Hai and Mukhmas. Hereabouts it becomes tortuous and rough; and in the last five miles it climbs nearly 1000 feet. Formerly, no doubt, it connected with Ai as now with the modern village of Deir Diwan. But the direct route to Bethel, passing to the east of Kh. Haiyan, follows the valley to the west of Ai, from which accordingly it is invisible.

[1] See also Map, p. 79.

Both these routes are natural avenues of communication between the hill country and the plain, but the objections to their use for the placing of this ambush are apparent. The northern one where it winds up the opposite slopes of the valley on the northern side of Ai, crosses in its ascent large patches of open ground visible plainly from the city above. To approach Ai unseen it would be necessary to follow the ravine itself, clambering thence by the rugged pathway close to the east of the hill on which the city stands. But this alternative, possible to an active individual in daylight, was not practicable to a force of men by night. The more southerly route, though less exposed to view and at the outset not so steep, is much rougher underfoot, and in its later stages it passes through rocky defiles of the wildest sort,[1] equally impracticable for a silent march by night.

All these difficulties could, however, be avoided by taking a narrow track which follows up the middle of the ridge between these valley routes. From Jericho, as we have seen, this climbs directly up the Jebel Kuruntul, but it can be joined from Ain el Duk by a track which follows up the bed of a watercourse[2] behind that mountain and offers accordingly a much easier grade, the rise being not more than 1000 feet in a distance of three miles. Thence the way lay clear. It avoided any inhabited places, and its exposed course involved less likelihood of meeting shepherds or other individuals by night.[3] This track was also shorter than all others, being no more than eleven miles from the foot of the hills. On the other hand progress would necessarily be slow: not only was there the further ascent of fifteen hundred feet, but the rocky nature of the ridge is such that for the most part the track must be followed in single file. Little more than a mile an hour could be accomplished under such conditions. But night at this latitude usually affords at least nine hours of darkness, and time might be gained at

[1] Cf. Pl. XXXIII. [2] The Wady el Makûk. [3] See Pl. XXXI.

Pl. XXXI.

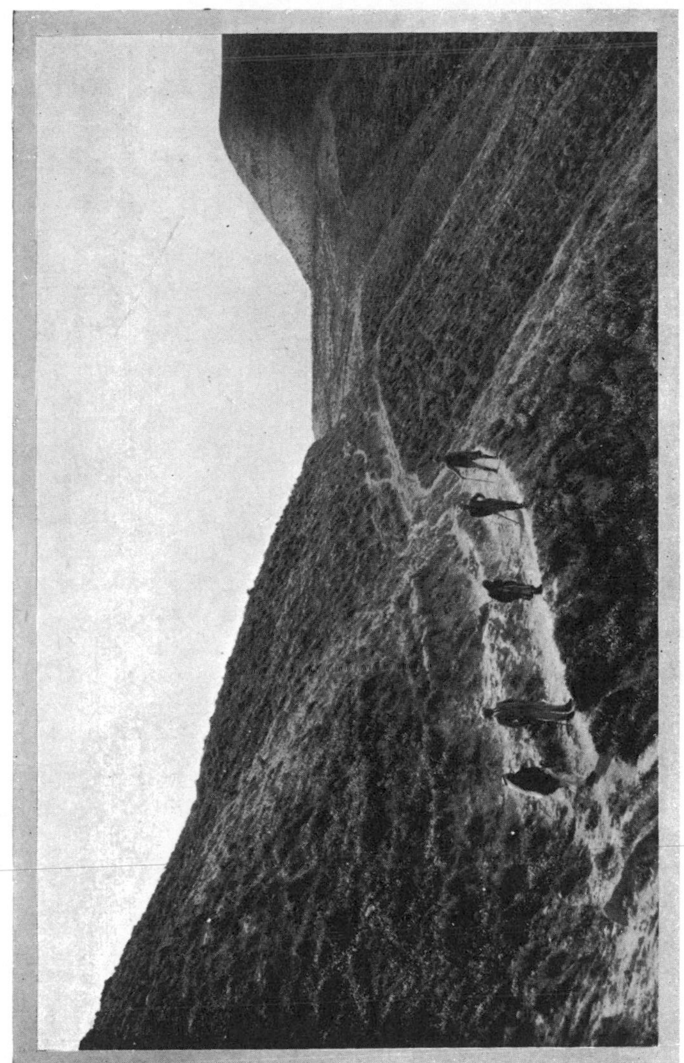

THE RIDGE TRACK BETWEEN JERICHO AND AI.

See p. 156.

the start by climbing the first thousand feet at twilight. This could be done with advantage and with safety; for the steepest part of the ascent by either way was invisible from the high ground beyond. The most difficult feature of the journey would be the crossing at about the seventh mile of the Wady Sikya; but even this does not involve rough climbing, and the track through the boulders is well defined. Once clear of this the site of Mukhmas is completely avoided by bending to the right around Tell el Suwan, leaving Ras el Tawil on the left. The critical moment would be the last mile of approach to the appropriate position on the west of Ai, but instead of crossing, as now, the broken ground immediately below the city, it would be possible to keep under the cover of a small valley to the south of Dêr Diwan and so gain the hidden road that leads towards Bethel. It must, moreover, have been past midnight, and evidently no warning reached the sleeping city.

JOSHUA viii

9 And Joshua sent them forth: and they went to the ambushment, and abode between Beth-el and Ai, on the west side of Ai: but Joshua lodged that night among the people.[a]
10 And Joshua rose up early in the morning, and mustered
the people, and went up, he and the elders of Israel, before
11 the people to Ai. And all the people, even the men of
war that were with him, went up, and drew nigh, and came before the city, and pitched on the north side of Ai: now there was a valley between him and Ai. [J]

The ridge track, so helpful to the setting of the ambush, approached the west of Ai from the south. Clearly Joshua's further plan would be to gain the north side of the city from a different direction, and there to take up such a position that the first light of morning would disclose the hosts of Israel to the inhabitants. Secrecy was not so essential as their arrival at the appointed hour.

[a] *Or,* In the midst of the Vale.

For this purpose the main north-western route was entirely favourable. From the mound of Ai and from the higher place of ambush, it could be traced from afar, while the opposite slopes of the valley which it followed formed the immediate foreground of the northern landscape: this was just the position that Joshua sought. This northern route had also the further advantage of a broader track and easier grades, more suitable for the movement of the larger body that Joshua accompanied. The distance was not much greater, being about fifteen miles from Gilgal. Seven or eight hours would be necessary, but advantage might be taken of the abundant water supply at Ain el Duk to advance in the evening as far at any rate as the valley there, so reducing the final stage of the journey by about three hours. Some such movement is indeed suggested in one version of the narrative,[1] and tactically might have been used to cover the detachment of the ambush party.

The stratagem was successful. The first morning light striking the opposite slopes would disclose Joshua's forces at once to the villagers of Ai, whose chief hastened down with his fighting men to gain a position towards the Jordan-valley, seeking thus to get between the Israelites and the road by which they had ascended. Before this first manœuvre of the men of Ai, the Israelites fled by the way of the wilderness towards the north and the east; and by so doing they retained the advantage which the higher ground would afford for launching their counter-attack as soon as the ambush had set fire to the city, in accordance with Joshua's instructions.

JOSHUA viii

21 And when Joshua and all Israel saw that the ambush had taken the city, and that the smoke of the city ascended,
22 then they turned again, and slew the men of Ai. And the

[1] Cf. viii 13 [JE]: 'In the midst of the Vale.' The purposeless phrase 'among the people,' in v 9 [J], may be amended by the addition of one letter to the Hebrew, to agree with this version. Cf. Cooke, *Joshua*, p. 65.

THE PLACE OF AMBUSH TO THE WEST OF AI. Joshua viii, 9, 12.
(The Scale is given by the standing figure with parasol among the rocks on the R.)

WEST SIDE OF EL TELL, THE SITE OF AI, TO-DAY.
'Joshua burnt Ai, and made it a mound forever, even a desolation unto this day.' Joshua viii, 28.
See p. 154.

**other came forth out of the city against them; so they
were in the midst of Israel, some on this side, and some on
that side: and they smote them so that they let none of
29 them remain or escape. And the King of Ai he hanged on
a tree until the eventide; and at the going down of the
sun Joshua commanded, and they took his carcase down
from the tree, and cast it at the entering of the gate of the
city, and raised thereon a great heap of stones, unto this
day. [J]**

So Joshua burned Ai, and made it an heap for ever even a desolation unto this day.[1] viii 28. [D]

THE SITUATION AFTER THE FALL OF AI

The destruction of Ai removed one of the two barriers between the Israelites and the plateau. Bethel alone now stood in the way. It might be thought that as the Bethelites had been drawn into the battle in support of Ai, Joshua would naturally have followed up his victory by assailing their city. This sequel, however, is not suggested in the Bible. On the contrary, in the first chapter of the Book of Judges, which contains several passages derived apparently from the same sources as the Book of Joshua,[2] we are told that Bethel fell to the House of Joseph as a result of treachery on the part of one of its inhabitants.[a] This event is related in the narrative after the capture of Hebron by Caleb, and would seem therefore not to have followed immediately the destruction of Ai, but to have been deferred for some reason until the first stage of the invasion had been accomplished. Archaeologically the evidence of a short excavation,[3] though corroborative as to the main fact that Bethel suffered destruction about 1400 B.C., cannot discriminate between two possibilities so near to one another in point

[a] Judges i 22-26 [J].

[1] Cf. Pl. XXXII. [2] See the Introductory Section, pp. 7, 26.

[3] Albright, *Zeits. Alttest. Wiss.* vi, 1929; i, p. 11. See also p. 54.

of time. It is significant, however, that Joshua does not appear to have attempted to establish himself as in conquered territory, but returned with his forces to his base at Gilgal near Jericho, as if to await a further opening.

The situation was manifestly difficult. A row of fortresses lining the eastern ridge commanded all the direct avenues of approach from Jericho. The northernmost of these was Bethel itself.[1] Three miles towards the south, upon Tell Nasbeh,[2] stood one of the strongest cities of the day, probably Beeroth, whence four and a half miles to the south, upon Tell el Ful,[3] rose the castle-like fortress known later as Gibeah.[a] Lastly, at a distance of three and a half miles farther south the series ended in Jerusalem.[4] Three of these were walled cities strongly placed, and all four were protected by stone ramparts, the great strength of which has been disclosed by excavation during recent years. The position of each had a strategic purpose, so that from a military standpoint the destruction of Ai still left before Joshua and the Israelites a formidable situation which would be fraught with danger if these cities should enter into combination. The area of that on Tell Nasbeh was about eight acres, while that of Jerusalem seems to have been about eleven acres, so that the total population of these two cities alone may have amounted to five thousand people. And though the size of the others is uncertain they may have claimed fully half that number, raising the combined fighting strength to nearly two thousand men, without counting any possible allied or dependent cities. The danger to the Israelites of such a combination is manifest.

The racial and political differences of these isolated units constituted, on the other hand, a factor in Joshua's favour. Bethel, deprived now of Ai, stood isolated, and was peopled, it would seem, by Amorites. The city on

[a] Judges xx 21 f [J].

[1] Pl. L. See the Map, p. 164. [2] Pl. XXXV and p. 164.

[3] Pl. XXXIII. Cf. Albright, *Ann. Am. S.O.R.*, IV. 1924. Pp. 28 f.

[4] Pl. XXXVIII and p. 169.

TELL EL FUL, A FORTIFIED POSITION TO THE N. OF JERUSALEM.

Excavations have traced the foundations of a stronghold attributable to the early Iron Age: site of Gibeah of Benjamin and Saul. Cf. Judges xx, 30.

THE WADY MEDINEH NEAR BURKAH.

View of the broken country to the S.W. of Ai, between Mukhmas and Tell el Nasbeh.

See pp. 156, 160

Tell el Nasbeh, whether Beeroth or Gibeon, belonged to the Hivite group; while Gibeah was to be counted probably with Jerusalem and the Jebusites. As between these three racial groups there was at this time of Egyptian apathy no co-ordinating power, albeit in general the news of Joshua's merciless victories, spreading throughout the length and breadth of the land, resulted as was to be anticipated in the tightening of any latent bonds of alliance between kindred cities. The terror inspired by Joshua's deeds in Jehovah's name brought indeed another factor into the situation, and it resulted almost at once in the group lying nearest to the pathway of conquest, the Hivites of Gibeon, making overtures for an alliance which was to determine the further development of the attack.

SECTION 7

THE RELIEF OF GIBEON

Joshua IX-X

Joshua ix.

3 **But when the inhabitants of Gibeon heard what Joshua**
6 **had done unto Jericho and to Ai, they . . . went to Joshua**
unto the camp at Gilgal, and said unto him, and to the men
of Israel, We are come from a far country; now therefore
14 **make ye a covenant with us. . . . And the men took of**
their provision, and asked not counsel at the mouth of the
Lord. And Joshua made peace with them, and made a
covenant with them, to let them live. [J]

THE HIVITE ALLIANCE

Although the identification of Gibeon is not without an element of difficulty, consensus of opinion has long associated it with the modern village of El Jib,[1] which is found some six miles to the north-northwest of Jerusalem, in a small plain, wherein it occupies an imposing position upon an isolated knoll.[2] Southwards its domain would be bounded by the ridge now crowned by the shrine called Nebi Samwîl. To the west its level lands reach out a mile or more and then break away into a stony valley, the Wady Selman, which leads down below Beth-horon into the Valley of Aijalon, near Yalo.[3] Towards its north and east appear a few low hills, through which there is easy communication.[4] It thus lay westward from the central spine of the country, along which were stationed, as we have seen, its nearest neighbours, the one on Tell Nasbeh four miles to the N.E. and the other

[1] In Arabic El Gib, the 'g' being soft. On the other hand the Biblical 'j,' as in Aijalon or Jearim, represents a *y* sound, thus Aiyalon, Yearim, etc.

[2] Pl. XXXIV. See also Pl. XLI.

[3] Pl. LII. See also below, p. 168.

[4] Pl. LX.

Pl. XXXIV.

EL JIB, THE SITE OF GIBEON, VIEWED FROM THE RIDGE TO THE SOUTH, LOOKING N.E.

'Gibeon was a great city, as one of the royal cities' Joshua x, 2.

See pp. 162, 179.

on Tell el Ful, three miles to the S.E. Through it ran in historic times the main road from Jerusalem to Jaffa, which offered to wayfarers the alternative of descending either by the Wady Selman, or by way of Beth-horon down the ridge that bounds this valley on the north.[1] The latter was probably the chariot way of the Roman period, for the former is rough and in places rather narrow. None the less, towards the foot of the hills, where the valley widens, its grade becomes gentle; and bending south-west below Yalo it gives ready access through the Shephelah to the coastal plain. For this reason the valley was probably early adopted as a line of route, and a passage in the Amarna Letters suggests that convoys from Jerusalem to Egypt might be sent that way.[2]

The fact that El Jib stands upon this Roman road helps to determine the site of Gibeon, which was stated by Josephus [3] to have lain on the route of Cestus from Lydda by way of Beth-horon to Jerusalem. The *Onomasticon* in this case fails to help, placing Gibeon four miles to the west of Bethel, a position which does not correspond with any known site of antiquity, and lies far from the road. On the other hand, the site of El Jib, particularly the south-eastern extremity of the knoll wherein lies the spring, in addition to its impressive appearance, possesses advantages both defensive and strategic. Though now unoccupied and completely denuded, its terraced scarps are well adapted for defensive walls, and the site has furnished investigators with proof of its antiquity and occupation in the Bronze Age.[4] At the foot of the hill there is record, moreover, of a large pool or reservoir,[5] such as evidently formed in later times a special feature of Gibeon.[a] Its situation at the meeting of the local roads, and the relative richness of its fields, made it the

[a] II Samuel ii 13, Jeremiah xli 12, etc.

[1] Cf. Pl. LI.

[2] Kn. 287. Above, p. 77.

[3] *Wars*, ii, 18, 1.

[4] See also 'Gibeon' in the Appendix.

[5] *P.E.F. Survey*, Vol. III, p. 99.

natural centre of the Hivite group associated with it in tradition, including the three cities of Beeroth, Chephirah, and Kiriath-Jearim. The passage referring to these places [a] shows traces of late editing,[1] but the topography of the sites is found on examination rather to favour the probability of such a combination.

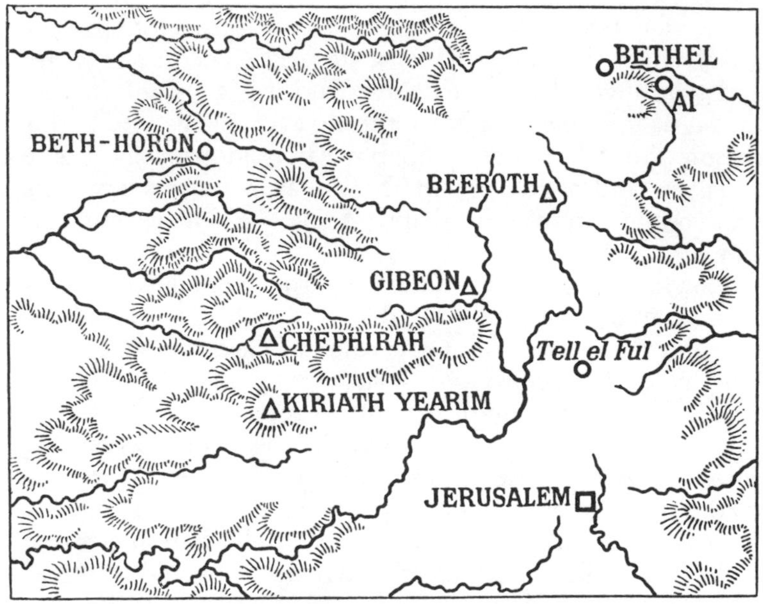

Map 11. Gibeon and the Hivite cities.

Beeroth, in accordance with accepted theory, occupied the great mound of Tell el Nasbeh, three miles to the north-east of Gibeon, and between the two there is ready communication by several minor valleys.[2] The identity of Beeroth, like that of Gibeon, rests entirely upon circumstantial evidence. In the first place, just to the north a trace of the old name seems to have survived in the modern name of Bireh, which indicates a well. At Bireh itself, however, there is no sign of a Canaanitish

[a] Joshua ix 17 [J].

[1] Cooke, *Joshua*, p. 79 *n*.

[2] Cf. Pl. LX.

POSITION OF TELL EL NASBEH, VIEWED FROM THE N.W.
The site commanded the high road from Jerusalem northwards.

TELL EL NASBEH, PROBABLE SITE OF BEEROTH, FROM THE E.
Excavations have disclosed exceptionally strong fortifications of the Middle Bronze Age. C. 1800 B.C.
See pp. 160, 164.

city, whereas at Tell el Nasbeh excavation has disclosed a fortress stronger and bolder than any other so far uncovered in the country.[1] Its massive walls were seventeen feet in thickness and are still preserved to a height of twenty-eight feet. Clearly it marks the site of one of the greatest strongholds of earlier Canaanitish times. For this very reason, alternatively, Tell el Nasbeh may be thought to represent more fittingly the ancient city of Gibeon itself,[2] which was apparently an imposing fortress 'as one of the royal cities greater than Ai.'[a] In support of this view it may be urged that the name 'Jib' does not adequately reproduce the spelling of Gibeon; and that the word Beeroth or Bireh might be applied to any site suitably supplied with water, so that it is not distinctive enough as a name to ensure identity. But excavation tends to show that, as in the case of Jericho and other Canaanite centres, the great day of the city on Tell Nasbeh was already past in the Late Bronze Age, the era of this narrative. Moreover, the later history of Beeroth favours rather the site of Nasbeh, just as we found El Jib to satisfy the requirements of the site of Gibeon. We therefore retain provisionally the old identification of these places.

Happily the question as to the particular identity of Gibeon and Beeroth, though difficult, is not vital to a correct understanding of the narrative. The two cities were evidently close together, being commonly associated with one another in Bible contexts.[b] Both occupied imposing positions of considerable strategic importance, and both might be approached from Jericho by the Wady Abu Retnah as far as the site of Mukhmas, whence a track leads westward past El Ram,[3] the site of Ramah;

[a] Joshua x 2 [J]. [b] Joshua ix 17 [J], xviii 25 [P].

[1] Badé, *P.E.F., Q.S.*, 1930, pp. 8 f.; also his *Excvns. at T. el Nasbeh*, 1926-7 (Pal. Inst., Berkeley, Calif.), pp. 15 ff.

[2] Cf., *inter alia*, Albright, *Ann. A.S.O.R.* (1922-3), pp. 90 f.; also *J.P.O.S.*, No. III, 1923, p. 111. Alt, *Palast. Jahrb.* 1926, pp. 11 f.; 1927, p. 22 Jirku, 'Wo Lag Gibeon?' in *J.P.O.S.*, No. VIII, 1928, pp. 187 f.

[3] See the Map, p. 171.

and as these places had not come into being in the age of Joshua, the way was open, the distance from the mouth of the wady being about fifteen miles.

Chephirah is to be identified with the impressive remains of an ancient city five miles to the west of Gibeon, now long uninhabited but still bearing its ancient name in the Arabic form, Kh. el Kefireh.[1] It crowned a spur of the plateau which juts out towards the coastal plain between two steep watercourses of the Wady Kotneh; and the village of Kutanneh nestles at the foot of the southern valley immediately below the ancient site.[2] In this bold position it commanded the approaches towards Gibeon from the west, which under the changed conditions are preserved only as bridle paths and to-day little used, but anciently claimed evident importance in the local organisation. The city stood like others of the Bronze Age on the summit of an ascending series of terraces, each readily defended[3]: without excavation it is hardly possible to say which line was followed by the fortifications of the period, but the city may be estimated to have comprised an area, more or less oval in form but of irregular surface, some four or perhaps five acres in extent, indicating a population of possibly 1250 people.

Kiriath Jearim occupied a similar position some two miles towards the south, upon the summit of a hill now called Dêr el Azar, above the village of Kiryat el Enab.[4] It thus lay nearly six miles, as the crow flies, in a south-westerly direction from El Jib. The position in this case also had its strategic value, commanding the route which is followed in modern times by the main road from Jerusalem to Jaffa. This site is not so bold as that of Chephirah, which in other respects it resembles, rising in a series of natural terraces, crowned by the remains of the ancient city.[5] Without excavation the ramparts are

[1] Pl. XXXVI. [2] Pl. LXXI. [3] Cf. Pl. LI.

[4] Pl. XXXVII.

[5] Soundings show that the debris of occupation has a depth of more than five metres.

Pl. XXXVI.

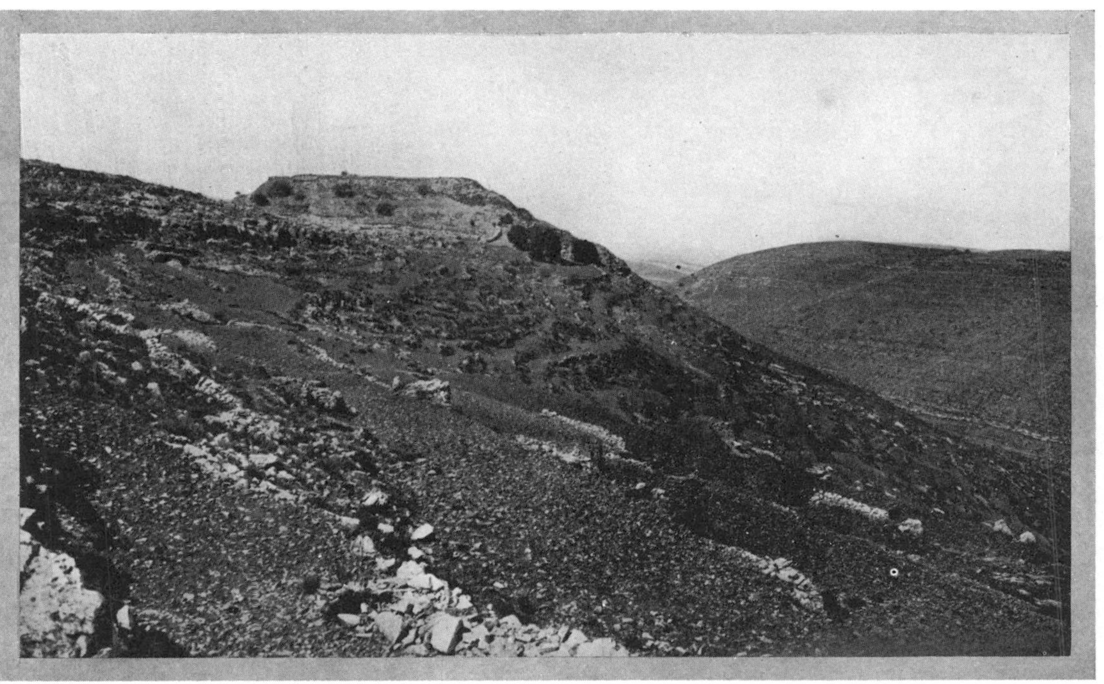

KH. KEFIREH, THE BOLD SITE OF CHEPHIRAH, FROM THE EAST.

The position overlooks the maritime plain from the western edge of the plateau.

See p. 166.

no longer traceable, though the configuration of the ground and the presence of potsherds of this period in the soil indicate their probable line. Consequently it is only possible to form an approximate idea of the city's size, but it seems to have been somewhat larger than Chephirah, covering an area of five to six acres with a population of perhaps 1500 people.

This group of cities, of which Gibeon occupied the central position, was linked up, then, by strategic bonds. It covered a defined territorial area, separated in marked fashion from the district of the Jebusites around Jerusalem by the upper valley of the Wady Surar.[1] Beeroth guarded its approaches from the north and to a certain measure from the east; while its western border was held in similar fashion by the dominating positions of Kiriath Jearim and Chephirah There is no reason, then, to doubt the original authenticity of the passage which associates these cities with Gibeon in a separate local alliance.

Assigning tentatively to these cities their maximum apparent size and adopting 250 per acre as the coefficient of population, we gain a rough idea of the possible strength of the 'Hivite' combination.

	Acres	Population	Warriors
Gibeon, at El Jib - - -	10	2500	625
Beeroth, on Tell el Nasbeh -	8	2000	500
Chephirah, Kh. Kefireh -	5	1250	300
Kiriath Jearim, Dêr el Azar -	6	1500	400

This estimate indicates a total maximum population for the four cities of 7250 people, representing a possible fighting strength of about 1800 men. It is, however, probable that the cities and the coefficient of population were both smaller in reality than this calculation has assumed,[2] and three-fourths of these figures may be nearer the truth.

[1] See the Map, p. 171.

[2] Statistics supplied by the Liverpool School of Geography show that 193 per acre is the highest comparable coefficient in modern times. The present population of Sileh (Pl. LXVII) is 1635, while El Aåje, a typical village on a hill, claims only 550 people.

Notwithstanding the subtle means by which the Hivites secured their alliance with the Israelites, their adhesion at this juncture was both timely and helpful. Not only did it increase the effective force at Joshua's disposal to an appreciable extent, but it placed in his hand a key to the central plateau which in the sequel made it unnecessary for the time being to resume his effort to force an entry by way of Bethel.

One other site mentioned in the narrative which follows, namely Beth-horon, is physically so linked with this area, that a measure of economic and political relations would seem to have been inevitable, though the implied difference of race would hold it ultimately apart. From the archaeological indications the upper city of that name had not, as yet, come into being, but Beth-horon the Lower occupied a Bronze Age site, and was placed, like other cities of the period, on a low isolated hill encircled by rock ledges which facilitated its defence.[1] This city was relatively extensive, covering as much possibly as eight or ten acres of ground, so that its population may have attained the number of two thousand or two thousand five hundred people. It lay athwart the main road from Gibeon north-westward, and overlooked to the south the Wady Selman, down which, as we have seen, ran an alternative track in the same general direction. In this position Beth-horon commanded a wide view of the coastal plain below, with which it communicated by the two roads mentioned and also by a third which descends due west to the foot of the hills, where, turning south, it enters the valley of Aijalon. Beth-horon thus occupied a central position on these lines of communication between the plateau and the plains, equally in touch with Gezer as with Gibeon.[2] It appears to have remained aloof and neutral in the struggle between the Israelite-Hivite combination and the Jebusites, which is next described in the narrative, notwithstanding that the battle seems to have rolled past its very gates.

[1] Pl. LI. [2] See the Map, p. 171.

THE MOUND OF DEIR EL AZAR, THE SITE OF KIRIATH JEARIM, FROM THE N.

The position dominates the high road from Jerusalem towards Jaffa.

THE SITE OF KIRIATH JEARIM, NEAR THE VILLAGE OF KIRYAT EL ENAB, FROM THE E.

Located by Eusebius nine miles N.W. of Jerusalem.

See p. 166.

DEFEAT OF A SOUTHERN LEAGUE

Joshua x.

1 **Now it came to pass, when Adoni-zedek King of Jerusalem heard how Joshua had taken Ai, and had utterly destroyed it . . . Adoni-zedek King of Jerusalem sent unto Hoham King of Hebron, and unto Piram King of Jarmuth, and unto Japhia King of Lachish and unto Debir King of Eglon, saying, Come up unto me, and help me, and let us smite Gibeon ; for it hath made peace with Joshua, and with the children of Israel.** [J]

The organisation of a League to resist the further Hebrew invasion was to be anticipated, and this group included several powerful cities. Jerusalem itself, which it is necessary to dissociate from the later city and its suburbs, stood almost at the head of the Wady el Nar, more familiarly known as Brook Kidron[a], a valley which falls steeply towards the Jordan rift. Placed like Ai on the eastern edge of the plateau, just below the highest part, it guarded the junction of the main roads north and south with those which lead from the coast by Jericho to the east of Jordan. The form of the city must have been curiously long and narrow,[1] for it occupied a sharp ridge between the Kidron itself on the east and its small tributary, the Tyropoeon valley, in the west. The latter is now hardly traceable, being filled with debris, but formerly it joined the Kidron near the position of the later pools of Siloam. This point marked the south end of the city, which extended northwards along the ridge almost up the wall bounding the platform whereon now rises the Dome of the Rock, once the Temple area. All these names and features, however, were non-existent at that time. The city stood isolated, protected like the older Jericho by a stout stone wall with sloping foundations which research has traced for considerable distances on each side of the

[a] II Samuel xv 23.

[1] See Pl. XXXVIII and the Plan in the Appendix, No. 9, p. 389.

hill.[1] The enclosed area, though not completely defined, may be estimated in broad terms at about ten or twelve acres, and the population accordingly at some 2500 to 3000 souls. Though so little of the ancient defences can be seen, the city long proved impregnable;[a] and doubtless its strength, coupled with its central situation, had led to it becoming an accepted centre of political influence and authority under Egyptian rule.[2]

Hebron, the second city of the group, occupied a similar position on the central spine of the country, about nineteen miles south and somewhat west from Jerusalem. It there dominated the junction of the main route north and south along the ridge with those which led by way of the western valleys towards the coastal plain. Judging by tradition which assigned to the building of Hebron a date several years before that of Zoan,[b] it was probably fortified like Jericho and other cities of Palestine at the beginning of the Middle Bronze Age, about 2000 B.C., and like them it would appear to have flourished chiefly during the centuries that followed. It is associated in Hebrew legend with Abraham[c] and is still called El Khalil, the Friend (of God) in remembrance of the fact. The situation of the present town is not, however, characteristic of that age, for it sits in a hollow, though occupying generally one of the highest parts of the central plateau. Doubtless the city of Kiriath-Arba would crown the ridge which overlooks the present site from the south-east, called Deir el Arbain, whereon substantial fortifications of megalithic appearance may be observed; but local circumstances have restricted methodical research. Now and again travellers have profited by exceptional circumstances to glean some little information

[a] II Samuel v 6. [b] Tanis in Egypt. Numbers xiii 22 [JE].

[c] Genesis xiii 18 [J].

[1] For the results of Excavations see *P.E.F. Annual*, IV-V (1923-7) and the *Q.S.*, 1924, sqq.: also Weill, *La Pointe Sud de la Cité de David et les Fouilles de 1923-4*: *Rev. des Études Juives* (1926), pp. 103 f.

[2] See further below, p. 218.

OPHEL, THE SITE OF JEBUSITE JERUSALEM.

Between the pools of Siloam and the old Temple area.

BRONZE-AGE RAMPART OF JEBUSITE JERUSALEM.

Overlooking the Kidron Valley.

See p. 169, 218.

about the caves, the reputed burial places of the patriarchs, which certainly exist,[1] and are now covered by the chief Moslem sanctuary of the area.

Jarmuth, the third city of the group, appears to be correctly identified with the ruins named Kh. el Yarmuk,

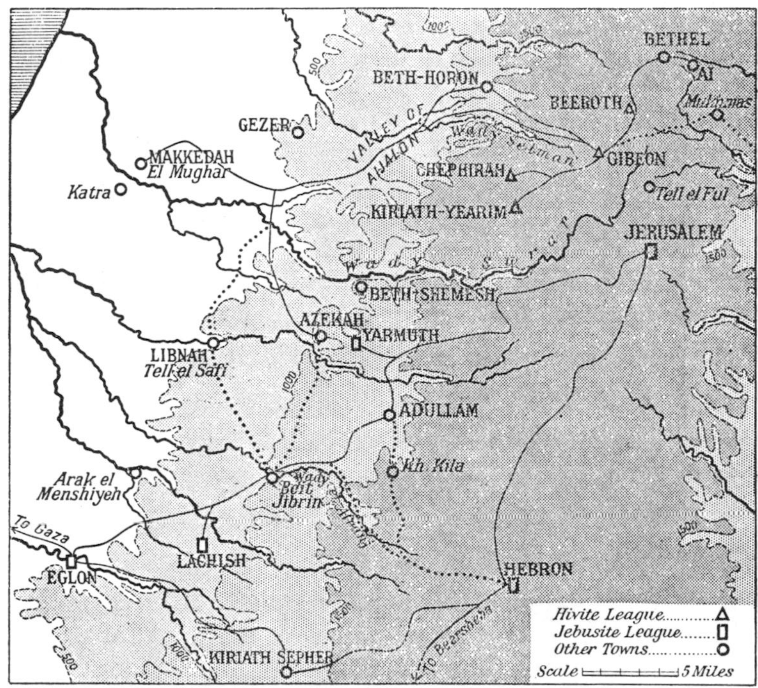

Map 12. Defeat of the Jebusite allies at Gibeon and Joshua's pursuit.

which crown a hilltop enclosed by two small tributaries of the Wady el Sûrâr and overlooking on the south-west the Wady Sunt, sixteen miles as the crow flies westward and somewhat south from Jerusalem.[2] The position is a bold one, dominating Tell Zakariya (Azekah) and Tell el Safi (Libnah) in the west, with a wide view over

[1] On this question see T. R. P. Vincent, *La Sépulture Des Patriarches*, *R.B.*, 1920, pp. 525 ff.

[2] Map, No. 12.

the coastal plains as far as the sea by Gaza, and in the other direction commanding at the same time an extensive panorama of mountain and valley among the southern highlands. It rose like a watch-tower and outpost on the edge of the plateau.[1] At the western foot of the hill a subterranean water supply seems to supplement a plentiful spring below, giving life to the valley and enriching it with a growth of trees. On the face of the ascent it is possible to trace an ancient ramp winding upwards, suggesting a chariot way, like that which may be seen on the slopes of Taanak.[2] Towards the top, the hill rises in terraces which are well defined and were evidently protected by masonry now hidden from view. The area of the open summit is not more than three or four acres, but it is probable from the disposition of numerous potsherds that the second terrace at least would be enclosed by the Bronze Age city, giving an area possibly of six to eight acres. Thus Jarmuth, though now completely deserted, was evidently a strong city at the time, with a population possibly of 1500-2000 people. The site lies two miles off the line of the Roman road from Jerusalem to Gaza by way of Beit Jibrin, and it is still connected with this road by a track which from the vicinity of Beit Nettîf follows up the ridge between the two enclosing valleys. Supposing that the ancient route of communication between Jerusalem and Jarmuth followed generally the line later taken by the Roman road, the distance between them would be about eighteen miles. Other roads pass along the two valleys at its foot forming part of the main arterial system of the country's communications: the one linked the cities of the hills with those of the plain by way of Tell Zakariya and Tell el Safi; the other, skirting the foot of the hills from north to south, collected numerous side-tracks on its way.

Lachish, the fourth city of this group, is to be identified in all probability with an ancient mound of exceptional

[1] Pl. XXXIX. [2] Pl. LXVI.

THE HILL OF KH. EL YARMUK, PROBABLE SITE OF JARMUTH.

Located by Eusebius ten miles from Eleutheropolis, Beit Jibrin, on the road to Jerusalem.

TELL EL DUWEIR, THE PROBABLE SITE OF LACHISH.

Located by Eusebius as six miles from Eleutheropolis on the road to Daroma.

See pp. 171, 173.

size and appearance, called Tell el Duweir,[1] which rises almost in the bed of a broad valley four and a half miles south-west from Beit Jibrin. It is true that Lachish is more familiarly associated in the minds of English readers with the small mound called Tell el Hesy,[2] which lies about eleven miles west and south from Beit Jibrin; but this identification seems to be ill-founded. Tell el Hesy is a site of small importance, incompatible with the position accorded to Lachish in contemporary history; and the fact that a letter from the King of Lachish has been found at Tell el Hesy seems opposed to the identity of these two places. The position, moreover, is at variance with the statement of the *Onomasticon*,[3] that *Lakeis*, the Roman city which had replaced that of earlier history, lay at the seventh milestone, that is six full miles from *Eleutheropolis* in the direction of *Daroma*. The former is found at Beit Jibrin, the present road centre of the vicinity; the latter near the coast, well to the south of Gaza.[4] It is true that a main road leads by Tell el Hesy towards Gaza, but if this had been meant it would surely have been so stated; whereas Tell el Duweir lies on the line of route towards Tell Sharieh and thence across to the Negeb westward to *Daroma*. Following the Roman road, which at first led southward from *Eleutheropolis* for some two miles and thence westward, the prescribed distance of six miles brings one exactly to the Roman and Byzantine ruins lying to the south-east of Tell el Duweir, which indicate the city of Lachish at the time when the notes for the *Onomasticon* were compiled, a correspondence which seems conclusive.

Tell el Duweir is one of the great mounds of Palestine, as befits the reputation of the city of Lachish. As it stands in a hollow little more than its pronounced acropolis

[1] Pl. XXXIX. This identification was suggested by Dr. Albright: see his notes in *Zeits. f. d. Alttest. Wiss.* (Giessen, 1929), vi 1, p. 3.

[2] Petrie, *Tell el Hesy*. Report of Excavations, 1891. Bliss, *A Mound of Many Cities*, 1893. See further under 'Eglon' in the Appendix.

[3] Ed. Klostermann, 1904, pp. 120-121.

[4] See the Map, p. 67.

is visible above the level of the plateau. But its steep sides are not less than sixty feet in height and traces of ancient walls may be seen along their broken face. The extent of the enclosed Bronze Age city cannot, of course, be determined with any exactitude without considerable excavation: though its general appearance is that of a round or oval Tell, its surface tends to be somewhat square in outline, with an area of about ten or twelve acres, and a possible population accordingly of 2500 to 3000 people.

Eglon, the fifth and last city mentioned is not included in the group as described by the Septuagint, in which it is replaced by Adullam.[1] Its position is uncertain. The *Onomasticon* would locate it one mile to the east of *Eleutheropolis*, but the indication would appear to be faulty, as it does not lead to any ancient site. The Egyptian record of cities conquered by Thutmose III also possibly mentions the place by name,[2] but gives no topographical information. Conceivably it is to be identified with Tell el Hesy, formerly supposed to be Lachish, a theory to some extent warranted by its position near and proved relations with Lachish, corresponding to the association of the two places in the Bible text, and by the presence in the vicinity of ruins called Kh. Ajlan, in which the ancient name is perfectly preserved. Excavations have shown that the history of Tell el Hesy as a fortified city dates from the Middle Bronze Age and that it remained in occupation till the early fourteenth century.[3] It thus conforms in all respects with what is known of Eglon, though the evidence is not sufficient to constitute a proof of its identity.

Though the position of Eglon remains open to some doubt, the other four constituent members of the group are known, and they all ranked among the great cities of

[1] Pl. XL. [2] No. 89, *Hykrym*.

[3] The third town, which was totally destroyed, is well dated by the inscribed Tablet from Zimrida, probably the King of Lachish who is known from the Amarna letters. Cf. Kn. 288.

KH. 'ID-EL-MA, PROBABLE SITE OF ADULLAM.

In the LXX Adullam replaces Eglon as fifth member of the combine raised by the King of Jerusalem against Gibeon.

EL MUGHAR, POSSIBLE SITE OF MAKKEDAH.

Now occupied by a village: the hillside contains great caves.

See pp. 174, 181.

the south. Apart, however, from their individual strength, there are features in the purpose and composition of the league summoned by the King of Jerusalem which attract attention. In the first place, its objective appears to have been punitive and directed against Gibeon, rather than defensive and directed against the Israelites. In the second place, the territory covered by the members of this league is relatively large and, as may be seen by a glance at the map,[1] conforms with no particular physical features of the country. It is true that the Wady Surar, one of the boldest landmarks of the southern highlands, separates the area of the Hivites from that covered by this new alliance. But the territory delimited by the triangle of which Jerusalem, Hebron and Lachish form the angles, lies partly in the hill country and partly in the Shephelah, while if extended beyond Lachish to include Tell el Hesy, it would enter the coastal plains. The routes connecting these five places lie across mountain, valley and plain, except that between Jerusalem and Hebron, which follows thus far the main watershed of the country. The leaguing of these cities is not wholly explained by their physical associations.

We must look, then, for some other explanation to account for the composition of this group. It is to be seen at a glance that the line Jerusalem, Jarmuth, Lachish, Eglon, indicates in fact a main route, almost the most direct, from Jerusalem to Gaza and Egypt, while that from Jerusalem by Hebron, thence west by Kiriath Sepher, leads in the same direction. Now Gaza had long been recognised as the headquarters of the Egyptian administration in the country,[2] and was by its very position the natural centre of Egyptian political authority. It is, therefore, significant that the cities responding to the call of the King of Jerusalem lined the principal routes that lead to Gaza. In this connexion it is of interest to observe that if the LXX version of this alliance, replacing Eglon by Adullam, be adopted, the same observation

[1] P. 171. [2] Cf. Breasted, *Anct. Rec.* ii 417.

applies, for the site of the latter at 'Id-el-Ma in the Wady Sunt lies on the most direct route from Jerusalem to Lachish. Investigation shows, indeed, that Adullam was a fortress of the period,[1] strongly placed on a rounded hilltop with a very copious supply of water at the foot. That it should figure in the narrative of this struggle is appropriate, and it evidently played a more important local rôle than the small city at Tell el Hesy.

The events already described, the destruction of Jericho and the sack of Ai, seem to have followed very rapidly on one another, possibly indeed during the spring of the same year. The summoning of the Amorite allies by the King of Jerusalem appears to have been designed to counter the Hivite alliance with the Israelites, and this in its turn formed a sequel to the fall of Ai. It would seem, then, that no long interval of time can have elapsed between the events already related and the summoning of the Amorite league to the punishment of Gibeon. This episode must then be assigned, on the basis of Biblical chronology already considered, to the last years of the fifteenth century, somewhere between 1410 and 1400 B.C. Now the political organisation of the country under Egypt at this time stands revealed by the official letters found at Tell el Amarna, to which place the capital of the Pharaoh Akhenaton was removed about the year 1375 B.C. Though pertaining, then, to the next generation and relating to the troublous state of affairs in Palestine from 1380 to 1360 B.C., these documents clearly reflect a system of administration that had long been in vogue. By that time one Abd-Khipa had been appointed by the Pharaoh to represent Egyptian interests in Jerusalem. He was not the hereditary ruler,[2] indeed the composition of his name suggests that he may have been a member of the Hittite community.[3]

[1] G. 1928. See Pl. XL and p. 87.

[2] Kn. 286.

[3] Compare Gilu-Khipa and Tadu-Khipa, the names of Mitannian princesses married respectively to Amenhotep III and Akhenaton; also Putu-Khipa of Kizzuwadna who shared the throne of Hatti with Hattusil III in the

In any case he proved loyal and zealous, and seems to have been entrusted with a wide political responsibility. He is found indeed at one time joining hands with the distant chiefs of Acco and Achshaph [1] against the forces of disorder, and deemed it his duty to keep the Egyptian Pharaoh informed of local developments hostile to his cause. Thus, in addition to general warnings, 'the lands of the king are going to ruin,' [2] 'the Ḥabiru are devastating all the lands of the king,' [3] 'the Ḥabiru are seizing the cities of the king, . . .' [4] there is mention of particular incidents. Two personages had been slain at the gate of Zilu.[5] A caravan and convoy had been despoiled in the fields of Aijalon [6]; and of special interest are references to Lachish itself and Gezer, including the news that the people of Lachish had themselves become Habiru and slain their king.[7] These developments belong, we believe, to the next generation; but the letters in general show clearly the exceptional position of responsibility and the range of influence of the Chief of Jerusalem in the Egyptian organisation, already long established, and help to explain the initiative taken by Adonizedek on this occasion.

We have already realised that the composition of the league assembled by Adonizedek could hardly be explained merely as the banding together of neighbouring cities for their mutual protection; and it now becomes fairly obvious that this combine represents a political organisation, the rally under a responsible head of cities still faithful to the Pharaoh, in a punitive expedition against the chieftains who had entered into alliance with the Hebrews, one of the disturbing elements of the day.

early thirteenth century B.C. Cf. Ezekiel xvi 3. A Hittite jar-seal has been found in the excavation of the site. *P.E.F. Annual*, IV, Fig. 203 ; cf. G., *H.E.*, p. 333, n. 2. Araunah, II Sam. xxiv 16, is also a Hittite name.

[1] Louvre Mus., Tablet AO 7096.
[2] Kn. 286.
[3] Kn. 286.
[4] Kn. 288.
[5] Kn. 288.
[6] Kn. 287.
[7] Zimrida, Kn. 288.

JOSHUA X

5 Therefore the five kings of the Amorites, the King of
Jerusalem, the King of Hebron, the King of Jarmuth, the
King of Lachish, the King of Eglon, gathered themselves
together and went up, they and all their hosts, and en-
7 camped against Gibeon, and made war against it. So
Joshua went up from Gilgal, he and all the people of war
9 with him, and all the mighty men of valour. Joshua
therefore came upon them suddenly : for he went up
from Gilgal all the night. [J]

Quickness of decision and the rapid movement of troops characterize Joshua's leadership throughout these campaigns, and explain in great measure his success. In this case, the forced march which he accomplished through the night from Gilgal to Gibeon involved a climb of 4000 feet, over a distance, as the crow flies, of eighteen miles.[1] The nearest road lay by the Wady Abu Retnah, but the way was rough. We have already seen that the northern route by way of Ain Duk was more favourable for such a journey; but apparently it was still barred by Bethel, and any attempt to avoid that city would lead into defiles impassable by night, besides involving a long detour. It may be regarded then as probable that the route employed would be that which follows up, as described, the Wady Abu Retnah as far as the site of Mukhmas. From that point a track descends, and, crossing the valley, climbs an easy grade on the western side, finally topping the ridge in the vicinity of El Ram. The modern road goes through that village, but the natural line lies just to the north. It will be recollected that hereabouts the ridge was guarded by two fortresses, at Tell el Ful and Tell el Nasbeh, which are about five miles apart;[2] but the track which emerges to the north of El Ram is invisible from both these sites. It passes, in fact, rather nearer to Tell el Nasbeh than to Tell el Ful, and we have shown reason to

[4] See the Map, p. 155.

[2] See p. 160 and Map No. 11.

THE MOUND OF EL JIB, PROBABLE SITE OF GIBEON, L.; THE RIDGE OF NEBI SAMWÎL, R.

In the foreground extending westward, the plain of El Jib, which leads towards Bethhoron, cf Joshua x. 10. 11.

See pp. 77, 179.

believe that the former, if not the site of Gibeon itself, must have been that of Beeroth and, therefore, in either case a 'Hivite' city. It may be safely concluded, then, that Joshua's march if not indeed directed to Tell el Nasbeh would incline in that direction, avoiding Tell el Ful, which appears rather like an outpost of Jerusalem itself. At this stage of the journey from Mukhmas westward, there would be light from the waning moon, as appears from the further details of the narrative, from which it is to be inferred that the sun and moon were both visible during the morning.[a] Under these conditions Joshua's march would be unimpeded and a further distance of two and a half miles would bring his forces by one of several easy valleys suddenly in sight of Gibeon at El Jib. The surprise of the Amorites was complete:

JOSHUA X

10 **The Lord discomfited them before Israel, and he slew them**
with a great slaughter at Gibeon, and chased them by the
way of the ascent of Bethhoron and smote them to Azekah,
11 **and unto Makkedah. And it came to pass as they fled from**
before Israel, while they were in the going down of Beth-
horon, that the Lord cast down great stones from heaven
upon them, unto Azekah, and they died : they were more
which died with the hailstones than they whom the children
of Israel slew with the sword. [J, E]

These two verses describing the defeat and rout are assigned by critics to separate early sources. The one refers to the 'ascent of Beth-horon' and the other to the 'going down of Beth-horon,' a distinction which may possibly trace its origin to the fact that two different routes led down from the plains of Gibeon towards the coast. Alternatively it may be thought to indicate the upper and lower portions of one of them, and this interpretation would explain how Beth-horon enters into the narrative though not drawn into the conflict. For it was

[a] Joshua x 12 [J].

the valley route, by the Wady Selman, that offered to the routed Amorites their nearest avenue of escape; and this as we have seen passes below Beth-horon, which remains in fact out of sight, being perched on the further slope of the northern ridge. Lower down, at the foot of the hills, this valley opens out, as has been mentioned, into that of Aijalon, a broader stretch with arable plains lying between the Shephelah and the hills. The name Aijalon[1] still clings with little change to the small village of Yalo which seems to occupy the same ancient site, while the prominent mound of Tell el Kokah[2] above carries back the history of this settlement to a much earlier period in the Bronze Age. The town thus stood on the foothills well above the route through the valley, and equally removed as Beth-horon from the track of the pursuit.

Both versions agree about the pursuit to Azekah, the older source [x 10, J] alone introducing Makkedah where the final scene is placed. Azekah is reasonably identified with Tell Zakariya,[3] a bold site filling a strategic position below Jarmuth, where the Wady Sunt opens as it emerges from the hills. This place has been examined. It covers the summit of a low hill, and the ancient fortress occupied a fairly level plateau about 1000 feet in length by 600 in breadth, giving an area of about an acre. Shafts sunk through the debris traced its origins to the Bronze Age, so that the archaeological indications, in addition to the name, are not unfavourable to this identification. It stood, moreover, at a distance of twelve miles, on the direct line of retreat from the

[1] The name is very ancient, appearing as *I'h.n.w.* in an Egyptian record of 2000 B.C. In the T.A. Letters it is spelled *Ia.lu.na.* Kn. 287. Cf. Dussaud, *Syria*, viii, p. 230.

[2] Pl. LII.

[3] Pl. XLII. Cf. I Samuel xvii 1, where the Philistines are said to have gathered together at Socoh, and to have pitched between Socoh and Azekah. Socoh corresponds well with Kh. Suweikeh, an Iron Age site some four miles higher up the valley. The excavation of Tell Zakariya was described by Dr. Macalister for the *P.E.F.* in a report of excavations for the years 1898-1900.

TELL ZAKARIYA, POSSIBLE SITE OF AZEKAH, VIEWED FROM THE N.E.

In the background the Philistine plain : R., Tell El Safi. possibly Libnah

See p. 180.

Valley of Aijalon towards Lachish and Jarmuth, by way of Latroun and Ain Shems.[1]

Makkedah is equated by most students with Moghar, which lies by contrast out on the plain almost westward from the Valley of Aijalon at a distance of fourteen miles. The modern village occupies the south-eastern slope of a low limestone ridge, famous for its caves.[2] It stands apparently on the same site as of old, for in the accumulation of the town debris there may be picked up fragments of Bronze Age pottery.[3]

If, then, these identifications are correct, it is noticeable that neither Beth-Shemesh nor Gezer was drawn into the struggle, nor is either mentioned in the old narrative, although the one at Ain Shems and the other on Tell Jezar commanded the direct routes from the foot of Aijalon to Azekah and to Makkedah. It may be inferred from this that the retreat must have taken a direction between these two places, aiming at some such point in the Wady Surar as Khuldeh, or better 'Ain el Sejid, before parting in its two separate directions. It is indeed faintly suggested, as we have seen, that after the first shock the routed Amorites may have become separated into two groups, some turning southward at the foot of the valley, seeking to regain their homes, while others may have been cut off by their pursuers and driven out on to the plain, being finally run to earth with their leaders at Makkedah. This alternative explanation conforms equally with the local topographical requirements, but like the other it is not capable of confirmation. None the less it may be noted that no irreconcilable element pervades the essential details of this episode, though the two sources of the narrative are apparently based upon separate traditions.

16 And these five kings fled, and hid themselves in the cave
17 at Makkedah, and it was told Joshua. . . . And Joshua

[1] Pl. LXXIII, and see 'Beth-shemesh' in the Appendix.

[2] See Pl. XL. 'Moghar' is the Arabic for 'cave.'

[3] G., 1928, L.I.A.

18 said, . . . Stay not, pursue after your enemies and smite
the hindmost of them. . . . [J]
24 And it came to pass when they brought forth those kings
unto Joshua, that Joshua called for all the men of Israel
and said unto the chiefs of the men of war which went
with him, Come near, put your feet upon the necks of
these kings, and they came near and put their feet upon
26 the necks of them. And afterwards Joshua smote them,
and put them to death. [J]

The victory was complete as it was momentous. The Israelites had traversed the plateau victoriously from the Jordan valley to the plains by the sea. An armed wedge had been thrust between the disunited cities of the south and those of the north. The ' inheritance ' of Judah was carved out, and the Hivite alliance protected its northern frontier. The first stage of the Promise seemed to be fulfilled.

This epoch-making victory in the infancy of the Nation became the favourite theme of folk-song and legend. Numerous glorious exploits clung to it, some of which grew in time till they bordered on the supernatural. Thus later redactors of the text credited Joshua with having followed up his crushing victory by a prolonged expedition against each of the combined Amorite or Canaanite cities in turn, which he successively reduced, slaying the whole population of each. The Judaean narrative, pertaining to the ninth century B.C., incorporated from the earlier songs of triumph collected in the lost book of Jashar an old lay, which is stated to have fallen from the lips of Joshua himself:

JOSHUA X 12, 13

Sun, stand thou still upon Gibeon ;
And thou, Moon, in the Valley of Aijalon.
And the Sun stood still, and the Moon stayed,
Until the Nation had avenged themselves of
their enemies. [J]

SECTION 8

THE FALL OF HAZOR

JOSHUA XI

1 **And it came to pass, when Jabin King of Hazor heard**
thereof, that he sent to Jobab King of Madon, and to the
2 **King of Achshaph. And they went out, they and all their**
hosts with them, much people, even as the sand that is upon
the sea shore in multitude, with horses and chariots very
5 **many. And all these kings met together ; and they came**
and pitched together at the waters of Merom, to fight with
6 **Israel. And the Lord said unto Joshua, Be not afraid**
because of them : for to-morrow at this time will I deliver
them up all slain before Israel : thou shalt hough their
7 **horses, and burn their chariots with fire. So Joshua came,**
and all the people of war with him, against them by the
waters of Merom suddenly, and fell upon them. . . . [J]

THE NORTHERN LEAGUE

HAZOR was the leading city of the Canaanites in the North. Its political influence ranged southward by the side of Jordan to Pahel beyond Bethshean and westward to the coastal plain near Acco, while it is associated in a passage of the Amarna letters with Sidon.[1] Standing in the south-west of the Huleh Basin, at the meeting-point of the main road from Sidon to Beisan with that from Damascus to Megiddo, it occupied the most strategic position in the land, the real key to Palestine. Its situation and character accorded fully with its importance.

[1] In one of the letters (Kn. 148), the King of Tyre reports to the Pharaoh that the Kings of Hazor and Sidon had made common cause with the Ḥabiru (SA-GAZ). In another (Louvre AO 7094, pub'd in 1922 by Thureau-Dangin, *Rev. d'Assyriologie* xix, p. 96), Aiab (of Bi-HI-SI, Kn. 256) complains that the King of Hazor had taken three of his towns. Pi-HI-SI has now been recognised by T. R. P. Dhorme as Pi-hi-lim and identified with Pahel or Pella, at Kh. Fahil, mentioned with Bethshean and other towns on the Beisan Stela (p. 271).

The name Hazor, meaning strictly an enclosure, signifies in this context a fortified camp. The site, *El Kedah*,[1] occupies a level plateau about 1200 yards in length and 600 yards in width, naturally protected on two sides and partly on the third by steep watercourses. This advantageous position was further surrounded by stupendous ramparts of beaten earth [2] on all sides except the south-east, where it was dominated and at the same time closed by a city mound [3] or Tell, rising 165 feet above the road which runs past its foot. It thus comprised at one and the same time a permanent city of large size and an associated camp enclosure. The former with an area of sixteen acres may have contained a population of some 4000 people; and the camp-enclosure was large enough to accommodate in emergency 30,000 men with a corresponding number of horses and chariots. But excavations [4] have shown that, as in the case of Jericho, the great day of Hazor was already past. During the Middle Bronze Age, about 1800 B.C., it had attained already the zenith of its prosperity and extension. Not only had the city been refortified at that time with a stout stone wall, which has been traced all around the Tell, but such had been its activity in those days that houses had arisen in numbers even inside the camp enclosure, disclosing a city of proportions altogether without parallel in southern Syria. The necessity for a vast enclosure of this kind is traceable here as elsewhere to the Hyksos invasions, with which tradition associates great hordes. The armies of the Pharaohs on campaign never involved numbers requiring so large a camp ground.

In the fifteenth century B.C. in which the story of Joshua begins, this exceptionally intensive period had given way to more normal conditions, under which Hazor

[1] Discovered by the writer in 1926 and described in *Liv. A.A.* xiv, pp. 35 ff.

[2] Pl. XLIII, XLIV.

[3] Pl. XVIII.

[4] Extensive soundings were made on the site in 1928: for the plan and further details see below in the Appendix. Cf. Pl. LXXII.

Pl. XLIII.

HAZOR: THE GREAT CAMP-ENCLOSURE VIEWED FROM THE N.W.

The western rampart extends 1000 yards and ends at the acropolis, El Kedah, cf Pl. XVIII.

See pp. 104. 184.

remained still pre-eminent by the very fact of its strength and dominant situation, while the great enclosure was apparently occupied only by temporary structures, for troops or travellers passing through, whether tents of goat-hair or maybe huts built of papyrus reeds after the fashion still much in vogue in the locality. The change does not necessarily indicate a period of decline, but rather an alteration of circumstances, which apparently preceded the conquest and annexation of Hazor by Thutmose III in 1478 B.C., and may be attributed here and elsewhere to the political upheaval consequent upon the defeat of the Hyksos kings by the first Pharaohs of the XVIIIth Dynasty. But though the repercussion of this event was general, and though Gaza had replaced the Hyksos capital as the centre of administration, Hazor at the time of Joshua still retained its leading place among the Canaanitish cities of the north.

The place was well known to the Egyptians,[1] and its king was a vassal of the Pharaoh; indeed his allegiance was vital to the maintenance of the Pharaoh's land communications with his Empire in Syria. The routes that converged upon Hazor were alone suitable for chariots, while its gateways opened directly to the plain; so that in addition to its strategic situation it presented special advantages to a power relying upon its chariotry. The Canaanites themselves, as we have seen, were well furnished with this arm, so that whether as the ally of Egypt or in independent action, the power of the King of Hazor was sustained by an appropriate force. Relying upon the security of his position and the strength of his alliances, he was at times able to assume a somewhat independent outlook towards political developments. Thus early in

[1] In the fifteenth century B.C. Hazor appears as H-ḏ-r (otherwise Ḥ-ṣ-r) in the List of Thutmose III, No. 22 (Sethe, *Urkunden*, 782, 30); in the fourteenth century as Ha-zu-ra or Ha-zu-ri (Amarna Letters, Kn. 148, 227, 228, Louvre AO 7094); and in the thirteenth century as H-ḏ(w)r (otherwise Ḥ-ṣ-ur) in the *Pap. Anast.* I, 21, 7. In the last-mentioned reference the would-be courier is chaffingly asked: 'The Maher—where does he make the journey to Hazor? what is its stream like?' (ed. Gardiner, p. 23*). See further Burchardt, *Fremdworte*, No. 709 and cf. No. 710.

the next century, *c.* 1380 B.C., when the Hittite advance darkened the northern horizon and troubles with the Habiru were attaining the proportions of a general insurrection, the King of Hazor at that day, Abdi-Tirsi, was able to assure the Pharaoh that he would hold the cities of the Pharaoh pending the latter's arrival.[1] None the less he and the King of Sidon were denounced by the Prince of Tyre for making common cause with the Ḥabiru and abandoning their trust.[2] Abdi-Tirsi protested his loyalty, however, and affirmed that he was protecting Hazor with its cities for the King. His protestation concludes with the significant words: [3] '*Let my Lord the King recall all that Hazor and its King have already had to endure*,' an allusion which seems clearly to evoke the recollection of some disaster still vivid in local memory.

Whatever may be the precise significance of this reminiscence, the correspondence in general reflects the special position of Hazor in political and military affairs. It was indeed the natural centre of the northern Canaanites, and the topography of the country indicates the general lines of its connexions. We have already noticed that it marked the junction of the two main north roads from Sidon and Damascus. Towards the south and south-west it was linked at a day's ride by a series of radiating routes with Bethshean, Ibleam, Taanak and Megiddo, that row of fortresses which also at this time owed at least a nominal allegiance to the Pharaoh, while communication was fairly direct with Acco and other places in the coastal plain by the routes that traverse the Galilean highlands. Probably the later editors of the narrative did not greatly err in stating that there rallied to the call of Hazor on this occasion, at any rate the kings of the hill country in the north, and in the Arabah south of Chinnereth and in the lowland, as well as those who dwelt under Hermon in the land of Mizpeh.[a] But we shall find reason to doubt on tactical grounds

[a] Cf. Joshua xi 2, 3 [D].

[1] Kn. 227. [2] Kn. 148. [3] Kn. 227.

HAZOR, THE GIANT EARTH RAMPARTS, WESTERN ANGLE.

On the N.W. side the enclosure is also protected by a watercourse.

HAZOR, THE RAMPARTS ON THE EAST, RISING ABOVE THE PLAIN.

In the background the Galilean plateau and Wady Hindaj.

See pp. 104, 184.

TELL KEISAN, POSSIBLY THE SITE OF ACHSHAPH (Joshua xi, 1).

The mound stands in the plain about six miles to the S.W. of Acre.

TELL SEMUNIYEH, ON THE NORTHERN BOUNDARY OF ESDRAELON.

Frequently identified with Shimron (Joshua xi, 1) but see p. 189.

See pp. 65, 98, 189.

whether the frontier cities like Taanak, Megiddo, Jokneam and Dor sent contingents northward to the appointed place of meeting.

Though the site of Hazor, the centre of this combination, is now known, it is not possible as yet to locate with any precision the principal allied cities which are named in the early documents, namely Madon, Shimron and Achshaph. Theory commonly associates Madon with the great fortress of Hattîn [1] which dominates lower Galilee, Shimron (LXX Sumoōn) [2] with Semuniyeh [3], to the west of Nazareth, and Achshaph with Kefr Yesif or some other site in the northern plain of Acre. Such a combination would indeed seem upon the map to form a defensive ring round lower Galilee, effectively constituted to resist the Israelite penetration towards the north. But, on consideration, the military aspect of the situation evokes certain doubts. In the first place it would seem unlikely that the rallying point of the Canaanites would lie far to the north, out of ready touch with the advanced cities of the combination, since in that case much of the territory that it was desired to protect would have to be evacuated, and the withdrawal of the fighting men from the fortress cities mentioned would leave the surrounding country at the mercy of the enemy. Considerations of this kind have led some students to seek for the Waters of Merom, where the encounter took place, in the vicinity of the Plain of Esdraelon, and possibly account for the fact that Eusebius suggested identity with the springs of Merrus,[4] which lay according to his statement even further to the south near Dothan. But the equation is doubtful; and it is a good thirty miles from Dothan to Hattîn, while the more distant focus of Hazor in the Huleh Basin, fifty miles away,

[1] Pl. XVI.

[2] Variants in the LXX: Sumurōn, VE; Sumoōn, E; Somorōn, S; Somerōn, PC. Dr. Margolis, after an exhaustive study of the sources, adopts Sumoōn as the correct reading.

[3] Pl. XLV.

[4] See the Map No. 13, p. 188.

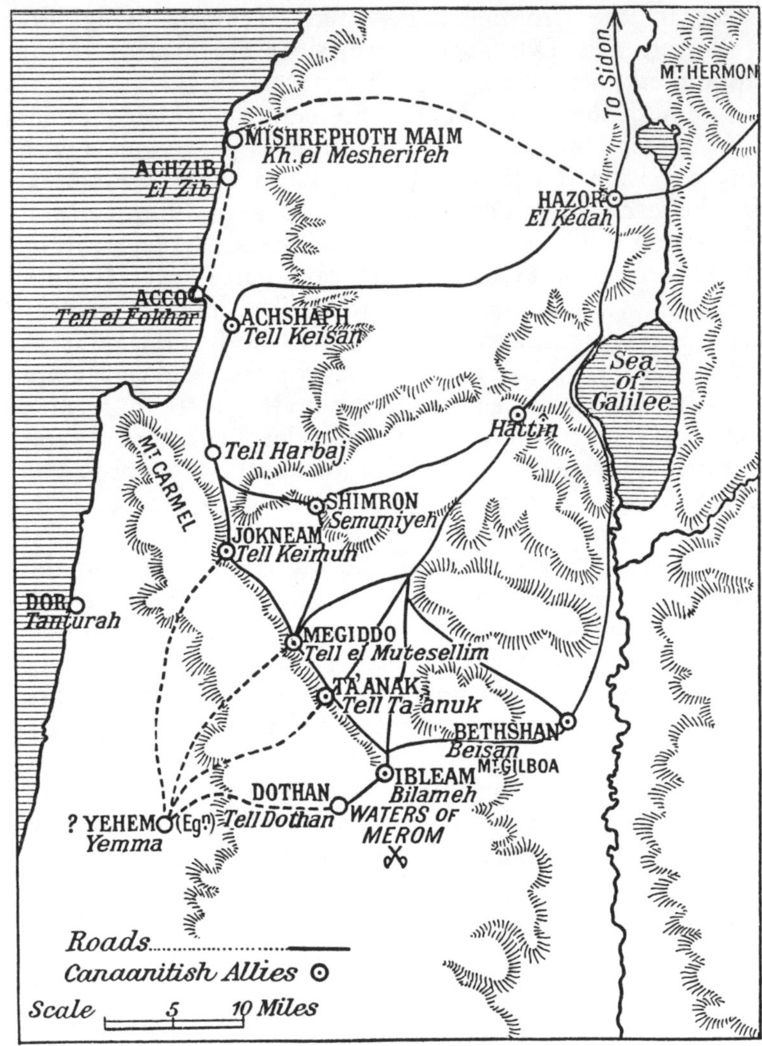

Map 13. Hazor and the Canaanite Frontier. (*Waters of Merom, after Eusebius.*)

would leave all further details of the battle outside the picture. Moreover, the popular identifications of Madon with Hattîn, and of Shimron with Semuniyeh are based upon similarity of name-sounds alone and are of doubtful

THE GORGE OF THE LITANY R. WHERE THIS BREAKS WESTWARD.
Viewed from the N.E.: the road towards Sidon crosses the river, R.

KALAT EL SUBEIBEH, PROBABLE SITE OF MIZPEH. Joshua xi, 8.
Viewed from the mouth of the valley, near Banias, by which climbs an old road towards Damascus. *See pp. 190, 196.*

value. The ruins to the west of Hattîn, with which the name Madon is often associated, are of Byzantine origin and called in Arabic Madîn, in which the penultimate letter is a consonantal *y*. The similarity of names is therefore not very close: indeed it is open to belief that the word Madon, which finds no clear counterpart in the ancient or modern names of the locality [1] is only an erroneous transcription of Maron,[2] the form which replaces Madon in the versions of the Septuagint, and is a well-known Galilean name to-day.[3] It would seem more likely that the majestic Bronze Age site of Hattîn represents some fortress city destroyed by Thutmose III.[4]

Shimron is replaced by Sumoōn in the LXX, and several scholars would identify it on philological and historical grounds with the Šamhuna of the Amarna Letters,[5] which left its name in the Huleh Basin as the classical *Samachonitis* and survives to-day as Summaka, a village to be found on the edge of the plateau some six miles eastward of the Huleh marshes, as well as at the spring, Ain Sumakh, not far to the north-west. The general position of Achshaph is well indicated by several later references in the Bible, and by its association with Acco

[1] The Egyptian M-d̲-n is nearest. It appears, No. 20, in the List of Thutmose III, following *B.y.r.t.*, *Bi'-y-rw-tu*, in a seemingly Syrian context. (Cf. Sethe, *Urk.*, 782, 20. Burchardt, *Fremdw.*, 550.) It would be pronounced Mazon, or rather Mazen, the middle letter being equivalent to Sade as in Hazor, whereas the corresponding letter in the Hebrew Madon is a Daleth followed by a Waw.

[2] The difference in Hebrew between Madon and Maron is so slight that confusion is always possible. The Greek versions supplied by Dr. Margolis are E, Marron; S, Maron. P.C. alone reads Madon, borrowing the Hebrew form.

[3] See below p. 194.

[4] It is tempting to see in the name Hattîn a derivative from the Egyptian Ḥ-t̲-y, otherwise Ḥ-t̲'-y, Hethy, which occurs as No. 3 in the List of Thutmose III, in the proper place immediately after Megiddo, notwithstanding the initial hard breathing in the latter (Burchardt, *Fremdw.*, No. 756). The form H-t̲-y-n actually occurs, and is associated with a fortress, in *Pap. Anast.* I (27, 5). Dr. Gardiner is disposed from the context to locate this on the route from Egypt to Gaza (p. 28, n. 21), but the only real indication refers to 'the extremity of the land of Canaan.'

[5] Kn. 224-225, Weber, p. 1299.

in the Amarna Letters. It cannot be identified with Kh. Iksâf on the north-east of the high plateau of Galilee, for the ruins now known by this name proved on examination to be of Byzantine origin.[1] On the other hand it was a chariotry centre and a situation in the plain of Acre satisfies the contexts: the strategically placed site of Tell Keisan accords well with its obvious importance.[2] In seeking to locate these sites and so explain the nature of their combination, we cannot overlook the known factors in the problem, namely the positions of Hazor and of Sidon, which we know lay in the north. We may lay aside then the theory of Eusebius and the battle in the south as not satisfying the indications of the narrative.

Turning again to the Bible text and remembering that three chief allies are named in the early sources, we note now with special interest that the pursuit after defeat takes three directions:

> **xi. 8 And they smote them, and chased them unto Great Zidon, and unto Misrephoth-Maim, and unto the valley of Mizpeh eastward. [J]**

The possibility suggests itself that these three lines of the flight and pursuit of the defeated Canaanites indicate severally the directions towards their homes. As Sidon lay in the north and Mizpeh in the east, it is reasonable to look first for Misrephoth-maim in the west. This name is peculiar and suggests the vicinity of hot springs.[3] It so happens that just to the south of Ras el Nakura, the rocky headland which forms the northern boundary of Palestine between Tyre and Acre, there lies a deserted Bronze-age site called Kh. el Mesherefeh,[4] in which not only the name but the presence of warm springs not two hundred yards away, seems to justify its identity with the ancient city. It lies, moreover, on the coastal road, with direct access to Achzib and other cities of the plain of Acre; and it may be reached from Hazor or the Huleh

[1] G. 1928. Pottery L.I.A.
[2] Pl. XLV. Map No. 7, p. 97.
[3] Cooke, *Joshua*, p. 103.
[4] Pl. XLVII.

KH. EL MESHÉREFEH, POSSIBLE SITE OF MISREPHOTH-MAIM.

On the R. the mound of ruins : On the L. the springs. The position is just south of the Ladder of Tyre.

EL ZIB, THE REPUTED SITE OF ACHZIB. Judges i, 31.

On the Mediterranean coast between Acre and the Ladder of Tyre.

See pp. 190, 241.

Basin by an established route which traverses the plateau from east to west by Kades, Bint Um el Jebeil and Dibl. The pursuit towards the west seems, then, to be accordant with the suggestion that the route taken may indicate the return of the western contingent towards Achshaph.

Mizpeh lay eastward, and its very name, the 'watch-tower,' points to the towering height now crowned by the Saracens' fortress called Kala't el Subeibeh,[1] which looks down on the north-east of the Huleh Basin from above Banias, and affords, by common consent, the most impressive and far-reaching view in the whole country. Moreover, we have seen that from Hazor, in the south-west of the Huleh Basin, the road leading northwards to Sidon throws off a main branch north-eastwards towards Damascus past Banias and the foot of Hermon.[2] It is important then to observe that in order to reach Summaka it is necessary to make the detour around the marshes of Huleh by way of Banias, whence the distance is about ten miles in a south-easterly direction. In this case again the direction of the line of flight seems to lead in the right direction, and it is worthy of mention that the traditional association of the Hittites (or the Hivites) from under Hermon[a] in this great combine against Joshua seems to be reconciled with the facts of the situation.

BY THE WATERS OF MEROM

Before trying to follow the line of flight towards Sidon in the north, it is necessary to determine, if possible, the scene of the battle. This must clearly be sought near some point from which radiated the several routes followed by the pursuit, while offering at the same time ready access from the south. Theory again has usually sought the Waters of Merom in the springs or marshes of the Huleh Lake, in particular the copious sources

[a] Joshua xi 3 [D]; LXX, 'Hittites'; cf. Judges i 26.

[1] Pl. XLVI. [2] Map, p. 195.

known as Ain el Mallahah, just north of Hazor, on the border of the plains. At first sight this identification seems to determine satisfactorily the rallying-point of the Canaanitish allies. Looked at more attentively, however, certain difficulties appear and seem insuperable. If Joshua's base were still near Jericho, as we are left to suppose, the surprise attack must have involved a forced march of more than 100 miles; indeed Josephus states that Joshua came up with the enemy on the fifth day,[1]

Fig. 3. *Merem*, possibly Merom, captured by Ramses II.

and from any point of view it is fairly clear that the Israelites did in fact accomplish some momentous feat of that kind. But the vital objection to this theory lies not in the question of distance but in the fact that Joshua with his infantry coming from the south would have had to march through the plains, past the site of Hazor, and there to attack the assembled Canaanites, where the chariotry and cavalry would have an immeasurable advantage. In short, neither the site near Dothan nor the Huleh Basin satisfies completely the circumstantial data as to the scene of the conflict.

It is to be noted that the word Merom is not necessarily the name of a place, but indicates a height or high

[1] *Antiq*. V, i 18.

place.[1] Moreover, if we turn to the LXX we find it to be stated categorically that Joshua attacked the enemy in the hill country. This variant reading retains indeed other significant details which may provide the solution of the problem.

JOSHUA xi

1 And when Jabis the King of Asor heard, he sent
to Jobab King of Maron,[a] and to the King of
Sumoon,[b] and to the King of Aziph.[c]
5 And all the kings assembled in person, and came
to the same place, and encamped at the waters
6 of Maron to war with Israel. And the Lord
said to Joshua, Be not afraid of him, for to-
morrow at this time I will put them to flight
before Israel: thou shalt hough their horses, and
7 burn their chariots with fire. And Joshua and
all the men of war came upon them at the water
of Maron suddenly; and they attacked them in
8 the hill country. And the Lord delivered them
into the power of Israel. [LXX.]

The main story thus remains the same; but the names Madon and Merom of the Hebrew are both replaced in this version by Marōn, a name still familiar in the hill country of northern Galilee in the form Mârûn.

The problem is now simplified. Somewhere in Upper Galilee, if this version provides the clue, there should exist a natural route-centre and a neighbouring water supply of somewhat special character, where possibly there still lingers the local name Marōn. Now to-day, we have seen, all the roads through Upper Galilee meet at Bint Um el Jebeil,[2] a village which lies at the northern foot of a prominent ridge called by that precise name, the

[a] Variant Marron. [b] Variant. Cf. p. 87, n. 2. [c] Variant Aksaph.

[1] See Fig. 3. The Egyptian drawing suggests a small hill-fortress. Cf. Lepsius, *Denk.* III 31, 156.

[2] P. 102, cf. Pl. XLVIII.

Jebel Mârûn, with the village of Mârûn el Ras near its highest point (3050 feet). For long the natives of Galilee and of southern Lebanon have met once a week at this place for market purposes; and so firmly is this custom established that the present administrations of these mandated territories have found it desirable to grant exceptional frontier privileges to those attending this weekly market. From a wide area people resort as a matter of course to this old-established centre; and early on Thursday mornings, or even overnight, streams of peasants with animals and produce may be seen making their way towards this point, where no fewer than nine bridle tracks converge. The site of Hazor lies to the S.E. at a distance of five hours only. Sidon is further away, east of north at a full day's ride. The western coasts between Tyre and Acre may be reached in about seven hours.

Jebel Mârûn dominates Upper Galilee, though not itself the highest mountain (which is Jebel Jermuk, 3900 feet, at a distance of ten miles southward), because it stands isolated on the highest portion of the plateau. At the north foot of the hill, below the village of Bint Um el Jebeil, a large collecting tank gathers the waters from Jebel Mârûn and from the hillsides around,[1] for the village stands as it were in a cup. The origin of this tank is unknown, but by general consent it is older than the village, which indeed appears quite modern. The question cannot well be tested without digging in its banks, and as these have been strengthened in recent times and are constantly in use, such an investigation is not practicable. Outside the village half-way up the slopes there is found a copious perennial spring now called 'Ain Jozeh.

An exceptionally plentiful supply of water is found also to the south of the Jebel Mârûn near the village of Yârûn, the Biblical Iron. This village boasts a hundred wells; and immediately to its north is an area known as

[1] Cf. Masterman, *Studies in Galilee*, p. 15.

BINT UM EL JEBEIL, THE MODERN ROAD CENTRE OF UPPER GALILEE.
The weekly market attracts peasants of Syria and N. Palestine for twenty miles around.

YARUN, A MODERN VILLAGE ON THE SITE OF IRON.
The city which in the Iron Age replaced El Khurbeh, whence the view is taken, looking West.
See pp. 102, 193.

Khurbet el Biâr, the Ruin of the Wells, while several isolated springs are found in the vicinity.

Here, then, in the heart of Upper Galilee are found all the elements for explaining the account of Joshua's victory by the Waters of Maron as described in the LXX. The permanence of the name Mârûn, the concentration of roads in this vicinity, and the unusual supply of water

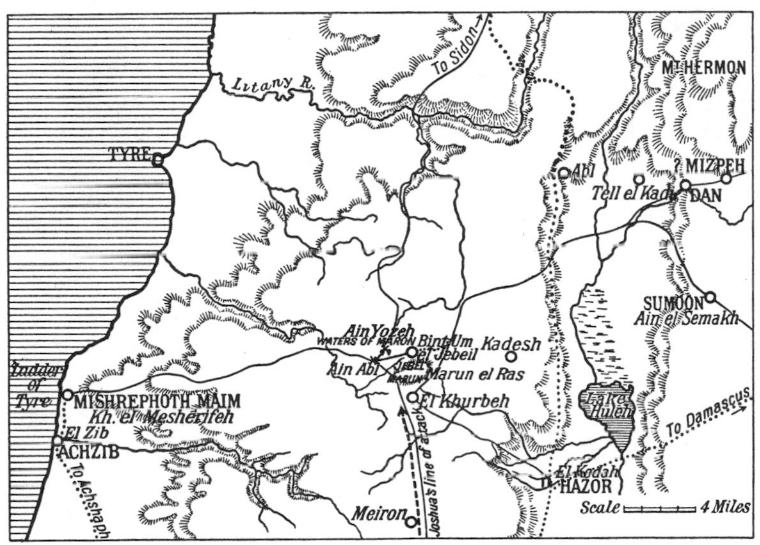

Map 14. The Battle by the Waters of Merom. (*After the LXX.*)

on either side of the hill, form a combination of features which correspond uniquely with the details of the narrative. Further to the north the name Mârûn recurs in several places, notably Kulat Mârûn, and in this vicinity it may be anticipated that research will ultimately locate the parent city of the Bronze Age, Marōn of the LXX, Madon of the standard (Massoretic) Hebrew text.[1]

Upon this clue the strategic details of this battle can now be reconstructed and explained.[2] The King of Hazor summoned his allies from the north and east and

[1] See above, p. 189, n. 1. [2] See Map, No. 14.

west to meet at the central rallying-point near Marun, the first step in a war against Israel. Their chariots would be dismantled and packed upon their animals for the mountain journey, and they would pitch their camp as they assembled in the vicinity of the waters of this area. Joshua, informed of their plans and realizing the vital importance of forestalling their next move, with characteristic energy led his troops northwards over the hills in a forced march. There is no mention of his mustering-point, but later tradition suggests that he may have been already at drawn swords with the cities of Esdraelon,[a] as seems likely; and from a position there (thirty miles away) the distance might be accomplished within twenty-four hours. Coming suddenly upon the enemy he caught them at a disadvantage, surprised in their camp and unable to employ their familiar arm, while the Israelites fought with their own weapons and methods. A quick manœuvre of men detailed for the purpose, running up and down the tethering lines, enabling them to maim and perhaps liberate the horses, would produce a commotion that could not be quelled, leading to stampede and panic. As at Gibeon the suddenness and impetuosity of the attack gave Joshua the victory.

From the scene of battle the chief roads led in three directions, northwards across the Litany Valley towards Great Sidon, westwards by Dibl as far as El Misherifeh to Achshaph in the coastal plain, and north-eastwards, skirting the Huleh marshes, towards the valley of Banias at the foot of Hermon.

The topography of the district thus affords a complete explanation of the details of the battle and its issue, as narrated in the Septuagint. The very simplicity and cohesion of this version suggests that some errors of copying or interpretation may have crept into the Massoretic text, which replaces Maron by Madon in the list of allies, and the Waters of Maron by the Waters of Merom as the scene of the battle. The name Merom seems to be

[a] Joshua xii 21-22 [D].

HAZOR: EXCAVATIONS WITHIN THE CAMP-AREA.

In which were found houses of the Middle Bronze Age, c. 1800 B.C., and traces of surface occupation, as in tents or huts, of the Late Bronze Age, c. 1600-1400 B.C.

HAZOR: EXCAVATIONS ON THE ACROPOLIS, EL KEDAH.

Which proved to have been fortified in the Middle Bronze Age, with a stout rampart wall of stone. *See p. 184 and the Appendix.*

uncertain, and is only doubtfully equated with the *Merem* in the records of Thutmose III and of Ramses II; and it gives way in later tradition to the form Meron.[a] Possibly it was identified at that time with Meiron, now the site of a synagogue, some four miles west of Safed. This place stands upon the main cross-country route leading westward by Rama to Acre. It is placed upon a sharp hill, at the foot of which a copious spring pours as it were from the heart of Jebel Jermuk. The distance between Marun and Meiron is not more than seven miles, and the position might suit the strategic situation almost as well. Certain details of the narrative, however, would not be so readily explained: the nearest camp-ground, for example, is a good half-mile from the water supply of Meiron, and less exposed to a surprise attack, being approached by a steep climb from the south. On the whole, therefore, the version in the Septuagint, which adheres to the name Marun, seems not only better authenticated but to lend itself to a more satisfactory interpretation.

The Septuagint and later Hebrew legend are agreed that after the pursuit into the valley of Mizpeh eastward, Joshua 'turned back' and took Hazor.[b] An independent examination of the site has shown in fact that the whole of the camp area was destroyed by a conflagration about this date.[1] The sloping ramparts that protected the camp-enclosure could not hold back the onslaught of the victorious Israelites. It was different perhaps with the city proper which stood on its own hill encircled and protected by stone walls; for though some buildings in this part of the area also show signs of destruction and burning, in places where it has been explored, the precise date of that event has not been determined independently, and it may pertain to some other period of conquest, such as that of Thutmose III earlier in the century or even of Ramses II.

[a] Joshua xii 20 [D]. [b] Joshua xi 10 [D].

[1] G. 1928. See 'Hazor' in the Appendix.

However that may be, the destruction of the camp enclosure with its contained tents or huts, is found to have been complete and final. The objects discovered in the examination of the area attest that it was in occupation till about 1400 B.C., when it was abandoned, and never re-inhabited. Subsequent occupation was confined entirely to the Acropolis. There seems to be no doubt then about the thorough nature of this victory, which must have broken up for the time being the combination opposed to the penetration of the northern tribes, for Hazor beforetime was the head of all those Kingdoms. The way was now open, not, indeed, for the occupation of the cities of Esdraelon and Galilee, which would still be too strong for the Israelites to take, but for the same process of infiltration which secured for their kinsmen a footing in the centre and the south. This victory, with its strategic consequences, was the crowning incident to Joshua's military career.

JOSHUA xi

10 Joshua turned back at that time and took Hazor.
11, 13 . . . And burnt Hazor with fire. . . . But as for
the cities that stood on their mounds, Israel
burned none of them, save Hazor only, that did
Joshua burn. [D]

THE SETTLEMENT OF THE TRIBES

SECTION 9

ALLOTMENT OF THE TRIBAL AREAS

Joshua xiii

1a Now Joshua was old and well stricken in years. [J]

The importance of this reference to Joshua's age, coming between his northern campaign and his allotment of the tribal portions to Judah with Caleb and to the House of Joseph, is twofold. It suggests a considerable lapse of time after the fall of Hazor, during which the lack of further information from the early sources implies the continued immobilization of the Israelites at Gilgal, as indeed is indicated more positively by later tradition.[1] This conclusion would introduce a changing background to the remainder of Joshua's career, during which his headquarters were advanced by stages from Gilgal to Bethel,[a] thence to Shiloh,[b] and eventually to Shechem.[c] The vigour of his active leadership until the fall of Hazor implies that he was not more than eighty years of age at the entry of the Israelites into the country, nor more than eighty-five when he led their forced march to the Waters of Merom.[d] Now the old sources of both books agree in stating that he lived to the ripe age of 110 years,[e] so that he still enjoyed twenty-five years of quieter leadership after the fall of Hazor. According to the Biblical dates,[2] the northern campaign must have taken place, then, about the year 1405 B.C., and Joshua's death about 1377 B.C. The importance of this conclusion lies in the

[a] Joshua xvi 2 [J], Judges i 22 [J], and Judges ii 1 [J].
[b] Joshua xviii 9-10 [JE]
[c] Joshua xxiv 1 [E].
[d] Joshua xi 7 [J].
[e] Joshua xxiv 29 [E].

[1] Cf. Joshua xi, 18 [D]. 'Joshua made war a long time with all those Kings.' Also Joshua xiv 6 [D]: 'The children of Judah drew nigh unto Joshua in Gilgal.'

[2] See pp. 61-62, also p. 254.

possibility that Joshua's last years may in that case have overlapped the period of the Amarna letters (*c.* 1380-1360 B.C.).[1]

Unfortunately, there is no information from the early sources as to Joshua's age at the time he settled in Shechem. Were it not for later tradition associated with Caleb, we should be predisposed to regard the figure of eighty-five as already too high for his age when leading the vigorous assault against the league of Hazor in the north, and be inclined to reduce the figure by a number of years. In that event his old age and sojourn at Shechem would necessarily overlap with the period of the Amarna letters, and possibly with the Ḥabiru invasion. But Caleb, his life companion, according to a later tradition embodied in the fifteenth chapter of the Book of Joshua, subsequent to the passage we are discussing, is made to state[a] that he had been forty years of age when sent with Joshua to spy out the land from Kadesh Barnea, forty-five years before, and in the second year of the Exodus. He claims, moreover, to be still vigorous, though eighty-five years of age; while Joshua, as we have seen, is already regarded as 'stricken in years.' The tendency of the later tradition, then, does not favour the reduction of Joshua's age. If he were contemporary with Caleb, and the latter's age be correctly indicated by D, then he must have been thirty-eight years of age at the Exodus,[2] forty at the sending of the spies, seventy-eight at Hor, on the death of Aaron, eighty at the entry of Israel into Canaan by Jericho, eighty-five at the burning of Hazor, and 110 at death. These figures based on the later tradition D agree, as we have seen, with the general indications of the earlier sources.

[a] Cf. Joshua xiv 7, 10 [D].

[1] See further, pp. 253 f.

[2] The allusion to Joshua's youth in Exodus xxxiii 11 is clearly misplaced and appears to be a gloss: cf. Exodus xvii 9, 10, 13, etc. On this question see further below, p. 254.

JOSHUA xiii

1b There remaineth yet very much land to be possessed. [J]

The campaigns led by Joshua do not appear from the early sources to have resulted directly in the possession of territory. At the most they appear to have broken the organised and co-ordinated resistance to the Israelite penetration, and to have secured for them certain avenues of approach. In the south the rout after the relief of Gibeon, extending through the valley of Aijalon into the coastal plain, and in the north the scattering of the Canaanitish forces by the Waters of Merom, followed by the assault on Hazor in the Huleh Basin, are in sum the two great achievements described in the records. We are left in darkness as to any further attempts at conquest, until, in accord with Caleb, co-ordinated tribal movements are set in action against the south and centre, and ultimately in the north, as though to make good the footings already won. To explain the gaps in the sequence of events it seems at first sight necessary to suppose that before and after the fall of Hazor the Israelites must have been involved in other wars, the narrative of which is lost. Late tradition supports this obvious contention, 'Joshua made war a long time with all those kings'[a]; but the details of the struggle and the summary of victories[b] embodied in later texts are found upon comparison with the earlier sources to introduce fresh problems[1] without suggesting a radical solution of the main difficulty.

On the other hand it may be urged with reason that if any further contest of strategic importance equal to those

[a] Joshua xi 18 [D]. [b] Joshua xii [D].

[1] Compare, for instance, the summary of victories in Trans-Jordania, in xii 1-6, from the hand of D, with the earlier and more modest claims of Jephthah, Judges xi 12-26 (E2). The list of kings whom the children of Israel smote beyond Jordan westward (xii 9-24, D) introduces the names of places not yet mentioned in the narrative; and while it may help after further investigation to fill in the gaps, it cannot be accepted in evidence at this stage of our enquiry.

of Aijalon and of Hazor had really been fought out with success, it is unlikely that no reminiscence of such a struggle would be traceable in either of the old sources, in the ample tradition of later times, or in the numerous snatches of folk tale and song embodied in the Books: nor is there any conceivable motive for expunging such a record. When we turn the remaining pages of the Book of Joshua and the early chapters of the Book of Judges in search of a solution, we find the root of the problem to be embedded in the fact that notwithstanding the admittedly incomplete nature of the conquest, a process of tribal penetration is deemed opportune and meets eventually with success. As noticed already, the abrupt allusion to Joshua's great age (in xiii. 1) indicates a considerable lapse of time between the fall of Hazor and the initiation of this movement. Meanwhile, it would appear that the Israelites were constrained to bide their time at Gilgal in anticipation of developments.

JOSHUA xiii

7 Divide this land for an inheritance. [J]

Though very much of the land remained to be possessed, Joshua, no longer able to lead the Israelites in battle, proceeded to apportion to the leading tribes their respective areas for ultimate occupation.[1] At the same time the project seems to have been formed for a concerted tribal action, commencing with two main movements, Judah and certain tribal elements with Caleb towards the south, the 'house of Joseph' and others with Joshua[a] towards the centre and the north. The military advan-

[a] Cf. Joshua xviii 2-6 [JE].

[1] Later tradition embodied in ch. xiv, xv, holds that Judah and the southern tribes now all received their portions; but the narrative is attributed to the late documents, P, and contains anachronisms. (See further below, p. 222.) Early tradition has, however, left record in Joshua xvi 1-3 [J] of the southern boundary to the territory of the 'house of Joseph' (ultimately that of Ephraim); and from this fact it may be inferred at least that the highlands south of this border were assigned at the same time to the Calebites and the associated tribal elements, as their sphere of action.

tages already attained would alone hardly have justified such a change of plan. It is true that the blows dealt by Joshua against the southern and northern leagues, those centred on Jerusalem and on Hazor respectively, had probably broken for the time being the power of these combines to organise an effective opposition to the further penetration of Joshua and his Hivite allies. But the division of the Israelite force into detachments at this juncture suggests a diminishing resistance, a changing political state which favoured rather the process of infiltration, and offered to the tribal units the prospect of spreading their tents unchallenged and of securing pasturage for their flocks. Clearly such a situation must have developed as the controlling power of Egypt waned in the reign of Amenhotep III, from 1390 B.C. onwards, culminating about 1375 B.C. when the Ḥabiru invasion began to spread disorder and dismay, driving the inhabitants to the shelter of their city walls.[1] Under such circumstances probably the methods of diplomacy and proffered friendship might prove more effective than threat or direct attack. The latter alternative was in any case practically useless, as the Israelites proved themselves unable to overcome any of the greatest fortified places. Thus we find the house of Joseph with Joshua advancing stage by stage from Gilgal to Shiloh, and eventually to Shechem, without trace in the narrative of any struggle, their progress apparently only challenged when the northern tribesmen of Manasseh found themselves confronted by the line of Canaanite fortresses extended across the country from Dor to Bethshean.[a]

In the south, however, the opposition was general. The first attempt of the Israelites to enter the country from the Negeb, and their subsequent defeat at Hormah, had displayed the hostile attitude of the Amalekites and their neighbours.[b] On this occasion, from the sparse records which have survived, it would appear that the action

[a] Joshua xvii 11, 12 [J]. [b] Numbers xiv. 45 [JE].

[1] On the Habiru see further below, p. 252.

against the south country was developed from several directions in three concerted movements, as between elements of the tribes of Judah and Simeon together, the Kenites allied with other elements of the tribe of Judah, and, separately, Caleb with his clan of Kenizzites.

These actions are described in fragmentary excerpts which in the Book of Joshua (xiii-xxiii) have become separated by more lengthy passages added at later times in an endeavour to amplify and elucidate their meaning. In the opening chapter of the Book of Judges, they appear, evidently from the same source, almost in their original form; some of the passages are consequently duplicated, while some few occur only in the Book of Judges. The latter source, being the more complete and undisturbed, may serve as a guide to the sequence of events.

SECTION 10

JUDAH AND SIMEON WITH CALEB IN THE SOUTH

JUDGES i. *Bezek*

1 The children of Israel asked of the Lord, saying, Who shall
go up for us first against the Canaanites, to fight against
2 them? And the Lord said, Judah shall go up: behold,
5 I have delivered the land into his hand. . . . And they
found Adoni-Bezek in Bezek. . . . [J]

THIS opening incident of the Book of Judges, is not easy to explain, and does not find any parallel in the Book of Joshua. Though reading in some ways like a sequel to the campaigns of united Israel, it appears as the first of the organised tribal movements, the record of some early struggle with the Canaanites in which the brunt of the affair was borne, in accordance with the decision of the oracle, by Judah. Critics sometimes escape from the difficulties of the passage by supposing that it really reproduces a variant version of the sequel to Joshua's campaign against the league assembled by Adoni-Zedek of Jerusalem.[a] But the setting is different; also the name of the king in this case is Adoni-Bezek, the latter element being the name of a place,[1] and the context indicates that this should be sought in the southern highlands: 'And Judah said unto Simeon his brother, come up with me into my lot . . . and I likewise will go with thee into thy lot.'[b] No place with a name like Bezek can be recognised, however, in the locality indicated, and herein lies the real difficulty. The nearest is that now called Ibzek, identified with the Bezek of I Samuel xi 8, but this lies north-east of Shechem on the road to Beisan. Curiously

[a] Joshua x 1 [J]. [b] Judges i 3 [J].

[1] But see Cooke, *Judges*, p. 5; Burney, *Judges*, p. 4.

enough, the introduction of Perizzites into the narrative seems also to point in the same general direction, for these people are encountered elsewhere only as inhabiting the wooded highlands to the north and east of Shechem.[a] If these indications are worth considering, they suggest an encircling movement of Judah with Simeon from the Jordan valley by way of the Wady Farah, in which case the whole incident would seem to be reminiscent of some expedition at an earlier phase of the struggle. Though this explanation might help to fill one of the obvious gaps in the records of Joshua's campaigns, *e.g.* between the relief of Gibeon and the fall of Hazor, it would seem to be improbable, for such a movement could hardly be associated with the occupation of the south as the narrative implies. The identification of Bezek is essential to a proper understanding of the episode.

HEBRON AND DEBIR

JOSHUA XV.

13 And unto Caleb he gave a portion among the children of Judah, even Kiriath Arba, the same is Hebron. [? J]

The most successful share in the attack upon the south is attributed to Caleb, who seems to have waged his battles independently of the children of Judah, though doubtless in concerted action. A later version in the Book of Judges [b] certainly introduces Judah into the narrative, but the Book of Joshua [c] is explicit in ascribing this campaign to Caleb. He himself was one of the tribe or clan of Kenizzites who had early thrown in his lot with the Israelites, and now reaped the reward of his loyal service. Supported by his alliance with Joshua he took this opportunity to possess himself of Hebron and the district lying south-westward down to the foot of the hills. The main lines of his attack are recorded in both Books, almost in duplicate terms.[1]

[a] Joshua xvii 15 [J]. [b] Judges i 10 [P]. [c] Joshua xv 14 [J].

[1] See the Text, pp. 24-25.

JOSHUA XV

14 And Caleb drove out thence the three sons of Anak, Sheshai and Ahiman, and Talmai. [J]

Hebron occupied a site of strategic importance, being the most southerly road-centre of the highland system, where the routes from Moab, the southern Negeb, Egypt and the coast met those of the interior and the north.[1] It was a city with very ancient traditions, built seven years after Zoan in Egypt, the resort in the Patriarchal age of a Hittite colony (P), and occupied at this time by 'Anakim,' children of Anak,[2] great in stature, whom Caleb dispossessed. Its name in Egyptian is not evident, though a credible hypothesis would equate it with *Rubute* of the Amarna Letters. In one of these Abd Khipa of Jerusalem reports to the Pharaoh that Milkili of Shechem and Shuardata of Keilah in open revolt had hired soldiers from Gaza, Gimti and Kilti and had taken the territory of Rubute. The land of the king was being lost to the Ḥabiru. The identity of Hebron, the city of Arba, with Rubute is favoured by several scholars.[3] Notwithstanding the doubt as to Egyptian relations with this place in common with nearly all others of the plateau, the antiquity of the site so strongly indicated by tradition can hardly be doubted. It must be said, however, that archaeological evidence is almost entirely lacking. The caves certainly exist which are reputed to be the burying places of the Patriarchal families : [4] but apart from this there are no definite traces of a great walled city such as befit the reputation of a City of Refuge.[a] It seems possible that, as with Jerusalem and Shechem, the enclosing walls and other

[a] I Chronicles vi 57.

[1] See also pp. 75, 170 ; and Map No. 4, p. 76.

[2] Iy'nq occurs on an Egyptian record, *c.* B.C. 2000 ; cf. *Syria*, viii, p. 218.

[3] Zimmern, *Zeits. Deut. Pal. Ver.* 13, p. 142, n. 2 ; and Hommel, *Gesch. des alt. Morgen.*, i p. 82 ; cf. Weber, *Anmerk.*, p. 1342. Kn. 290.

[4] Cf. p. 170 ; also Vincent in *Rev. Bibl.* 1920, pp. 525 ff.

remains of the Late Bronze Age have been obliterated by the later occupation of the site. The position of the city in this case was somewhat exceptional, for though relatively high in altitude, 3000 feet, it lies in a hollow overlooked by the surrounding hills. On the western side one of these, called El Rumeidah, also distinguished by the name Deir el Arba'în, is crowned with the remains of a small enclosure, strongly fortified, covering an area of about five acres. The surrounding walls are constructed in the massive style of the Middle Bronze Age, like the strong work of Hazor, Jericho and Beeroth; but for some exceptional reason the steep slopes of this knoll have not as yet produced any characteristic early potsherds, such as elsewhere enable us to appreciate almost at a glance the probable antiquity of each site. It is just possible that the old Hittite community originally organised this hilltop in accordance with local practice; and that the Anakim who next occupied the place, relying upon their own strength, preferred to dwell on the lower ground, where their city has gradually become obliterated by the modern town, while that of the Hittites, earlier evacuated, has survived the depredations of time until to-day.

JOSHUA XV

15 And he went up thence against the inhabitants of Debir :
17 now the name of Debir aforetime was Kiriath-Sepher : and
Othniel the brother of Caleb took it. [J]

Modern research has located Kiriath-Sepher at Tell Beit Mersîm, a mound situated not very conspicuously among the foothills that fringe the maritime plain 1600 feet above the sea, and some thirteen miles west south-west of Hebron, near the road towards Beersheba and Egypt. Here excavations have disclosed a walled city and other features that satisfy the several references to the place in Bible narrative. One minor discrepancy should, however, be noted at this point, in that the account of Caleb's movement in Joshua xv 15 states that he 'went up' to Debîr. This detail appears also in the LXX but is not insisted on in the Book of Judges.[a] Possibly it implies a preliminary action extending to the plains near Beersheba, in the process of driving out the Anakim, before proceeding against Debîr. However that may be, there remains little doubt about the identity of Debîr with Tell Beit Mersîm, especially as this site proves to have had an important status in the period of the monarchy, such as no other city than Debîr can claim. It was connected at one time with Hebron by a road, which, however, is now little used. Another route skirting the foothills passes in a north-westerly direction. But Beit Mersîm lies rather in tangled ground, amid patches of bare rock and shallow valleys, and its former importance has no counterpart in the modern economy of the area. The ancient Tell has been scientifically excavated down to certain levels.[1] Two gates, east and west, have been traced, and between them an enclosing wall of the Early Iron Age (*c.* 1200 B.C.). The uppermost city of the monarchy was cleared extensively of its debris. In the vicinity of the east gate four levels have been successively cleared and examined. The lowest stratum dates from the Early Bronze Age, before 2000 B.C. and at this time the houses appear to have been constructed largely of wood. In the Middle Bronze Age, about 1800 B.C. the time when so many cities of the country were fortified, this one was surrounded by a wall which in the section examined proved to be 3.25 metres or ten feet in thickness. During the Hyksos period (about 1700 B.C.) which was represented among the excavated remains by six characteristic scarabs, the place became an important Canaanitish town, which continued to flourish under the XVIIIth Dynasty of Egypt.

[a] Judges i 11 [J].

[1] Cf. Albright, 'The American Excavations at Tell Beit Mirsîm' in *Zeits. f. d. alttest. Wiss.*, Giessen, 1929, pp. 1-18; also in *Bull. Am. Sch. Or. Res.*, No. 23, 1926, pp. 2-14, with 9 photographs. Also Vincent in *Rev. Bibl.* 1927, No. 3, pp. 408 ff. and *ibid.* 1929, No. 1, pp. 103 ff.

The latter period is well marked in the archaeology of Palestine by the presence of Cypro-Phoenician objects, and the absence, on the other hand, of Mykenaean products,[1] such as later impressed themselves upon the local culture. The houses of the Canaanite city previous to this dividing line furnished abundant testimony to the high standard of art prevailing in the latter part of the Middle Bronze Age, which seems indeed from the evidence of all excavated sites, like Jericho, Beisan, Hazor and Shechem, to mark the zenith of the Canaanite civilisation. In this era Kiriath-Sepher shared; and at this time its defensive walls were for the most part about ten feet thick, but attained in places as much as thirteen feet, and these were further strengthened on the outside, in characteristic fashion, by a sloping revetment of stonework.[2] In detail of construction this masonry was less massive than the contemporary work of Shechem or Hattîn, but is comparable with much of that of Jericho, which it also rivalled in size. The excavator found evidence which seemed to indicate a period during which the place had remained unoccupied, and thinks it may have been overthrown as early as the expulsion of the Hyksos from Egypt, *c.* 1550 B.C., and not reoccupied until after the time of Thutmose III a hundred years later. The date of its destruction, however, is not ascertained with precision, and the excavator in reviewing the historical situation would await further evidence before pronouncing a final opinion; but the potsherds of this level, viewed independently, may bring the occupation down to about 1500 B.C. When finally reconstructed the new city showed indications of relative poverty: the houses were poorly built and separated by open spaces containing grain pits. In this period the derelict fortifications of

[1] Cf. Wace, *J.H.S.* xlvi, p. 116, also Albright, 'Am. Excvns.' *loc. cit.* p. 4. On the general question see further, Vincent, 'La Peinture Céramique Palestinienne,' in *Syria*, 1924, pp. 81, 186 ff.; and the same scholar's *Canaan d'après l'Exploration Récente*, pp. 326 ff.; also Macalister, *Gezer*, ii, pp. 138 ff., and *Pal. Mus. Bull.* No. 3, Pl. VII.

[2] Cf. pp. 130, 249; and Pl. XXXVIII.

the earlier period were restored, and the east gate was entirely rebuilt, on the same general plan. The occupation of this city (level C) is found to have lasted well into the second half of the Late Bronze Age (*i.e.* after 1400 B.C.) and so enters into the period of the narrative. It is consequently of highest interest to note that 'the destruction of this city was accompanied by a terrific conflagration, and by the complete demolition of its fortifications'.[1] Though the date of this catastrophe is not determined with precision,[2] it is properly ascribed by the excavator to the handiwork of 'Othniel' or his clan, from the striking accordance of details in the subsequent history of the site. The city was rebuilt at once upon the ashes and débris which mark its capture. Its outline remained much the same, but its defensive walls were not so strong. The occupation of this new city was found to cover three consecutive phases. The first was characterised by a decadent local civilization, in which the last stage of the Late Bronze Age (1300-1200 B.C.), though well represented by pottery and other objects, shows no trace of foreign relations. This phase is believed to have covered roughly 50 to 100 years. The second phase, though succeeding the first without shock, brought an entirely new culture, that of the Early Iron Age, with an abundance of Philistine wares and a maintenance of Egyptian influence. The third phase was marked by the disappearance of Philistine and Egyptian traces, and a transition to purely local culture. These discoveries not only throw a vivid light upon the fortunes of the city at this time, but serve to illustrate the further development of local history during the period of The Judges, in particular the rôle played by the Philistines in the Egyptian administration of the area.[3]

[1] Albright, *op. cit.* p. 8.

[2] See below under 'Debir' in the Appendix to this volume.

[3] See below, pp. 285, 311, 338

JOSHUA XV

19 And [Achsah] said : Give me a blessing [a]; for thou has set me in the land of the South, give me also springs [b] of water. And he gave her the upper springs and the lower springs.[c]

As regards the further allusion in the narrative to the Upper and Lower Pools, it is to be noted that the word Gullath, which is rendered 'springs' in the English translation, here rather connotes something rounded or enclosed, like a reservoir, or a spring walled round.[1] The alternative reading 'pools' better represents the sense of the original. It is then a fact of striking interest, supporting indeed the identification of the site, that two large reservoirs of the type peculiar to this region are to be seen in the immediate vicinity, and in the positions indicated, the one at a distance of three kilometres above the mound, and the other one kilometre below it.[2]

ARAD AND HORMAH

JUDGES i

16 And the children of [d] the Kenite, Moses' brother in law, [e] went up out of the city of palm trees with the children of Judah into the wilderness of Judah, which is in the south [f] of Arad [f]; and they went and dwelt with the people.[g] [J]

This brief record of the settling of the Kenites and some of the children of Judah in the Negeb south of Arad,[h] though but a fragment, contains several helpful suggestions. The 'City of Palm Trees' in later times was a

[a] *Or* present. [b] *Or* given me the land of the South. [c] *Or* pools.

[d] *Supply* Hobab (J and LXX B). [e] *Or* father in law.

[f] *Supply* at the descent (LXX, A and B).

[g] *I.e.* of Amalek (cf. I Samuel xv 6, Numbers xxiv 20, 22).

[h] Cf. Numbers xxi 1, 2, 3 ; xxxiii 40 ; xiv 45.

[1] Cooke, *Joshua*, p. 143.

[2] Albr., *Am. Excavs. at Tell Beit Mersim*, p. 3; Kyle, *Bibl. Sacra*, 1928, 381-408.

familiar epithet of Jericho,[a] and it appropriately describes the cultivated area below the spring eastward of the now deserted mound. As the name of the city is not mentioned otherwise in the Book of Judges, there is no reason to doubt the identity in this case, especially as we are left to infer that Gilgal in the immediate vicinity was the starting-point of these expeditions. It is true that the expression might equally denote any one of several cities in the south, *e.g.* Beersheba or Rafa, and various theories have been founded on such a possibility. But when we last heard of the Kenite leader he was living in Gilgal; and the alternatives involve an interpretation of the Bible story not justified by the records. One cogent factor cannot be ignored, namely that the combined movement of the Kenites with Judah from the City of Palm Trees was *upwards* and that the destination was the wilderness or desert plain to the south of Arad.[1] The LXX indeed describes the objective explicitly as 'the wilderness that is in the south of Juda, which is at the descent of Arad.' This land is on the normal lėvel of the whole region, not more than a thousand feet above the sea, and there would be no sensation of climbing when approaching it from Beersheba or any city of the Negeb, whereas the starting point near Jericho would lie nearly 1 000 feet below sea level.

Arad itself stands somewhat higher, overlooking the plain.[2] Its situation and appearance are alike of interest. The Tell which marks the site and still bears the ancient name, though not prominent, is well defined amid an area of extensive ruins, among which there seem to be distinguishable the traces of an inner and an outer ramp. Whether these fortifications belong to the Bronze Age it is not possible to say without excavation; but there is evidence that the site was in active occupation at that time, and to judge from its position and known history it was presumably one of the fenced or walled cities of the period. It commands the meeting of numerous

[a] Deuteronomy xxxiv 3; II Chronicles xxviii 15.

[1] Cf. Adam Smith, *Hist. Geog.* p. 277.

[2] See Pl. VII.

desert routes, including the chief line of approach to the plateau from the south-east. From its summit may be seen towards the south and to the west miles of plain reaching away to the horizon. The land is not sterile, but produces enough scrub for Bedouin life; while the more favoured areas may be ploughed and in years of good rain reward the labour with abundant crops. The same features prevail from Beersheba almost to the Dead Sea. In these lands the Kenites spread their tents, but to judge from later incident[a] they were not settled; and probably circumstances compelled them, like the Bedouin of that region to-day, to seek new pastures at certain seasons even far afield, while regarding this area to the south of Arad as their natural centre and chief resort. This main fact has in itself significance, as indicating a less hostile attitude or lessened power of resistance among the dwellers in that area than had been the case forty years before,[b] though on that occasion, it is true, their adversaries had secured support from the peoples inhabiting the cities upon the higher ground.[c]

JUDGES i. *Hormah*

17 Judah went with Simeon his brother, and they smote the Canaanites that inhabited Zephath, and the name of the city was called Hormah. [J]

Thus did the Israelites avenge the defeat of forty years before. The place is unknown, and we can only suggest the deserted site called Tell el Melh, which is found with an active well about ten miles to the south-west of Arad, in the vicinity of other ruins. This episode reads like a continuation of that described in the opening passage of the Book of Judges (1-7) concerning Bezek, and leads again to the conclusion that the latter place is to be sought in the south-east, the area of these campaigns.

[a] Judges iv 11 [E]. [b] Cf. Numbers xxiv 20, 22; also I Samuel xv 6.
[c] Numbers xiv 45 [JE].

Looking back at these sparse records, while recognising their obscurity and the possibility of filling up the gaps by enticing theories, we find certain facts emerging none the less to light. In the first place, Judah was not alone in the attempt to secure the southern highlands, but received indispensable support from the allied non-Israelitish clans of the Kenite and the Kenizzite, in addition to the association of the tribe of Simeon, which was too weak to take independent action. In the second place, the area and places secured for settlement, looked at as a whole, lay around the fringe of the southern highlands, with Hebron as its advanced northerly point. It is reasonable to infer that the whole of this part of the settlement resulted from a joint movement of all concerned from Jericho southward by the shores of the Dead Sea at least as far as Engedi, whence Caleb might climb the heights towards Hebron, while those who were bent on settling, and were presumably driving their flocks before them, would move around the foothills on the easier contour. Indeed the order of incidents as recorded in Judges i, wherein Caleb does not appear until after the attack on Arad and Hormah (v. 20), makes it possible to suppose that the attack on Hebron was the penultimate incident of a long encircling movement, which, proceeding south and west from the City of Palm Trees, wound around the borders of the southern highlands, and finally secured an entry by Debir. Tactically this movement, in which all the threads of the narrative are gathered together in sequence, would seem more practicable than a series of disjointed actions: it was successful in a measure as far as Hebron, but the final effort, the attack on Jerusalem, hitherto postponed, ended admittedly in failure.

JERUSALEM NOT CAPTURED

JOSHUA XV

63 **And as for the Jebusites, the inhabitants of Jerusalem, the children of Judah could not drive them out: but the Jebusites dwelt with the children of Judah at Jerusalem, unto this day. [J]**

JUDGES i

21 **And the children of Benjamin did not drive out the Jebusites that inhabited Jerusalem: but the Jebusites dwelt with the children of Benjamin in Jerusalem, unto this day. [J]**

The Egyptian state archives confirm the tenour of these records. In the reign of Akhenaton (1375-1358 B.C.), when all Palestine was falling away before the advance of the Ḥabiru, Jerusalem remained loyal to the Pharaoh; indeed the king Abd-Khipa proved himself a stout and faithful ally, not only by keeping the Egyptian court informed of the changes and dangers of the times, but even by sending to other loyal vassals such reinforcement as lay within his power and control.[1]

Looking again at the record of these achievements as a whole, we recognise that the only cities captured were secured by the Calebite allies. Judah and Simeon, with the exception of the act of punishment or revenge at Hormah, were seemingly content to remain as goatherds in the undisputed lands between Arad and the Wady Arabah. The process of infiltration and settlement was slow, and the time had evidently not yet come for further penetration of the plateau. Nor is it necessary to suppose that all the conquests of 'Caleb' were accomplished immediately. In the early documents Caleb does not appear as a leader with that strength of personality which gives reality to the life of Joshua; and if his name were lent to the clan of his kinsmen and descendants as was not unusual, some of these events also may overlap the period of the Amarna letters. These documents show that the Egyptian strong centres like Gezer, Ke'ilah, Lachish, Askalon, and Gaza, in addition to Jerusalem, were at

[1] *T.A. Letters*: Kn. 285-290; Louvre A.O. 7096.

first still wholly loyal to the Egyptian cause, but found themselves increasingly menaced by the Ḥabiru invasion,[1] and in informing the Pharaoh their chiefs did not disguise the peril of the moment. Even the prince of Gezer, one of the key positions, appealed almost in despair for help [2]: 'Let my lord, the king, the Sun of heaven, care for his land, for the Ḥabiru are very powerful against us: and let my lord, the king, extend his hand to me, and rescue me from the hand of the Ḥabiru, in order that the Ḥabiru may not destroy us.' Then came the day when the pressure of the marauders became too great, and Abd-Khipa of Jerusalem, almost surrounded by enemies, reported to the Pharaoh [3] that 'the territory of Gazri (Gezer), that of Askalon, and the city of Lachish had given them food, oil, and all necessaries.' Ke'ilah,[4] on the road between Jarmuth and Hebron to the south of Adullam, overlooking the main way of ascent from the plain, and so nearest of all to Kiriath-Sepher, lay equally within the invaded area, for a letter from its chieftain said: 'Know that the SAGAZ (Ḥabiru) are carrying war into the territory which the king has given me. . . . Moreover, that all my brothers have forsaken me, and that I and Abd-Ḥiba are making war on the SAGAZ. . . . The ruler of Akka and the ruler of Aksaph are the helpers to me with fifty chariots.' But the situation worsened. The king of Lachish was murdered by his own servants,[5] themselves turned Ḥabiru: and Lachish is not ten miles from Kiriath-Sepher. At the same time the soldiers of Gezer, Gimti (Gath) and Kilti (Ke'ilah) are reported to have taken the territory of Rubute, the place which more likely than any other is to be identified with Hebron [6]: 'The last of the Kings is lost to the Ḥabiru.' At the same time Abd-Khipa reported the loss of a city in the territory of Jerusalem, called Bit-Ninib, one of the cities

[1] On the Ḥabiru see Sect. 13, below, p. 25[illegible].

[2] Kn. 299.

[3] Kn. 287.

[4] Kh. Kila. See Map 12, p. 171.

[5] Kn. 289.

[6] Kn. 290.

of the king, to the people of Kilti or Ke'ilah. Lastly came the news that the city of Rubute had fallen[1] and that Jerusalem was menaced. 'Shall we then let Jerusalem fall?' enquired the despairing vassal. 'Let the king know that there is no garrison with me. . . . Let the king send fifty garrison men to protect his land. The whole land of the king is going in revolt.'

These brief extracts give a vivid impression of the movement that was rapidly gaining ground and undermining the established order in the land. Other letters suggest that the revolution had been pending for some years before the arrival of the Ḥabiru precipitated the crisis. If Rubute be really identical with Hebron then there is a marked parallelism between the local developments of the Ḥabiru invasion, as described in the letters—the defection of Lachish and Ke'ilah on either side of Debir, the loss of territory around Hebron, the capture of that city and ultimately the menace against Jerusalem itself—and the movement of the Caleb-Judah alliance in the Bible narrative. Now 'Ḥabiru' and 'Hebrew' are regarded by scholars as philological equivalents.[2] When we consider further that the native chieftains, having no special knowledge of the Israelites, and meeting them only as invaders and marauders, would see little if any difference between them and the Ḥabiru, we may well believe that some of the deeds and movements of the Israelites within the Egyptian zone at this time would be duly reported to the Pharaoh as incidents of the invasion as a whole. Some of these letters may then in this case actually relate to activities of the Hebrew-Israelites. Let us not deceive ourselves, however. It is necessary to establish the historicity and approximate date of these episodes before we can look confidently for further information about them in the Amarna letters. Meanwhile we cannot afford to overlook the obvious similarity

[1] Kn. 289.

[2] Burney, *Judges*, lxxiv; *Israel's Settlement*, p. 68; Langdon, *Expos. Times*, xxxi. p. 327. See further below, p. 255.

of the incidents and their setting as recorded in the two different sources, and we recognise once again the exceptional opportunity which the general decline of Egyptian authority afforded the Israelites to make good their footing upon the plateau.

SECTION 11

EPHRAIM AND MANASSEH IN THE CENTRE

Joshua XVI-XVII

JOSHUA xvi

1 **And the lot for the children of Joseph went out from the**
Jordan at Jericho, at the waters of Jericho on the east, even
the wilderness, going up from Jericho through the hill
2 **country to Beth-el; and it went out from Beth-el (to) Luz**
and passed along unto the border of the Archites to
3 **Ataroth; and it went down westward to the border of the**
Japhletites, unto the border of Beth-horon the nether, even
unto Gezer: and the goings out thereof were at the sea.
[J]

SOUTHERN BOUNDARY

THESE verses, quoted from Joshua xvi, contain the only authentic record from the early sources of a tribal boundary. The extract is of special value: not only does it show that the apportioning of the land among the tribes to a certain extent was really attributed to Joshua by the most ancient sources of the Book, but it indicates clearly when read with other early passages, which we shall presently consider, that this apportionment was made in anticipation, not as a result of conquest.[1] Other boundaries like those of Judah[a] and that between Ephraim and Manasseh,[b] which were later described in detail by priestly hands, though they can be traced upon the map, contain recognisable anachronisms,[2] making use for descriptive purposes of place-names familiar at the

[a] Ch. xv 1-12. [b] Ch. xvi 6-8; xvii 7-10.

[1] Cf. Cooke, *Joshua*, pp. 115, 153, n. 1.

[2] Cf. Phythian-Adams, 'The Boundary of Ephraim and Manasseh,' in *P.E.F., Q.S.*, Oct. 1929, pp. 228 ff.

BEITIN, THE SITE OF BETHEL, VIEWED FROM THE E.

Excavations have disclosed fortifications of the 15th century B.C.

KH. SEILUN, POSSIBLE SITE OF SHILOH, APPROACHED FROM THE S.

Excavations have attested the Bronze Age origins of the site.

See pp. 225, 251.

time of writing, as was quite natural after the changes of a thousand years. In these cases it is difficult to estimate without exhaustive archaeological research whether and to what extent the descriptions reflect the political organisation of some later and nearer age, on which, if rightly handled, they might throw much light, or whether they merely repeat in new words the original story of the partition of the land. In this text the description is straightforward, the line followed being roughly that traced by Joshua's first and second campaigns. Starting from the Jordan east of Jericho, and including the water supplies of that town, Ain el Sultan and presumably Ain el Duk,[1] it seems to have followed the high ridge which bounds on the north the route towards Bethel. This can be traced up the track later taken by the Roman road towards Rummon, below which it branches westward towards Bethel, separated from the deserted site of Ai by the intervening valley of the Wady Muheisin. Thence by the watershed between the Wady Hamis, which falls north-westward, and the Wady el Deir, which flows south to join the Wady Surar, the boundary would pass naturally between Ain Arik (? Archi) and Beth-horon the Lower.[2] Descending still westward, it would find the northern boundaries of the valley of Aijalon, after which it is said to have gone even unto Gezer and beyond that city to the sea. This last allusion to the sea, though exceeding the accomplished fact,[a] does not necessarily indicate the priestly hand as often supposed; for, as we have said, the old sources all tend to show that the original partition of the land by sacred lot admittedly preceded the further final efforts of the tribes at conquest and settlement. Though nothing substantial is known about the Archites, Ataroth, or the Japhletites, four places mentioned in this text, namely Jericho, Bethel, Beth-horon the Lower, and Gezer, were among the leading cities of the age. The special allusion to Beth-horon as

[a] Cf. xvi 10 [J].

[1] See Pl. XXIV, Map, p. 155. [2] Pl. LI, and Map, p. 171.

'the nether' does not necessarily indicate a redactor's hand: for although Upper Beth-horon apparently only came into existence in the Early Iron Age, it had become well known in the ninth century when the records 'J' took written form. The boundary, then, so far as it can be followed, is defined in general terms by natural features or by the position of contemporary cities.

The first stage in the occupation of the territory thus assigned was evidently the capture of Bethel, already long deferred, and this was now undertaken by the tribes of Ephraim and Manasseh, working still together as the house of Joseph. No record of the event is preserved in the Book of Joshua, and we quote the relevant passage from the first chapter of the Book of Judges.

JUDGES i. *Bethel*

22 And the house of Joseph, they also went up against
23 Bethel: and the Lord was with them, and the house of
24 Joseph sent to spy out Bethel. And the watchers saw a
25 man come forth out of the city. . . . And he shewed them
the entrance into the city, and they smote the city with the
edge of the sword. [J]

No record of any victory in this part of the highlands has survived, other than this tardy capture of Bethel. Although this passage occurs in the Book of Judges in an appropriate geographical sequence, after the narrative of the taking of Hebron and before the further problems of Manasseh in the north, there is no reason to suppose that the movements of Ephraim and Manasseh (*i.e.* the house of Joseph) to possess the central highlands were not commenced at the same time as those of Judah, Simeon and Caleb to possess the south. The site of Bethel has been described. It lay barely two miles west of Ai, and though its people had been drawn out in the conflict when the latter place was burned,[a] no attack seems to have been made at the time on the city itself.

[a] Joshua viii 17 [J].

BEIT UR EL TAHTA, BETHHORON THE LOWER, FROM THE EAST.

The site is ancient, and shows signs of occupation in the Bronze Age.

BETHHORON: DEFENSIVE TERRACE SCARPS ON THE NORTH SIDE.

The lower terraces preserve traces of megalithic walls.

See pp. 168, 179.

A short excavation made upon the site of Bethel, still largely occupied by the modern village of Beitîn, has determined that, like all other strong places of the time, the city was surrounded in the Late Bronze Age by a stout defensive wall of stone. The section examined proved to be preserved to a height of thirteen feet. A layer of destruction was disclosed, which the excavator dated on evidence in round figures to 1400 B.C.[1] Though so closely agreeing with observed facts the brief record of the capture of Bethel leaves much unexplained, and arouses further questions. It was for Israel an event of first importance. Bethel held for them ancestral memories and deep religious associations; yet the account is meagre compared with that of the taking of Ai, a relatively uninteresting place. Between these two sites there may be seen, at a point on the edge of and overlooking the deep descent to the Jordan valley, a small platform of rock and earth, bearing to-day the name Burj Beitin, with which is associated in modern times, but from what antiquity we cannot say, the old story of Jacob's dream. This position corresponds with that of the mountain on the east of Bethel, 'having Bethel on the west and Ai on the east,' where Abram pitched his tent and built an altar to Jehovah.[a]

JUDGES i. *Luz*

26 And the man went into the land of the Hittites, and built a city and called the name thereof Luz: which is the name thereof unto this day. [J]

In some contexts Hittites are regarded as settled at the foot of Hermon[b]; but the 'Land of the Hittites,' from the point of view prevailing when this narrative took form, would refer to the Orontes valley or the territory farther north, lying between the range of Amanus and the

[a] Genesis xiii 3 [J]. [b] Joshua xi 3 [LXX].

[1] Albr., *Bull. Am. S.O.R.*, N. 29, February 1928, pp. 10-11, and *Zeits. f. alttest. Wiss.* 1929, i. p. 11.

Euphrates. It is true that in 1400 B.C. the Hittite Empire, centred hitherto in Asia Minor, was on the eve of a great expansion under Subbiluliuma, a warrior-king who, during the early part of the fourteenth century, overran Mesopotamia and wrested from Egypt the suzerainty of Syria. The story of his conquests, reaching southward, is told in parallel both in the Tell El Amarna Letters, and in the archives of the Ḥattic kings of Asia Minor, which have been recovered only this century from the ruins of the palaces in their far-off capital beyond the Halys River.[1] With the Hittites were associated the SA-GAZ or Ḥabiru, probably as mercenary troops.[2] The evidence of discoveries made during excavations on the sites of Bethshean, Shechem, Jerusalem and Gerar, suggests that the Hittites possessed themselves at this time of Palestine.[3] Their effective occupation or domination appears to have lasted, however, only a short time (perhaps from 1375 till 1360 B.C.). Tutenkhamon through his general Harmhab, about 1360 B.C., took steps towards restoring the Egyptian authority; but the sculptures illustrating the campaigns of his successors Seti I and Ramses II, at the close of the century, still show a strong Hittite element among the population of the country. This interlude, though it may explain how the traitor of Bethel was able to travel in safety and take up his abode in the land of the Hittites, was probably not present in the mind of the first archivists of Israel when they set down the records of tradition. In their day, during the ninth century B.C., the Hittite Empire was a faded memory of the past; for about 1200 B.C. the military and social organisation of Asia Minor gave way before a great migration of Iron Age peoples from Europe, which carried all with fire before it.[4] Thereafter the most active centres of the old Hittite influence are

[1] By the late Dr. Winckler: cf. G., *H.E.*, p. 5, n. 5.

[2] On this question see below, Sect. 13, p. 256.

[3] Cf. G., *H.E.*, p. 333.

[4] Breasted, *A.R.*, iv. 64: see further below, p. 308.

found in the far north of Syria on the south side of Taurus. Cities and palaces of Hittite kings of these later centuries, down to 700 B.C., have been found and in some cases excavated, at Marash, Sinjerli, Sakje-Geuzi and Carchemish, the last-named being possibly the most important of these now disunited centres.[1] These were the homes of the kings of the Hittites, whose fame in war found its echo later in the Chronicles of Israel.[a] Cities like Hamath, Homs, Kadesh and Katna, in and near the valley of the Orontes, had been at times subject to the Hittite kings and had become imbued to some extent with Hittite methods and organisation; but their population, so far as can be seen, was rather Amorite than Hittite. There is no trace, moreover, of any city in that vicinity by the name of Luz.[2]

The capture of Bethel by the house of Joseph, which placed a key to the central highlands in possession of the Israelites, remains, however, the one military success on record affecting the penetration of the tribes of Ephraim and Manasseh. That they made progress in their advance northwards is certain, as we shall see, but the method and process are unknown, nor is there any record of further fighting. Certain non-successes, however, are mentioned, and these show clearly that whatever progress may have been made along the highlands northward, the efforts of the Josephites and other tribes to establish themselves upon the western plains ended in complete failure.

[a] II Kings vii 6.

[1] Cf. G., *H.E.*, pp. 11, 278, 334.

[2] There remains the possibility of a confusion between Luz and Laish (Judg. xviii 27), otherwise written Leshem (Josh. xix 47). In the list of cities conquered by Thutmose III (*c.* 1475 B.C.), No. 31 appears as *L'.wy.s'*, or more briefly *Lws*. It precedes a group of names, *Hazor*, *Pahel*, *Kinneret*, which belong to the Upper Jordan valley, and would seem therefore to represent Laish, indicating at the same time a native pronunciation with a *u*-sound following the initial letter, corresponding to the Hebrew spelling in *Luz*. The 'Land of the Hittites' would in that case refer to the country around the S.E. foot of Hermon (above, p. 103). A Hittite residence of this period stood at Sheikh Sa'd upon the eastern plateau above Laish (G., *H.E.*, p. 327 and Pl. LIII).

Gezer not captured

JOSHUA xvi	JUDGES i
10 **And they drave not out the Canaanites that dwelt in Gezer: but the Canaanites dwelt in the midst of Ephraim unto this day, and became servants to do taskwork. [J]**	29 **And Ephraim drave not out the Canaanites that dwelt in Gezer; but the Canaanites dwelt in Gezer among them. [J]**

These passages are of interest in two ways. In the first place, both records agree that Ephraim, the southern constituent member of the house of Joseph, was unequal to the task of driving out the Canaanite inhabitants of Gezer. This city was strongly placed, and occupied a key position astride the main north-south road,[1] commanding the approaches from the plateau, notably those by the Bab el Wad and the Vale of Sorek, to the coast at Jaffa. Moreover, Gezer was governed by an Egyptian vassal and ally, who held firm before the advancing Ḥabiru, until they appeared at his gates demanding provisions.[2] Indeed, the archaeological remains discovered in the excavation of this city[3] attest uniquely, among the general surrender or disaffection of the surrounding cities, that relations with Egypt were maintained throughout the two reigns most concerned, those of Amenhotep III and IV. It was not until the age of Solomon that this Canaanite city lost its independence; even then its fall was brought about by Egyptian troops.[a] No city in the central part of the coastal plain could claim so wide a range of influence, nor a position politically and historically so assured: it may safely be said that while Gezer stood the central area of the coastlands was denied to Israel.

The two verses quoted, when compared, disclose the building of the record to its present form. The account

[a] I Kings ix 16, 17.

[1] Map No. 5.

[2] *T.A. Letters*, Kn. 298-300 and 287.

[3] Macalister, *The Excavation of Gezer*, i. p. 136; ii. p. 100.

in the Book of Joshua, beginning with the sentence 'they drave not out,' follows naturally the sequence of xvi. 3, and regards the movement as a joint action of the children of Joseph. The second sentence, like the passage from the Book of Judges, shows knowledge of the subsequent separation of Ephraim from Manasseh, and of the territory assigned to each. The words 'unto this day' bring the redaction down at any rate to the ninth century B.C.; while the last sentence, 'and became servants to do taskwork,' suggests the Deuteronomic hand of the sixth century, and certainly could not have been said truthfully until the age of Solomon.

Non-success of Dan

That the occupation of the coastlands and even of the western slopes was not effective appears from further extracts describing the non-success, and ultimately the migration, of the tribe of Dan.

JOSHUA xix	JUDGES i
47 **And the border of the children of Dan went out beyond them. [J]**	34 **And the Amorites forced the children of Dan into the hill country: for they would not suffer them to come down to the valley.**
	35 **But the Amorites would dwell in Mount Heres, in Aijalon, and in Shaalbim.**

These passages contain the first mention of Dan, for there is no reference hitherto of an allocation of territory to this tribe. Tradition embodied in this same chapter of the Book of Joshua,[a] and ascribed to the post-exilic school (P), defines the border of Dan by a number of sites already allocated in xv 33 [P] to Judah, including Zorah, Eshtaol and Ekron (45). These passages, however, we have already found to require examination before their value can be gauged. It included further, according to the same source, Irshemesh, Aijalon,

[a] Joshua xix 40, 41 [P].

Timnah, and even the port of Joppa.[1] This allocation, as we see from the old sources, was never realised, and the tribe of Dan migrated to the north. None the less the names Mt. Heres,[2] comparable with Ir-Shemesh, and Aijalon, occurring in the record of Judges i 34 from the early source, show that the description of the boundary by the post-exilic writer, P, was founded upon more ancient tradition, though introducing names of places that had sprung up meanwhile. The fact is stated in the one extract and confirmed in the other that the Israelites represented by Dan failed at that time to occupy the coastlands, and were not allowed even to come down into the valley of Aijalon, notwithstanding Joshua's previous victory. The strong arm of Gezer had apparently been roused to intervene in an area so intimately concerned with its own trade interests and the military policy of Egypt.

To sum up, we have been informed by the early sources of the allocation to the House of Joseph of the territory lying northwards of a line that passed by Bethel and Gezer, of the occupation of Bethel, and of the failure of Ephraim to possess itself of Gezer. The experience of Dan confirms the impression already created by other passages, that in fact the Israelites gained no appreciable footing in the coastal plains. The next record takes us to the northern boundary of the House of Joseph, where Manasseh found its northward penetration barred by a row of fortresses reaching from the Jordan to the sea. There is no light whatever on the method of progression thus far; apart from the taking of Bethel there is as yet no indication of the occupation of any large towns, nor even the suggestion anywhere of a struggle or of opposition. Yet it is obvious that the House of Joseph was establishing itself and expanding northwards, and we are

[1] *Yapu* of the Amarna letters, the modern Jaffa, which with Gaza seems to have held out against the Ḫabiru : Kn. 294, 296.

[2] The Mount of the Sun : Cooke, *Judges*, p. 21, n. 35 ; Burney, *Judges*, p. 32, n. 35. The site of Beth-Shemesh (temple of the sun) is still associated with the name 'Ain-Shems, Spring of the Sun. The Legends of 'Samson' are associated with the same locality. Cf. Plates LXIX, LXXIII, and p. 334.

THE WADY SELMAN BELOW BETHHORON.

The gorge which links the plain of Gibeon with the valley of Aijalon. cf. Joshua x, 12.

TELL EL KOKAH, THE ORIGINAL SITE OF AIJALON, FROM THE S.W.

The valley of Aijalon, traversed by a road, is seen opening out on the L.

See pp. 87, 180.

left to infer that the movement was one of peaceful penetration; the spreading of tents in a depopulated area, where walled towns were few, and the inhabitants under the circumstances of the day might respond to friendly overtures. It is not necessary to assume that at this stage they must have formed any definite alliance, the record of which has been expunged. The Israelites would find blood relatives established in these parts, and in the neighbourhood of Shechem may have made good their title to their patrimony. The silence of the records in this case is eloquent, and it would seem impossible that the memory of any conflict in this area would have totally escaped notice in both the Books of Joshua and Judges. The fact that Joshua and the House of Joseph were able in succeeding years to remove their headquarters and the Ark from Bethel to Shiloh and eventually to Shechem,[1] confirms the supposition that peaceful relations of an accepted and helpful character developed without serious interruption.

THE NORTHERN BOUNDARY

JOSHUA xvii

11 And Manasseh had in Issachar and in Asher Beth-shean and her towns, and Ibleam and her towns, and the inhabitants of Dor and her towns, and the inhabitants of En-dor and her towns, and the inhabitants of Taanach and her towns, and the inhabitants of Megiddo and her towns, even the three heights.[a]
12 Yet the children of Manasseh could not drive out the inhabitants of those cities; but the Canaanites would dwell in that land. [J]

JUDGES i

27 And Manasseh did not drive out the inhabitants of Beth-shean and her towns, nor of Taanach and her towns, nor the inhabitants of Dor and her towns, nor the inhabitants of Ibleam and her towns, nor the inhabitants of Megiddo and her towns: but the Canaanites would dwell in that land.
28 And it came to pass, when Israel was waxen strong that they put the Canaanites to taskwork, and did not utterly drive them out. [J]

[a] Possibly 'districts.' A.V. 'countries.'

[1] See further below, pp. 250 f.

The row of fortresses which barred the further progress of Manasseh towards the north reached from the River Jordan to the sea, comprising in order Bethshean, Ibleam, Taanak, Megiddo and Dor,[1] the last-named upon the coast. These places were all strongly fortified, and we have already seen that they were disposed along the natural frontier of the Canaanite area centred on Hazor.[2] Each city guarded a strategic pass.[3] Two of them, namely, Ibleam and Bethshean, lay directly across the northward tracks of Manasseh. The one on Tell Bilameh looked down on the central road from Bethel and Shechem, where this descended by the Wady Bilameh from the plain of Dothan past Jenin into Esdraelon.[4] The other, as we have seen, commanded the Jordan valley at its juncture with the valley of Jezreel. Between Bethshean and Ibleam rose the bold sweeping slopes of Mt. Gilboa. Taanak[5] and Megiddo were stationed along the ridge which separates Esdraelon from Sharon, and above them towers the volcanic cone of Um el Fahm. Dor, if rightly identified with Dora at Tantura on the coast, lay practically at the foot of Carmel; and Endor, which is associated with it in one context,[a] should be sought on the slopes of that mountain.[6] Viewed from this aspect in the sequence of the passage from the Book of Joshua, the system composes itself into

[a] Joshua xvii 11 [J].

[1] Plates LIII, LXVI, XX, and IX respectively.

[2] P. 105 and Map 13. [3] P. 89 and Map 6. [4] Cf. Pl. XII.

[5] *Bibl.* Taanach ; *Arab.* Tell Ta'anuk.

[6] Though we accept provisionally the identification of the Canaanite Dor with the coastal Dora, the name of which appears in the Egyptian story of Wen Amon (*c.* 1110 B.C.), the equation still seems open to doubt and gives rise in its turn to difficulties. The familiar Endor of the 1st Book of Samuel (xxviii 7) on the northern slopes of Jebel Duhy or Little Hermon, seems not to be a Bronze Age site ; but hardly a mile towards the west, upon an isolated knoll called Tell el Ajjul, there may be seen the traces of an important city of the period, subsequently deserted and later reoccupied by a Roman garrison. We cannot elude the possibility that this may mark the site of Dor, though the ancient name now appears only in that of its associated spring 'Ain Dor or Endor, which is found above the present village. In this case the order of the names in the Book of Joshua (xvii 11 J) would be correct, and Little Hermon would replace Carmel as the third of the heights or Naphoth.

TELL HUSN, THE SITE OF BETHSHEAN; WITH THE BRONZE AGE NECROPOLIS L.

In the background, the Jordan valley: on the R., the village of Beisan.

See pp. 71, 271.

three groups by pairs, each pair with its associated height, on the left wing Bethshean and Ibleam with Gilboa (1650 feet), on the right wing Dor and Endor with Carmel (1800 feet), in the centre Ta'anak and Megiddo with Um el Fahm (1700 feet).

It is not possible to appraise the value of the suggestion that the word *Naphoth* read as 'heights' in the R.V. and 'countries' in the A.V. may connote administrative districts.[1] Independent details as to the early organisation of the area are not available. All five places are mentioned as conquered cities in the lists of Thutmose III. In the Amarna letters, Bethshean and Megiddo appear clearly as centres of Egyptian authority, but Dor lay off the track and we are without evidence of its status at that time. On this matter we must await further light. The insufficiency of scientific explorations makes it also impossible to point out the sites of the smaller towns which evidently were dependent upon these several parent cities. The Tell el Amarna letters in the case of Jerusalem and of Hazor disclose similar local organisation; but until each village site of to-day and every Khurbeh or ruin of antiquity has been scientifically examined, it will not be possible to give a reliable picture of the territorial organisation of those days. One small tell, called Abu Kudeis, in the vicinity of Taanak, a large one Abu Shusheh, on the edge of the ridge near Megiddo, and a few tells lying to the south of Beisan are all the sites that can be said at the present time to have been certainly in occupation in the fourteenth and fifteenth centuries B.C., and presumably they would be grouped with the greater cities in the scheme. These places lie in the plains, and it would not be surprising if search for others among the neighbouring hills proved fruitless. Even to-day the country to the north of Shechem is much more wooded than the south,[2] and there

[1] Cf. Albright, 'The Administrative Divisions of Israel and Judah' in *J.P.O.S.* v (1925), pp. 17 ff.

[2] See Pl. LIV.

still remain traces both N.E. and N.W. of great forests. Towards the north-west in particular, along the broken ridge that separates Esdraelon from the coast, scrub oak is widespread, and this seems to have been the case in antiquity, as may be gathered from the purposely-exaggerated descriptions of an Egyptian courier in the thirteenth century B.C.[1] It may be believed that much of this region would have to be reclaimed from nature before it could be occupied. Consequently the plea of the House of Joseph for more space, the permission accorded, and the subsequent penetration of Manasseh eastwards assume a fresh reality.

JOSHUA xvii. *Eastward expansion authorised*

14 **And the children of Joseph spake unto Joshua, saying,**
Why hast thou given me but one lot and one part for an
inheritance, seeing I am a great people, forasmuch as
15 **hitherto the Lord has blessed me ? And Joshua said unto**
them, If thou be a great people, get thee up to the forest,
and cut down for thyself there in the land of the Perizzites
and of the Rephaim; since the hill country of Ephraim is
16 **too narrow for thee. And the children of Joseph said,**
The hill country is not enough for us: and all the Canaan-
ites that dwell in the land of the valley have chariots of
iron, both they who are in Beth-shean and her towns, and
17 **they who are in the valley of Jezreel. And Joshua spake**
unto the house of Joseph, even to Ephraim and to Man-
asseh, saying, Thou art a great people, and hast great
power; thou shalt not have one lot only: but the hill
18 **country shall be thine: for though it is a forest, thou shalt**
cut it down and the goings out thereof shall be thine: for
thou shalt drive out the Canaanites, though they have
chariots of iron, and though they be strong. [J]

The text shows that no expansion was practicable towards the north; and it must be recognised that any

[1] Above, p. 91. The face of the country has undergone great changes even since the Middle Ages: cf. George Adam Smith, *Hist. Geog.* p. 81.

Pl. LIV.

THE HILL COUNTRY OF MANASSEH, FROM THE N.

In the centre the hill of Shemer,' later the site of Samaria.

See pp. 234. 272.

advance towards the west and north-west would most probably be sternly contested on account of the political and military importance of the routes by which that region was traversed. With the ten thousand of Ephraim pressing from the south, and ultimately enfolding Shechem, only one immediate outlet presented itself to Manasseh, namely, the wooded hill country lying away over the inner slopes of Gilboa, between Dothan and the Jordan valley. Cutting their way in that direction, Manasseh might ultimately occupy the valleys and passes, the 'goings out,' that led down to the Jordan, and so secure access to the wider territory on the farther side. Such an eastward expansion seems to be reflected in the age of Seti I by the stela found recently in excavation at Beisan.[1]

[1] P. 73. See further below, p. 272, and cf. Cook, S.A., in *C.A.H.*, ii. p. 370.

SECTION 12

TRIBAL PORTIONS IN THE NORTH

Issachar, Zebulun, Asher, Naphtali and Dan

JOSHUA xviii. *Joshua at Shiloh*

2 **And there remained among the children of Israel seven**
3 **tribes which had not divided their inheritance. And**
5 **Joshua said . . . Judah shall abide in his border on the**
south, and the house of Joseph shall abide in their border
6 **on the north. And ye shall describe the land into seven**
portions, and bring the description hither to me; and I will
cast lots for you here before the Lord our God. [JE]

THOUGH the wording of this instructive passage, as it stands, is deemed by critics to be no earlier than the first half of the seventh century B.C. when the old documents, J and E, were welded together, the independent evidence of those older sources shows no reason to mistrust the bearing of the record upon the early separation and settlement of the tribes. As we have seen in the three preceding chapters, priority is given in both Books to the claims of Judah with Caleb and of the House of Joseph, and the latter is regarded as separating into the two tribes of Ephraim and Manasseh, so that three tribes have received their portions at this stage. Two others, Reuben and Gad, according to recognised tradition which can be traced back in the Book of Joshua to a pre-exilic origin,[a] had their inheritance on the east side of Jordan, having received it already, according to this record, from the hand of Moses; and they are therefore not included in the 'seven tribes' of our quotation. But in one way or another these seven tribes are all mentioned in the older documents. Thus in the Book of Judges we find Simeon to have been associated with Judah in two early expeditions,[b]

[a] Joshua xviii 7 [D]. [b] Judges i 3, 17 [J].

while in connexion with the northern boundary of Manasseh there is mention in the Book of Joshua [a] of both Issachar and of Asher. It is true that the allusion seemingly anticipates the allocation of their territory and is strictly speaking anachronistic, nor does it appear in the parallel passage from the Book of Judges.[b] There is to be found, however, independent testimony as to the existence and position of Issachar,[c] while Asher is the subject of a separate paragraph [d] in the first chapter of the Book of Judges. This last context speaks of difficulties which that tribe encountered, while adjoining paragraphs make mention of Zebulun and Naphtali and also of Dan in a similar connexion. The subsequent migration of Dan is mentioned in the Book of Joshua,[e] and exceptionally full details concerning this event are preserved in a sort of appendix to the Book of Judges,[f] which is largely derived from the oldest sources. The tribe of Benjamin is not mentioned at all in the old sources of the Book of Joshua, nor in the Book of Judges until during the second oppression, from which Israel was delivered by Ehud the Benjamite.[g] The tribe responded, however, to the call of Deborah; and its subsequent misadventures are the subject of a long and ancient legend embodied likewise in the concluding chapters of the Book of Judges.[h] These several contexts thus indicate independently the separate existence in the earliest tradition of the seven tribes of Simeon, Issachar, Zebulun, Asher, Naphtali, Dan and Benjamin, completing, with the three tribes whose territory has already been assigned and the two tribes beyond Jordan, the number of twelve tribes corresponding with tradition; so that, though the passage quoted above [i] appears only to date from the early part of the seventh century B.C., it demonstrably embodies more ancient memories. It would appear probable, indeed, that some substantial portion of the Book of

[a] Joshua xvii 11 [J]. [b] Judges i 27 [J]. [c] Judges v 15 [E].
[d] Judges i 31 [J]. [e] Joshua xix 47 [J]. [f] Judges xviii.
[g] Judges iii 15 [E2]. [h] Judges xix-xxi. [i] Joshua xviii 2 ff. [JE].

Joshua at this place has been lost, or submerged by later explanations, for the old sources as such tell us independently little or nothing as to the subsequent fortunes of the tribes. We are left with only a few isolated paragraphs describing the difficulties they encountered in taking up their allotted territory.

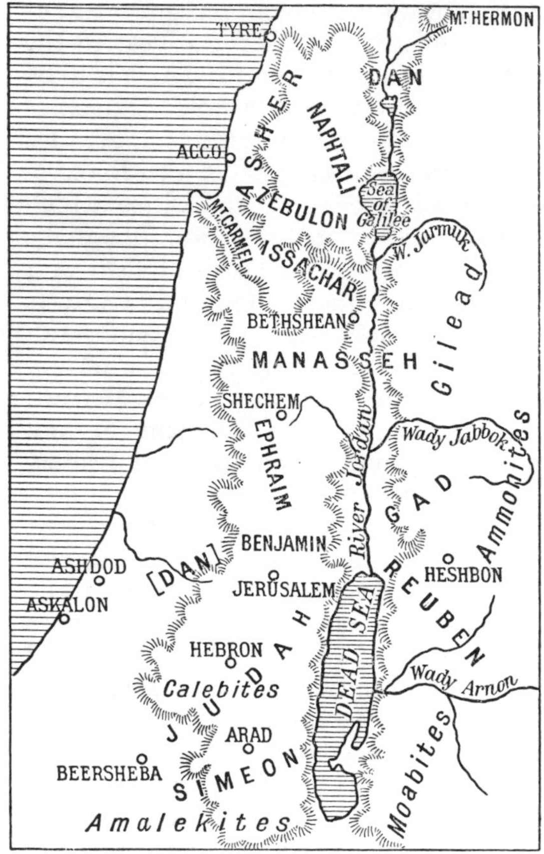

Map 15. The Tribal Portions.

The setting of these paragraphs and the belated appeal to the sacred Lot suggest indeed that the settlement of these northern and southern tribes was a slower, and more difficult process than that of the House of Joseph in the centre. Until the age of Deborah, nearly a hundred and fifty years later, Biblical narrative contains indeed no further indication that their settlement had been effected. In the meanwhile, however, there appears independent allusion in the Egyptian records of the early thirteenth century B.C. to the tribe of Asher,[1]

[1] *Pap. Anast.* I, xix 23, 8. Ed. Gardiner, p. 25 and n. 12; Leps., *Denk.* III. 140a. Meyer, *Israeliten*, p. 540. Müller, *Asien*, p. 236.

while the establishment of the other northern tribes before the end of that century seems also to be confirmed by the well-known reference to 'Israel' on the stele of Merneptah.[1] Both these allusions will be found discussed below.[2]

The only information about the tribes to be derived from the old sources of the Book of Joshua at this early stage of their separation is a record of unsuccessful efforts. These allusions have, however, their value. We can recognise from the places mentioned that the area of each tribe's activities conforms in a general way with its traditional boundaries as defined much later by the priestly redactors.[a] The organised administrative areas of the monarchy in subsequent centuries should not, however, mislead us as to the realities of the situation in the age of Joshua. We must rather picture these tribal detachments as moving off in small groups, profiting by political circumstances and supported by Joshua's own acquired position and reputation, feeling their way through untold difficulties by slow stages towards their allotted portions.

ISSACHAR

Issachar we have already met on the northern border of Manasseh.[3] The impregnable fortresses of Beth-shean, Ibleam, Taanak and Megiddo, which at all times played a leading part in the Egyptian or Canaanite control of this area, separated it from the territory of Manasseh. They fringe the southern border to the valley of Jezreel and the plain of Esdraelon, wherein later allusions also regularly place this tribe. The Lot had reserved to Issachar the choicest area in all Palestine for camp life; and the fact is reflected by the words used in the Blessing of Moses:[4] *Rejoice . . . Issachar, in thy tents.*[b]

[a] Joshua xix 10 ff. [b] Cf. Deuteronomy xxxiii 18.

[1] Breasted, *Anct. Rec.* iii 617. [2] See pp. 242, 291. [3] Above, p. 231.

[4] On the historical value and antiquity of this poem see the instructive paper by Phythian-Adams in *J.P.O.S.* iii, pp. 158 ff.

On the other hand, the strength of the Canaanite cities clearly restrained the people of Issachar for many generations from securing territorial rights, and the privilege of settling in the region seems to have been obtained at the price of their personal servitude:

He saw a resting place that it was good,
And the land that it was pleasant ;
And he bowed his shoulder to bear
And became a servant under taskwork.[a] [J]

JUDGES i

ZEBULUN

30 Zebulun drave not out the inhabitants of Kitron nor of Nahalol. [J]

Kitron is unknown. Nahalol may be identified with Malul, which occupies an ancient site in a situation corresponding well with later tradition. This place overlooks the plain of Esdraelon from the north, being one of the boundary cities on that side, and it would mark the southern limit to the zone of Zebulun. It stands on high ground among wooded slopes, to the north-east of a broad fertile extension of Esdraelon, which here stretches out, as it were, a hand towards the north. In that direction Zebulun would comprise the inland plain of the Buttauf, which was traversed by the most useful trade route of antiquity, the ' Way of the Sea.' This, coming from beyond Jordan by way of Tell Abeidiyeh,[1] led straight across lower Galilee, and descended by the Wady Abellin upon Acco, nature's seaport for Canaan and Damascus. ' Rejoice Zebulun in thy going out! '[b] Its boundary on the north at this time cannot be ascertained, but the scope originally intended is clearly indicated by the early sources of other Books:

Zebulun shall dwell at the haven of the Sea
And he shall be for an haven of ships,
And his border shall be upon Zidon.[c] [J]

[a] Genesis xlix 15 [J]. [b] Deuteronomy xxxiii 18. [c] Genesis xlix 13 [J].

[1] See above, pp. 73, 99 f.

ACRE, THE SEA-WALL, FROM THE N.W.
In the background Haifa and the slopes of Carmel.

ACRE, THE MODERN TOWN AND BAY.
The ancient Acco stood inland, on Tell el Fokhar.

See pp. 96, 241.

ASHER

JUDGES i

31 Asher drave not out the inhabitants of Acco nor of Zidon nor of Achzib. The Asherites dwelt among the Canaanites, the inhabitants of the land: for they did not drive them out. [J]

The information in this case is definite. These three places are known, being still called by much the same names, Acre, Sidon and El Zib.[1] Four other places mentioned in the texts, Ahlab, Helbah, Aphik and Rehob, are less certain, indeed Ahlab and Helbah may prove to be only variant forms of the same name, which appears as Mahalab in other versions,[a] and seems to be recognisable as *Maḥalleba* mentioned by Sennacherib[2] together with Achzib and Acco. Rehob again may be identical with a place north of the Kishon mentioned by the Egyptian records as *Raḥubu*.[3] The suggestion is that these places lay inland along the edge of the border hills of the plain of Acre.

The southern boundary of Asher seems from earliest times to have comprehended Mt. Carmel; the words,[b] 'Manasseh had . . . in Asher . . . the inhabitants of Dor and her towns, and the inhabitants of Endor and her towns,' imply at least that, while the city of Dor lay possibly within the confines of Manasseh, the territory allocated to Asher included parts of the lands of Dor and its dependent towns. Later tradition adheres to Carmel as the southern boundary[c] and confirms the northward extension of the Lot even unto great Zidon.[d] A further reference, 'and the goings out thereof were at the sea, by the region of [or, from Hebel to] Achzib: Ummah also and Aphek and Rehob,' helps to define the general position of the last-named places. Asher touched thus

[a] *Var.*, Joshua xix 29 [E]. [b] Joshua xvii 11 [J].
[c] Joshua xix 26 [P]. [d] Joshua xix 28 [P].

[1] See Plates XLVII, LV. [2] Cf. Cooke, *Joshua*, p. 181. Burney, *Judges*, p. 28.
[3] Otherwise *Ra-ḥ-bu*; cf. Müller, *Asien*, p. 153, quoting *Pap. Anast.* IV, 17, 3.

upon the Phoenician seaboard, and lay entirely within the active political and commercial zone of Canaan and of Egypt. In such a situation the Asherites were probably more exposed to cultural and racial absorption than any other tribe. 'Out of Asher his bread shall be fat. And he shall eat royal dainties.'[a] The princes of Acco and Achshaph were staunch supporters of Egyptian rule; and the prosperity of their country, borne in by caravans, depended upon the maintenance of order and good relations.[1] Consequently, the penetration of Asher, when once a footing had been established, proved relatively easy, so that from the year 1300 B.C. onwards the tribe was sufficiently consolidated, and its independence so far recognised as to obtain separate mention in the records both of Seti I and of Ramses II, in the Egyptian form *'A-sh-r*.[2] Within a century, however, the situation had changed, and Deborah called on the tribe in vain.[3]

NAPHTALI

JUDGES i

33 Naphtali drave not out the inhabitants of Bethshemesh nor the inhabitants of Beth-anath; but he dwelt among the Canaanites, the inhabitants of the land. [J]

Naphtali, though not located by the early text of Joshua, is known from well-substantiated tradition to have occupied the eastern part of Upper Galilee. According to the post-exilic description,[b] it touched Asher on the west and Zebulun on the south. In the Jordan valley at that late date, it was regarded as embracing Chinnereth, identified with Tell 'Oreimeh on the north-west shore of the Sea of Galilee, as well as Hazor in the Huleh Basin. But at this time its inheritance was still limited

[a] Genesis xlix 20 [J]. [b] Joshua xix 34, 36 [P].

[1] Cf. *Amarna Letters*, Kn. No. 8, in which the king of *Karadunias* [Babylonia] complains to the Pharaoh of the robbery of his caravans at *Ḥinnatuni* (? Tell El Bedeiwiyeh, p. 100) near Acre. Cf. also Weber, *Anmerk*. p. 1027.

[2] See above, p. 98, n. 2. [3] Below, p. 305.

to the Galilean hills. The two strongholds Beth-Shemesh and Beth-Anath, which the tribe could not occupy, clearly dominated the situation. These places

Fig. 4. Kedesh [Naphtali] taken by Seti I, *c.* 1310 B.C.
[*Site of a Sun temple, and possibly to be identified with Beth-Shemesh of Judges* i 33.]

have not hitherto been located: the names are in fact those of sanctuaries, the one of a sun-god and the other of the Canaanite goddess Anath; so that possibly the cities themselves which claimed these holy places were called by other names. Now the two most powerful Bronze Age cities that have been recognised upon the eastern plateau of Upper Galilee were at Kedesh (Kades) and at El Khurbeh.[1] It is consequently significant to find that at Kedesh, the name of which implies the presence of a sanctuary, there survive to this day traces of a solar cult in the Roman remains still visible upon the site.[2]

Fig. 5. Beth-Anath, taken by Ramses II, *c.* 1289 B.C.

The area of ancient Kedesh is divided into two parts, one of which may prove to have been devoted to the sanctuary, the other to the civil community. Egyptian scenes represent Kedesh as a powerful fortress, which was not finally demolished until the reign of Seti I, *c.* 1310 B.C.[3]

The identity of El Khurbeh with Beth-Anath is indicated only in a general way by its situation and the strength of its position,[4] but no other site has been discovered which will satisfy the archaeological and

[1] See p. 101, and Pl. LXI.

[2] Sculptures associated with the 'Temple of the Sun' at Kadesh recall certain details at Ba'albek. There is, moreover, record of a 'winged deity, the sun' (*P.E.F.*, Survey I, p. 227), and also of an altar, since lost, upon which the deity is represented as solar-radiate; cf. Cook, S. A., *The Religion of Ancient Palestine in the Light of Archaeology*, 1930, Pl. XXXV.

[3] See our illustration drawn from a photograph of a relief at Medinet Habu, p. 243, and cf. Wreszinski, *Atlas*, No. 53.

[4] Cf. above, p. 101.

strategical conditions of the contexts. The Egyptian representation of Beth-Anath in the age of Ramses II, which we reproduce,[1] shows the place to be defended after the usual fashion of the Canaanite cities by a migdol or battlemented tower, but the inhabitants wear distinctive features of dress. The worship of the old Syrian war-goddess Anath[2] in this part of Galilee, reflected possibly, but not with philological certainty, in the local name 'Ainitha,[3] may indicate a special element in the population surviving from Hyksos times, and so throw more light upon the application of the word 'Goyyim' to this region, as seen in the familiar expression, Galilee of the Gentiles,[a] and extending in the case of Harosheth of the Gentiles,[b] to the coastal plain. However that may be, the identity of Beth-Anath with El Khurbeh seems likely, and the strength of its position would explain the difficulty with which the tribe of Naphtali remained confronted until in the thirteenth century Ramses II destroyed the city and dismantled its fortifications.[4]

DAN

Joshua xix

47 The children of Dan went up and fought against Leshem, and took it, . . . and possessed it, and dwelt therein, and called Leshem, Dan, after the name of Dan their father. [J]

The attempt of Dan to settle in the valley of Aijalon and the Shephelah, to the west of the Hivite territory, and their non-success, have already been discussed.[5] This passage introduces the sequel, confirmed and amplified

[a] Isaiah ix 1. [b] Judges iv 2 [E].

[1] Fig. 5 after Lepsius, *Denkmäler*, III, B. 1, 156.

[2] On this cult see Cook, S. A., *The Religion of Ancient Palestine*, pp. 104 ff.; also Vincent in *Rev. Bibl.* 1928, p. 541 f.

[3] 'Ainitha is the name of a modern Mutaweleh village to the north of the Jebel Marun. The philological relation of 'Ainitha with Anath is, however, open to some doubt, and is disputed by Albright: *Bull. Am. S.O.R.* No. 35, p. 9.

[4] Below, pp. 279 f. [5] P. 229.

by the old legend of Judges xviii,[1] indicating the migration of the tribe northwards to a territory less difficult to secure. The general direction of the new quest is briefly described in the Blessing of Moses.[a]

> Dan is a lion's whelp
> That leapeth forth from Bashan.

All later tradition regards Dan as the most northerly settlement of the Israelites,[2] pointing towards the upper Huleh Basin in which to seek for their new home. There the deserted site of Tell el Kadi, the mound of the Judge,[3] seems to satisfy the indications of the old city of Leshem. It lies near the edge of the broad valley, just below the outlet of the Wady Banias, at the source of the gentler stream of the Wady el Leddan. Nothing remains of the old city but the long low mound which hides its ruins. This is roughly quadrangular in form, with its sides about 500 and 600 yards respectively in length, and it rises only about thirty or forty feet above the surrounding plain. The general line of its ancient ramparts may be traced all around except towards the south-west where the stream fed from the exceptionally bounteous spring and pool, the 'Ain el Leddan, actually within the site, has in course of time worn away the mound in that direction. The site furnishes ample evidence of its occupation down to the Late Bronze Age; but it is difficult to say where the Danites established themselves after taking possession of the place. The traces of habitation to be seen a few hundred yards to the north, called the Kh. el Menkheileh, are probably of Byzantine date. Most students are of opinion that the tribe eventually established its chief town at the foot of the hill, by the source of the Nahr Banias, on the site which later became well known as Caesarea Philippi,

[a] Deuteronomy xxxiii 22.

[1] Quoted on p. 29.

[2] Cf. the familiar expression 'from Dan to Beersheba,' 1 Samuel iii 20, etc.

[3] Dan means Judge, cf. Genesis xlix 16 [J].

THE UPPER HULEH BASIN VIEWED FROM THE S.
In the R. foreground the site Abel Beth Maacah, Abil el Kamh.

THE UPPER HULEH BASIN FROM BANIAS IN THE N.E.
In the Centre, low-lying, Tell el Kadi, the site of Laish (Dan).

See pp. 103, 246.

though the fact that even without excavation Tell Kadi shows traces of reoccupation in the Early Iron Age II, about 800 B.C., compared with the early tradition [a] that they rebuilt the city, suggests that they at first reoccupied the old site of Laish, or Leshem, on Tell Kadi, and that their removal or expansion to the foot of the hills indicates a later development.

JUDGES xviii

27 And they . . . came unto Laish, unto a people quiet and
secure, and smote them with the edge of the sword, and
28 they burnt the city with fire. And there was no deliverer,
because it was far from Sidon. [J]

The position of the tribe thus isolated must have involved quite special relations with the neighbouring peoples. The fact that it passed in the migration beyond the site and sphere of Hazor tells mutely of the temporary decline in the prestige of that old Canaanite centre, or at any rate of the respect inspired by Joshua's vigorous campaign in the neighbourhood. It would appear however probable, in view of all the circumstances, that the migration of Dan was effected about the same time as the final settlement of Naphtali, after the conquests of Seti I and Ramses II, but before the oppression of Sisera, since an allusion in the Song of Deborah implies that the tribe then found itself unable to leave the neighbourhood of the lake: [b] 'And Dan, why did he remain in ships.' Possibly it is the situation of Dan alongside the main connexions between Canaan and the north and actually upon the route from Hazor to Damascus, that is reflected in the old song:

Dan shall be a serpent in the way.
An adder in the path,
That biteth the horses heels.[c] [J]

[a] Judges xviii 28 [J]. [b] Judges v 17 [E]. [c] Genesis xlix 17 [J].

SECTION 13

DEATH OF JOSHUA AND THE ELDERS

JOSHUA xxiv. *Joshua at Shechem*

1 Joshua gathered together all the tribes of Israel to Shechem. [E]

WHILE there is no means of determining the exact place of this last recorded meeting of the tribes, the general situation of Shechem is established by unanimous and apparently continuous tradition.[1] It occupied, generally speaking, the position of modern Nablus, now a pleasant well-built town with 17,000 habitants which spreads along the slopes of the narrow valley between Mts. Ebal and Gerizim.[2] This strategic and geographic centre had harboured from remote antiquity one of the greatest cities of the highland region. As early as the XIIth Dynasty of Egypt (*c.* 2000), which corresponds in round terms with the Patriarchal age, it was singled out for mention by name *Sekmem* in one of the oldest accounts of Egyptian campaigning in the country.[3] Later, under the Imperial Pharaohs, within the period covered by this volume, it appears as *Sakmi* in the Tell el Amarna letters, *c.* 1375 B.C., and as *Sekem* on a papyrus generally attributed to the reign of Ramses II, *c.* 1250. The latter adds a touch of topographical realism in an allusion to the hill of Shechem,[4] doubtless Mt. Ebal. No traces of an ancient walled enclosure have been observed on the present site of Nablus; but the mound of Balata, which

[1] Cf. Josephus, *Antiq.* IV, viii, 44; Eusebius, *Onomasticon*, ed. Klostermann, p. 151.

[2] Pl. IV and p. 79. Cf. Map No. 5, p. 78.

[3] The Stele of Sebek-khu found by the writer at Abydos in Egypt in 1901, translated by Professor Newberry in G., *El Arâbah* (1902), ch. v, collated with notes by Professor Peet in Handbook 75 of the Manchester Museum, 1914.

[4] *Pap. Anast.* I, 21, 6. (Ed. Gardiner, p. 23.)

stands about a mile to the S.E., and hence at the entrance to the valley, proves on excavation to contain the remains of a stoutly defended city.[1] This in all probability marks the site of Shechem at the time of Joshua, for it shows clear trace of occupation in the Late Bronze Age; but the matter is complicated by the recent discovery within the area of a revetted platform, in the form of a truncated pyramid, such as might have served as the basis of a tower. Reference to the Book of Judges[a] will show that at the date of Abimelech, some 250 years later, a distinction seems to have been drawn between the walled city of Shechem and the tower of Shechem, and it is to be conjectured that the city proper then stood nearer to the modern site of Nablus, protected at its S.E. approach by this detached fortress-tower. However that may be, the archaeological evidence shows that the tower had not yet come into being in the fourteenth century B.C., while, as has been said, the walled area, within which it arose later, was at that time in active occupation.

Though the whole outline of the walls has not yet been traced, the enclosed area appears to have been oval in form and to have covered as much as twelve or even fourteen acres, thus exceeding in size all other cities of the period that have been examined. In general its development shows a marked parallelism with that of Jericho.[2] Its original ramparts, dating from the Middle Bronze Age, were constructed of megalithic blocks with the solidarity and precision which characterise the work of that period elsewhere.[3] As at Jericho, Tell Nasbeh, and Jerusalem, they presented a high, sloping revetment on the outer side. An inner contour on the same general outline was followed by the ramparts of the Late

[a] Judges ix 45, 46 [E].

[1] Sellin, 'Die Ausgrabung von Sichem,' in *Zeits. Deut. Pal. Ver.*, 1926-7; cf. especially the plans, Bd. 49 (1926), Taf. 29 and 32.

[2] Information in 1930 of Dr. Welter, who has recently directed the excavations.

[3] Cf. pp. 130, 165.

Bronze Age, and during that period one of the chief gateways was remodelled upon a plan familiar in the Hittite area of North Syria and Asia Minor.[1] With the erection of the tower in the Early Iron Age, after B.C. 1200, the interior underwent a radical reconstruction, the precise nature of which is still under investigation.

For the Israelites, Shechem retained ancestral associations, some trace of which may still survive upon the site. 'Jacob's well' and 'Joseph's tomb' are two features pointed out to visitors to-day, though the authenticity of these popular identifications is not established.[2] The name Balata may conceivably be derived from the Aramaic *Ballut* meaning Oak, and so perpetuate the memory of the venerable tree which, according to consistent Israelitish tradition in Ephraim, formed a central and seemingly sacred feature of an ancient sanctuary of the place.[a]

Previous to this gathering of the tribes at Shechem Joshua is last found at Shiloh,[b] where he allocated by Lot the territory of the northern tribes. Nothing is said in either Book that will explain his presence at Shechem[3]; nor indeed is it known under what circumstances or at which stage in the development of events his headquarters had been removed from Gilgal. Being himself an Ephraimite he may have accompanied the 'house of Joseph' at the taking of Bethel,[c] the one recorded achievement which would open the pathway towards Shiloh and the north. On the other hand, in view of his great age, it may be thought more probable that he would

[a] Genesis xxxv 4 [E]; Joshua xxiv 26 [E]. [b] Joshua xviii 9 [JE].

[c] Judges i 22 [J].

[1] Sellin, *loc. cit.* Taf. 33; *ib.* vol. l, Taf. 2. Cf. G., *H.E.*, p. 127 and Figs. 24, 29, 32, 40.

[2] The legendary site of Joseph's tomb (Joshua xxiv 32, [E]), as pointed out in the early centuries of our era (*Onomasticon*, p. 151), was not necessarily that of the present domed structure. In 1913 a tomb was opened in the vicinity and was found to contain a semi-regal deposit, Egyptian in character, pertaining to the XVIIIth Dynasty, 16-1400 B.C. See Böhl, *De Geschiedenis der Stad Sichem*. Amsterdam, 1926, pp. 20 ff.

[3] The LXX reads Shiloh.

BALATA, THE ANCIENT SITE OF SHECHEM, BETWEEN EBAL AND GERIZIM.

Where excavations have located the tower of Shechem.

See pp. 78, 248, 327.

accompany the Ark, which from the old record of Judges ii seems to have been moved independently after the fall of Bethel.—

1 And the angel of the Lord came up from Gilgal to Bochim.
5 And they sacrificed there unto the Lord. [J]

Bochim, the 'place of weeping,' is unlocated. But the ultimate destination of the Ark was Shiloh,[a] whither it would seem indeed to have been conveyed previous to the allocation of territory to the northern tribes,[b] as narrated in Joshua xviii, for on that occasion it is recorded that:

10 Joshua cast lots for them in Shiloh before the Lord. [JE]

The direct way from Gilgal to Shiloh, assuming the latter to be correctly placed at Kh. Seilun,[1] would take the route of the later Roman road by the Wady Taiy'beh towards Turmus Aya, or by the lower valley of the Wady Samieh. The course of the latter is marked by numerous holy places,[2] together with plentiful traces of occupation in the Late Bronze Age, and it would appear well placed for a stage in the moving of the Ark to Shiloh. 'Bochim' is, however, an unusual name, and there appears some doubt as to its original form and meaning. Indeed the version of this incident in the LXX contains the additional words 'and to Bethel,' which would make it appear that the Ark followed in the wake of the army, and that

[a] I Samuel iv 3. [b] Cf. Joshua xviii 1 [P].

[1] Cf. Judges xxi 19 [P], where the position of Shiloh corresponding exactly to Kh. Seilun ('on the east side of the road that goeth up from Bethel to Shechem and on the south of Lebonah') is carefully described as though to distinguish it from Shiloh the familiar sanctuary of Israel. The passage is ascribed, however, to a late hand, and may have been inserted to preserve a record of the position. Excavations have removed any objection to the identification on archaeological grounds, by tracing the origin of the site to the Middle Bronze Age, and the foundations of a city wall to the Early Iron Age. There seem to be no structural remains of the period of Joshua (*c.* 1400 B.C. Late Bronze Age); cf. Albright, *Bull. Am. S.O.R.* 35, 1929, p. 4, supplementary to *ibid.* No. 9, p. 10. Also Hans Kjaer, 'The Danish Excavation of Shiloh' in *P.E.F., Q.S.* Oct. 1927; and Vincent, *Rev. Bibl.* 1927, pp. 418-9.

[2] Cf. Albright in *Journ. P.O. Soc.* III, 1923, pp. 38 f.

Bochim (if it had separate existence[1]) marked some holy place, associated maybe with a grove of trees,[2] on the way between Gilgal and Bethel.

Meagre and unsatisfactory as are these suggestions, there is found no other indication of the stages by which Joshua may have moved his headquarters from Gilgal to Shiloh, and thence to Shechem. Nor does the Text offer any explanation of the status which he and the Israelites had evidently secured at Shechem, where he appears to have settled amid peaceful relations with right of access to the local sanctuary.[3] If the priestly tradition of an old Hivite element among the ruling class at Shechem[a] could be confirmed, an explanation might be found in the treaty which Joshua had concluded with the Hivites of Gibeon. But the passage in question, even if it can be reconciled with the older tradition which describes the inhabitants of Shechem as Canaanites and Perizzites,[b] does not refer to contemporary events, and the suggestion is not supported by any other indication. It is more likely that the explanation should be sought in the ancestral associations of the Israelites with Shechem[4]; but for fresh light we must turn to external sources.

The Habiru and Shechem

It has already been noted that Joshua's last years, during which the Settlement of the Tribes began, may have overlapped to some extent the period covered by the Amarna letters.[5] The point is of great interest, as in some of these direct reference is made to Shechem and

[a] Genesis xxxiv 2 [P]. [b] Genesis xxxiv 30 [J].

[1] Cf. Burney, *Judges*, p. 37; Cooke, *Judges*, p. 23.

[2] Cf. Cooke, *ibid.* p. 25; who recalls the possible derivation of Bochim from *Bekaim*, balsam trees, of II Samuel v 23, a suggestion which again would point rather to the Wady Samieh as the site. See also G. A. Smith, *Hist. Geog.* p. 487.

[3] Baal-berith, the Lord of the Covenant. Cf. Judges viii 33 [E2], ix 4 [E]. Cf. Burney, *Judges*, p. 266, also Cooke, *Joshua*, xxiv 25.

[4] Cf. Genesis xii 6 [J]; xlviii 22 [E]. Driver, *Genesis*, p. 378.

[5] Sect. 9, p. 205.

the part played by its chief Labaya in the anti-Egyptian revolution of the day. In the foregoing pages frequent reference has been made to these documents without special comment, but the question of their precise relevance at this stage now claims closer consideration. The letters contain reports and appeals for help addressed mostly 'to the Pharaoh' by his vassal chieftains (local kings) from the cities of Syria and Palestine; but it is not clear in many cases for which Pharaoh they were intended. Though all of them were found in the deserted Palace of Akhenaton (Amenhotep IV) at Tell el Amarna, some of them were addressed by name to that Pharaoh's predecessor, Amenhotep III, whose reign ended not later than 1375 B.C.,[1] having possibly overlapped already that of his successor by a few years.[2] Reports from Akizzi of Qatna which lay near Homs upon the Orontes are found addressed to both these monarchs. Consequently, the acute phase of the revolution associated with the SA-GAZ or Habiru,[3] which forms the main theme of the letters concerning Canaan, may be held to cover the years from 1380-1365 B.C., while the period of political unrest caused by the steady progress southward of the Hittite invasion and intrigue, culminating in the menace to Damascus as reported to Amenhetep III by Akizzi,[4] must hark back a further five years at least. It may be safely

[1] This is Prof. Breasted's date. Dr. Hall adopted 1380 B.C. (*Camb. Anct. Hist.* ii, pp. 699-700). Drs. Gardiner and Langdon, from a study of Hittite and other synchronisms, arrive at 1383 B.C. (*Journ. Eg. Arch.* 1920, p. 204).

[2] Petrie, *Hist. Egypt*, ii (1899), p. 208; also *Syria and Egypt*, p. 13.

[3] That the professional fighting men represented by the ideograms SA-GAZ (Semitic *ḥabbatu*, warrior, plunderer) are to be identified with the Habiru or Habirites is now accepted. Cf. in particular Langdon, 'The Habiru and the Hebrews' in *The Expository Times*, xxxi, 1920, pp. 324 ff.; also *Camb. Anct. Hist.* ii, p. 733. The names interchange definitely in a series of Hittite treaties, readily seen in Jack, *Exod.*, schedule to face p. 72. On the general question of the Habiru, see further, Dhorme, *Rev. Bib.* 1924, pp. 12 ff.; Landsberger in *Kleinas. Forsch.* I, pp. 321 f.; also *Zeits. f. Assyr.* 35, p. 214, n. 1; Gustav in *Z.A.T.W.* 1926, pp. 25 ff.; Opitz in *Zeits. f. Assyr.* 37, pp. 99 ff. Also Burney, *Judges*, pp. lxxv ff.

[4] Kn. No. 120. 'Damascus in the land of Ubi stretches out her hand to your feet.'

postulated that political disturbance was spreading fast between 1385 and 1380 B.C. With these dates in mind it is natural to enquire whether Joshua's entry late in life into Shechem does not synchronize with some definite episode in the Amarna letters. But we are faced by an initial difficulty, in that the year of Joshua's death cannot be determined with the necessary exactitude to establish a reliable conclusion. When examining the question of Joshua's age [1] we found from the information given by the Bible, that, if contemporary with Caleb, his death would have taken place about 1377 B.C., and his sojourn at Shechem may, therefore, have overlapped the period of the letters. But this conclusion involves an initial assumption: if Joshua were older than Caleb, as appears from a comparison of certain passages,[a] one of which is not, however, derived from the old sources, then his death would have occurred earlier. Moreover there appears in the Book of Exodus [b] a reference to Joshua as a young man, which would bring down the date of his death much later if we are to believe that he really lived to be 110 years of age. This is, however, a passing allusion of doubtful authenticity, and it cannot be reconciled with the data of these Books. The only relatively fixed position is that of the end of Joshua's generation, the Elders who outlived Joshua,[c] which by computation backwards from the figures given by the old sources,[2] may be put down at approximately 1367 B.C.

Within the limits of reserve imposed by these considerations, however, the possible relevance of the letters may be usefully examined. The summoning by Joshua of the tribal representatives to Shechem and his farewell exhortation are the last recorded actions of his life, and it is clearly to be inferred that he was nearing his end.[d] The date of his entry to Shechem then may

[a] Joshua xiii 1 [J], xiv 7 [D]. [b] Exodus xxxiii 11.

[c] Joshua xxiv 31. Judges ii 7, 10 [E].

[d] Joshua xiii 1 [J]; xviii 3-9 [JE]; xxiv 29 [E].

[1] P. 201. [2] P. 65.

be estimated provisionally as between 1370 and 1367 B.C. and therefore may overlap the period of the Habiru revolution.[1] Now one of the undated letters, written 'to the Pharaoh' by Abd-Khipa of Jerusalem, actually reports the secession of Shechem to the Habiru. *Labaya and the Land of Shechem* [2] *have given (all) to the Ḫabiru.* [3] The cogent question arises as to whether Abd-Ḳhipa by this statement did in effect record the peaceful occupation of the neighbourhood of Shechem by Joshua and the Israelites with the concurrence of the local chief. In view of our preliminary reservation, the most that can be said in answer is that this coincidence is possible. The ruler of Jerusalem, beset by his own immediate problems, would hardly be able or interested to discern any difference between the Hebrew-Habiru from the north, and the Hebrew-Israelites from the east: both were invaders and hostile to the Egyptian cause. The one name Habiru would cover both without distinction.

It will be well to note at this point that though the words Habiru and Hebrew [4] may be philologically equivalent,[5] no historical connexion can be traced between the Habiru revolution and the original invasion of Canaan by the Israelites under Joshua. The two movements were essentially distinct. The Israelites launched their attack from the east by way of Jericho, whence they drove in a wedge across the highlands through Gibeon and Aijalon. The old Biblical tradition, as we have seen, places that event towards the close of the fifteenth century B.C., some twenty-five or thirty years before the development of the Habiru disturbance. This, on the other hand, came from the north: it was the sequel to the conquest of Syria by the Hittite king Subbiluliuma, whose campaigns and intrigue can be followed with certainty and in detail, by the parallelism of his own archives with those of Tell

[1] P. 205. [2] *Sakmi.* [3] Kn. 289.

[4] *ʿIbhri*, ʿEbher; LXX ʿEber.

[5] Burney, *Isr. Settlement*, p. 68. Langdon, *Expository Times*, xxxi, p. 327.

el Amarna.[1] Habiru warriors, who as a class had long been known in Babylonia,[2] and elsewhere figure among the guards at the Hittite capital in Asia Minor,[3] were associated with him in this invasion. Their gods were invoked, after the fashion of the day, in the treaties which he forced upon the various principalities of Mesopotamia and Syria.[4] The Habiru penetration of Canaan is seen from the Letters themselves to form the most southerly stage in the Hittite invasion of Egyptian Syria, and seems to have moved progressively from north to south.[5] Hazor, Yenoam, Acco, Megiddo, Shechem, Gezer, Lachish, are among the names which mark its course. Though the sequence of events lacks chronological landmarks, it would be contrary to the present weight of evidence, and in conflict with the known history of this period, to attach to the movement any other interpretation; or to assign to it a date outside the limits already indicated, 1380-1360 B.C.[6] The original invasion of

1 Cook, 'Syria and Palestine in the Amarna Age,' *Camb. Anct. Hist.* ii, pp. 296 ff. Hall, *Anct. Hist., Near East* (1912), pp. 341 ff. G., *L.H.* (1910), pp. 330 ff.

2 Langdon, *Expository Times, loc. cit.*

3 King, *Hittite Texts in the Brit. Mus.* Nos. 6, 37. Cf. Sayce, *J.H.S.* xlv, p. 163.

4 Weidner, *Pol. Dok. aus Kleinasien*, in VIII Bo. Stn. (1923), p. 31, l. 50; p. 51, l. 22; p. 69, l. 37; p. 75, l. 4; etc.

5 Cf. S. A. Cook in *Camb. Anct. Hist.* ii, 314 ff.

6 The chief difficulty involved in a study of the Amarna letters is the lack of fixed chronological points. One letter (Kn. 254) written by Labaya, the chief of Shechem himself, to the Pharaoh, bears the suggestion of a date, in the signs 'year 10+2 . . .' written upon it in ink, apparently by some scribe. If this refers to Akhenaton's reign (as read by Cook, *Camb. Anct. Hist.* ii, 313 n. and Ed. Meyer, *Gesch. d. Alt.* ii, p. 316) it indicates a date about 1364 B.C. and the secession of Shechem may have taken place not long before. But the year *c.* 1367 B.C., according to the Biblical dates, marks the end of the Elders who outlived Joshua; and the fact that they maintained apparently undisturbed the worship and regime which he had established, implies stability of political relations from his death until the end of their generation. In this case the Ḥabiru invasion might prove to have been the disturbing factor that heralded the first Oppression. On the other hand the date may refer to the reign of Amenhotep III (as read by Bilabel, *Gesch. Vorderas. u. Ägyptens*, 1927, i, p. 231) and so indicate that a much longer range of time is covered by the Letters than has hitherto been suggested. The date of this letter would fall about the year 1400, and so would point to a contact between Ḥabiru and Israelite about the time of the fall of Hazor, a fertile possibility which must, however, await further light.

Canaan by the Hebrew-Israelites under Joshua was thus distinct both in character and in date from that of the Hebrew-Habiru.

Though there seems from the foregoing considerations to be no possibility of any contact between these two movements until or after the settlement of Joshua at Shechem, various later episodes in the Settlement of Israel seem to reflect the changed political environment resulting from the Hittite-Habiru invasion, and to be supported in one or two cases by circumstantial details. Thus the broad fact that the Settlement of the Tribes was effected under relatively peaceful conditions is in strong contrast with the resistance offered by the Canaanite cities in the first instance while the Egyptian organisation was still in a measure effective.[1] The strong cities of Canaan, though still able to hold out invaders by their walls, were unable at this time to protect the land by concerted action as of old: their power of co-ordination was temporarily paralysed by some circumstance which Joshua's victories alone do not explain. In the second place a marked resemblance has been observed between the situation created by the attack of Caleb on Hebron and that of Othniel on Debir, followed by the menace to Jerusalem,[2] with that described in the letters from Abd-Khipa of Jerusalem to the Pharaoh.[3] Thirdly may be mentioned, though not coming within the scope of this volume, the similarity between the progress of the Habiru movement down the southern coastlands, affecting Gezer, Gath, Debir, Lachish and Askalon, and the record of conquests added by a later hand[4] to the older narrative of Joshua's victory in the plain of Gibeon and the valley of Aijalon.[5] Speaking generally, it does indeed seem possible, and for that reason to demand careful study, that D's additions to the older narrative of Joshua's invasion (J and E) may preserve a memory of the great

[1] Cf. p. 61. [2] P. 219. [3] Kn. Nos. 289-290.

[4] The Deuteronomic redactor : see p. 3.

[5] Above, p. 182. Cf. especially Joshua x 31, 33, 39 [D].

Hittite-Habiru penetration and conquest of Syria and Palestine [1] 'from Baal-gad in the valley of Lebanon even unto Mt. Halah, that goeth up to Seir' and 'from the valley of Arnon unto Mt. Hermon.' If the Canaanite chieftain could hardly distinguish at the time between these two bodies of Hebrews, and their activities, it would not be a matter for surprise that the editors of the older Hebrew records in the seventh century B.C. should fail to recognise the difference after a lapse of seven full centuries.[2] It is evident in any case that the fortunes of Israel were for a time and in a measure interlocked with those of the Habiru.

JOSHUA xxiv. *The Hornet*

12 I sent the Hornet before you which drave them out. [E]

Joshua's farewell exhortation to the tribes opens with a brief survey of national events, from before the coming to Canaan of Abraham their great ancestor down to the fall of Jericho. The document is of peculiar interest: read together with Jephthah's account in Judges xi, which also is derived from the early sources, it discloses a clearly defined Ephraimite tradition on the subject of the Exodus. The joint narrative covers the descent of the Patriarch Jacob and his children to Egypt, the subsequent escape of the Israelites under Moses, the destruction of the Pharaoh's pursuing force, the sojourn in Kadesh, the compassing of Edom and Moab, the defeat of the Amorites, the taking possession of their land between the Arnon and the Jabbok, and finally the destruction of Jericho. These initial achievements are ascribed by Joshua directly to Jehovah: the further stage in the

[1] See also Prof. Langdon in the *Expository Times*, xxxi, p. 329, who suggestively enquires: 'Were the heroic deeds of the Ḥabirites in the service of Larsa, Babylon and the Hittites also written in the Book of Jashar?'

[2] Several later passages in the Bible draw a distinction between the Israelites and other Hebrews, in particular I Samuel xiv 21. 'Now the Hebrews that were with the Philistines . . . turned to be with the Israelites that were with Saul. . . .' Cf. also Exodus i 15; I Samuel iv 6, 9; and xiii 3, 7. See further Sayce, *The Early History of the Hebrews*, 1897, p. 6 f.

penetration of Canaan is attributed to a divinely sent agency which is not defined but is symbolised by 'The Hornet.'

The religion of the Israelites, and in particular the ideals of those who set down and arranged these records, could not tolerate the notion that any power other than that of the God of Israel might influence their destinies. No direct allusion is made throughout these Books to the supreme temporal power in the land, that of the Pharaoh, which had held Canaan in vassalage almost continuously for four hundred years. That side of the picture is veiled from view, and only at rare intervals does a chance reflexion betray what is there concealed.

It has already been seen that Egypt had aimed at securing the servitude of the Canaanite cities by a consistent policy of tyranny and spoliation,[1] calculated in the issue to break their individual strength, and had now left them to their fate before the advancing Hittites and the Habiru; so that at the time chosen for the Settlement of the Tribes the land is found in the throes of a revolution, with the Egyptian organisation temporarily broken down.

The sovereignty of the Pharaoh over united Egypt was expressed by a hieroglyphic formula, *ny-swt-byt*, in which the second member, a reed, symbolises Upper Egypt, and the third member, which denotes in particular the kingship of Lower Egypt,[2] is probably a hornet though commonly taken for a bee.[3] In current hieroglyphs the bee and hornet were not distinguished, though the honey-bee was called the 'fly of honey.'[4] When drawn out pictorially, however, as in some of the Theban tombs,[5] the insect is seen to possess features

[1] Above, p. 112 ff.

[2] Cf. Erman and Grapow, *Wörterbuch d. Aegypt. Sprache*, i, p. 434.

[3] Translated the formula would thus read, 'He who belongs to the Reed and the Hornet'; though doubtless long usage had imparted to the signs a purely symbolic meaning.

[4] Erman, *loc. cit.*

[5] Facsimile copies of two examples have been made by Mr. de Garis Davis. In the one from the tomb of Kenamun (93), Pl. IX, the wings are striped with red and partly bordered with blue; in the other from the Tomb of Peh Su Kha, No. 88 at Thebes, blue spots are added, borrowing in this as in other

which in the opinion of zoologists are peculiar to wasps. 'It is safe to assume that the figure is not a bee (*apidæ*) but one of the *vespidæ*, and probably the Hornet.'[1] Our frontispiece epitomises this interpretation.

Not only did the devastating policy of the Pharaoh prepare the way for Israel's invasion, and the breakdown of his authority make possible their settlement; but, as will be seen from the Book of Judges, the activities of later Pharaohs seem to have removed one by one various other obstacles which beset the pathway of the tribes.

The remaining passages from Joshua's exhortation, vv. 14-27, are concerned with the Covenant which he made with the Israelites in Shechem, in confirmation of the people's reiterated decision to put away the strange gods and serve the Lord, the God of Israel [Jehovah]. There is no reference to any earlier Covenant of the sort. As witness Joshua is said to have taken a great stone and set it up there under the oak that was by the sanctuary of the Lord, saying '... it hath heard all the words of the Lord which he spake unto us.'

JUDGES ii 7.

And the people served the Lord all the days of Joshua and all the days of the elders that outlived Joshua. [E]

JOSH. xxiv. (cf. Judges ii 8.)

29 And it came to pass after these things, that Joshua the son of Nun, the servant of the Lord, died, being an hundred and ten years old. [E]

JUDGES ii.

10 And also all that generation were gathered to their fathers ; and there arose another generation after them which knew not the Lord, nor yet the work which he had wrought for Israel. [E]

details from the butterfly. But the distinctive markings and coloration of the lower body are the same in each case, viz. strong black bands upon a dark yellow ground.

[1] Communication of Professors E. B. Poulton and W. Garstang.

THE TRIBES UNDER THE JUDGES

SECTION 14

RESTORATION OF PEACEFUL CONDITIONS UNDER EGYPT

OPPRESSION BY CUSHAN

c. 1367-1359 B.C.

JUDGES iii

8 The anger of the Lord was kindled against Israel, and he sold them into the hand of Cushan-Rishathaim King of Mesopotamia[a] ; and the children of Israel served Cushan-Rishathaim eight years. [E]

THE eight years of oppression following upon the death of the elders who outlived Joshua synchronise in round figures with the closing years of Akhenaton's reign. The record as it stands is fragmentary and not easy to explain with satisfaction; for while the association of Cushan, elsewhere a Midianite tribe,[b] with Othniel, who as a Kenizzite dwelt in the southern highlands, seems reasonable, yet the introduction of the king of Mesopotamia into the story of a local disturbance seems out of focus. Possibly 'Aram,' which is coupled with 'Naharaim,' is a misreading for 'Edom,' for these words closely resemble one another in the Hebrew script. But apart from that possibility the chronology of the period [1] suggests another way in which this fragmentary record may have become confused. For at this time the Hittite King Subbiluliuma, having with the help of the Ḥabiru and his Amorite allies completed the conquest of Syria and Palestine, had also by a brilliant campaign overrun the land of Mitanni in Mesopotamia, and finally by astute diplomacy established his suzerainty over the whole eastern area, as well as Syria.[2] Some hold, however, that the words of the Hebrew text, Aram-Naharaim,

[a] *Hebrew*: Aram-Naharaim. [b] Habakkuk iii 7.

[1] Above, pp. 62-65. [2] G., *H.E.* p. 5.

would better be interpreted as Syria of the Rivers[1]; and indeed the Egyptians indicated the northern tract of Syria, lying between the Orontes and the Euphrates, by the name Land of *Naharîn* or *Naharên*, the land of the two rivers.[2] Politically, as we have seen, the precise value of the term is immaterial, for the Hittite king was master of both areas. Cushan, then, though probably a Midianite tribe or chief from Trans-Jordania, may have been a vassal in active relations with the Hittite King or his representative in the north of Syria; and in the process by which this record has been reduced to its present meagre form, the two chief personages may have become confused. The oppression evidently affected chiefly, if not entirely, the southernmost tribes, and did not call for a general effort to drive out the invaders. Commentators have sought to give the episode a wider significance by comparing the name Cushan-rishathaim with a Kassite name Kashsha-rishrt, which it certainly resembles, apart from the fact that the latter name is that of a woman. Kassite rulers had founded the Third Dynasty of Babylonia, and at this time still occupied the throne. Their patronymic appears to have been Kush,[a] the traditional father of Nimrod and of the Babylonian civilisation. The suggestion cannot, however, be sustained. It would involve a Kassite intervention in Trans-Jordania at the very time when the wide-reaching domination of the Hattic kings is disclosed by the Hittite records, which include several treaties with Syrian principalities and even with the Kassite kings themselves. Rishathaim, moreover, is a word susceptible of translation, signifying the 'doubly-wicked,' and so hardly a personal name. It seems then more probable that in an abridgment of the

[a] Genesis x 8. [J]

[1] As in the LXX. In the original unpointed Hebrew the spelling would read Naharim (plural) rather than Naharaim (dual); cf. Burney, *Judges*, p. 66; Cooke, *Judges*, p. 37. Hittite documents speak of a 'Land of Nine Rivers' (*K.U.B.* xv. p. 30, l. 38), but the district may have included the Eastern Taurus.

[2] Breasted, *Anc. Rec.* ii. 479 n.; ii. 583.

original records, the conquest of all Palestine by the Hittite King of the Land of Rivers, with a possible oppression of all Israel, has become combined with the reminiscences of a local struggle between the tribes of Cushan and Kenaz, who opposed one another across the Jordan, resulting in the ultimate victory of Othniel.

DELIVERANCE BY OTHNIEL.

c. 1359 B.C.

JUDGES iii.

9 The Lord raised up a saviour to the children of Israel, who
saved them, even Othniel the son of Kenaz, Caleb's younger
10 brother. . . . And he judged Israel . . . [E 2]

Othniel the Kenizzite is already known from the story of the capture of Debir.[a] The reference, therefore, provides an important link in the chronology of the period.[1] The generation of the elders of Israel who outlived Joshua was now past; the death of Caleb also may be presumed, for he was almost as old as Joshua and, according to tradition, had reached the age of eighty-five before his attack on Hebron.[b] Othniel is stated to have been a younger brother of Caleb, and even though the word 'younger' may be an interpolation, as some hold,[2] the fact that he married Caleb's daughter[c] suggests that he belonged to a younger generation. It would be fully accordant with oriental life to find forty years difference in age between the brothers but not more, and that number of years is more than sufficient to cover the interval between the fall of Hebron and the time when Othniel delivered his kinsmen and allies from this oppression, and was acclaimed as 'Judge.'

The Hebrew word for Judge, *shophat*, is not in this case to be interpreted in the English sense of law-giver or

[a] Judges i 13. [J]. [b] Joshua xiv 10 [D]. [c] Joshua xv 17. [J].

[1] Above, p. 56.

[2] Versions of the LXX. differ on the question of Othniel's relationship to Caleb; cf. Cooke, *Judges*, p. 9.

arbitrator between man and man, though susceptible of that meaning, but rather as Deliverer.[1] The estimated year of deliverance in this case almost coincides with the accession of Sakere and Tutenkhamon to the throne of Egypt, when Palestine was in great measure reconquered for the Pharaoh by Harmhab.

PERIOD OF PEACE

c. 1359-1319 B.C.

JUDGES iii.

11 And the land had rest forty years. And Othniel the son of Kenaz died. [E]

ALTHOUGH the text as it stands almost suggests that Othniel after delivering Israel from the oppression of Cushan continued to judge Israel throughout the whole ensuing period of forty years, yet the complete silence as to any subsequent achievements and the method of expression so different from the deliberate statement used in the case of Gideon [a] render this interpretation improbable. The ambiguity may indeed arise from nothing more than the interchanging of the two quoted sentences.

This period of forty years covers broadly the short reigns of Akhenaton's immediate successors, Sakere (1358-56) and Tutenkhamon (1356-1350), and most of the reign of Harmhab (1350-1314). Egyptian authority over Syria was re-established early in this period by Harmhab, while he was still commander-in-chief of the Egyptian troops. The evidence is found on a monument of Harmhab himself, but pertains to the days before that warrior had reached the throne, for he is still styled 'Hereditary Prince, wearer of the royal seal,' etc. . . . and 'general-in-chief.' He is further called the 'King's follower on expeditions in the south and north country,' and finally 'companion of the feet of his lord upon the battlefield on

[a] Judges viii 28 [E2].

[1] *or* Avenger: a different word *Moshi'a* is used for Saviour.

that day of slaying the Asiatics' (*St. tyw*).[1] Now the predecessors whom Harmhab served as general-in-chief could only have been Sakere or Tutenkhamon, so that the re-establishment of Egyptian supremacy in Syria and Palestine early in this period of Rest is well authenticated by Egyptian sources.

A monument of peculiar interest shows Harmhab in his earlier years giving instructions to certain Egyptian officials regarding a number of Asiatic refugees, whose arrival may be attributed to the reign of Akhenaton or just later.[2] The inscription states 'others have been placed in their abodes . . . they have been destroyed, and their towns laid waste. . . . Their countries are starving, they live like goats of the mountain. . . . They come begging a home in the domain of the Pharaoh [maybe from the oppression of Cushan] after the manner of their fathers' fathers since the beginning.'[3] This privilege of settling on the borders of Egypt was an established custom, and later records allude to a similar case in the reign of Merneptah, *c.* 1220 B.C., when again invaders overran the sea-board of Palestine.[4]

Another scene in the tomb of a high Egyptian official in the reign of Tutenkhamon shows the Pharaoh enthroned under a kiosk, receiving from numerous Asiatic envoys a magnificent array of tribute, chiefly gold and silver vessels, costly stones and horses. Accompanying the scene is an inscription stating that 'the chiefs of *Retenu the Upper* (Central or perhaps Northern Palestine) who knew not Egypt since the time of the god are craving peace from his majesty.' They say . . . 'there shall be no revolters in thy time, but every land shall be in peace.'[5] Objects found in the tomb of Tutenkhamon, in particular the carved staffs decorated with images of the Pharaoh's prisoners and vassals, give general confirmation to this text.

[1] Breasted, *Anct. Rec.* iii, 20. [2] *Ibid.* iii, 10. [3] *Ibid.* iii, 11.

[4] Cf. Gardiner, *Pap. Anast.* VI, 4, 13 ff. and 5 ff.

[5] Breasted, *Anct. Rec.* ii, 1028-1033.

After his succession to the throne, Harmhab was preoccupied with reorganising the provincial administration of Egypt, reforming the abuses which had sprung up under Akhenaton. None the less he appears from another monument to have maintained his authority over Palestine, and claims ascendancy over a number of northern peoples.[1] The inscription in this instance is not well preserved, and only eleven names can be read, but these are supplemented by a relief depicting three rows of captives, distinguished by their dress and faces as Asiatics, whom he presents to the Egyptian gods. The scene evidently commemorates a successful campaign in Syria. But, on the whole, records of military activities in Palestine at this time are rare: Harmhab seems to have been able to rely upon the efficiency of his organization in the country, and appears moreover to have assured peace by concluding with his chief adversary in northern Syria, the Hittite King Mursil, a treaty[2] by which Palestine also would be secured against that former source of disturbance and disaffection. There is, in fact, no further trace in the Egyptian records of disorder in Palestine during the active career of this soldier king.

[1] Breasted, *Anct. Rec.* iii, 34. [2] *Ibid.* iii, 377.

KERAK, PROBABLY KIR OF MOAB; BOLDLY PLACED UPON A KNOLL, E. OF THE DEAD SEA.

The ruined walls are mediaeval, but excavations have reached down to Graeco-Roman levels.

See p. 70.

SECTION 15

ESTABLISHMENT OF THE NORTHERN TRIBES

OPPRESSION BY EGLON OF MOAB

c. *1319-1301 B.C.*

JUDGES iii

12 **And the Lord strengthened Eglon the king of Moab against**
Israel, because they had done that which was evil in the
13 **sight of the Lord. And he gathered unto him the children**
of Ammon and Amalek; and he went and smote Israel and
14 **they possessed the City of Palm Trees. And the children**
of Israel served Eglon the king of Moab eighteen years.

[E]

THE period of rest which the land enjoyed after the deliverance by Othniel, though synchronising generally, as we have just seen, with the regime of Harmhab, came to an end according to the Biblical date about 1319, some five years before that Pharaoh died, whereas the records of Egypt only begin to tell of renewed disturbance in Palestine after his death. But Harmhab was an old man; his reign lasted about thirty-five years, and his official career went back at least twenty-four years earlier,[1] to the beginning, that is, of Akhenaton's reign. He must, therefore, have attained the age of eighty years before the close of his reign; and it is probable from the absence of all record, that he had ceased to take an active interest in the affairs of Palestine and Syria. The similar experience of Amenhotep III has shown that the country could not be left so long by the Pharaoh without danger of disloyalty among the vassal chieftains, particularly if tempted by the prospect of profitable adventure. That disorder was actually developing before the end of his

[1] Breasted, *Hist. Egypt*. p. 407. Harmhab's 59th regnal year is mentioned in an inscription of *Mes*.

reign seems manifest from the fact that Seti I, upon succeeding to the throne, was called upon in his very first year of rule to face the menace of open rebellion in Palestine, particularly upon its southern borders and in the Jordan valley near Beisan. The disturbance in southern Palestine seems to be that instigated by the King of Moab, in collusion with the Ammonites, whose territory lay opposite to Jericho,[a] and the Amalekites whom we have met in the vicinity of Arad and Hormah.[b] The situation described in the Book of Judges and that recorded in the annals of Seti I seem indeed to be one and the same, as may be seen by a comparison of the two accounts.

JUDGES iii. *Eglon*, *c.* 1319 B.C.	SETI I, Year I, 1314 B.C.
13 He (the king of Moab) gathered unto him the children of Ammon and Amalek; and he went and smote Israel and they possessed the City of Palm Trees.	The vanquished Shasu (Bedouin) plan rebellion: their tribal chiefs are gathered together, rising against the Asiatics of S. Palestine (Kharu), . . . and they disobey the laws of the Palace.[1]

Seti faced the situation promptly, and in his first year not only reopened the desert routes and brought the southern Bedouin to submission,[2] but pushed on northwards, making good his main lines of communication at Acco and Yenoam.[3] At Beisan the situation was serious, and he left there a monument to record the measures he was called upon to take. This has been recovered in excavation and now published in translation.[4] It relates, in lines 15-21, how 'the wretched enemy who was in the

[a] Cf. Judges, xi 33 [J]. [b] Cf. Numbers xiv 45 [JE].

[1] Breasted, *Anct. Rec.* iii, 101. [2] See figs. 4, 6.

[3] Breasted, *Anct. Rec.* iii, 84.

[4] By Mr. Alan Rowe, in the *Mus. Journ.*, *Phil.* 1929, p. 93. On the topography of this text see above p. 73 and Map 3.

city of Hamath had collected to himself many people; was taking away the town of Beth-shean; had made an alliance with those of Pahel and was not allowing to come forth the chief of Rehob outside his own city. Then his Majesty sent the first army of Amen (Powerful Bows) to the city of Hamath, the first army of Ra (Many Braves) to the city of Bethshean, and the first army of Sutekh (Strong Bows) to the city of Yenoam: and it happened that in the space of a day, they were overthrown by the will of his Majesty.' All of these places we have met before: the sites of Beth-shean and Pahel are known, the one at Beisan on the west, the other, the classical Pella, at Kh. Fahil on the east side of the Jordan. Yenoam lay to the north of Beisan,[1] while Rehob and Hamath may be plausibly located at Tell el Sarem and Tell Hammeh[2] to the south; and though these identifications remain unconfirmed, the area of the operations covered by this inscription is fairly clear. Seti stopped by his dispositions the chief crossings of the Jordan both north and south of Beisan, and apparently brought this rebellious combination to an end. The disturbance recorded on this monument at Beisan is evidently different from that in the south described in the two parallel passages quoted above. In this case the district involved, the joining of hands across the river, and the menace to Beisan itself, recall the subject-matter of Joshua xvii 11 and 18, already

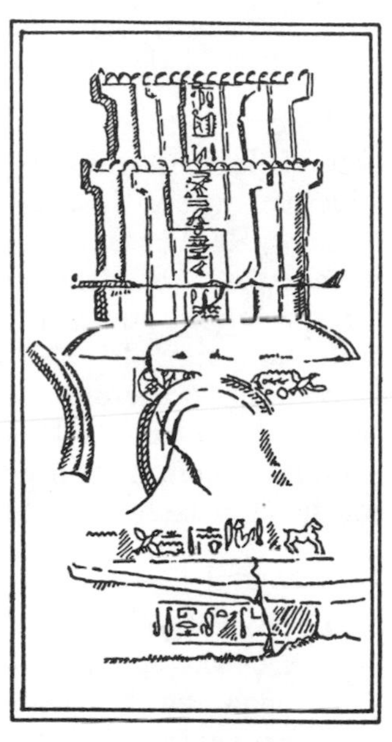

Fig. 6. Well-station on the way to Canaan recovered by Seti I.

[1] See above, p. 74, and Map 3. [2] Pl. LIX.

considered[1] in connection with the eastward expansion of Manasseh:

11 **And Manasseh had in Issachar Bethshean and her towns**
12 **and Ibleam and her towns. . . . Yet the children of**
Manasseh could not drive out the inhabitants of those cities. [J]

According to late tradition the inheritance of Manasseh east of Jordan was attributable to Moses[a] and became effective when Joshua at Shiloh dismissed with his blessing Reuben and Gad after the conquest and partition of the west.[b] But the old tradition does not bear out this interpretation, nor do the military results of the Israelites' early campaigns beyond Jordan justify such a conclusion.[c] According to the old sources the expansion of Manasseh eastwards began fairly late in Joshua's career, when he promised them not only the hill country of the Perizzites, but its approaches on the other side:

Joshua xvii

18 **The hill country shall be thine, for though it is a forest, thou shalt cut it down, and the goings out thereof shall be thine: for thou shalt drive out the Canaanites though they have chariots of iron. [J]**

The ' goings out ' of Manasseh in this context are the passes that descend to the Jordan valley from the hills lying south of Gilboa.[2] These lead directly down towards the sites of Hamath and Pahel and Rehob, the scene of the disturbances repressed by Seti I in the year 1305 B.C., less than a hundred years from the time when Joshua at Shiloh had laid down for Manasseh their plan of future expansion.

The settlement of Manasseh astride the river in this area seems to have been completed according to Eph-

[a] Joshua xiii 8, 29-31. [b] Joshua xxii 1-6.
[c] Cf. Joshua xxiv 8, 9 [E]; Judges xi 22 [E].

[1] Pp. 27, 232; cf. Joshua xvii 16 and Judges i 27. [2] See map, p. 72.

TELL HAMMEH, PROBABLY HAMATH, IN THE MID-JORDAN VALLEY.
Mentioned with Bethshean, Fahel and Yenoam, on an inscription of Seti I. from Beisan.

NOMAD ENCAMPMENT IN THE MID-JORDAN VALLEY.
At the foot of the hills between Tell Hammeh and Mt. Gilboa.

See pp. 73, 271.

raimite tradition (E) before the national rally under Deborah, a hundred years later than this episode, as is to be inferred from a line in the great epic of Judges v :

14 Out of Machir came down governors. [E]

Whatever may have been the exact stages of Manasseh's expansion, it seems clear that their movement across the river is reflected by the details of this narrative. Thus two different episodes in the tribal history of Israel at this time seem to be traceable in the independent records of the contemporary Egyptian Pharaoh.

Notwithstanding the vigour and promptitude of Seti's action, it was not for nine years that the situation was completely redressed, and Egyptian authority restored. Troubles on his Libyan frontier monopolised his attention for some time,[1] and the state of affairs in Palestine and Syria involved at least four campaigns.[2] These covered all Canaan or northern Palestine, from Tyre and Acco on the coast to Yenoam by the Jordan, including also, according to the records,[3] the cities of Beth-anath[4] and Kedesh of Naphtali,[5] in addition to the cities mentioned independently on the Beisan stele. Some of his expeditions carried him into the Hittite country of the north as well as beyond Jordan, where he erected another monument at Tell el Shihab.[6] The result of his efforts and policy seems to have been lasting. Possibly he also patched up his difficulties in Syrian politics by a further treaty with the Hittite king,[7] for after his ninth year (1306 B.C.) we hear no more of wars or troubles in Palestine throughout his reign. The local struggle

[1] Breasted, *Anct. Rec.* iii, 82.

[2] *Ibid.* iii, 40, n. *a.*

[3] *Ibid.* iii, 88.

[4] *Ibid.* 114.

[5] *Ibid.* 141. The destruction of Kedesh by Seti on this occasion made it possible for Naphtali to occupy the site. Cf. Judges iv 6.

[6] Discovered by Prof. Sir G. Adam Smith in 1901 and reported in the *Athenæum* of July 6, 1901. Cf. Breasted, *Anct. Rec.* iii, 140.

[7] Called *Metella* (*Mu-t-n-l'*) in Egyptian, Hittite *Muwatallis*, son of Mursil. The breaking of this treaty led to the battle of Kadesh in 1288 B.C. Cf. Breasted, *Anct. Rec.* iii, 377.

between Moab and southern Israel, though suppressed by Seti in the south, may have continued for some time

Fig. 7. Hill-fortress of Canaan * stormed by Seti I.

in the Jordan valley and the vicinity of Jericho almost unperceived, or may not have been deemed of sufficient

* This scene, taken from a monument at Karnak in Egypt, is described as the 'slaughter among the enemies of *Shasu*-land as far as the Kanaan Land.' It may therefore represent the assault of one of the hill fortresses of Galilee, though some would locate it nearer the Southern Negeb, on the frontiers of the Bedouin (*Shasu*) country. Cf. Gardiner, *J.E.A.* vi (1920), p. 100.

importance to call for repressive measures. However that may be, as a result of Ehud's action, this too was brought to an end some five years later.

DELIVERANCE BY EHUD OF BENJAMIN,

c. 1301 B.C.

JUDGES iii

15 . . . the Lord raised them up a saviour Ehud the son of Gera, the Benjamite.

27 And it came to pass, when he was come, that he blew a trumpet in the hill country of Ephraim, and the children of Israel went down with him from the hill country, and he before them.

28 . . . And they went down after him, and took the fords of
Jordan against the Moabites, and suffered not a man to
29, 30 pass over. . . . and there escaped not a man. So Moab
was subdued that day under the hand of Israel. [E]

The relatively full detail of this episode,[1] which finally delivered the neighbouring Israelites from the Moabite aggression, not only throws light upon the tribal situation in the south, but affords an insight into the essentially local character of many records in the Book of Judges. This oppression from the first, as we have seen, had menaced primarily south-eastern Palestine, by the alliance of Moab, Ammon and Amalek around its border; and it would seem in its latter phase, after the campaign undertaken by the Pharaoh in the south, to have resolved itself into a purely local struggle centred around the site of Jericho. Though this city lay in ruins, the position was manifestly of strategic interest to those who dwelt nearest to it upon both sides of the river, and cannot long have remained unoccupied. After the evacuation of Gilgal by the united Israelites it had fallen to the King of Moab, to whom, as previously with Joshua, it had served as base for the further penetration of the west and south. The city, we have ascertained, was not rebuilt at this time: a

[1] For the full text see pp. 34, 35.

few houses at the north end of the ancient mound bear witness, it is true, to a partial occupation[1]; it was not, however, Jericho, but the ' City of Palm Trees ' of which Eglon took possession, and this name would more suitably describe a new settlement in the cultivable area below the spring towards the east. The record (v. 28) shows, indeed, that the whole of the narrated incidents took place on the west bank of the river, which the Moabites must have occupied in force. The Summer Parlour whither Eglon had retired alone when slain by Ehud may well have been an arbour situated upon the river itself, such as may be seen to-day, and are favourite resorts in hot weather. It may be reasonably inferred that the Moabites were busied on some raid or operations in the south country at the time that Ephraim, roused by Ehud with the news of Eglon's death, descended from the highlands and secured the fords, so cutting them off from their base and their line of retreat. This disaster to the Moabite forces, added to the death of their king, evidently caused them to desist from further attempts to hold the ground they had gained in Palestine, and brought this period of oppression to an end.

The special significance of this narrative lies, however, in the fact that it is apparently concerned only with those Israelites who dwelt in the south-east of the country. Benjamin and their neighbours of southern Ephraim alone are mentioned by name in the record of the deliverance, but the previous oppression clearly affected also the southern highlands. That Judah and Simeon are not mentioned may indeed be attributed to the fact, borne out by other passages,[2] that these tribes were among the last to develop their political independence. Already in the Book of Joshua we have seen that exceptional difficulties lay across their path; and now it appears that the two first oppressions recorded in the Book of Judges were directed primarily against these tribes of the south country and their allies, whose settlement cannot fail to have

[1] See pp. 147-8. [2] See pp. 305, 340.

THE TERRITORY OF BENJAMIN, FROM THE N.

View from Tell Nasbeh looking towards Jerusalem.

THE TERRITORY OF BENJAMIN AND THE HIVITE AREA.

View from Tell Nasbeh looking towards El Jib.

See pp. 179. 237.

been retarded by these circumstances. But this explanation cannot be applied to those children of Joseph who bordered on Mt. Ephraim to the north, nor to the northern tribes, all of whom seem to have remained unmoved by the Moabite incursion. It is true that each group of the Israelites had at this time to face its particular problems; moreover, common action not only was restrained by the dispersal of the tribes, but under the political circumstances of the day would inevitably have been followed by punishment and reprisals on the part of Egypt, now fully re-established in its suzerainty.

Generally speaking, it is found that the historical narrative in the Book of Judges is concerned for the most part only with transient local episodes, and throws little or no light upon the activities of the tribes in other areas. Looking farther, we find that long periods of rest are dismissed in single lines, though collectively they cover more than half the whole period of the Judges.[1] The conclusion is obvious, that the records preserved in the Book of Judges are for the most part only fragments from the traditions of the tribes: and that further light upon the Israelites as a whole is only to be gathered by reflexion from the history they shared in common with other subject peoples of the Egyptian Empire.

PROLONGED PERIOD OF PEACE

1301-1221 B.C.

JUDGES iii

30 The land had rest fourscore years [E 2]

The oppression of Israel by Eglon of Moab had lasted eighteen years, and though the narrated episodes suggest mostly local trouble, it seems evident from the fact that the Ephraimites responded to the call of Benjamin to drive out the invaders, that most of central Palestine had

[1] See the Schedule on p. 58. Of the three opening judgeships, the periods of rest cover 160 years in a total of 206 years, the difference of 46 years being covered by the three oppressions.

been involved, while the Egyptian and Biblical records both indicate that the south of Palestine had been invaded at the same time. Released from this oppression, Israel began to enjoy an unparalleled period of rest from wars and troubles; and during this time, it would appear, the tribes at last found the opportunity under the *Pax Aegyptiaca* to make good their inheritance in the land.

The period of peace which the early efforts of Seti had secured for the latter half of his reign still endured at his death, about 1292 B.C., and was inherited by his successor Ramses II, sometimes called the Great. Even the wars which this Pharaoh waged in Syria, particularly the battle of Kadesh, though among the most vaunted episodes of Egyptian history, affected Palestine very little. His quarrel lay with the Hittites, who doubtless had established themselves more firmly than ever in central Syria, where their continued presence menaced the Pharaoh's prestige farther south. Ramses found himself obliged to challenge their pretensions. Kadesh, where the issue was decided, lay in Amorite country near the head of the Orontes valley, at a point which commanded the natural route from that area towards the coast. Ramses' lines of communication are not stated; possibly he profited by the experience of his great predecessor Thutmose III and employed the sea route as far as practicable. The army he led to the famous contest is estimated at 20,000 men of all ranks,[1] cavalry, infantry and Sherden, an unprecedented force. The Hittite king also mustered every available ally and mercenary from central Syria to the Troad. The issue crippled both powers; and Ramses left the scene without any apparent effort to secure even the country which he had hitherto held towards the south. Consequently, while songs celebrating his brave exploits were being composed at Thebes, Hittite and allied bands pushed forward into Palestine, which as of old was immediately stirred to disaffection. The chief trouble seems to have

[1] Breasted, *Hist. Egypt.* p. 435.

centred once more around the main highroad from Gaza to the north. Even Ascalon fell into the hands of rebels and had to be recaptured by the Pharaoh.[1] Most of the names of cities taking part in this revolt are now unreadable,[2] but one which is clear is that of Beth-Anath

Fig. 8. Sherden mercenary troops in the army of Ramses II at the battle of Kadesh on the Orontes, *c.* 1288 B.C.

in Upper Galilee. The descriptive reference, 'the city on the Mount of Beth-Anath, named Kerpe[t],'[3] while appropriate to the Bronze-age site now called El Khurbeh, suggests that, as in the case of Kedesh, the Sanctuary or *hieron* of Anath was distinct in some way from the town, to which was attached a separate name.[4] Hitherto

[1] See Fig. 10.

[2] Three, Inmyn, Rawr, Kemnat, are quite legible but unplaced. A fourth, M—r—m, suggests Merom of Joshua x 17 and appears in the list of Thutmose III. Fig. No. 12. Cf. Müller, *Asien*, p. 220. Lepsius, *Denk.* III, 156.

[3] Breasted, *Anct. Rec.* iii, 356. In Lepsius, *loc. cit.*, the signs for 'mountain' are not clear, but Müller's reading adequately restores the text.

[4] Cf. also Kadesh, p. 243.

Naphtali had been constrained to dwell among the Canaanites, the inhabitants of the land, but the fall of Beth-Anath [1] following the destruction of Kadesh [2] by Seti I, removed from the pathway of the northern tribes the two great stumbling-blocks of Upper Galilee, and from this time 'the inhabitants of Beth-Shemesh and Beth-Anath became tributary unto them.' [a] The tribe of Naphtali 'like a hind let loose' was now enabled to advance its borders and to possess the west and the south [b]; and at the end of this, the thirteenth century B.C., it is found taking a leading part in the first national effort of Israel to be free. Asher too, as we have seen [3] from the archives of Seti and Ramses, had already established itself as an organised unit, and occupied a district near the coast.

In all, the campaigns of Ramses II occupied him for about sixteen years, a relatively short proportion of the longest reign on record. It will also be gathered that with the exception of the three years following the Battle of Kadesh, his preoccupation was largely with the Hittite area of the north; and even during those years he was concerned directly with the after-effects of the Hittite penetration, if not in some cases actually with Hittite foes. His campaigns, while redressing the political situation to the temporary satisfaction of Egypt, inevitably dealt one of the deathblows to the Canaanite power and civilisation, and so furthered the continuous attempt of the Israelites to consolidate their position in the country. In accordance with established custom, clearly seen in the case of the Shasu and of the other Asiatics,[4] the Israelites themselves must have paid for their immunity a regular tribute to the coffers of the Pharaoh, providing also at the will of the local Resident or Chief food and fodder for the passage of the Pharaoh's troops. Here and there tribal elements by failure to conform with established practice, or from other

[a] Judges i 33 [J]. [b] Deuteronomy xxxiii 23.

[1] P. 243 and Fig. 5. [2] P. 244 and Fig. 4. [3] Above, p. 242.

[4] Breasted, *Anc. Rec.* ii, 101 ; iv, 219.

TELL KADES, THE SITE OF KEDESH NAPHTALI.

The mound was in occupation during the Late Bronze Age, after which the neighbouring site of the present village came into being.

TELL EL KHURBEH, POSSIBLE SITE OF BETH-ANATH.

The position overlooks the Wady Fara' at the foot of Jebel Marun.

See pp. 243, 279.

cause, might incur the wrath of the Egyptian representative, and doubtless in one way or another a number of Israelites might be led off to Egypt as civil or military prisoners.[1]

But on the whole the eighty years that followed the period of Seti's campaigns until the death of Ramses II

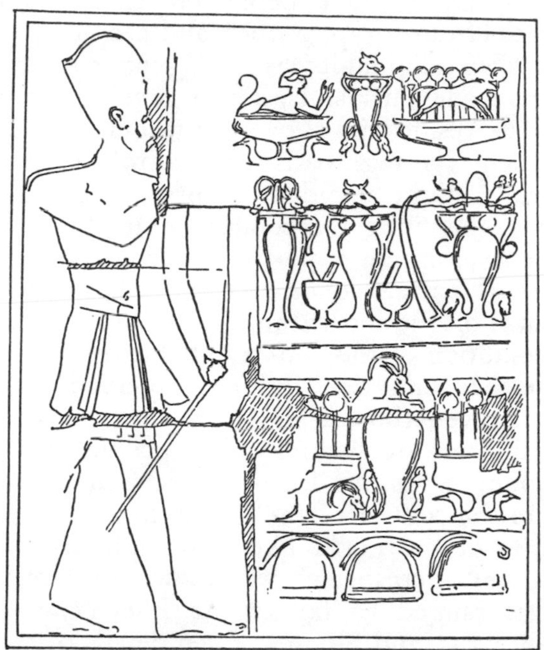

Fig. 9. Ramses II receives tribute from Syria.

(1305-1225 B.C.),[2] may be regarded as a time of unbroken peace, during which the children of Israel enjoyed rest and multiplied, and the tribes were enabled to re-weld their broken relations; so that early in the next reign the

[1] Israelite prisoners seem to be depicted among other Semites upon a painted relief from Thebes, exhibited in the Metropolitan Museum of New York, and attributable to the age of Ramses II.

[2] The discrepancy of four years in the synchronism of Biblical and Egyptian dates is within the margin of error admitted by our basis of computation. See above, p. 61.

'people Israel' is found mentioned separately by name,[1] for the first time in contemporary history. The ill-founded theory which regarded the Israelites at this time as captives in Egypt engaged upon the construction of Pithom and Ramses,[2] has long hid this reality from view.

The whole of Palestine was administered as a frontier province of Egypt; but being in Asia, separated by desert tracks from Egypt proper, and peopled by Semites with their own religion, it was not Egyptianised, any more than it was made Turkish by a later government. Egyptian officials resided in the country, officers and troops passed along its highroads and patrolled its byways. Racial feuds might smoulder or break occasionally into flame, and the hungry Bedouin on its borders would always be awaiting an opportunity for pillage; but these were internal matters concerning the police: the external horizon was bright and without clouds.

The condition of the country at this time is well seen from the Maher's descriptions preserved in *Papyrus Anastasi*, I, even though these are mingled with good-humoured chaff, for which allowance must be made. This account shows that Palestine and Canaan were quite familiar to the courier of the day, and not only were the great cities of the north like Achshaph, Acco, Hazor, Hamath, and Bethshean well known to him, but his knowledge ranged as far as the Phoenician cities of Byblos, Berytus, and Sidon. Even details of the routes, as described by him, can be recognised at once by anyone who is familiar with them.[3] 'The crossing over to Megiddo,' where 'the narrow defile is infested with Bedouin' (Shasu), applies well to the two known passes by the Wady Arah, and the Bab el Ebweib,[4] while the steep descent by the Wady Farah [5] to the Jordan at Damieh is clearly the route where 'a ravine is on one side and the

[1] On the stele of Merneptah, see below, p. 290.

[2] Cf. Peet, *Egypt and the Old Testament*, p. 108.

[3] Ed. Gardiner, *Egyptian Hieratic Texts*, Pt. I. Sec. xix, pp. 24-27.

[4] Plates X, XI.

[5] Plate XI *b*.

mountain on the other.' These tracks are described so vividly, and their dangers so playfully exaggerated, as to leave no doubt that the narrator was not only intimately acquainted with the main roads of the country, but had travelled through them at all hours and under varying conditions. At a number of points stood fortresses manned by Egyptian mercenary garrison troops: that of Bethshean has been excavated, and proof has been found that it remained in almost continuous use as an Egyptian station for nearly three hundred years. There also in his seventh year Ramses, like his predecessor, set up a memorial tablet. With the progress of excavation no doubt further illuminative detail will come to light, but it will probably fill in, rather than modify, the clear outline of Egyptian rule in Palestine during this prolonged period of rest.

SECTION 16

SHAMGAR BEN ANATH AND THE PHILISTINES

c. 1230 B.C.

JUDGES iii

31 And after him was Shamgar the son of Anath which smote of the Philistines six hundred men with an ox goad: and he also saved Israel.

A GLANCE at the chronological chart (p. 344), which compares the dates of the periods given in the Book of Judges with the contemporary reigns of Egyptian Pharaohs, will show that the period of fourscore years now drawing to a close, while conforming in broad outline with the facts of Egyptian history, is not in precise agreement as to date at the beginning and the end. We have already observed that while Seti I appears to have re-established order in Palestine by his ninth year, *c.* 1305 B.C., the period of Rest does not begin, according to these round dates, until four years later, in 1301 B.C. The difference is small, and as has been said, it may even be explained away by the remoteness of the scene of Eglon's death at the hand of Ehud from the centre of Egyptian authority. The end of the period falls in the fourth year of Merneptah, about 1221 B.C., two years after the peace of Palestine is known to have been broken by a disturbance which involved Israel itself. In this case also the apparent discrepancy is negligible, for the computation of dates admits a possible error of eight years. We have, however, to take into account the passage quoted above,[a] even though critics generally regard it as a gloss. This records the discomfiture of the Philistines on their first appearance in an undated

[a] Judges iii 31.

episode, which apparently is not of sufficient duration to break into the chronological scheme. The wording 'after him,' meaning 'after Ehud's death,' though vague, seems to point to a date within the fourscore years, therefore probably during the reign of Ramses II.

The mention of Philistines thus early has generally been regarded as anachronous, and not without reason. For it was not until about 1190 B.C. that a great movement of peoples in the North drove the Philistines and other bands as migrants towards the coast of Egypt, where they were successfully opposed by Ramses III; and the triumph scenes of the Pharaoh are among the best-known sculptures of the temples by the Nile. Yet the matter merits re-examination in the light of two recent discoveries. A photographic registration of the familiar sculptures of Medinet Habu at Thebes, where the most complete series of these scenes is preserved, shows that the army of Ramses III at the time of this great inroad already contained Philistine soldiers,[1] as well as Sherdens, so that these must have been taken prisoners, or joined the army as mercenaries, at an earlier date. Again, certain tombs recently excavated in the vicinity of Tell Fara [2] in Southern Palestine were found to contain the distinctive Philistine pottery associated with Egyptian objects of the period of Ramses II, together with Canaanite pottery characteristic of the last phase of the Late Bronze Age, a combination consistent within itself, and indicating a date estimated by the excavator Sir Wm. Flinders Petrie at about 1240 B.C.

These archaeological suggestions of a Philistine infiltration into Palestine before 1200 B.C. invite a careful review of the literary evidence. The Philistines and their comrades, whom Ramses III dispersed, came by land as well

[1] Nelson, *Medinet Habu* (Or. Inst. of Univ. of Chicago). 1924-28. P. 5 and Fig. 4.

[2] Petrie, *Catalogue of Egyptian, Hyksos and Philistine Antiquities found at Beth-pelet, Palestine, 1929*. P. 5, tomb 552, 1240 B.C. The evidence of tomb 542, which suggests an earlier date, is less reliable owing to the possibility of admixture or intrusion arising from the superposition of the burials.

Fig. 10. The fortress of Askalon retaken by Ramses II.

as by sea, and it becomes significant to find that in the record of his successful resistance the Pharaoh alludes to some Philistines as actually living within the area of conflict, 'The Peleset are hung up in their towns,'[1] and therefore not farther than the Phoenician frontier which marked the limit of his preparations.[2]

This fact brings back to memory the allusions to Philistines settled in the vicinity of Gerar as early as the Patriarchal age in the xxvith chapter of the Book of Genesis which is ascribed to an early source (J). But in this case the name of the king and the incidents narrated do not reveal the Philistines in the same light as they appear in history, when finally established upon the plain and sea-board, so that these references may be dismissed as anachronisms based on subsequent developments, and similar to expressions like 'the way of the land of the Philistines' and the 'Sea of the Philistines' in the Book of Exodus.[a] Accordingly we do not take these passages into consideration.

Whatever may lie behind these suggestions of earlier settlements of Philistines in Palestine, one thing seems certain, they were not at that time organised as found later in the age of Samson at the beginning of the eleventh century B.C. Nor do the inhabitants of Askalon overcome by Ramses II (*c.* 1290 B.C.), as represented in the art of Egypt,[3] be they Canaanites or Hittites, bear any resemblance in facial type or armour to the Philistines of the time of Ramses III, a century later. The coming of their vanguard may thus be ascribed on the evidence to the last years of the reign of Ramses II, *c.* 1230 B.C.[4] They were smitten, and Israel was saved, according to the Bible narrative, by Shamgar Ben Anath. It is then peculiarly significant to find that 'Ben Anath' was the name of a Syrian sea-captain upon whom Ramses II

[a] Exodus xiii 17 and xxiii 31.

[1] Breasted, *Anct. Rec.* iv, 71. [2] *Ibid.* iv, 65. [3] Fig. 10, p. 286.

[4] A date not far removed from that of Sisera is indicated by the association of the two episodes in the same setting in Judges v 6 quoted below.

bestowed the signal favour of a royal alliance.[1] If this coincidence in date and circumstance and name indicates the truth, we secure a solution of several interesting questions. It would be the protecting arm of Egypt that warded off this Philistine invasion from Palestine, and it is instructive to note that Shamgar is not claimed by the Israelites as a Judge. The combat having taken place at sea, or by the shore, the area most involved would be the coastlands that looked towards Egypt. Apparently Israel was saved on this occasion from the menace of invasion rather than an actual aggression. Hence the fact that this deliverance plays no part in the chronological scheme of the period, and does not interrupt the long period of rest under Ramses II; nor is the incident recorded as an oppression. None the less the terror inspired by this menace evidently left behind a deep impression, which found its echo in the nation's songs as the memory of a time of fear and danger:

JUDGES V

> **6 In the days of Shamgar the son of Anath,**
> **In the days of Jael, the highways were unoccupied.**
> **And the travellers walked through byways. [E]**

In Egypt a similar deliverance from national danger under Merneptah was celebrated in words which present a noticeable similarity of thought and expression:[2]

> Sit down happily and talk and walk far out upon the way, for there is no fear in the heart of the people. The strongholds are left to themselves, the wells are opened again. . . . One comes and goes with singing. . . . The towns are settled again anew.[3]

[1] Breasted, *Hist. Egypt*, p. 449. From an ostracon in the Louvre Museum N. 2262, publ. in the *Receuil*, xvi, 64.

[2] Merneptah. Breasted, *Hist. Egypt*, p. 470.

[3] Breasted, *Anc. Rec.* iii, 616.

SECTION 17

REUNION OF THE TRIBES UNDER DEBORAH

OPPRESSION BY SISERA

1221-1201 B.C.

JUDGES iv

1 **And the children of Israel again did that which was evil in**
2 **the sight of the Lord, when Ehud was dead. And the Lord**
sold them into the hand of Jabin King of Canaan, that
reigned in Hazor; the captain of whose host was Sisera,
3 **which dwelt in Harosheth of the Gentiles. And the**
children of Israel cried unto the Lord: for he had nine
hundred chariots of iron; and twenty years he mightily
oppressed the children of Israel. [E2]

THE political calm which had enfolded the Egyptian world during the last fifty years of Ramses II was so fixed and widespread that even the change of ruler at his death brought about no reactionary disturbance. Merneptah succeeded peacefully to the throne of the Pharaoh about 1221 B.C., and it was not until the third year of his reign that the long peace was broken. Looking back we see that from 1287 B.C. when Ramses had set up his monument at Bethshean, no incident is on record that might have jeopardised the period of rest vouchsafed to Israel. During this time, on the contrary, we find Asher recognised as an established unit on the extreme north-west, and the fall first of Kedesh, and then of Beth-Anath to have removed the great difficulties that beset the path of Naphtali to their inheritance.[1] Expeditionary forces had brought order by way of the roads between Acco and Yenoam, passing thus through the territory allotted to Zebulun.[2] It may safely be concluded that it was during these sixty-five years of uninterrupted peace, that

[1] Pp. 244, 280. [2] Pp. 240, 270.

the northern tribes made good their footing. In the central highlands also, from the date when Upper Retenu had been last brought to tribute,[1] there is no record of further disturbing factors, and this very name soon disappears from history. Amid the evident decline of the old Canaanite power, upon which successive Pharaohs had levelled blow after blow, it would appear that at this time the House of Joseph also came to enjoy the blessings which Jacob,[a] their great ancestor, had reserved for them, and had been promised again by Moses. They had survived the great perils.

> The archers have sorely grieved him,
> And shot at him, and persecuted him,
> But his bow abode in strength.

The bough was becoming fruitful: the strength of Ephraim was measured by ten thousands, and that of Manasseh by thousands. Not only had the children of Joseph found the opportunity to extend their inheritance 'unto the utmost bound of the everlasting hills' which encircled their horizon,[2] but we have seen on the stele from Beisan [3] a suggestion of the expansion of Manasseh beyond the Jordan towards the east.

These developments in the centre and the north prepare us to appreciate at their full value the words and significance of Merneptah's victory stele,[4] the monument which tells us nearly all we know about his campaign in Asia; for upon this occurs the first and only independent historical reference to Israel:

> The HITTITE LAND is pacified,
> Plundered is the CANAAN, with every evil,
> Carried off is ASKALON,
> Seized upon is GEZER.
> YENOAM is made as a thing not existing,

[a] Genesis xlix 23, 24.

[1] Breasted, *Anct. Rec.* iii, 366. [2] Pl. LIV. [3] P. 271 f.

[4] Breasted, *Anct. Rec.* iii, 617.

ISRAEL is desolated, her seed is not,
S. PALESTINE[1] has become a (defenceless) widow
for Egypt,
All lands are united, they are pacified;
Everyone that is turbulent is bound by king
Merneptah.

This inscription is dated to *c.* 1223 B.C. and is contemporary with the events described: it is thus some three or four hundred years older than the earliest documentary sources which criticism has traced through the pages of the Bible itself.[2] The reference to Israel is therefore of paramount importance. Though details are lacking, the general tenour of this inscription is obvious. Circumstances had called for an expeditionary force into the north of Palestine, and it appears from rough notes made by an Egyptian officer at the time, and happily preserved,[3] that the period of military activity and the moving of troops in the area began in Merneptah's third year, at which time a captain of infantry was posted at Tyre and a royal steward in southern Palestine. The troops followed the time-honoured coastal route by Gezer and Askalon. The extent of the disturbance is apparent from the fact that it was necessary to recapture even these frontier cities. Possibly the Philistines or other sea peoples were already hammering at their gates. But Yenoam lay in the north, one of the key positions frequently contested.[4] 'Israel' in this context refers apparently to the northern tribes in Galilee; but it may include the central plateau where the Joseph tribes were now settled in the hill country around Shechem, if we are to read *Kharu* as referring exclusively to southern Palestine or Judah.

The cause of this disturbance is not clear, but it hardly arose as a spontaneous rebellion. The sea was bearing rovers and pirates in threatening numbers from the Aegean world. Some of these leagued themselves with

[1] Egn. *Kharu* or *Ḥaru*. [2] Except the lost Book of Jashar: see p. 4.
[3] Breasted, *Anct. Rec.* iii, 630, 633, 634. [4] Pp. 73, 99; Maps 3, 7.

the Libyans, and their united raids upon the western delta of Egypt, though resisted by Merneptah with the strongest force which he could muster, created widespread alarm.[1] Among these raiders were some who had previously fought with the Hittite king at Kadesh, and the Pharaoh's problem was not simplified by the fact that units of his own army were recruited from the same sources. Familiar detachments were the Lycians and Sherdens, while among the newcomers are found Ekwesh, Shekelesh, and Teresh.[2] Who exactly these were, or whence they came, cannot be regarded as certain; but the Ekwesh seem clearly to be identified with the Aḥiawans of the Hittite texts,[3] the Achaeans of Homeric legend, who for a hundred years or more had already been harassing the coasts of Asia Minor,[4] and at this time had gained a footing on the island of Cyprus.[5] Their association with the Lycians (Luka) in adventures a generation before the siege of Troy is reflected in the Homeric poems.[6] The other bands no doubt were kindred tribes united in this common enterprise. The Luka and Sherdens had fought, as we have said, on the side of the Hittite king at Kadesh, and the present disturbance can best be explained by supposing that these sea-rovers, before joining hands with the Libyans in their raids on Egypt, had landed on the coasts of Syria and there stirred up a similar outbreak among their one-time comrades in arms. The activity of the Pharaoh's troops at Yenoam and at Tyre favours this hypothesis.

Such were the conditions under which Sisera, whose name betrays a northern connexion,[7] seems to have made good his footing in the plain of Acco,[8] presumably

[1] Breasted, *Anc. Rec.* iii, 580 *sqq.*

[2] Breasted, *Anc. Rec.* iii, 579. Cf. *C.A.H* ii, pp. 281 ff.

[3] Forrer, *M.D.O.G.*, 63, p. 9. [4] Götze, *Maduwattas*, pp. 147 ff.

[5] *K.V.B.* xiv, No. 1; cf. Forrer, *loc. cit.* pp. 21 f.; Götze, *loc. cit.* pp. 10 f.; G., *H.E.*, pp. 10, 43.

[6] Homer, *Iliad*, ii, 815-7.

[7] Cf. Burney, *Judges*, p. 84; *C.A.H.* ii, p. 386.

[8] Below, p. 296; Pl. LXIII.

after the Pharaoh had withdrawn his troops to stem the Libyan invasion. There by alliance with the King of Hazor,[1] in the form perhaps of mercenary service, he

Fig. 11. Type of Aegean or western warrior, designed from contemporary monuments.

not only bolstered up thc failing powers of the old Canaanitish centre but established firmly his own position on the prestige and organisation of his chief.

Notwithstanding that Merneptah staved off the more serious inroads of the allies in the west, affairs went badly for the Pharaoh. The Egyptian sun was setting, and now a series of internal shocks shook the throne, plunging the country into disorder and even anarchy. During these troublous times there could be no question of

[1] For the strategic position see the Map No. 13, p. 188.

succour for those in Palestine who looked to Egypt for protection. On the other hand the records tell of the admission of refugee Bedouin tribes from Edom at the pools of Pithom, in order to sustain them and their herds in the domain of the Pharaoh.[1] There are no further records as to Palestine, but even these benign intentions were rudely arrested by fresh disturbances that broke out in Egypt on Merneptah's death. Finally in 1205 B.C. a Syrian usurper seized the throne and held it for five years; so that for about twenty-one years Sisera was able to exercise his tyranny without restraint. This state of affairs plunged Israel in jeopardy, threatening with disruption the growing prospect of reunion at the very time when the tribes had attained their goal. It was at this crisis, the gravest which had menaced the growing nation, that Deborah the prophetess arose and gathered the tribes together, 'a mother in Israel.'

DELIVERANCE BY BARAK OF NAPHTALI

JUDGES iv

4 Now Deborah, a prophetess, . . . judged Israel at that time. . . . [E2]

6 And she sent and called Barak the son of Abinoam out of Kedesh Naphtali, and she said unto him, hath not the Lord, the God of Israel, commanded, saying, Go and draw unto Mount Tabor, and take with thee ten thousand men of the children of Naphtali and of the children of Zebulun ?

7 And I will draw unto thee to the River Kishon Sisera, the captain of Jabin's army, with his chariots and his multitude; and I will deliver him into thine hand. [E]

Esdraelon

THE references to Taanach, Tabor and the Kishon, in the further description of this stirring episode, bring us to the plain of Esdraelon. The boundaries and physical character of this plain have been described ;[2] it will,

[1] Breasted, *Anct. Rec.* iii, 638. [2] Pp. 92 ff.

THE PLAIN OF ESDRAELON, TOWARDS THE WEST.

Viewed from Megiddo: the heights of Carmel on the L.

PLAIN OF ESDRAELON, TOWARDS THE EAST.

Viewed from near Nazareth. In the Centre the Jebel Duhy; on the R. the crest of Mt. Gilboa.

See pp. 92, 295.

however, be helpful to our understanding of the narrative to recall some of its special features.

The plain, though generally level, is not altogether flat, but gains character particularly towards the west from the long and low undulations of its soil; and this feature is sharpened by the attrition slowly taking place along the banks of the numberless stream-beds that break its surface like the veins of a leaf. To-day,[1] except in the vicinity of certain villages, it is given over mostly to herds of cattle, which in summer-time walk miles for their daily allowance of water; and so little is its natural peace and partial desolation disturbed that deer and gazelle may occasionally be seen browsing on the scanty herbage.

The area of this historic plain is small: it may be regarded as triangular in shape, with its apex in the north-east at Tabor. Thence its northern and eastern borders lie away, seventeen miles in either case, as far as its southern angle at Jenin and its western angle at Tell Kussîs, this last being an ancient site upon the river's course at the foot of Carmel. The south-western side of the triangle, which joins the angles so defined, is longer and measures perhaps twenty miles.

An old road coming from the plain of Acco past Kussîs connects Megiddo and Taanach with Jenin; and where it hugs the foot of the border ridge, its course is marked here and there by chariot wheel-ruts in the rock. The ancient highroad from Egypt, traversing this ridge from Sharon by the defile of the Wady Arah, emerged at Megiddo into the plain, which it crossed direct upon the foot of Tabor, whence by Han Tujjar, Hattin and Tell Oreimeh it continued its way towards Hazor and Damascus.[2]

The tribe of Issachar, to whom this district had fallen by Lot, was presumably still eking out a more or less nomadic existence upon and around the plain, while doubtless taking advantage of every opportunity to settle.

[1] Notes written in 1926-7.

[2] Cf. Map No. 13, p. 188.

We have already found reason in the Egyptian records to believe that the other tribes of the north, Zebulun and Naphtali, though scattered throughout Galilee, and Manasseh to the south, after passing through similar experiences, had begun to emerge from the difficulties of their situation, and to make good their footing,[1] when the tyranny of Sisera suddenly arrested their development.

Harosheth

The development of the political situation that aroused so many tribes to a common effort cannot well be understood, nor can the details of the ensuing battle be followed, without locating Harosheth, the starting point of Sisera's movements. Certain indications are given in the text. From the narrative[a] it is clear that the routed charioteers took flight in the direction of Harosheth, and from the Song[b] that ultimately they were swept away by the River Kishon. Now we have seen that while the plain of Esdraelon is traversed by numerous tributaries of the Kishon which come down from all its borders, these streams are for the most part small, many of them being little more than shallow channels. Even the bed of the Kishon itself as it wanders north-westward through the plain, hardly ever attains a greater depth than three or four feet. Indeed along its course there is found within the plain no place sufficiently deep even in flood time to satisfy the conditions of the narrative. For such a position we must look at its exit from the plain between the foot of Carmel and the south-west point of the Galilean hills, a passage not a mile wide, through which run at the present time river, road, and railway. This is marked at its eastern extremity by Tell el Kussîs and its western end by Tell Amr.[2] In this corridor the waters of the Kishon are all collected into a single bed which in places is six yards deep or more, and twenty yards across.

[a] Judges iv 16. [E] [b] Judges v 21. [E]

[1] Above, pp. 272, 280.

[2] Cf. *B.S.A.J.*, Bulletin No. 2, 1922, pp. 9 ff. and Map, Pl. I.

TELL HARBAJ, PROBABLE SITE OF HAROSHETH, WITH CARMEL IN THE BACKGROUND.

Republished by courtesy of the British School of Archæology in Jerusalem.

See p. 297.

THE RIVER KISHON. WHERE IT ENTERS THE PLAIN OF ACRE.

Numerous streams of the Nahr Muketta which water the plain of Esdraelon are here united in a single channel.

MT. TABOR, AS SEEN FROM THE NORTH-EAST.

In the foreground Han el Tujjar, a station on the old road to the north.

See pp. 92, 294.

This channel, usually dry, or containing only stagnant pools, fills up rapidly after rain and becomes a formidable torrent. Hereabout also Nature has designed a ford, at a place no doubt where the rock rises sufficiently near the surface, for it seems to be permanent; and until the route was modified in recent years this passage was much used during the dry season. Only two other crossings are found and these are much higher up the course of the river, one immediately opposite Megiddo on the way across the plain towards Semunieh, and the other opposite Taanak[1] on the road from that place or from Megiddo to Afuleh.

It is already clear that the site of Harosheth must be sought near the exit of the Kishon from the Plain of Esdraelon: and indeed the name seems to have survived or reappeared in the form Harithiyeh among the foothills on the side of Galilee quite close to the ford. On examination in 1922, however, it was found that the village of that name rested upon bare rock, and did not mark a historic site; indeed it has now disappeared and been replaced by a settlement upon the plain. It was thus probably a case of name transference from some more ancient place. The nearest such site lies on the south bank of the river, not more than a mile away, and it is called Tell Amr. Excavations do not show this to have been an important or defended site in the thirteenth century B.C., and furthermore, its situation on the same side of the Kishon as Taanak could not be well reconciled with the context. However, some three miles from the name-site Harithiyeh, a more imposing tell, called El Harbaj, stands by a small tributary of the Kishon on the north side of the parent stream. On excavation it proved to have been occupied intensively during the latter centuries of the Bronze Age, when indeed it was further protected by an encircling wall of stone.[2] Though rising some twelve yards only above the plain, its length is fully two hundred

[1] *Bibl.* Taanach.

[2] *B.S.A.J.*, Bulletin 2 (1922), pp. 12 f.; further, *ibid.* No. 4, pp. 45 f.

yards, and being round in shape its surface covers an area of about six acres, so that in its greatest period of prosperity it may have contained some 1500 people. Its history came to an end about this time, for there is very sparse indication of occupation during the Iron Age, after 1200 B.C., and the flat shape of the mound shows that there can have been little building upon any part of its surface from that time onward. This position then seems to satisfy all the conditions of the narrative. The site fulfils the archaeological requirements of the period; and it is sufficiently near to the name-site of Harithiyeh to justify its identity with Harosheth.

BARAK DEFEATS SISERA

c. 1201 B.C.

JUDGES V.

19 The Kings came and fought;
Then fought the Kings of Canaan,
In Taanach by the waters of Megiddo:

. . . .

20 The stars in their courses fought against Sisera.
21 The river Kishon swept them away. [E]

The location of Harosheth enables us to examine the further development of the struggle and its political consequences. Throughout the battle itself there may be traced the studied tactics of Deborah and her kinsmen who knew the plain. In arranging the campaign with Barak she had promised to 'draw out Sisera to the river Kishon,' [a] and later when the concentration of the northern tribesmen upon the slopes of Tabor was complete it was she who determined the moment for action: 'Up, for this is the day.' [b]

It is obvious that under the normal conditions of dry weather the chariots of Sisera would have had a pronounced advantage over the unmounted Israelites when fighting upon the plain. But after rain the situation

[a] Judges iv 7 [E]. [b] Judges iv 14 [E].

would be reversed. During the Great War experience showed that a quarter of an hour's rain on this clay soil endangered the issue of all cavalry manœuvres. This was evidently the determining factor in Deborah's plan, and it is reflected in the Song.[a] The tactical move was to

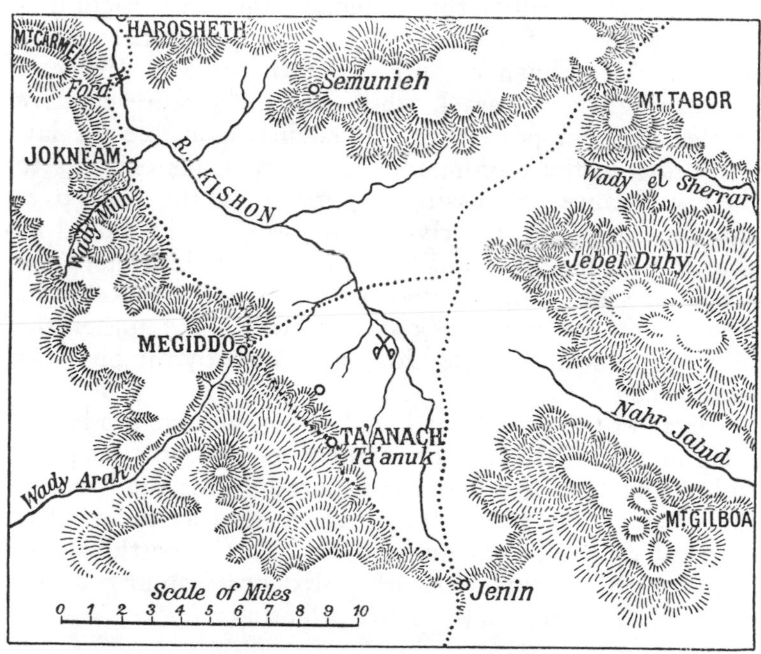

Map 16. The plain of Esdraelon: scene of the decisive battle 'at Taanach by the waters of Megiddo' where Barak defeated Sisera.

draw Sisera with his chariotry to the valley when rain was imminent. No attempt was made to disguise the assembling of the northern tribesmen on Tabor. The news was told to Sisera, who gathered together all the chariots and warriors under his command 'from Harosheth unto the river Kishon.'[b] This point of concentration commanded the ford at the foot of Carmel.

Meanwhile, the warriors of the southern tribes who had responded to Deborah's call, entering the plain at the

[a] Judges v 22-23 [E]. [b] Judges iv 13 [E2].

usual place by Jenin, would find themselves almost at once in the fields of Taanach by the Kishon. There apparently they were joined at once by Barak and the leaders of Issachar.[a] In this selected spot and, as it seems, at Deborah's chosen moment, the Canaanitish Kings whose territory this gathering menaced, including doubtless those of Taanach, Megiddo, the nameless city on Tell Abu Shusheh, and Jokneam on Tell Keimun, came to fight with Israel, while Sisera, the representative of the northern power, and as such responsible for law and order in the region, moved out with his chariots to their assistance. Crossing the river by the ford over against Harosheth, the river being still dry, he would be able to join his allies and approach the point where the Israelites were concentrated near the south bank of the Kishon, by the well-marked road which led under the hills by Jokneam to Megiddo and thence by the highway across the plain.

Detail of the actual battle is lacking, and we are left to imagine the swift series of infantry movements, designed to lure the chariotry more and more towards the basin of the river. One thing seems clear, that at the critical moment rain fell sufficiently to reduce the battlefield to a quagmire, in which the affrighted horses plunged and reared in their efforts to secure a footing:

> **Then did the horsehoofs stamp**
> **By reason of the pransings.**[b]

The advantage was now with the infantry, before whose impetuous onslaughts the chariotry, already in difficulties, lost their formation, then broke and fled. Pursued and harassed in the retreat by Barak,[c] the routed charioteers, making for Harosheth, would find the now swollen river between themselves and safety. An indescribable confusion of men and horses plunging into the dangerous ford to escape from the worse fury of the

[a] Judges v 15 [E]. [b] Judges v 22 [E].
[c] Judges iv 16 [E2].

TELL ABU KUDEIS, PROBABLE SITE OF KEDESH, Judges iv, 11.

The small mound lies between Ta'anak and Megiddo near the edge of the Plain of Esdraelon, and bears trace of occupation in the Late Bronze Age.

THE APPROACH TO TELL ABU KUDEIS AND THE BATTLEFIELD OF ESDRAELON.

In the background the hills of Galilee and Mt. Tabor, R.

See pp. 233, 301.

victorious Israelites completed the havoc of the day. The River Kishon swept them away.[a]

When the chariot line broke, Sisera became separated from his force. Lighting down from his chariot he fled away on his feet[b], and took refuge in the tent of Jael, the wife of Heber the Kenite, who had pitched his tent by Kedesh.[c] This place is not far to seek. The name Tell Abu Kudeis clings to a small mound of Bronze-age origin which is to be found in the plain near the field of battle, some three miles from Taanach or Megiddo,[1] and about the same distance from the nearest crossing of the Kishon, which lies almost due north. Every year there may be seen in the autumn the tents of certain Bedouin Arabs from the Negeb of Beersheba (the old Kenite area) who come by rotation of families to graze and glean this quarter of the plain. This is an established custom, older than human memory, which has survived all known political changes and is one of a number of such annual movements up the coastal plain.[2] A position near Tell Abu Kudeis for Heber's tent would suit the context perfectly. Sisera, wearied by his long day and his defeat, though invited into the tent to avoid detection seems to have violated the women's quarters, a breach which under Bedouin law would probably involve death. In any case, Jael, strange as it seems, without waiting the return of her men-folk, killed the sleeping guest and was hailed by the Israelites as a national heroine. Unless Jael acted purely in defence of her good name, it is only possible to explain this dramatic sequel to the battle by the supposition that the bond between Jael and Israel, for whom she struck the blow, was nearer and deeper than the newly established peace between Sisera's overlord, the King of Hazor, and the house of Heber, in other words that Jael was herself an Israelitess.

In other respects the narrative speaks for itself. With Sisera dead, the chariots put to rout and largely destroyed,

[a] Judges v 21 [E]. [b] Judges iv 15 [E]. [c] Judges iv 11 [E].

[1] The site marked by a circle on Map 16. [2] See above, p. 82.

the faded power of Hazor would hardly be able for some time to redress the situation, which left the Israelites thus temporarily masters of the plain with its approaches, and reunited as between north and south.

DEBORAH'S SONG OF TRIUMPH

As translated by the late Rev. C. F. Burney, D.Litt.

JUDGES V

6 From the days of Shamgar ben-'Anath,
From the days of old, caravans ceased.
And they that went along the ways used to walk by crooked paths.
7 Villages ceased in Israel;
. . . . ceased;
Till thou didst arise, Deborah,
Didst arise as a mother in Israel.
8 Armourers had they none;
Armed men failed from the city:
Was there seen a shield or a lance
Among forty thousand in Israel?
12 Awake, awake, Deborah!
Awake, awake, sing paean!
Rise up, Barak, and lead captive
Thy captors, O son of Abinoam!
9 Come, ye commanders of Israel!
Ye that volunteered among the people, bless ye Yahweh!
10 Let the riders on tawny she-asses (review it)
And let the wayfarers (recall it to mind).
11 Hark to the maidens laughing at the wells!
There they recount the righteous acts of Yahweh,
The righteous acts of his arm in Israel.
13 Then down to the gates gat the nobles;
Yahweh's folk gat them down 'mid the heroes.
14 From Ephraim they spread out on the vale;
After thee, Benjamin! 'mid thy clansmen.

Pl. LXVI.

TELL TA'ANUK: TAANACH BY THE WATERS OF MEGIDDO.

See pp. 231, 300.

From Machir came down the commanders,
And from Zebulun men wielding the truncheon.
15 And thy princes, Issachar, were with Deborah;
And Naphtali was leal (to) Barak:
To the vale he was loosed at his heel.

(Utterly reft) into factions was Reuben;
Great were his searchings of heart.

16 Why sat'st thou still amid the folds,
To hear the pastoral pipings?
17 Gilead beyond the Jordan dwelt,
And Dan abideth by the ships.
Asher sat still by the shore of the seas,
Dwelling beside his creeks.
18 Zebulun is the folk that scorned its life to the death,
And Naphtali on the heights of the field.
19 On came the kings, they fought;
Then fought the kings of Canaan;
In Ta'anach, by the rills of Megiddo;
The gain of money they took not.
20 From heaven fought the stars;
From their highways they fought with Sisera.
21 The torrent Kishon swept them off;
It faced them, the torrent Kishon.
Bless thou, my soul, the might (of Yahweh).

The Book of Judges, pp. 103-4.

The Political Situation

c. 1200 B.C.

JUDGES V

14 Out of Ephraim came down they whose root is in Amalek;
After thee, Benjamin, among thy peoples;
Out of Machir came down governors,
And out of Zebulun they that handle the marshal's staff.
15 And the princes of Issachar were with Deborah;
As was Issachar, so was Barak.
Into the valley they rushed forth at his feet.
By the watercourses of Reuben
There were great resolves of heart. [E]

THIS episode marked the first recorded effort of the tribes to unite in a common enterprise since the campaigns of Joshua two hundred years before, though it is true that their development had already attained a stage of consolidation which had gained for Israel separate mention in the annals of the Pharaoh Merneptah.[1] On this occasion, according to the prose narrative,[a] a prominent part was taken by the northern tribes of Zebulun and Naphtali, which evidently had securely established themselves in their 'inheritance' during the long period of Peace under Ramses II, and multiplied, so that they now were able to muster ten thousand fighting men.[b] These figures may be taken as a general index to the increased numbers of the tribes as a whole at this epoch, which transpire with due proportion in one of the opening verses of the Song:

8 Was there a shield or spear seen
Among forty thousand in Israel. [E]

This allusion implies a total population at this time of some 200,000 people as compared with 5000 or 6000 eight generations previously. The high coefficient of increase involved can hardly be admissible even under oriental

[a] Judges iv 10 [E]. [b] Judges iv 14 [E].

[1] P. 290.

conditions, unless allowance be made for alliance and intermarriage with kindred native elements of the population.[1]

Whatever may have been the precise figures, it is evident that the Israelites were multiplying in numbers, and that neither the long period of waiting nor the oppressions had deadened the conscience of the nation. The Song, which is no doubt older in structure than the prose narrative and takes a broader view, shows that four other tribes responded to Deborah's call, namely Ephraim and Benjamin from the south, Machir representing Manasseh, which may already have extended to the east of Jordan,[2] and Issachar, whose lot lay within the zone of conflict. Of Judah there is no mention, and indeed throughout the Book of Judges there is hardly more than a reflection of this tribe, the emergence of which as a unit from the difficulties of its political environment must be regarded in consequence as not yet having become effective, a conclusion accordant with what is known of its chequered history.[3] The Trans-Jordanian tribes, Reuben and Gad, also took no part in the struggle. Dan, presumably at this time already established on the borders of the Huleh Lake,[4] would find itself cut off by the dominion of Hazor from its tribal neighbour of Naphtali, a fact which answers plausibly the pointed question, 'Dan why did he remain in ships?'[a] The tribesmen of Asher also found themselves in an even more embarrassing situation. The stronghold of Sisera, and his lines of communication with Hazor, lay between them and the scene of battle, while their position near the seaboard doubtless brought them into daily contact with those who owed allegiance to Sisera himself. To move might have proved fatal:

Asher sat still at the haven[b] of the sea
And abode by his creeks.[c]

Making due allowance for the special circumstances

[a] Judges v 17 [E]. [b] *Or*, shore. [c] Judges v 17 [E].

[1] Cf. pp. 281, 326. [2] Cf. pp. 272-3. [3] Cf. p. 276.

[4] Cf. Burney, *Judges*, p. 143.

affecting the absentees, this rally of six leading tribes indicates a definite movement of the Israelites towards reunion. Their victory, by clearing the pathway, must have given impetus to the further development and closer cohesion of the nation. The Bronze Age with its Canaanitish civilisation was drawing to a close, while the coming of the Sea-rovers, heralded as it would appear by Sisera, and culminating in the Philistine invasions, marked an influx of fresh life and vigour with the Iron Age of which they formed the vanguard. The advent of these peoples in the issue affected the political and social organisation more profoundly than any movement which had stirred the country for five hundred years.

The episode of Sisera's defeat and the final downfall of the Canaanite regime falls approximately about the year 1200 B.C. The occasion was timely, for in the next year the crowning of a new Pharaoh brought to an end the regime of the Syrian usurper *Yarsu*, who had 'overthrown the land of Egypt from without and plunged the whole country into anarchy.' The new monarch Set-Nekht quickly restored the prestige of the Pharaoh's throne. 'He set in order the entire land and slew the rebels.' [1] The re-establishment of authority and order with Egypt's revival would aid the Israelites to secure in peace the fruits of their victory.

PERIOD OF PEACE

c. 1201-1161 B.C.

JUDGES V

31 The land had rest forty years. [E]

Set-Nekht reigned only about two years, but the measures taken by him to set order in the land seem to have been effective in Palestine as well as Egypt, for when his successor was called upon to face a grave crisis in the early years of his reign, the scene of greatest military activity lay northward on the Phoenician coast; and

[1] Breasted, *Anct. Rec.* iv, 399.

although the immediate seaboard of Palestine may have been involved, and witnessed at any rate the passage of the Pharaoh's troops, there is no indication that the inland areas were disturbed by this event; while thereafter 'only a revolt of the Bedouin of Seir interrupted the peaceful government of the Pharaoh in Asia from this time forth.' [1] Indeed, Ramses III, the Pharaoh who was called upon to face this menace of invasion, after the successful issue of his campaign, took pains to leave a record of the complete re-establishment of peace.[2]

'I made the woman of Egypt to go . . . to the place she desired; no stranger nor anyone on the road molested her. I made the infantry and chariotry to dwell (at home) in my time; the Sherden and Kehek were in their towns, lying (the length) of their backs: they had no fear for there was no enemy from Kush (Nubia) nor foe from Syria. The land was well satisfied in my reign.'

Ramses III reigned for thirty-one years, from 1198 to 1167 B.C. The first signs of danger to Egypt appeared from the west, in the fifth year of his reign, when the Libyans, accompanied as in the reign of Merneptah by Sea-rovers, made inroads upon the Delta, evidently with the intention of seizing land to settle. At the same time, unless this record be misplaced,[3] bands of Philistines and their companion Thekels are found raiding the river mouths of the Egyptian Delta, where as it is graphically said, they were 'like wild fowl creeping into the net.' [4] Some 'came by land, but Amon-Ra was behind them, destroying them.' Then in 1191 B.C., the eighth year of Ramses' reign, the threatening storm burst upon Egyptian Syria, in the form of a great movement of peoples from the north. This time the Philistines and Thekels were definitely involved, borne on, it would seem, by the irresistible torrent of a general migration out of eastern Europe which, coming by land as well as by sea, had already swept through Asia Minor and north Syria,

[1] Breasted, *Hist.* p. 484.
[2] *Ibid. Anc. Rec.* iv, 410.
[3] *Ibid.* iv, 44.
[4] *Ibid.* iv, 44.

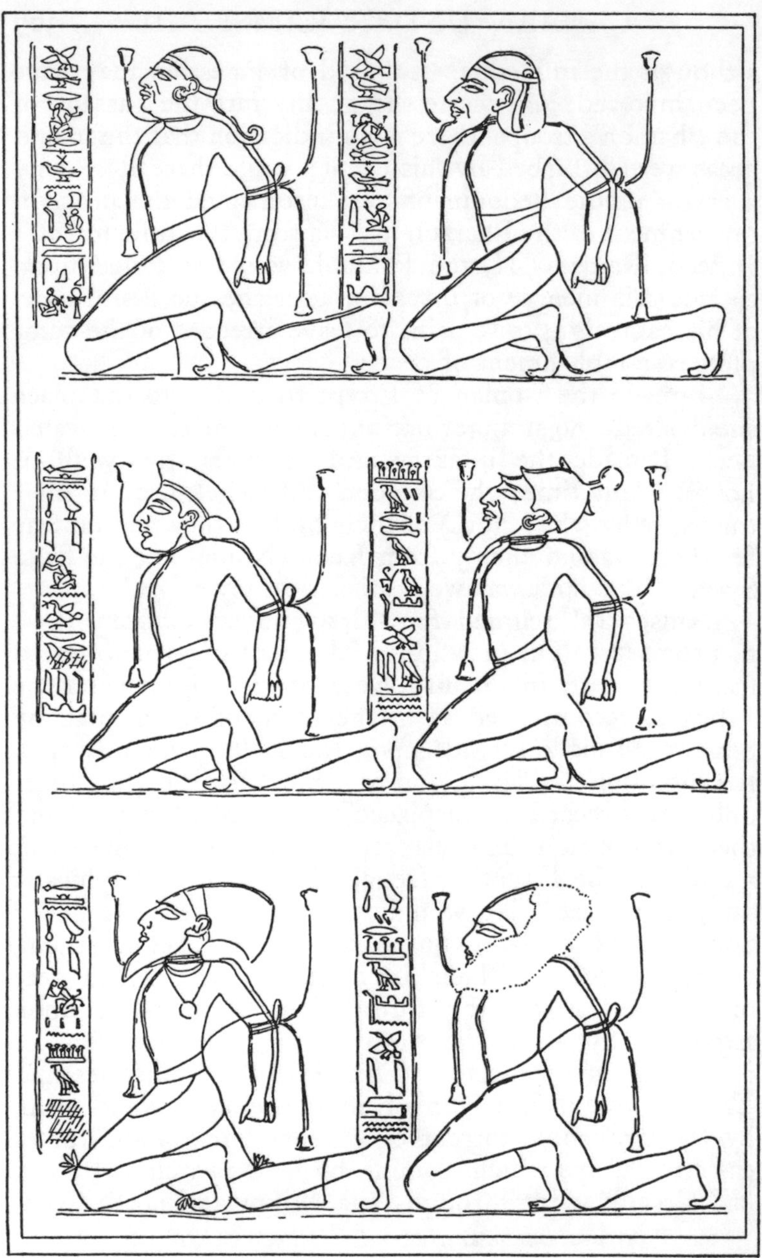

Fig. 12. Prisoners taken together with Philistines by Ramses III.

destroying the Hittite empire, and now menaced even the frontiers of Egypt. The Pharaoh's annals give a succinct but graphic description of this epoch-making movement.

'The countries . . . of the northerners in their isles were disturbed. . . . Not one stood before their hands, from Ḥatti, Kode, Carchemish, Arvad and Alasa they were wasted. (They set up) a camp in Amor.[1] They desolated his people and his land like that which is not. They came with fire prepared before them, forward to Egypt. Their main support was Peleset, Thekel, Shekelesh, Denyen, and Weshesh. These lands were united, and they laid their hands upon the land as far as the Circle of the Earth.'[2]

The Pharaoh, duly warned, made adequate preparations in Zahi, upon the Phoenician coast; and finally in one of the creeks along the shore he met and repelled the invaders both by land and sea. A scene sculptured upon the pavilion of the temple which Ramses set up at Medinet Habu in Thebes shows a line of seven captives typifying this horde, with their racial peculiarities and costumes clearly depicted.[3] They include:

(i) A Hittite, 'the wretched chief of Ḥatti as a living captive.'
(ii) An Amorite, 'the wretched chief of Amor.'
(iii) An Asiatic, 'Chieftain of the foe of Thekel.'
(iv) A Sherden,[4] 'Sherden of the Sea.'
(v) A Bedouin, 'Chieftain of the foe of Shasu.'
(vi) A Teresh, 'Teresh of the Sea' (? Tursian or possibly Trojan).
(vii) (A Philistine), 'Chieftain of the Peleset' (Philistines).

[1] Possibly at El Mishrefeh near Homs in Central Syria. Cf. G., *HE.*, p. 324.

[2] Breasted, *Anct. Rec.* iv, 64.

[3] *Ibid.* iv, 129. Lepsius, *Denk.* vii 209. Our Fig. 12. The figure of the Philistine being mutilated is replaced by a separate drawing on p. 313, Fig. 14.

[4] So also in the Harris Papyrus (Breasted, *Anct. Rec.* iv, 603), though in the passage quoted above from the temple of Medinet Habu the fifth group in the

In these records and in the further details of this episode from Egyptian sources, we find no mention of 'Kharu,' *i.e.* inland and southern Palestine, which would hardly be disturbed by this movement down the coast. The issue of the struggle, nevertheless, must have affected the Israelites indirectly, for from about this time there is evidence that Philistines lived and died in some of the towns of the Shephelah and the southern plain, where they are found settled when first mentioned in later Bible narrative. The Thekels also reappear within the century settled upon the coast of Sharon.[1] The presence of these erstwhile raiders and foes in undisturbed possession and even in positions of authority, within the frontier zone of Egypt, indeed astride the coastal road from Egypt into Syria, calls for an explanation, which may at the same time throw light upon the subsequent political developments. Three facts derived from Egyptian sources seem to be of special significance in this connexion. Firstly, the sculptures of Medinet Habu show Philistines, no less than Sherden, as already enlisted in the ranks of the Pharaoh's armies.[2] Secondly, one record reads 'The Peleset are hung up in their towns.'[3] Thirdly, the prisoners of the Denyen, Thekel, Peleset, Sherden and Weshesh, 'brought as captives to Egypt, like the sand of the shore,' are said to have been settled by the Pharaoh in strongholds, bound in his name.[4] It is to be inferred from these indications that Philistines were living already on the frontiers of Egypt, whence some may have been drawn into this affray on the side of the invaders, while others had evidently taken service in the imperial army,

combination is named Thekel (or Zakkara). The Sherdens were already familiar in pictures of the Egyptian army in which they formed a special detachment of light armed infantry. As such they were included among the troops mobilised to meet this invasion (Breasted, *Anct. Rec.* ii, 402), and in the scenes of this conflict they actually appear fighting on both sides. Cf. Fig. 8.

[1] In the story of Wen-Amon. 'I arrived at Dor, a city of Thekel,' Breasted, *Anct. Rec.* iv, 565.

[2] Nelson, *Medinet Habu, cit.* p. 5 and Fig. 4.

[3] Breasted, *Anct. Rec.* iv, 71.

[4] *Ibid.* iv, 403.

after the fashion of the day. This earlier settlement is accordant with the appearance of Philistines in the age of Shamgar and with the archaeological indications.[1] The third allusion renders it possible that the unchallenged presence of Philistines in later times in the strong places on the coast of Palestine is really to be explained by the fact that they had been placed there by the Pharaoh himself as Egyptian garrison troops. In this connexion it may be noted that a hundred years later, at the very time when the Bible makes mention of the Philistines as ruling over the Israelites in the age of Samson,[2] Egypt still laid formal claim to the suzerainty of the land, as is to be seen in an inscription of Herihor,[3] 'The chiefs of Retenu do obeisance to his fame every day.'

With this explanation of the position originally held in Palestine by the Philistines in relation to the Pharaoh, their suzerain, it is possible to understand much in regard to their rôle as depicted in the O.T. that would otherwise remain enigmatic; and this aspect of the subject will be considered in due course. This solution covers that part of the Philistine problem which directly concerns this volume. It is none the less of interest, and natural, to enquire at this stage, who were the Philistines? And though a definite answer to this question is not forthcoming, and can indeed only be found by wide archaeological investigation,[4] the general indications can be readily and usefully reviewed. This single issue has nearly always been complicated by subsidiary problems,—is Caphtor the same as Crete? and can either or both of them be the Egyptian *Keftiu*? Avoiding this complication, it may be said at once that the Philistines were not like the Minoan Cretans, nor Keftians, either in dress or armour or facial type.[5] It is true the Philistines do not appear upon the horizon of Egypt, and so in Palestine, until about

[1] P. 285. [2] See below, p. 337. [3] Breasted, *Anct. Rec.* iv, 623.

[4] See the suggestive paper on 'Philistine Origins' by W. J. Phythian-Adams in *B.S.A.J.*, Bulletin No. 3, 1923, pp. 20 ff.

[5] See also Dr. Hall in *Camb. Anct. Hist.* ii, 286.

1200 B.C., while the Cretans and Keftians are known chiefly from the frescoes and other representations of an earlier age.[1] While, therefore, it may properly be inferred that the Philistines did not trace their ancestral home to Crete, the possibility remains that they may have visited that island, or even sojourned there, previous to

Fig. 13. Arimaspian figure carved in ivory.
From Cyprus, date about 1300 B.C. *Brit. Mus.*

their descent upon the Palestinian coast. Some colour is lent to this possibility by the theory that two of their comrade bands, the Thekels (Zakkara) and the 'Weshesh' of the Sea may have been so called from the names of two places in Crete, respectively Zagros and Waxos. But though it has gained credence, this theory lacks material support: indeed the name Zagros or Zagro does not appear in classical writing.[2]

[1] See in particular the exhaustive study by Wainwright, *L.A.A.* vi, 1914, pp. 75 ff.

[2] Hall, *loc. cit.* p. 284, etc.

The Philistines, to judge by their arms and organisation, were akin to the Iron Age peoples of the Achaean world, and particularly those of the Homeric age. They

Fig. 14. The Philistines in Battle, period of Ramses III, *c.* 1190 B.C. *

wore laminated body armour [1] of a kind which is found on an Arimaspian figure carved in ivory, found in the island of Cyprus and pertaining to the Late Bronze Age. They further protected themselves with small round

* Designed from contemporary materials and drawn by Miss Gertrude Levy. The armour is that depicted at Medinet Habu. The sword comes from Gaza. The shield devices are taken from early Iron Age pottery found on Philistine sites in Palestine.

[1] See Figs. 13-14.

shields, such as were already known in the Aegean world, and are seen with the Sherdens on Egyptian representations of the thirteenth century B.C.[1] Their offensive weapons comprised a great broadsword also like that of the Sherdens. Their headdress was distinctive, being of the nature of a feathered tiara, which may be compared with the classical allusion to the Carian crested helmet.[2] So that though differing in detail, the Philistine represents a type of armoured warrior already familiar in the Aegean area. Indeed two representations in Crete suggest that the type may have been present or known there at an even earlier date. These indications are all consistent with the view that the Philistines were akin to the Achaean warrior type described in Homeric legend, and may have been seen within the Aegean horizon some two hundred years before they appeared upon the coastlands of Palestine. The Achaeans themselves present an interesting parallel. As early as the fourteenth century B.C. Achaean armies were at drawn swords with the Hattic Kings of Asia Minor, and their activities through the thirteenth century are familiar from the Hittite archives; but it was not until the reign of Merneptah [3] (1225 B.C.) that they are found advancing within the horizon of Egypt in the south-eastern Mediterranean. Significantly they were accompanied on that raid, amongst others, by two of those bands which a generation later are found associated with the Philistines. Some of them, it is true, had already been encountered by the Egyptian troops at the battle of Kadesh, 1288 B.C., to which the Hittite King had enticed his allies and confederates from the far coasts of Asia Minor; but that encounter took place in Central Syria, beyond the purview of the chroniclers of Israel.

It results from these general considerations that though the Philistines appear newly upon the threshold of Egypt and in the records of the Book of Judges at the close of the

[1] Cf. Fig. 8, p. 279. [2] Strabo, XIV, ii, 327.

[3] Breasted, *Anc. Rec.* iii, 579, 588, 601; also above, p. 292.

thirteenth century B.C. they are of a type already long familiar in the Aegean world including the western and southern coasts of Asia Minor, where indeed they may have been domiciled for generations before being swept away by the great migration that left their remnants upon the southern coasts of Palestine. Deeper investigation of their origin, though admittedly of great interest, would affect little our enquiry. With their re-settlement under Egypt in Palestine their story began afresh. There for long they held themselves aloof, not mingling with the people, maintaining their own religion, organisation, and institutions; but in the end they were absorbed, leaving little impress upon the civilisation of the land in which politically they played a leading part for several hundred years.

SECTION 18

THE QUEST FOR A LEADER

OPPRESSION BY THE MIDIANITES

c. 1161-1154 B.C.

JUDGES vi

1 **And the children of Israel did that which was evil in the
sight of the Lord: and the Lord delivered them into the
2 hand of Midian seven years. And the hand of Midian prevailed against Israel: and because of Midian the children of
Israel made them the dens which are in the mountains, and
3 the caves, and the strongholds. And so it was, when
Israel had sown, that the Midianites came up, and the
Amalekites, and the children of the east; they came up
against them; and they encamped against them and
destroyed the increase of the earth till thou come unto Gaza,
and left no sustenance in Israel, neither sheep, nor ox, nor
ass. [E2, JE]**

THE oppression by the Midianites falls approximately in the reigns of the Pharaohs Ramses IV and V, the two immediate successors of Ramses III. The scene now changes. The Ramessides proved to be weak rulers, and under them Egypt rapidly lost control over the remnants of its Syrian Empire in Palestine. The seeds of its downfall had been sown as far back as the XVIIIth Dynasty, when mercenary troops were enrolled in the imperial army, so that already in the XIXth Dynasty under Ramses II the foreign element had grown to a majority. The measures taken by Ramses III, after he had successfully resisted the great migration from the north, to shore up the tottering fabric by settling groups of these warlike invaders in the Egyptian strongholds [1] in the issue only assured the irretrievable character of its fall. The statue of that Pharaoh at Bethshean [2] forms the last monument of

[1] Breasted, *Anct. Rec.* iv, 403. [2] *Mus. Journ., Phil.*, 1922, pp. 32 ff.

the imperial age; and though a 'fiction of Egyptian sovereignty' over Palestine was still maintained at the court of the Pharaoh until the reign of Herihor,[1] about 1090 B.C., there is evidence to show that Egyptian prestige in the country began even now rapidly to fade from memory. Internally Egypt was passing through political and religious crises, and the withdrawal from Sinai about this time [2] is a further indication of its inability to cope with external problems.

We must visualize Palestine in this age, with the old Canaanite civilization almost at an end, as a somewhat depopulated and forlorn land, its terraces neglected and its cultivation limited to the necessities of life. Upon the coastlands the Philistines in the south and the Thekels in the north upheld half-heartedly the shadow of Egyptian authority; but in the interior, as the raid of the Midianites shows, this protection was insufficient to ensure the safety of the inhabitants. As in past times the Midianites from Trans-Jordania pressed in by the valley of Jezreel, where evidently Bethshean no longer presented an effective barrier,[3] while in the south country the Amalekites again reaped the broad cornlands of the Negeb 'till thou come to Gaza.' Israel was brought very low at this time, and there emerged from the necessities of this situation an increasing need for an organized defensive system and a leader.

[1] Cf. Breasted, *Hist. Egypt*, p. 522. [2] *Ibid.* p. 507.

[3] An Egyptian garrison was maintained at Bethshean until the reign of Ramses III, *Mus. Journ., Phil.* 1922, 1929. Cf. also Adam Smith, *Hist. Geog.* pp. 358 ff. As recently as 1920, in the early days of the British Occupation, a raid from Trans-Jordan was checked by a small British outpost at Beisan.

DELIVERANCE BY GIDEON OF MANASSEH

JUDGES vi

33 Then all the Midianites and the Amalekites and the children
of the east assembled themselves together; and they passed
34 over, and pitched in the valley of Jezreel. But the spirit
of the Lord came upon Gideon, and he blew a trumpet; and
35 Abiezer was gathered together after him. And he sent
messengers throughout all Manasseh and they (also) were
gathered together after him: and he sent messengers unto
Asher, and unto Zebulun, and unto Naphtali, and they
came up to meet them. [E, JE]

THE Midianites were tent-dwellers, whose favourite habitation lay to the east and south-east of the Dead Sea.[1] The fact stated in several passages[a] that the Amalekites from the south and other peoples from the east were associated with them, suggests that a wide area was affected by a common disturbing element. Their incursions into Palestine would appear to have been not so much an organised raid of warring tribes, as a general movement of nomads in search of food and pasture,[b] impelled maybe by the failure of the rains in their own districts and profiting by the breakdown of Egyptian authority.

The events of Gideon's successful leadership, narrated with unusual fullness in chapters vi-vii, are derived almost entirely from the early sources;[2] and the two strains of tradition which these embody, though varying to some extent, on the whole are parallel and supplementary to one another.[3] Though much of the graphic detail is concerned with local incidents, and several of the places mentioned are not identified,[4] the main lines of the central

[a] Judges vi 3 [JE], 33 [E], vii 12 [E]. [b] Judges vi 4, 5 [JE].

[1] Musil, *The Northern Hegaz*, pp. 282-3. [2] See pp. 38-40.

[3] See Burney, *Judges*, pp. 126 ff.; Cooke, *Judges*, p. 69.

[4] Some of the names may be variants of more familiar forms, *e.g.* Zererah (vii 22) for Zarethan (Jos. iii 16) and, less probably, Tabbath (vii 22) for Thebez (ix 50).

EL AAJE, A MODERN VILLAGE ON A HILL.

The place lies between Nablus and Dothan : its present population is about 500 souls.

SILET-EL-DHAHR, POSSIBLY THE SITE OF OPHRAH, Judges vi, 11.

The village occupies an ancient site, and to-day has a population of 1635 people.

See pp. 79, 319.

episodes concerning the Midianites' invasion and their flight can be followed in a general way from the topographical indications of the record.

The Midianites seem to have overrun the plain of Esdraelon and to have passed southward into the fertile areas around Dothan, where, according to the meagre indications of the text,[a] should probably be sought the site of Ophrah. Among the places tentatively proposed, Ferrata, which is found in somewhat broken country six miles to the west of Shechem, lies outside the picture, which does not extend as far as Shechem. The resemblance of name-sound in this case has no significance, Ferrata being the modern form of a Greek word meaning springs.[1] Arrabeh, sixteen miles to the north, is more suitably placed, but its antiquity is doubtful, though going back beyond the Middle Ages: it seems to have succeeded Dothan in the ownership of the fertile plain that lies to their north and west. The most ancient site of the neighbourhood is apparently that of Sileh, more fully Silet el Dhahr,[2] six miles nearer Shechem, a situation which seems to satisfy the context. It will be noted that all the northern tribes, including Asher, rallied to the call of Gideon, himself a Manassite. There is no mention of Issachar, which usually dwelt in the plain of Esdraelon and its neighbourhood; it may be assumed, therefore, that this tribe, like the adjoining portion of Manasseh, had been constrained to find a refuge in the highlands. Ephraim also joined in the operations towards the close. The southern tribes, Judah, Simeon and Benjamin, of whom there is no mention, would be overburdened already by the pressure of the Amalekites on their own borders.

The Midianites after the night alarm in their camp, seem to have fled down the Jordan valley, seeking to out-

[a] Judges vi 11, 15, 33, 35 [J]; vii 1 [E]; viii 31 [E]; ix 1 [E].

[1] Ferrata or Far'ata stands upon a mound which is partly natural, but dates back at least to E.I.A. ii (*c.* 900 B.C.). Presumably it marks the site of Pirathon; 1 Samuel xxiii 30, etc.

[2] Sileh stands partly upon a great bank of town debris, in which may be found potsherds of E.I.A. i. (*c.* 1200 B.C.). Cf. Pl. LXVII.

distance their pursuers. Meanwhile the tribesmen from the hill country of Ephraim, in response to Gideon's call [a] had secured the fords of Jordan, presumably those within immediate reach of the Wady Farah, their nearest avenue of descent, namely the well-known ford of El Damieh at its foot, and that of Abu Sidrah somewhat higher up. The Midianites, caught in a trap, sought safety beyond the river, which can be crossed in dry weather at numerous places in its middle course. The two leaders with their following made good their escape, but some parties were overtaken, including, according to one tradition, the two 'princes' Oreb and Zeeb.[b] Once across the river the nomad hosts moving over familiar tracks would quickly melt away; while the leaders, Zebah and Zalmunna, when next heard of, had reached their retreat at Karkor, two hundred miles away. The narrative states that they were accompanied by fifteen thousand men,[c] but as before allowance must be made for inaccurate preservation of figures in the record, especially in view of the reiterated statement that Gideon retained only his three hundred selected men. The route taken by the Midianite leaders is not described: but as Karkor is found far up the Wady Sirḥan—the desert highway towards El Jowf—which may be approached directly from the Jordan by an old established track up the Wady Kafrinji past Ajloun and Jerash, they would presumably take advantage of this ready avenue of escape. That Gideon followed eventually the same way, after his meeting with the Ephraimites,[d] is fairly clear from the further details of the narrative.

[a] Judges vii 24 [J].
[b] Judges vii 25 [J] and viii 3 [J].
[c] Judges viii 10 [E].
[d] Judges viii 1-3 [J].

Gideon's Pursuit of the Midianites

JUDGES viii

4 **And Gideon came to Jordan, and passed over, he and the
three hundred men that were with him, faint, yet pur-**
10 **suing. . . . Now Zebah and Zalmunna were in Karkor, and**
11 **their hosts with them. . . . And Gideon went up by the
way of them that dwelt in tents on the east of Nobah and
Jogbehah, and smote the host; for the host was secure,**
12 **And Zebah and Zalmunna fled; and he pursued after them
and he took the two kings of Midian, Zebah and Zalmunna,
and discomfited all the host. [E]**

Though Nobah and Jogbehah are unknown, the suggestion of name would place the latter at El Jubeilhat, northwestward from Amman, while the great centres of nomad concentration lie eastward of the upper Zerka. If, moreover, Succoth [a] be correctly located at Tell Deir-Allah,[1] near the mouth of that river, the details of the narrative assume a definite cohesion. Penuel, unlocated as yet, would in that case be best sought at Kalat el Rabat, where to-day still rises the boldest ruined castle on the eastern ridge of Jordan. These tentative indications would have little value, were it not that the further topography of this episode has been more satisfactorily established by recent exploration.[2] The 'way of the tent-dwellers' corresponds clearly with the route actually called to-day 'the road of the nomads.' It passes through the 'gateway' between the south-eastern spurs of the Hauran and the broken hills in which Zerka has its source. Camel-breeders from the desert to-day make

[a] Judges viii 5, 14 [E].

[1] The identification seems probable. It is pointed out by T. R. Père Abel (*Rev. Bibl.* 1910, pp. 555 ff.) that the ancient name is perfectly preserved at one of the mounds of the site called Tell el Ekhsas, Mound of Booths, *Heb.* Succot; while both mounds date back on the evidence of their potsherds to E.I.A. i, or earlier. Cf. Holscher in *Z.D.P.V.* xxxiii, p. 20, and *M.D.O.G.* xxiii, 33; also Albright, *Bull. A.S.O.R.*, No. 35, 1929, pp. 13, 14.

[2] Musil, *The Northern Hegaz*, pp. 283 ff; also his *Arabia Deserta*, App. ii, pp. 494 ff.

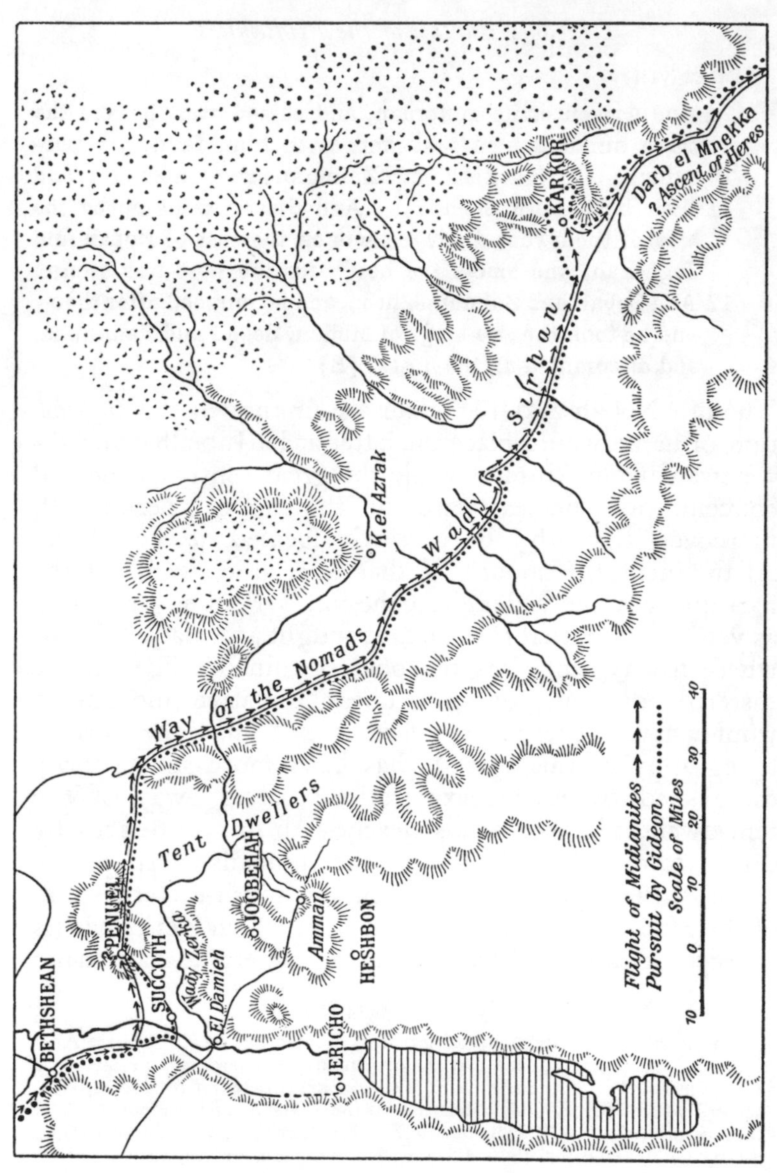

Map 17. Flight of the Midianites to Karkor and Gideon's pursuit.

regular use of this route, which is well known to all desert-born peoples of the Near East. It leads by the Wady Sirḥan, as we have said, directly to the site of Karkor, which lies fifty miles to the S.E. of Kasr el Azrak where may be found both pasturage and water.

The wells of Karkar or Keraker are situated in a capacious basin surrounded by almost impassable limestone hills, from which only a single convenient but not very broad outlet leads to the depression of Sirḥan.[1] The suggestion is that Gideon, having stationed some of his men at this opening, might with others climb the hills surrounding the basin, and so take the camp by surprise.[2] Thence he pursued them as far as the 'ascent of Heres,' which seems to identify itself with the well-known feature of the route called Darb al Mnekka.

JUDGES viii

13 **And Gideon the son of Joash returned from the battle from the ascent of Heres. [E]**

PERIOD OF REST UNDER GIDEON

c. 1154-1114 B.C.

JUDGES viii

22 **Then the men of Israel said unto Gideon, Rule thou over**
us, both thou, and thy son, and thy son's son also: for thou
23 **hast saved us out of the hand of Midian. And Gideon said**
unto them, I will not rule over you, neither shall my son
28 **rule over you: the Lord shall rule over you. . . . So**
Midian was subdued before the children of Israel, and they
lifted up their heads no more. And the land had rest forty
years in the days of Gideon. [E2]

THOUGH the records of Egypt are silent as to the precise nature of the relations of that country with Palestine throughout this time, one or two factors must enter into our consideration. Evidence is not wanting to show that

[1] See Map No. 17, which is based on Musil's observations.

[2] Musil, *Northern Hegaz*, p. 284; also *Arabia Deserta*, p. 495.

the Philistines, as we have surmised, were already established in the cities of the southern plain. Excavations at Askalon [1] have revealed the traces at this age of their familiar pottery, which is found to have permeated fairly generally the border cities of the Shephelah [2] and the south; while towards the close of the century contemporary literature mentions that the Thekels had already been established some generations in the ancient city of Dor [3] upon the coast. It is then remarkable that no mention of the Philistines appears in the Biblical writings of this age, nor indeed any reference to the coastal areas. The record of the Midianite oppression and the deliverance by Gideon, while demonstrating again the capacity for joint action among the tribes, is concerned chiefly with the eastern territory of Manasseh and the adjacent valley of Jezreel. The apparent freedom of the Israelites from other difficulties suggests indeed a not unfriendly attitude on the part of their Philistine neighbours. Already it appears certain from the allusions to this period in the story of Wen Amon, that the power and prestige of Egypt were in rapid decline, since a number of Egyptian envoys are said to have been detained in prison for seventeen years, and there to have died, without any retaliation on the part of Egypt.[4] From this it may be inferred that both Philistines and Thekels, even though stationed originally in the cities of the plains as garrison troops of Egypt, had ceased to entertain a strict sense of responsibility towards their former masters, but were drifting tacitly into a state of armed independence. Their growing freedom, however, had not yet given place to ambition, and from the absence of any indication to the contrary in the narrative, it may be believed that they still retained for the Israelites the habit

[1] Conducted by the writer and Mr. Phythian-Adams for the *P.E.F.* in 1920-2; see the reports in the *Q.S.* for 1921-23, in particular 1921, p. 12, p. 76; 1922, p. 112; 1923, pp. 11, 18.

[2] Notably Ain-Shems, Gezer and Tell el Safi: see *Bull. No.* 4 of the Palestine Mus., Pl. II, with notes by Miss G. Levy.

[3] Breasted, *Anc. Rec.* iv, 565, from the *Golénischeff Papyrus*, Pl. I, l. 9.

[4] *Ibid.* iv, 585.

of toleration instilled during the period of their common vassalage to the former Pharaoh Ramses III.

Under these circumstances, the rally of the tribes around Gideon and the successful effort to release the oppressed territory of Issachar and Manasseh appears in a new light. It discloses the Israelites for the first time as the strongest element in the population of the plateau, and accepting responsibility for the protection of the land they occupied. Thrown upon their own resources before the menace of invasion, the tribes proved again the value of union: the desire to make Gideon their king and common leader gave expression to the growing need for mutual support which foreshadowed the future welding of the tribes. The experience of centuries had taught them the value of an efficient kingship, since the periods of Rest which they had enjoyed had been won for them by the effective control and often the active intervention of the more powerful Pharaohs. On the other hand the weakening of Egypt and the uprising of Assyria under a warrior king only exposed their own weakness and lack of cohesive organization.

SECTION 19

MOVEMENT TOWARDS A KINGSHIP

ABIMELECH AND SHECHEM

c. 1114-1111 B.C.

JUDGES ix

1 **And Abimelech the son of Jerubbaal went to Shechem unto his mother's brethren, and spake with them, and with all the family of the house of his mother's father. [E]**

6 **And all the men of Shechem assembled themselves together, and all the house of Millo, and went and made Abimelech king, by the oak of the pillar that was in Shechem. [E]**

22 **And Abimelech was prince over Israel three years. [E2]**

THE discontinuous and fragmentary nature of the preserved portions of the Book of Judges is well seen by comparing the contents of Chapters ix-xii, which are devoted to the events of about five years, with the record of viii 28, in which a period of forty years is dismissed with a single sentence. Moreover, the career of Abimelech, which occupies Chapter ix, concerned primarily the people of Shechem and its immediate vicinity; while the leadership of Jephthah (x-xii) himself a Gileadite, arose out of the difficulties of his people in Trans-Jordania, the scene of his exploits, and aroused opposition among the people of Ephraim. Both stories none the less throw light upon various aspects of the Israelite development at this stage; and while emphasizing the growing need for a common leader, they disclose the inherent obstacle of inter-tribal jealousies, which tended to delay the reunion of Israel under a mutually acceptable king.

The attempt of Abimelech to secure succession to the unique position held by his father Jerubbaal (Gideon) is told in the narrative itself.[1] Though topographical details

[1] Pp. 42-43.

are uncertain it seems clear that the episodes described were confined to the immediate vicinity of Shechem. The city itself, as we have seen,[1] was probably situated in the pleasant valley between Ebal and Gerizim, on the site now occupied by modern Nablus, protected at the entrance by a fortified position, the tower of Shechem,[2] which Abimelech destroyed by fire.[a] Ophrah, Jerubbaal's home, lay, it would seem probable, to the north, possibly on the site of Silet el Dhahr.[3] Arumah, which Abimelech chose for his headquarters, is usually located on Kh. Ormë, on account of the similarity of name sound, and the identity seems possible. The site named occupied a height some seven miles to the south-east of the tower of Shechem at Balata; its position dominates the expanse of plain which marks the upper course of the Wady Kanah and the entrance to the valley of Shechem, with wooded hills on either hand. A fortress of mediaeval character now crowns the site and renders difficult a thorough investigation of the soil. For this reason, possibly, no potsherds or other traces of the period are in evidence. Thebez, where Abimelech met his death, is located with more circumstantial probability at Tubas,[4] a strategic point on the highland tracks that connected Shechem and Dothan with Bethshean and the Jordan valley. The fact that there was a strong tower within the city indicates a place of some importance. To-day the town which occupies the site boasts a population of nearly 4000 people, a fact which attests its permanent importance as an agricultural and trading centre. Indeed few towns in the highlands of Palestine, except those by the main road, can claim so large a population. The area of the ancient city would be much smaller, and is now obscured by modern buildings. If this location be correct, the attack on Thebez by Abimelech assumes a new interest. For Thebez, though lying in the hill country, would mark the

[a] Judges ix 49 [E].

[1] Pp. 79, 248, Pl. V. [2] Pl. LVII. [3] Pl. LXVII.
[4] Map No. 5.

most central as well as the most populous township to the west of Jordan of the tribe Manasseh, to which Abimelech himself belonged by birth,[a] and the fact that it provoked his hostility shows clearly how little hold the usurper had on the affections and loyalty of his own clansmen.

One further aspect of Abimelech's short-lived endeavour to establish a kingship is worthy of consideration. While his father Jerubbaal (or Gideon) was a Manassite, his mother was a native woman of the old population of Shechem.[b] The relations between Israelite and Canaanite were evidently so intimately established by this date that not only had Gideon's leadership proved acceptable to the population as a whole, but his son's partial kinship with the Shechemites was deemed sufficient ground for proclaiming him their king. A section only of the community resisted the usurpation of their time-honoured prerogatives.[c] It would appear then that the Israelites had so far consolidated their position as to secure a certain ascendancy even in political affairs over the older inhabitants of the land. The extent to which they may have relied upon their personal relations with Zebul, the governor of the city, cannot be estimated owing to the lack of information as to the latter's source of power. Presumably he represented the regime with which Israel had succeeded in establishing relations. If he had been placed in office by the Pharaoh, and could still rely upon the support of Egypt, an intelligible explanation would be forthcoming, not only as to the situation at this time but as to the whole course of events of which it was the outcome; and in this connexion it may be recalled that both Ephraim and Manasseh could claim by birth an Egyptian blood-relationship.[d] However that may be, the narrative throws direct light upon the practical meaning of the familiar statement to the effect that the Israelites drave not out the Canaanites but dwelt among them.

[a] Judges vi 15 [J].
[b] Judges viii, 31 [E].
[c] Judges ix 28 [J].
[d] Genesis xli 50 [E].

OPPRESSION BY AMMON

c. 1110 B.C.

JUDGES X

7 **And the anger of the Lord was kindled against Israel and he sold them into the hands of the Philistines and into the hands of the children of Ammon. . . . [E2]**

THOUGH the oppression of the Israelites by the children of Ammon is the chief feature of this age, the allusion to the Philistines should not be allowed altogether to escape our notice. About eighty years had passed since the Philistine invasion had been stayed by Ramses III,[1] and during the latter half of that period we have seen the power of Egypt in rapid decline, so that Sinai had to be evacuated and Egyptian envoys could be detained with impunity in Syria.[2] The deathblow to Egyptian prestige was delivered about this time by the Assyrian king Tiglath Pileser I, who, extending the range of his conquests west of the Euphrates with an irresistible armed force reached even the Phoenician coasts, where he wrested finally from Egypt the vassalage of the rich seaports of Arvad, Byblos, Simyra and Sidon.[3] He left, it is thought, upon the rocky passage by the mouth of the Nahr el Kelb an inscribed representation of himself, where formerly the image of the Pharaoh had stood alone. The long dispute between Egypt and the Hittites for the possession of Syria was thus ended with almost dramatic suddenness, and the Assyrian remained unchallenged in the field. The repercussion of this critical episode was immediate and profound. An Egyptian envoy of the Pharaoh Ramses XI, putting in at Dor,[4] was there robbed and treated with scant respect; while at Byblos,[5] his destination, the Thekel chieftain Zakar-Baal refused for some time to receive him, but day after day sent messengers bidding him begone.

[1] Above, p. 309.
[2] Breasted, *Anc. Rec.* iv, 585.
[3] *Camb. Anct. Hist.* ii, p. 250.
[4] Breasted, *Anc. Rec.* iv, 566.
[5] *Ibid.* 569.

Now the Egyptian archives already considered show that the Philistines not only had their settled townships in Palestine under Ramses III, but were among those who

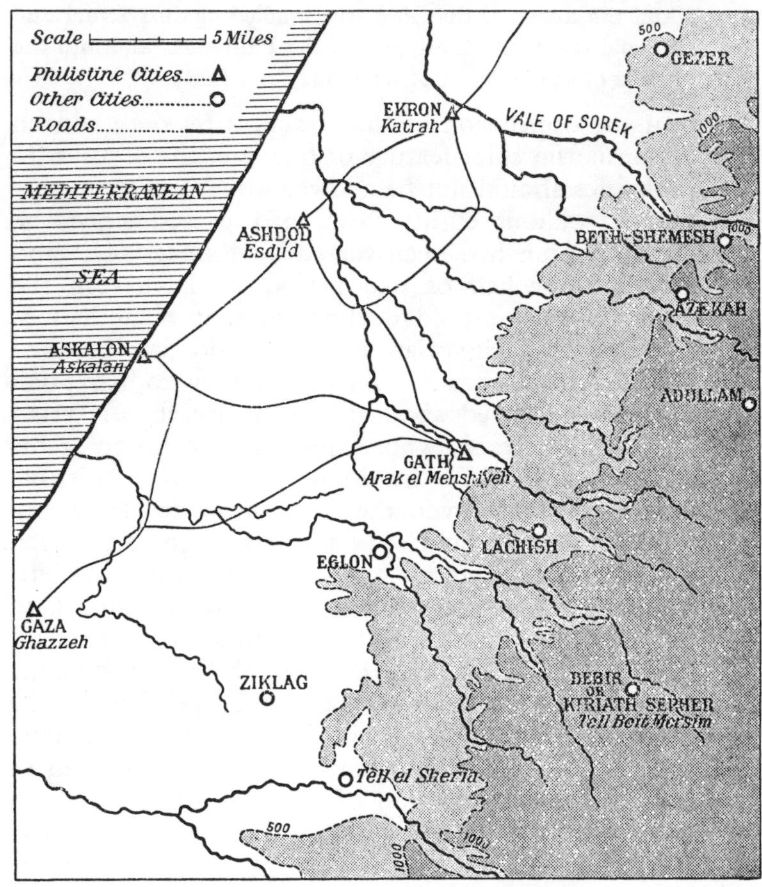

Map 18. The Philistine Plain and the Shephelah.

after the great sea battle were placed as garrison troops in Egyptian strongholds.[1] We have suggested that it was the Pharaoh himself who stationed them in the fortress cities of Gaza, Askalon, Ashdod, Ekron, and Gath, to

[1] Above, p. 311.

maintain order on behalf of Egypt. It is impossible to explain in any other way their undoubted and apparently unchallenged presence on the seaboard of Palestine in the early days of the Iron Age, soon after 1200 B.C., and, therefore, not long after the Pharaoh's victory. Indeed evidence has been found in the excavation at Beisan that people with Aegean customs, presumed to be the defeated Achaeans or Sherdens, had been stationed and ultimately buried there in the previous generation.[1] The practice was characteristic of the age. Once established, the Philistines would evidently enter into relations with the inhabitants, who from the first would not fail to treat them with respect. We may see, then, in this chance allusion a reflexion of the day when the Philistines, freed of the Egyptian yoke, and thrown also upon their own resources, established their dominion over the Israelites and other elements of the population, collecting for themselves the tithes and exacting the other dues formerly pertaining to the Pharaohs.

The oppression of Israel began in Trans-Jordania, where according to the narrative the children of Ammon had oppressed the children of Israel eighteen years[a] before carrying the warfare over to the west, where they vexed and oppressed the children of Israel that year. The significance of this distinction in the chronology of the period has already been discussed.[2] A new feature in the development of Israelite unity is the appearance of a deliverer from among the Trans-Jordanian tribes, in the person of Jephthah, a Gileadite.[b]

[a] Judges x 8 [E2]. [b] Judges xi 6 [J].

[1] *Mus. Journ., Phil,* 1922, pp. 22 ff.; *Rev. Bibl.,* 1923, pp. 430 f.; 1924, pp. 426 f.; P. Thomsen, *Reallexikon,* ii, 1925, pp. 7 f.

[2] P. 57.

DELIVERANCE BY JEPHTHAH

c. 1110-1104 B.C.

JUDGES x

9 And the children of Ammon passed over Jordan to fight also against Judah, and against Benjamin, and against the house of Ephraim, so that Israel was sore distressed. [E2]

The ground of this invasion, elicited by Jephthah from the King of Ammon, was the claim that Israel when coming up out of Egypt, under the leadership of Moses, had taken lands belonging to the Ammonites, between the Arnon and the Jabbok and unto Jordan,[a] which lands, it was now demanded, should be peaceably restored. Jephthah's reply, as recorded in Chapter xv 10-27 attributed to E, constitutes an historical document of unique antiquity and interest, which not only gives the oldest account of the last stages of the Exodus,[1] but throws direct light upon the political state of the country at that time (*c.* 1410 B.C.) while contributing in verse 26 an important factor, already discussed,[2] to the chronology of Israel during the foregoing period of the Judges.

JUDGES xi

15 Thus saith Jephthah: Israel took not away the land of
16 Moab, nor the land of the children of Ammon: but when
they came up from Egypt, and Israel walked through the
17 wilderness unto the Red Sea, and came to Kadesh; then
Israel sent messengers unto the king of Edom, saying Let
me, I pray thee, pass through thy land: but the king of
Edom hearkened not. And in like manner he sent unto
the king of Moab: but he would not: and Israel abode in
18 Kadesh. Then he walked through the wilderness, and
compassed the land of Edom, and the land of Moab, and
came by the east side of the land of Moab, and they pitched
on the other side of Arnon; but they came not within the

[a] Judges xi 13 [E].

[1] Cf. p. 258. An illuminative study of the topography of the Exodus appears in *P.E.F.*, *Q.S.*, 1930, pp. 135 and 192 ff., from the pen of the Rev. W. J. Phythian-Adams, M.A., D.S.O., M.C., with a map to face p. 193.

[2] Pp. 58-59.

TELL HESBAN: THE SITE OF HESHBON, Judges x, 26.
Seen from the north, at a distance of two miles.

TELL HESBAN: HESHBON, FROM THE SOUTH.
Potsherds lying on the slopes of this site tell of its occupation in the Late Bronze Age.

See p. 332.

border of Moab, for Arnon was the border of Moab.
19 And Israel sent messengers unto Sihon king of the Amorites,
the king of Heshbon; and Israel said unto him, Let us pass,
20 we pray thee, through thy land unto my place. But Sihon
trusted not Israel to pass through his border; but Sihon
gathered all his people together, and pitched in Jahaz, and
21 fought against Israel. And the Lord, the God of Israel,
delivered Sihon and all his people into the hand of Israel,
and they smote them: so Israel possessed all the land of the
22 Amorites, the inhabitants of that country. And they
possessed all the border of the Amorites, from Arnon even
unto Jabbok, and from the wilderness even unto Jordan.
23 So now the Lord, the God of Israel, hath dispossessed the
Amorites from before his people Israel, and shouldest thou
24 possess them? Wilt not thou possess that which Chemosh
26 thy god giveth thee to possess? . . . While Israel dwelt in E
Heshbon and her towns, and in Aroer and her towns, and
in all the cities that are along by the side of Arnon, three
hundred years; wherefore did ye not recover them within
that time?'

. . . .

32 **So Jephthah passed over unto the children of Ammon to**
fight against them; and the Lord delivered them into his
33 **hand. . . . So the children of Ammon were subdued** **J**
before the children of Israel.

. . . .

JUDGES xii

7 **And Jephthah judged Israel six years.** **JE**

SECTION 20

THE PHILISTINES RULE OVER ISRAEL

1105-1065 B.C.

JUDGES xiii

1 **And the children of Israel again did that which was evil in the sight of the Lord; and the Lord delivered them into the hand of the Philistines forty years. [E2]**

Samson, c. 1085-1065 B.C.

THE consecutive narrative of the Book of Judges closes with the well-known epic of Samson, which embodies evidently some old hero tales, but reflects hardly at all the position of a national leader. Nevertheless, the announcement of his birth so like that which heralded the career of Gideon, and the twice-repeated statement that he judged Israel twenty years, show that he was venerated in memory as a national hero, even though the incidents attributed to him in life seem to be based upon a cycle of independent legends arising to some extent maybe out of his great physical strength.

The scene of his familiar exploits takes us to the region of the Vale of Sorek,[a] to-day recognised as the Wady el Surar.[1] Where this emerges from the Judaean hills, some fifteen miles to the west of Jerusalem, the valley opens, so that from a low mound upon its left bank the old Canaanite city of Beth-Shemesh, which guards the pass, looked northwards over a small plain.[2] On the opposite side the sites of Zorah and Eshtaol[b] may be recognised in the modern villages of Surah and Eshua respectively.[3] The latter stands upon a platform of rock at the head of the northern end of this opening: the present village does

[a] Judges xvi 4 [J 1] [b] Judges xiii 2, 25 [J 2].

[1] Pronounced Es-Surar. See note 4, p. 70.

[2] See Maps 18, 19, also Pl. LXXIII. [3] Pl. LXIX.

ESHUA, PROBABLE SITE OF ESHTAOL, FROM THE S.E.

The modern village occupies part of the ancient site.

MAHANEH-DAN, BETWEEN ZORAH AND ESHTAOL, Judges xiii, 25.

Viewed from the heights of Surah (Zorah) to the west.

See p. 335.

not entirely fill the ancient site, which is small, however, in size, and apparently dates back only to the period of overlap between the Bronze and Iron Ages, about 1200 B.C. Surah by contrast stands upon a sharp hill, and the ancient site is well seen as a low tell extending beyond the modern village and crowning the ridge. Potsherds found in its slopes also give token of a somewhat earlier origin,

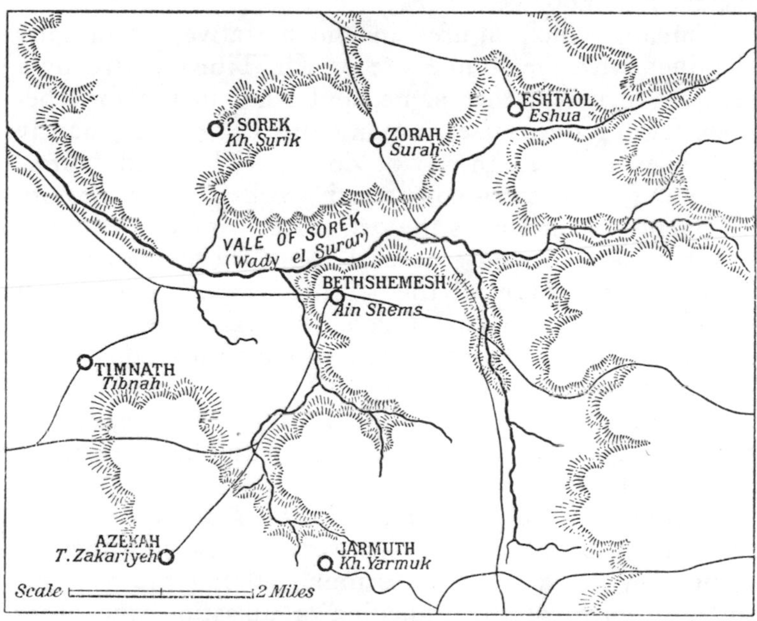

Map 19. The Vale of Sorek : scene of Samson's exploits.

in the last phase of the late Bronze Age, although superficially it has not the characteristic appearance of an old Canaanite fortress-city.

So situated, Zorah dominated the immediate surroundings, and at a distance of two miles from Eshtaol and from Beth-Shemesh looked down to the east upon the small plain between them, picturesque with its border of scrub, boasting now an olive grove upon the hillside and a copious well at the foot, an ideal camping ground.[1] On

[1] Pl. LXIX, *b*.

the westward side a small valley breaks away past the ruined site of Kh. Surik, which from its name might be thought to indicate more precisely the Vale of Sorek itself. These ruins, however, are not earlier than Byzantine date; but a small hamlet just at the head of the valley about half a mile away seems to stand upon an accumulation of town debris that may mark a more ancient habitation.

Timnah, which figures in the narrative,[a] is usually identified with the ruined site of Kh. Tibneh, hard by a modern village of that name, and lying in the fork between two watercourses, among broken ground, hardly four miles to the south-east of Zorah. The Wady Surar, continuing its western course as it works its way through the Shephelah, separates the two places from one another, and may have formed a natural boundary to the original Philistine occupation of the southern area. The site of Kh. Tibneh bears traces of defensive walls, the origin of which cannot well be estimated without excavation; but various indications including potsherds point to the occupation of the place in the Early Iron Age, a fact which seems to warrant its identity with the Timnah of this legend.

Askalon and Gaza, already known as Canaanitish cities under Egyptian control, are disclosed as in Philistine occupation.[b] Later they are found among the five important centres of the Philistine organisation, the other three being Ashdod at Esdud, Ekron presumably at Katrah, and Gath possibly at Arak el Menshiyeh.[1] All five mark the sites of Bronze Age cities. Askalon traces its origin from the middle of that period, *c.* 1800 B.C., when apparently it was encircled on the land side with a rampart of beaten earth like the camp enclosure of Hazor.[2] Later the fortified area was reduced in size. The Egyptian artists pictured it as defended by a characteristic 'migdol' or tower, with battlemented walls and

[a] Judges xiv 1 [J1]. [b] Judges xiv 19 [Gl.], xvi 21 [J1].

[1] See Map No. 18. [2] Cf. Pl. XLIV.

ASKALAN: THE GARDENS AND CITY-MOUND OF ASKALON.

The site is enclosed by a rampart of earth crowned by Byzantine Wall, except on the west where it fronts the Mediteranean Sea.

GAZA: NORTHERN SCARP OF THE ANCIENT CITY.

Soundings have disclosed brick ramparts of Egyptian style.

See p. 337.

a gateway.[1] Excavations in the central area of the site, its highest feature, show that this fortress must have been small in plan, but the extent of the walled city of that age has not been determined. Later, when occupied by the Philistines, the inhabited area seems to have covered the whole of this central hill, for fragments of pottery of characteristic style were found well down in the level ground at its foot.[2]

Gaza is still in occupation, and no extensive excavation has been made upon the site. None the less, soundings made around the slopes of its vast Tell have shown clearly the great age and strength of this famous city,[3] and the long period during the XVIIIth and XIXth Dynasties, when it formed the headquarters of the Egyptian occupation of the country, seems to be well indicated by stout defensive walls built in brick after the Egyptian fashion. The examination showed also traces of the Philistine occupation and later periods.

JUDGES xiv

At that time the Philistines had rule over Israel. [J]

The coming of the Philistines, their kinship, and their probable rôle in the Egyptian organisation, have already been considered.[4] After being almost lost to sight for nearly a century, during which Egyptian prestige in the country reached its lowest ebb, they now reappear in the Biblical narrative with an established position. Meanwhile, the trend of political circumstances has prepared us to find them, no less than the Israelites, developing a spirit of independence as Egyptian authority and protection declined.

[1] See Fig. 10, p. 286.

[2] See the Plan, No. 1, p. 358, which shows the later Byzantine walls to have followed the original course of the Bronze Age ramparts. For further details see the Appendix, below, p. 357, also the writer's summary in *P.E.F., Q.S.*, 1922, p. 112.

[3] See the reports by Mr. Phythian-Adams, *ibid.* 1923, pp. 11, 18.

[4] Pp. 285, 311 f.

Events were clearly leading towards a final struggle for ascendancy between these two peoples. The issue, if left to time, could hardly be doubtful. Though the Philistines were armed and organised, they were limited in numbers. Few only of their women-folk are known to have accompanied them in the first instance [1] and their existence probably depended upon their intermarriage with the native peoples of the Plain. The Israelites, on the other hand, though not disciplined, must have been already greatly superior in numbers if united, and were multiplying all the time. But at the era covered by the legends of Samson, when the conflict of interest first becomes apparent, the Philistines are disclosed as accepted masters of the situation, at least in the south of Palestine. Apparently they exercised their function without calling forth any expression of dissatisfaction or mistrust on the part of those Israelites from the neighbouring parts of Judah with whom they came into contact. 'Knowest thou not that the Philistines are rulers over us,' [a] is an argument used by men of Judah against Samson himself, who in these stories is pictured as the provoker of quarrels, revelling in his strength. Except indeed for the bare statement of Judges x 7, which possibly marks the date when the Philistines began to assume their independence and assert their domination over the adjacent tribes,[2] there occurs as yet in the narrative no incident or record which would stamp them as oppressors in the sense previously applied to that term. Their presence as a disciplined and armed community might be deemed oppressive, but in their acts and relations with the Israelites at this time they appear, from details provided by the narrative, as reasonable rulers, conscious of their authority and power,

[a] Judges xv 11 [J].

[1] Egyptian mural decorations of Ramses III show that women travelling in ox-carts upon the shore accompanied the great migration (p. 307); from the fact that they were protected by a Philistine bodyguard it may be inferred that they represent the chieftains' wives and families.

[2] Cf. p. 329.

but not as tyrants or invaders. Nor do they evince as yet any desire to extend their suzerainty beyond the Plain.

The story of Samson and his vain struggles thus fitly closes the period of the Judges, while presaging a more ominous future. The remaining chapters of the Book of Judges do not form part of the connected narrative, and so far as they seem apposite they have been considered in their context.[1] If, however, we turn further and open the Book of Samuel, we find Israel no longer submissive under foreign rule, but struggling for its national existence amidst a net of hostile garrisons. The change in the political situation then becomes radical and marks the beginning of a new era, when the tribes are driven at last in the extremity of their need to seek and find in union under a central monarchy their freedom and their future.

As yet, however, this situation had not developed. Two tribes only, namely Dan and Judah, are mentioned in the stories associated with Samson. The references to Dan (the tribe of Samson himself) suggest at first sight that this tribe had not yet migrated to the north;[2] and indeed it may reasonably be thought that the circumstances under which the city of Laish was destroyed without reprisals 'because it was far from Zidon'[a] betoken a period of Phoenician rather than Egyptian domination in the Huleh area, and hence a somewhat later date than the age of Samson, when the withdrawal of Egypt had become a *fait accompli* and even the nominal suzerainty of the Pharaoh could be no longer claimed.[3] On the other hand Zidon may be mentioned in that

[a] Judges xviii 28 [J].

[1] The migration of the Danites to the north, described in Ch. xviii, is discussed on pp. 245, 305. The story of the punishment of Benjamin (Ch. xx-xxi) appears from the details of the narrative to be anachronous and misplaced, suggesting a stage of tribal development and organisation out of keeping with the rest of the Book. It seems to pertain at the earliest to the age of Eli and Samuel.

[2] Cf. p. 247.

[3] Cf. p. 317.

passage as representing Egypt,[1] and in view of the allusions in the Song of Deborah which we have considered,[2] a more probable explanation is to be found in the fact that not all the tribe migrated, but that some families retained the footing they had already gained in Zorah and its vicinity.

The mention of the 'men of Judah' is even more instructive; for from before Joshua's death when it was decided that Judah, Simeon and Caleb should move towards the south, there is found no further reference to this tribe in the old sources until the time of Jephthah,[a] a lapse of more than 250 years. Even then the allusion tells only of the menace of an Ammonite invasion, directed against the S.E. highlands, which Judah shared with Benjamin and Ephraim; and it will not be forgotten that the full weight of the first oppressions had fallen upon the same area of the south and east. In the meanwhile the tribe of Judah had responded to none of the great national calls.[3] It would appear then that only now had the people of Judah begun to emerge from their early vicissitudes and form an independent unit, even though still submissive to an alien regime. The field of Samson's activities being limited to the neighbourhood of the Vale of Sorek and the adjoining Plain, no further light is shed by the narrative upon the state of the other tribes of Israel at this time. However, their varying fortunes and their development throughout the period of the Judges can be followed, as we have seen,[4] from the series of disconnected episodes and the occasional calls to union which form the main subject-matter of the Book.

[a] Judges x 9 [J E]. Cf. p. 332.

[1] Sidon was a vassal city of the Pharaoh: cf. Kn. 144-5. One alternative possibility, of the episode belonging to the period of the Habiru revolt, when the Kings of Sidon and Hazor were accused of throwing in their lot with the enemy (p. 186) and so repudiating their allegiance, seems to be ruled out by the reference to Geshur and Maacah (Joshua xiii 13 [J]), which according to the true text of II Samuel xx 18 appear to have included the area of Abel and Dan (*C.A.H.* ii, p. 369).

P. 305. [3] Above, pp. 275, 305, 318. [4] Sect. 12.

Read as incidents in the history of the Egyptian Empire, these narratives become imbued with a fuller meaning and their discontinuous character becomes less apparent. Compared with our knowledge of other portions of the Egyptian Empire, the records concerning the Israelites appear in fact to be exceptionally full and reliable. Not only do the numerous recorded episodes find their natural setting inside the broad outline derived from Egyptian sources, but their historical value is enhanced by chronological coincidences at various epochs, seen, for instance, in the intervention of Ben Anath[1] in the reign of Ramses II, and the disturbance in southern Palestine in the first year of Seti I,[2] in addition to the general correspondence of the alternate periods of rest and unrest discussed in the opening Section of this volume.[3] Moreover, the narrative gains interest and clearness from the fact that it can now be plentifully illustrated from contemporary materials, and this advantage will increase all the time with the progress of archaeological research.

Turning over the pages of this volume in a critical but commonsense frame of mind, we find no reason to doubt that the historical narrative contained in the Books of Joshua and Judges, so far as it was derived from the old sources J and E, was founded upon fact. Further, in view of the remarkable accuracy and fulness of topographical detail in the earlier portion of the Book of Joshua, and the parallelism of certain passages in the Book of Judges with contemporary Egyptian archives, it is difficult to believe that these records were not written down in any form until the ninth or eighth century B.C., to which period the early documents, J and E, are attributed, that is from 300 to 500 years after the events described. The lost Book of Jashar twice mentioned in the Bible[a] is evidence to the contrary, and there is literary indication that if only for the purposes of minstrelsy

[a] Joshua x 13 [J] ; II Samuel i 18.

[1] Sect. 16, p. 287. [2] Sect. 15, p. 270. [3] Pp. 64-5.

the 'Book of the Wars of Jehovah' early took that poetical and therefore semi-permanent form,[a] which is seen in the Song of Deborah. It would seem indeed probable that the religious leaders of Israel, soon after their entry into Canaan, adopted the system of writing already well developed in the land,[1] and commenced at any rate a series of sacred archives. The old text, which we have found in all other respects so trustworthy, implies clearly that Joshua set down in writing at Shiloh the description of the tribal portions,[b] and later at Shechem the terms of the Covenant to serve Jehovah which he made there with the People.[c]

Remarkable as may appear the proved historical reliability of the documents upon which is based the world's oldest connected narrative in the history of human and national endeavour, the conclusion we have reached is not altogether astonishing in view of the fact that both the Egyptians and the Hittites, whose influence permeated Canaan at that time, had already established a system of State archives. But these Books are at the core the record of a religious movement, as recognised at the outset of this work in the discussion of Joshua's Vision before Jericho, and from that aspect of the matter, of which we cannot altogether lose sight, there is indeed room for wonderment. Throughout the centuries we have been reviewing, frequent political changes and recurring crises swept the country; yet, in spite of the dispersal of the tribes, and their prolonged association with peoples worshipping strange gods with attractive rites, the flame of Israel's religion was kept alive. Our wonder is only increased when we picture to ourselves the realities of nomad life in the highlands of Judaea or Galilee with the winds of winter moaning and whistling through the dripping

[a] Numbers xxi 14 [J]; Joshua x 13 [J]; Judges v 2-31 [E].

[b] Joshua xviii 8 [JE]. [c] Joshua xxv 25 [E], 26 []?.

[1] Modern discoveries illustrate the development both of early Hebrew and even of an alphabetical system in the Late Bronze Age. Cf. *Syria* III, 1922, pp. 273 ff.; X, 1929, pp. 304 ff.; and XI, 1930, pp. 2 ff.; also *Camb. Anct. Hist.* ii, pp. 334 f.

tents, and try to appreciate something of the untold hardships which the various groups and individuals must have suffered during this long period of vigil. Yet, in spite of all, though the years drew out into centuries, somewhere, 'between Ramah and Bethel,' the spark was kept glowing, ready when the propitious moment returned to burst anew into flame, and so guide the People farther along the unknown path they followed at the bidding of their God.

Cf. I. Samuel XVII, 5-7

EGYPT AND ISRAEL

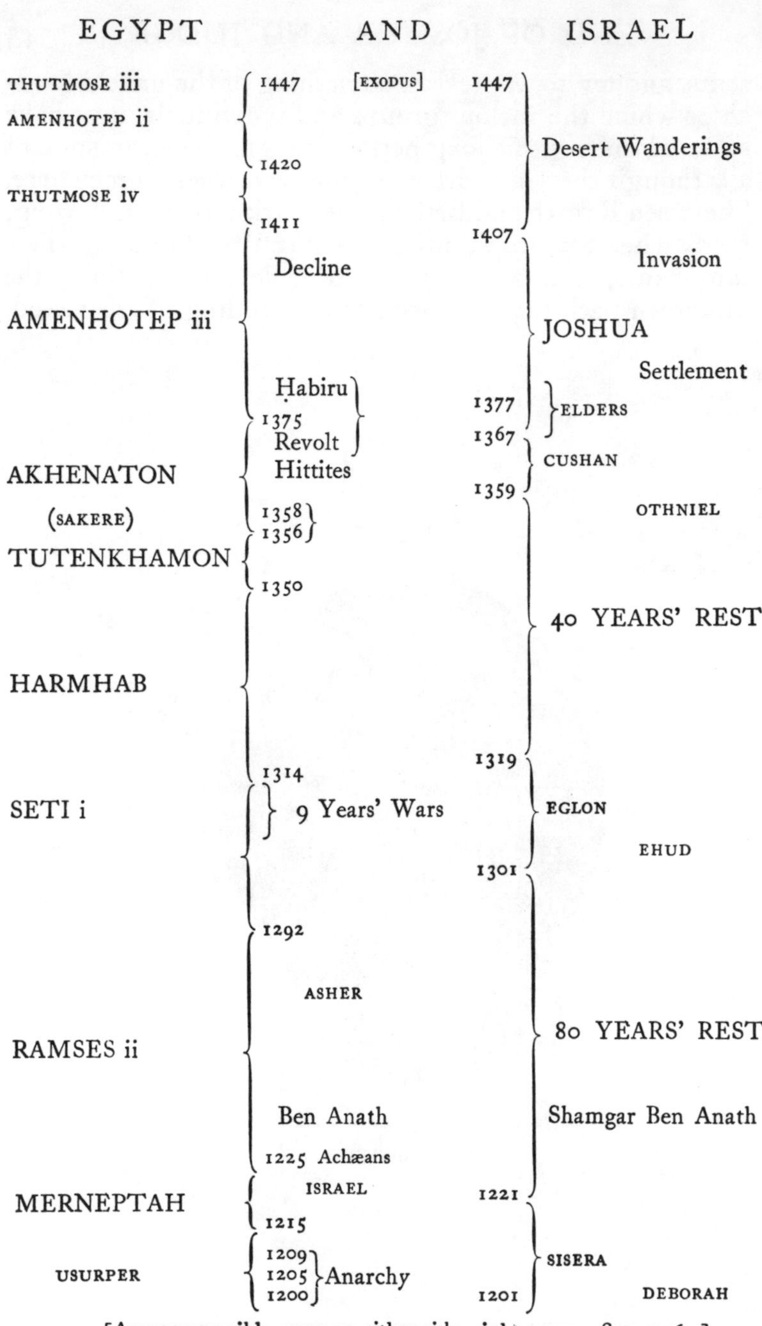

[Average possible error on either side, eight years. See. p. 61.]

CHRONOLOGICAL OUTLINES

Egypt		Events		Israel
SET-NEKHT	1200 1198	Restoration.	1201	BARAK AND DEBORAH
RAMSES iii		Migration of Northerners and Philistines.		40 YEARS' REST
„ iv	1167	Sinai evacuated.	1161	MIDIANITE OPPRESSION
„ v	1157	Decline of Egyptian power and prestige.	1154	
„ vi	1154			
„ vii	1152			
„ viii	1150			40 YEARS' REST UNDER GIDEON
„ ix	1142			
„ x	1123			
RAMSES xi	1118	Assyrian Conquests. Thekels in Dor.	1114 1111	ABIMELECH JEPHTHAH
SMENDES	1100		1104	
HERIHOR, 1095				
PESIBKHENNO i	1085	Philistines have rule over Israel.	1085	PHILISTINE OPPRESSION SAMSON *End of Book of Judges*
PAYNOZEM i	1067		1065 1045	ELI SAMUEL
	1026		1025	SAUL, 1st King
AMENEMOPET				DAVID, 2nd King Treaty and Marriage relations with Egypt
SIAMON	976		970	SOLOMON, 3rd King TEMPLE

[Average possible error on either side, eight years. See p. 61.]

EPOCHS IN BIBLE HISTORY

B.C.

1500. *THUTMOSE III. Campaigns in Syria, 119 Cities of Canaan captured.*

Hazor annexed, p. 185. Megiddo despoiled (1478 B.C.), p. 112.

1450 *AMENHOTEP II* (1447 B.C.). *Spoliation of Canaan continued.*

Exodus of Israel from Egypt (1447 B.C.), p. 258.

Desert wanderings, p. 65.

1410. *AMENHOTEP III* (1411 B.C.) *No campaigns in Canaan.*

Desert wanderings under Moses continued, p. 119.

Israelites reach Heshbon, p. 333. Joshua becomes leader, p. 119.

Jericho sacrificed to Jehovah, p. 140.

Capture of Ai, p. 153. Hivite Alliance, p. 162.

Defeat of Jerusalem league, p. 178. Fall of Hazor (*c.* 1400 B.C.), p. 183.

1390. *Egyptian Apathy followed by unrest in Canaan.*

Israel at Gilgal, Joshua very old, p. 201.

Apportionment of the Highlands, p. 202.

Judah and Simeon with Caleb in the south, p. 207.

Ephraim and Manasseh in the Centre : Bethel, p. 220.

1380. *AKHENATON* (1375 B.C.). *Period of Amarna letters : Ḥabiru invasion.*

Allotment of territory to the northern tribes at Shiloh, p. 236.

Death of Joshua at Shechem, p. 260. The Tribes disperse, p. 31.

1370. *Habiru at Shechem*, p. 252. *Hittite ascendancy*, p. 263.

Oppression of the Southern tribes by Cushan (8 years), p. 263.

1360. Deliverance by Othniel, the Kenizzite, p. 265.

SAKERE, TUTENKHAMON and HARMHAB restore the Egyptian Empire.

Forty years of Peace for Israel, p. 266.

1320. *SETI I. suppresses revolts in S. Canaan and the Jordan Valley.*

Oppression of S.E. tribes by Eglon of Moab (18 years), p. 270.

THE ISRAELITES IN CANAAN

B.C.

1300. Deliverance by Ehud of Benjamin, p. 275.

SETI I. and RAMSES II. maintain the Egyptian Empire.

Eighty years of Peace for Israel, p. 277.

Kedesh and Beth Anath reduced : Asher, Naphtali and Zebulun established, p. 280.

Shamgar Ben Anath smites the Philistines and saves Israel, p. 285.

1220. *MERNEPTAH repels the Sea-peoples.*

Oppression of Israel by Sisera allied with Hazor (20 years), p. 289.

Closing phase of the Bronze Age and Canaanite civilisation.

Anarchy in Egypt and a Syrian Usurper.

Union of tribes by Deborah and defeat of Sisera, p. 298.

1200. *SET-NEKHT re-establishes order in Egypt.*

Forty years of Peace for Israel, p. 306.

1190. *RAMSES III maintains peace and frustrates in Syria threatened inroad of northern peoples.*

Philistines and Thekels in coastal cities of Palestine, p. 309.

1160. *RAMESSIDES lose control of Palestine.*

Midianites and Amalekites overrun Palestine (7 years), p. 316.

Rout of the Midianites and pursuit to Karkor, p. 318.

1150. Forty years of Peace under Gideon of Manasseh, p. 323.

Abimelech in Shechem, p. 326.

1110. *Egypt withdraws from Syria : Assyrian invasion.*

Oppression by Ammonites and Philistines, p. 329.

Deliverance by Jephthah of Gilead, p. 333.

1100. *Philistines have rule over Israel forty years*, p. 334.

Samson resists and becomes the national hero, p. 334.

Men of Judah acknowledge the Philistine rule, p. 338.

1060. End of the historical narrative in the Book of Judges.

APPENDIX

PLACES AND ARCHAEOLOGY

PLACE NAMES AND IDENTIFIED SITES

The names are derived from the Early Sources J, E, and JE, and are quoted as transcribed in the R.V. (Revised Version).

(* Sites excavated.)

Acco.	Acre, Tell el Fokhar.
Achshaph.	Possibly Tell Keisan.
Achzib.	El Zib.
Adam.	Tell el Damieh.
Ai.	El Tell, E. of Bethel.
Aijalon.	Yalo, Tell Kokah.
Arad.	Tell Arad.
Arumeh.	Possibly Kh. Ormë.
Ashkelon : Askalon.	El Askalan.
Azekah.	Tell Zakariya.*
Beeroth.	Probably Tell Nasbeh.
Beth Anath.	Possibly El Khurbeh.
Bethel.	Beitin.
Bethhoron.	Beit-Ur (the lower).
Bethshean.	Beisan, Tell Husn.*
Bethshemesh, N.	Possibly Kadesh.
Bethshemesh, S.	‘Ain Shems.*
Debir : K. Sepher.	Tell Beit Mirsim.*
Dor.	Possibly Dora, Tanturah.*
Eglon.	Probably Tell el Hesy.*
Eshtaol.	Probably Eshua.
Gaza.	Gaza : Ghaza.*
Gezer.	Tell Jezer.*
Gibeah.	Tell el Ful.*
Gibeon.	El Jib.
Gilgal.	Jiljulieh by Jericho.
Harosheth.	Prob. Tell Harbaj.*
Hazor.	Tell el Kedah.*
Hebron.	Hebron : El Khalil.
Heshbon.	Tell Hesban.
Ibleam.	Tell el Bilameh.
Jarmuth.	Kh. el Yarmuk.
Jericho.	Kom el Sultan * by El Riha.
Jerusalem.	Ophel,* S.E. of Jerusalem.
Kadesh Naphtali.	Kades (cf. Beth-shemesh).
Karkor.	Karkar ; Keraker.
Kiriath-Jearim.	Kiriath el Enab.
Kiriath-Sepher: Debir.	Tell Beit Mirsim.
Lachish.	Tell el Duweir.
Laish.	Tell el Kadi.
Libnah.	Tell el Safi.
Makkedah.	Possibly Moghar.
Megiddo.	Tell el Mutesellim.
Merom, Waters of.	Jebel Marun, Waters of.
Misrephoth-maim.	Kh. el Misherefeh.
Nahalol.	Possibly Malul.
Ophrah.	Poss. Silet el Dhahr.
Rehob.	Tell Berweh.
Shechem.	Balata : Nablus.
Shiloh.	Kh. Seilun.
Shimron.	Poss. Summaka.
Shittim.	Kh. el Kufrein.
Succoth.	Tell Deir-Allah.
Taanach : Taanak.	Tell Ta‘anuk.
Thebez.	Tubas.
Timnah : Timnath.	Kh. Tibnah.
Zidon.	Sidon.
Zorah.	Surah.

SCHEME AND CLASSIFICATION

REFS. = Textual References. *Jos.* = Book of Joshua. *Jud.* = Book of Judges.

VAR. = Variant Spellings. *AV.* = Authorised Version. *LXX.* = Septuagint. *EGN.* = Egyptian. *T*[3]. = Thutmose III, *c.* 1475 B.C. *A.* = Tell el Amarna Letters, *c.* 1375 B.C. (*Kn.* = *Ed.* Knudtzon). *S.* = Seti I., *c.* 1300 B.C. *R*[2]. = Ramses II., *c.* 1275 B.C. *M.* = Merneptah, *c.* 1220 B.C. *R*[3]. = Ramses III., *c.* 1190 B.C.

LOC. = Location. *Cont.* = Biblical contexts. *Onom.* = The Onomasticon of Eusebius (*Ed.* Klostermann, 1904).

IDENT. = Identification. DESCR. = Description and Archaeological Notes.

EXCVNS. = Excavations, particularly as regards the L.B.A. (Late Bronze Age, 1600-1200 B.C.) and E.I.A. (Early Iron Age, 1200-1000 B.C.).

BIBL. = Bibliography.

ABBREVIATIONS FREQUENTLY USED

Ann. (or *Bul.*) *ASOR.* = *Annual* or *Bulletin of American School of Oriental Research*, Jerusalem.

B. *Jud.* = Burney, *The Book of Judges* (1918).

Bul. BSAJ. = *Bulletin of the British School of Archaeology, Jerusalem.*

CAH. = *Cambridge Ancient History.*

C. *Jos.*, C. *Jud.* = Cooke, G. A., Cambridge Bible for Schools and Colleges. *Joshua* and *Judges.*

JPOS. = *Journal of the Palestine Oriental Society, Jerusalem.*

Kh. = Khurbeh, a ruin. Pronounced Khurbet if followed by a vowel.

PEF, QS. = *Palestine Exploration Fund, Quarterly Statement.*

PJ-B. = *Palästina-Jahrbuch.*

RB. = *Revue Biblique,* Journal of the École Biblique Française de St. Étienne, Jerusalem.

ZDPV. = *Zeitschrift des Deutschen Palästina-Vereins.*

For further abbreviations see pp. xxiii and xxiv.

FAMILIAR ELEMENTS IN ARABIC PLACE NAMES

Ain, Spring ; *El*, the ; *Khurbeh*, ruin ; *Nahr*, river ; *Tell*, mound ; *Wady*, valley, or watercourse usually dry.

In pronunciation the final letter of *el* is often assimilated to the following consonant, and that of *Khurbeh* becomes *t* before a vowel. Thus El Deir is pronounced *Ed-Deir*, and Kh. el Kefireh *Khurbet e'Kefireh.*

Abel-Cheramim. Jud. xi 33 [J]. Var. *LXX Ebelcharmim.*

Loc. The *Context* indicates a position in Trans-Jordania and probably in the district of Ammon. Jephthah smote the children of Ammon 'from Aroer (? Arair) until thou cometh to Minnith . . . and unto A.' Minnith is located by Eusebius (*Onom.* Kl. p. 133) at Maanith, 4 miles from Heshbon (Tell Hesban) and Abel-cheramin (*ibid.* p. 33) at *Abel-vinearum*, 6 miles from *Philadelphia* (Amman). The site is unknown, but is identified tentatively by Tristram with Kurm Dhiban, the 'vineyards of Diban,' a gentle depression with old dykes and grass-grown ridges, marking former vineyards where not a vine has grown for centuries, an instance of the persistence of topogr. nomenclature.

Bibl. Tristram, *Land of Moab*, p. 130; *Bible Places*, p. 416. C.*Jud.*, p. 123. Cf. further, Vigouroux, *Dict. Bibl.*, and Jacobus, *Stand. Bib. Dict.*

Abel-Meholah. Jud. vii 22 [J]. *LXX Abel Meula.*

Loc. Not far from the west bank of the Jordan in its middle course, between Beisan and the fords by El Damieh (Map 17, p. 322). In Gideon's pursuit of the Midianites 'the host fled as far as Bethshittah toward Zererah, as far as the border (lip) of Abel-meholah, by Tabbath' (see p. 318, n. 4). In 1 Kings iv 12 the name is associated with Bethshean as marking the boundaries of a tithe officer's district in a passage which is however somewhat confused, 'all Bethshean which is beside Zarethan, beneath Jezreel, from Bethshean to Abelmeholah.' Burney, *Judges*, p. 220, would rearrange this passage, reading 'Abel-meholah which is beside Zarethan.'

Ident. The site is not identified. Eusebius in *Onom.* proposed a place 9 Roman miles from Beisan down the valley, called Bethmaula, the position of which is lost but corresponds generally with the Ruins (*Khurbeh*) and Spring called El Maleh.

Bibl. B.*J.* p. 222, C.*Jud.* p. 88, *Kl. O.* p. 35. J., *S.B.D.* p. 16, *PEF. Mem.* ii. p. 231. Cf. further Holscher, *ZDPV.* 1910, p. 16; Abel, *Rev. Bibl.* (1913), p. 224; Albr. *JPOS.* v. 34 n.; and *Bull. ASOR.* Oct. 1925, p. 18.

Acco. Jud. i 31 [J].

Var. *AV. Accho. LXX 'Accho. EGN.* T^3 (No. 47), *Ak.* A (Kn. 8, 88, 111, 232, 236, 234, L.AO. 7096), *Akka*; S *Aka*; R^2 ? *Akn.*

Loc. *Cont.* assoc. with Asher, Zidon and Achzib. *A.* similar. *Onom.* 'Accho now Ptolemais.'

Ident. In name of modern Acre (*Gk.* Ptolemais, *Arabic* Akka, *French* St. Jean d'Acre) which, however, may formerly have been an island, like Tyre, just off the coast; ancient site probably Tell el Fokhar (the mound of pots), a contiguous Bronze Age mound now just inland, *i.e.* eastward from modern Acre, and perhaps once on the coast.

Descr. P. 96; Pl. LV; Map No. 7. 'Tell el Fokhar, an imposing site which lies East of Acre, near the spring *'Ain es Sitt*, is a large natural hill, the northern side of which is rounded, the southern irregular. On this there lies a quantity of debris 2½ m. in depth in the S.E., but in the N. and N.E. deeper. In that direction the mound is higher with steep slopes, but it descends gradually towards the S.W. Occupation originally covered the N.E. top of the mound, but later expanded towards the spring and the plain. . . . Sherds of M.B., L.B. and E.I.i.' Saarisalo, in *JPOS.* ix. 1929, p. 27 f.

Bibl. *Bull. BSAJ.* No. 2, 1922, pp. 10 f.; *JPOS. loc. cit.*; B. *A.R.* iii. 114, No. 13; Gard. *Anast.* 23.*

Achshaph. Jos. xi 1 [J].

Var. *LXX Aziph, EGN.* T[3] (No. 40) *y-k-s-p*, A. (*L.AO.* 7096), *Ak-ša-pa*, R[2] (*Anast.*) *'A-k-s-p.*

Loc. Undefined in *Cont.* According to later tradition (Jos. xix. 25 [P]) it lay on the border, probably the west border, of Asher, hence probably in or near the border of the Plain of Acre, a suggestion supported by its association with Akka in *A.* In *Pap. Anast.* it appears after Acco and lay apparently to the S. *Onom.* would locate it at *Chsalus*, seven miles from *Diocaesarea* at the foot of Tabor in the Plain of Esdraelon, in accordance with the theory of identifying Shimron with Semuniyeh (p. 180).

Ident. Uncertain: the site of Tell Keisan suits the general indications. Cf. pp. 99, 189 and Pl. XLV. Other suggestions are El Tell, in the northern part of the plain of Acre, and Kh. Iksaf in the N.E. of Galilee, which, however, proves on inspection to be a purely Byzantine site. (G. 1928.)

Bibl. *PEF, QS.* 1892, p. 207. *Rev. Bibl.* 1924, p. 11. Kl. *Onom.* p. 23. Gard. *Anast.* p. 23*.

Achzib. Jud. i 31 [J].

Var. *LXX Aschazi*[*b*].

Loc. The context groups Achzib with Acco, Sidon and other cities as a place from which the Canaanites were not driven out by Asher (Jud. i 31 [J]); and it was later counted (Jos. xix 29 [P]) on the border of Asher. The name appears in classical authors as Ecdippa (Ptolemy v 15, Pliny v 17, Josephus (Ecdippon), *Bell. Jud.* 1 xiii 4), which is placed by the *Onomasticon* 9 m. north of Ptolemais (Acre).

Ident. The modern El Zib, 9 miles to the north of Acre upon the coast. The present village covers the ancient site, in which, however, a section cut by a watercourse attests its Bronze Age antiquity (G. 1928. P. *LIA.*). See further, pp. 96, 190.

Adam. Jos. iii 16 [JE], I Kings vii 46 (?) Adamah.
VAR. *LXX* (the region of) *Kariathiarim*.

LOC. The context places 'Adam, the city that is beside Zarethan,' on the Jordan and a considerable distance from the crossing-place opposite Jericho.

IDENT. The one site satisfying the conditions is found at TELL EL DAMIEH, upon the east bank opposite the ford of Jisr el Damieh, sixteen miles above Jericho. This distance, being measured as the crow flies, is sufficient under the conditions of travel in this desolate region to justify the expression 'a great way off.' (See pp. 71, 127.)

DESCR. The Tell is small, hardly more than a mound, rising above a natural terrace towards the N.E. of a small plain. See Pl. III and p. 136; also Map, p. 126. Pottery L.B.A. and E.I.A. (G. 1928 P. *L.I.A.*).

Ahlab. Jud. i 31 [J].
VAR. *LXX Dalaph*.

LOC. This city, which is not named elsewhere (unless Helbah in the same verse is a doublet of it), appears in the list of Jud. i 31 [J] together with Acco and Sidon, between the latter and Achzib.

IDENT. Unknown. One of the unnamed Bronze Age Tells in the northern plain of Acre is possible, but the place may have lain further to the north.

Ai. Josh. vii 2-5 [J], viii 1-29 [JE]. *LXX Gai.*
VAR. ? *Aiath*, Isaiah x 28. ? *Aija*, Nehemiah xi 31.

LOC. Assoc. with Bethel and Michmas. The contexts of Josh. vii 2 [J] and viii 12 [E] place Ai definitely to the east of Bethel.

IDENT. EL TELL (Pl. XXVIII), a Bronze Age site upon a rocky, terraced mound 2 m. to the east of Bethel. Its situation is confirmed by certain topographical details, particularly the position of the Wady Muheisin on the north side, as indicated in vii 11 [J], and a hill with crevasses suitable for ambush overlooking the site from the west (*ibid.* 12 [J]). See Plates XXIX-XXXII.

DESCR. The situation, appearance and general character of EL TELL have already been described in Sect. 6 (see especially pp. 150-1 and Plates XXVIII, XXIX). Assuming the city of the L.B.A. to have followed the line of terraced scarp already protected by a stone wall in M.B.A. ii, its form would be roughly square, about 230 × 200 yards, with rounded corners, and an area of some 9 acres. Soundings made by the writer in 1928 showed the rampart wall to have been largely quarried away in Byzantine times, but traced its course along the southern slopes of the Tell for about 180 yards by following the line of stone chippings and the remains of its foundations, and on the west face exposed a stretch of walling (Pl. XXIX *b*), which was found preserved to a height of eleven feet over a distance of 40 yards. The masonry consisted of heavy unworked stones packed with small pieces, in the style characteristic of the

M.B.A.; and though the stones employed were on the whole smaller than are found in strong places like Tell el Nasbeh or Jericho, they were similar in size and setting to the contemporary walls of Jerusalem (Pl. XXXVIII) and Hazor (Pl. LXXII). In confirmation of date, a sherd of M.B.A.i technique was picked out of the bonding at the fourth course The origins of the defences were not tested, but evidence was found of the occupation of the site in the E.B.A. While, as usual, M.B.A. wares were most abundant, there was found a considerable proportion of L.B.A.i including (in the collection of the American School) a Cypriote wish-bone handle, but nothing of Mykenaean date or character, nor any local fabrics of a date later than 1400 B.C.

Bibl. Above pp. 150 ff., and Albr. *Zeits. f. d. Alttest. Wiss.* (*ZATW.*), vi 1929, p. 12.

Aijalon. Jos. x 12 [J], Jud. i 35 [J].

Var. *LXX Ailon*, *Aialon*. *EGN*. M.K. *I-'-h-n-w*; A. (Kn. 273) *A-ia-lu-na*, (Kn. 287) *Ia-lu-na*.

Loc. The oldest reference (Joshua's triumph-song, Jos. x 12 [J]) places the 'vale of Aijalon' in the neighbourhood of Bethhoron, westwards from Gibeon. It remained an Amorite city (Jud. i 35 [J]). It was apparently known to the Egyptians as early as the Middle Kingdom, *c.* 2000 B.C. (*Syria* viii, 216, 230), and its valley was traversed by Egyptian caravans (A, *Kn.* 287). *Onom.* repeats a current identification: near Nicopolis (Emmaus, Amwas), 1 mile towards Jerusalem.

Ident. The modern Yalo, a village standing upon a mound representing Late Bronze and subsequent ages. Tell el Kokah, near by, an Early Bronze Age site, may mark the original settlement. See further, p. 180 and Pl. LII.

Bibl. *PEF, QS* 1877, 26. *PEF, Mem.* ii 299. *Bul. ASOR* Oct. 1924, 10.

Aphik. Jud. i. 31 [J].

Var. *LXX Aphek*. *Naei*. *EGN*. T^3 (No. 66) *Y-p-k-n*.

Loc. In Asher, and probably in the Plain of Acre; one of the cities which remained Canaanite. *Cont.* names it between Helbah and Rehob, *q.v.*

Ident. Unknown: the name means simply 'fortress,' and is common. [The Aphek of the Egyptian list is Aphek of Sharon, possibly at Baka West, p. 85 and Pl. VIII.] Aphek of Asher may be one of the numerous Tells of the Plain of Akko: T. el Tantur has been suggested (Albr. *Cont. Hist. Geog. Pal.* p. 28), but there is no direct indication.

Bibl. *MVAG.* 1902, 51-60; *MNDPV.* 1911, 33-44; *PJ-B.* 1912, 21-22; 1914, 31, 53-99; *RB.* 1927, 398-400, 595; *JPOS.* ii 145-158, 184-9; *Bul. ASOR.* Oct. 1923, p. 6; Oct. 1929, p. 7.

Arad. Jud. i 16 [J].
VAR. *LXX Arad, Airath, Ader. EGN.* T^3 (No. 100) *Y-r-t.*

Loc. Arad is mentioned in connexion with the operations of the Kenites, Judah and Simeon, in the Southern Negeb, the *Cont.* being 'the wilderness of Judah, which is in the south of Arad.' There can be little doubt then as to its identity with Tell Arad which preserves the name.

IDENT. TELL ARAD, 17 m. south of Hebron (Map, p. 76). This is an extensive, deserted ancient site standing on the foothills, with a broad view over the southern plains (see p. 215 and Pl. VII). A line of fortifications is suggested by the present appearance of the mound, in which Bronze Age pottery gives independent evidence of its antiquity (G. 1921).

BIBL. *PEF. Mem.* iii pp. 403, 415.

Aroer. Jud. xi 26. VAR. *LXX Aroer (land of).*

Loc. In Trans-Jordania, north of the R. Arnon. Two places of this name occur in O.T.; the one, E. of Rabboth-Ammon, is excluded by the context, in which Jephthah denies the claims of Ammon to the site. The other, probably identical with KH. 'ARA'IR, stood on the N. bank of the Arnon, some 4 miles S.W. of Dibon (*Dhiban*), with which it is associated in Num. xxxii 34. It had fallen into possession of the Israelites under Moses by their defeat of Sihon, King of the Amorites, who at that time held the land between the Arnon and the Jabbok, with his headquarters at Heshbon, having apparently dispossessed the Ammonites (p. 332). This position suits the topographical indications, and an ancient mound with potsherds similar to those of Heshban is reported, among the Roman and later ruins upon the site.

BIBL. *PEF, QS.* 1879, p. 191.

Arumah. Jud. ix 41 [J].
VAR. *LXX Arema, Arima.*

Loc. The name only occurs here in the story of Abimelech, and the *Cont.* suggests that the town lay not far from Shechem. *Onom.* (s.v. *Ruma*) locates it in the neighbourhood of Diospolis (*i.e.* coastwards on the mountains of Ephraim), and mentions that 'some said' it was Arimathea.

IDENT. Very uncertain. Position and name sound admit the possible identity with EL ORMË (p. 78), on a prominent hilltop 7 miles S.E. of Balata (G. 1928).

BIBL. *PEF. Mem.* ii 387. *Bul. ASOR.* Apr. 1925, p. 6.

Ashkelon (Askalon ; Ascalon). Jud. xiv 19 [Gl. J]

VAR. *LXX Askalon. EGN.* MK. (*Syria* viii 227) *Isq'nw.* A. (*Kn.* 287, 320, 321, 322) *Aš-ka-lu-na.* R^2 *Is-k-lw-n.*

Loc. One of the five cities of the Philistines in the southern coastal plain accessible from Timnah (Jud. xiv 19). In the fourteenth century a vassal city of Egypt (Amarna letters); re-conquered by Ramses II (p. 287

and Fig. 10). Traditionally allotted to Judah (Jud. i 18 [P]), but the next verse (attributed to [J]) states that the Canaanites of the Plain, having

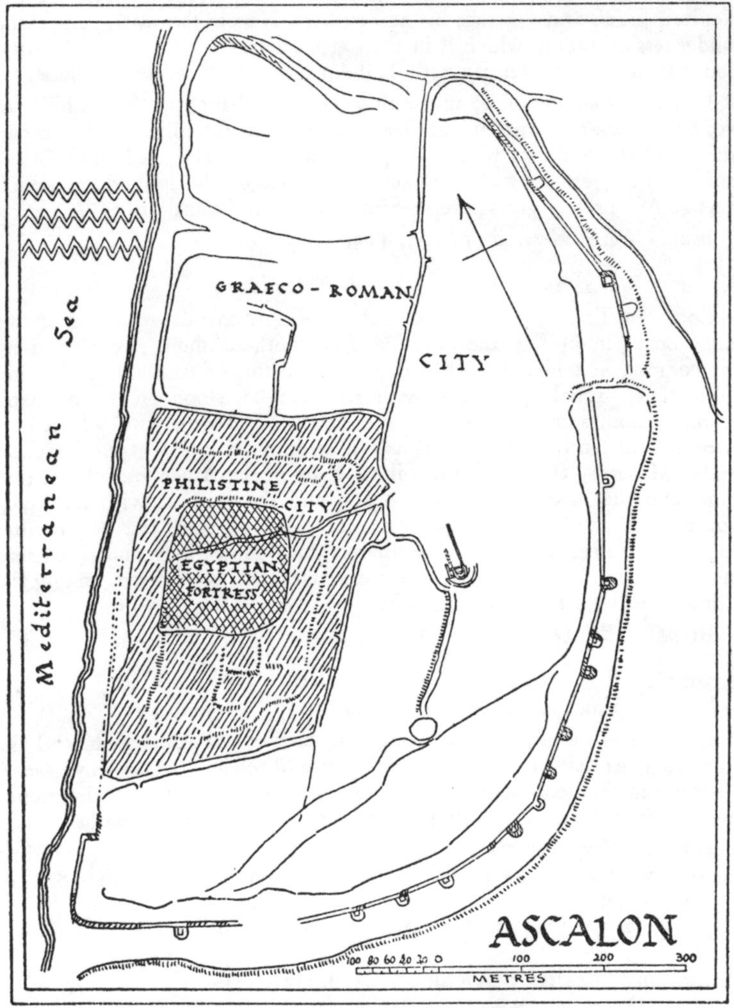

Plan No. 1. Site of Askalon at different epochs.

chariots of iron, could not be dispossessed. Later it became the Philistines' port (see below EXCVNS.). Josephus (*Bell. Jud.* III ii 1), the Peutinger Table, the Antonine Itinerary, Ptolemy (v 16) and Strabo (xvi 29), all give its exact location, modern Askalan, where the name survives with little change.

Descr. Askalan is a garden area by the sea, 17 miles to the north of Gaza. It boasts a hundred wells, and owes its fertility, indeed its existence, to a subterranean supply of gently flowing fresh waters, which can be reached upon the seashore by digging a foot depth into the sand. Its area has roughly the form of a half-circle, with its diameter, about a thousand yards in length, along the coast, as seen in Plan No. 1, p. 358.

Excvns. made during 1921-2 under the supervision of the writer for the P.E.F. have traced the history of the city in outline from E.B.A. down to mediaeval times, and the results illustrate the known history of the site (Cf. *Hist. of A.*, by Phythian-Adams in *PEF*, *QS*. 1921, pp. 76 f., and *The Excavns. of A.*, A Summary, *id*. 1922, pp. 112 f.). Civilized settlement seems to have begun in M.B.A., and in the latter part of that epoch (*c*. 1700 B.C.) the area was surrounded by a great rampart of beaten earth, similar to those of Hazor (p. 184, Pl. XLIV) and of Qatna (Misrefeh) in Central Syria. Such earthworks seem to be associated in some way with the Hyksos, the enclosed areas being much larger than the largest known Canaanite cities : the Hittite capital at Boghaz Keui in Asia Minor was defended on its more exposed side in a similar way (G. *HE*. pp. 81-2). The outline of Askalon in the L.B.A. has not been determined ; presumably it enclosed a portion of the high ground overlooking the coast near the middle of the site (see Plan, No. 1), and was commensurate with other cities of the period, which vary from 5 to 12 acres in area. It is known to have been dominated and defended in the time of Ramses II, *c*. 1290 B.C., by a tall tower or migdol (see Fig. 10, p. 286). To judge by the disposition of the potsherds of E.I.A.i (1200-1000), the Philistine city was more extensive, and it may have occupied the whole of the central hill. The most prosperous period of Askalon as yet known to history belonged to the early centuries of the Christian era, when the city once again spread out as far as its original ramparts. The Senate-house of the period, with its columned portico (presumably the famous peristyle with which Herod adorned his birth-place), as well as several fine pieces of architectural sculpture, were unearthed in the course of the excavations. At that epoch the city enjoyed the privilege of Roman freedom. Later a new defensive wall with external bastions was built around the enclosure upon the original line of earthern ramparts.

Though the solidarity and extent of the Roman remains baffled the project of excavating the Philistine city, various sections cut into the central mound threw light both on the local development and on various problems of wider interest. In a first cutting (*QS*. 1921, p. 163) the layer representing the period of Egyptian occupation under Ramses II (*c*. 1250 B.C.) was separated by a marked layer of ashes and debris from that of the Philistine occupation which immediately followed it. The line of cleavage thus falls about 1225-1190 B.C., corresponding with the rise of the Iron Age, and possibly with the Philistine invasion repelled by Ramses

III (p. 309). These indications were controlled and developed by Mr. Phythian-Adams, by a broad section cut scientifically upon the steep scarp above the seashore (*QS*. 1923, p. 60). The results were parallel, but additional light was thrown upon the archaeology of the L.B.A., in the earlier strata of which were found Cypriote and Aegean types, and above these, the abundant traces of Mykenaean trade relations and its effects. The notable influx of Mediterranean products suggests that Askalon in L.B.A.ii became a centre for foreign infiltration from the Aegean area, including Crete, Cyprus and the coasts of Asia Minor and Syria, and may account in some measure for the repeated defection of the city, as in the reigns of Ramses II and Merneptah. Compare the parallel results of excavation at Bethshemesh, Debir and Gerar.

BIBL. *PEF, QS*. 1921, 12-76, 102; 1922, p. 112; 1923, pp. 60-84. Thomsen, *Reallexikon, s.v.* Askalon.

Ataroth. Jos. xvi 2 [J]. VAR. *LXX Chatarothi.*

LOC. The context indicates a position between Bethel and Bethhoron. *Onom.* mentions several places of this name, locating this one 'near Rama.'

IDENT. Uncertain. Several sites have been proposed in the neighbourhood, where the name 'Atara appears in various forms, *e.g.* Kh. Aṭṭarah, 1 m. S. of Tell el Nasbeh; 'Athara near Bethel, 'Atara near El Râm.

BIBL. *PEF, QS*. 1905, p. 170. C. *J.*, p. 154. *Bul. ASOR*. Oct. 1929, p. 4.

Azekah. Jos. x 10 [J]. VAR. *LXX Azeka.*

LOC. In the Shephelah, as seen from the context, which places A. beyond Beth-horon, on the line of the Amorites' westward flight from Gibeon. The list of Rehoboam's buildings (II Chron. xi 9-10) and later references (Neh. xi 30, Jer. xxxiv 7) associate it with Lachish. It is also placed by *Onom.* between Eleutheropolis (Beit Jibrîn) and Jerusalem. A definite indication is supplied by I Sam. xvii 1, which shows that it lay like Socoh in the Vale of Elah (see p. 180, n. 3).

IDENT. TELL ZAKARIYA (Pl. XLII) satisfies the topogr. and archaeol. indications.

DESCR. TELL ZAKARIYA is an isolated mound rising 1200 feet above sea level upon a low spur in a loop of the Wady Sunt (the reputed Vale of Elah, I Sam. xvii 2), with a commanding view over the Shephelah across the Philistine Plain (Pl. XLII and p. 180). The summit or plateau of the mound measures only 1000 × 500 feet, with an area of about one acre, while a fortress or citadel in the south-east corner measures some 220 × 150 feet. It thus suggests a fortified outpost or migdol, like Gibeah on Tell el Ful (Pl. XXXIII).

Excvns. made for the P.E.F. by Drs. Bliss and Macalister, in 1898, showed that the 'citadel' and other towers on the south-west side belonged to the Seleucidan and Roman epochs. But soundings made in various positions gave proof that the occupation at one time spread over the whole surface, and dated at any rate from L.B.A.i, *c.* 1500 B.C., though no fortifications of that period were discovered. Egyptian beads, scarabs and amulets disclosed Egyptian connexions in the reigns of Thutmose III and

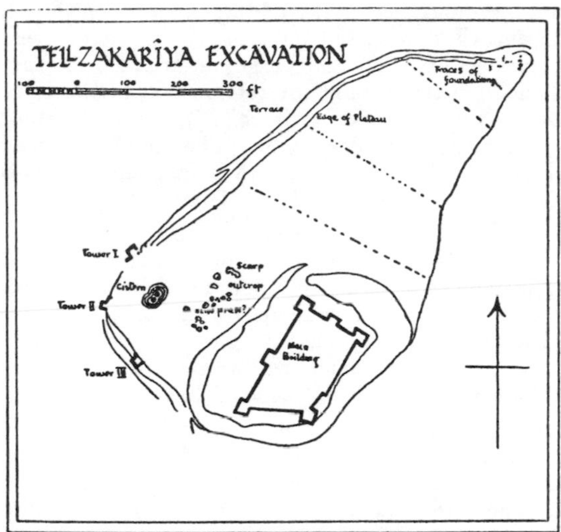

Plan No. 2. Tell Zakariya, probable site of Azekah.

Amenhotep III; while pottery of Cypriote and Mykenaean affinities showed that the place shared in the general culture influences of the age in this vicinity, as illustrated by the excavation of Askalon, 'Ain-Shems and Gezer, *q.v.*

Bibl. *PEF. Excavations in Palestine*, 1898-1900, pp. 12-27 and Plates 1 and 2, from which our Plan No. 2 is derived.

Baal-Tamar. Jud. xx 33 [J]. Var. *LXX Baalthamar.*

Loc. This one context indicates a site near to Gibeah of Benjamin (Tell el Ful). *Onom.* states that a village near Gibeah was still called Bethtamari.

Beer. Jud. ix 21 [E]. Var. *LXX Baier, Bera.*

Loc. The *Cont.* gives no indication, and the name does not occur elsewhere; *Onom.* suggests Bera, a village 8 miles east from Eleutheropolis (Beit Jibrin), and hence rather remote from the scene of the narrative.

Beeroth. Jos. ix 17 (? P).

VAR. *LXX Beroth*. *EGN*. (doubtful) T[3] (No. 19) *B-'-y-r-t*.

LOC. One of the group of Hivite cities allied with Gibeon (pp. 77-160). Placed by *Onom*. ' under the hill of Gabaon,' where it was pointed out as a village 6 miles from Jerusalem on the way to Shechem.

IDENT. Not certain, but probably TELL EL NASBEH. Cf. pp. 164-5, Pl. XXXV and Map No. 11

[It remains open to conjecture that Mizpah (Josh. xv 38 [P], Judg. xxi 1-20 [P], I Sam. vii 5) occupied the same site in later Israelitish times. In the early passages of Joshua and Judges as far as xxi the name Mizpah is not mentioned. There is only one reference in the historical books to Beeroth after Joshua ix 17 (exc. xviii 25 [P]), viz. in II Sam. iv 2, ' for Beeroth also was reckoned to Benjamin.' The site of the place referred to by the same name in Ezra and Nehemiah is uncertain. In II Samuel the name Mizpah is not mentioned. The references to the two names thus do not overlap or conflict with this possibility.]

DESCR. TELL EL NASBEH occupies a prominent knoll above the springs, about seven miles north of Jerusalem upon the highroad towards Shechem (Pl. XXXV). It commands a wide view of the territory allotted to Benjamin (Pl. LX), as far as the higher parts of Jerusalem to the south, and the ridge which descends thence westward, with the height of Nebi Samwil above the village of El Jib (Gibeon) towards the south-west.

EXCVNS. made for the Pacific School of Religion by Dr. W. Badé in 1926 and 1927, and still in progress, have shown that the mound of Tell Nasbeh must have been occupied from the beginning of the Bronze Age to the end. The pottery found is representative of each period : several cave tombs contained very varied and instructive groups dating from E.B.A., and an inner city wall is ascribed to the same early period. In M.B.A. massive stone ramparts surrounded the Tell upon a terrace just below the top, enclosing an area of about 8 acres. They were more than 40 feet in height with a thickness of 16 to 20 feet, and in places are still preserved to an unparalleled extent. This great rampart was built after the fashion of the M.B.A. (cf. Jericho, Shechem) of rough blocks, which towards the bottom were of great size, decreasing with the successive courses, and the whole rested upon a made platform of immense rocks. As usual the building joints were partly filled with small stones. The lower part of the wall face was found also to have been coated with a hard yellow plaster to a height of fifteen or eighteen feet, apparently as a further protection against scaling, which otherwise might have been possible owing to the roughness of the stones and the fact that, as usual, the wall face slopes inwards at a certain angle. External bastions, rising at a steeper angle, seem to have been added during the Bronze Age as an additional support. The early part of the Late Bronze Age is well represented by the pottery found, and the excavator is of opinion that the types betoken occupation during the whole of that phase (1600-1200 B.C.), though the latter half is not so well defined. Of the Early Iron Age (after 1200 B.C.), though considerable change took place, and the great fortress was dismantled, there remain abundant traces of occupation, including Philistine wares, and also a tomb containing a rich assortment of pottery with two Egyptian scarabs. In the interior the Bronze Age level in general has not been reached, but is still under excavation.

Bibl. W. F. Badè, *Excavations at Tell el Nasbeh*. Alt. *PJB*. 1910, 45. Ph.-Adams, *JPOS*. iii p. 13. Alb. *JPOS*. 1923, p. 113 f. Cf. Guthe, *ZDPV*. xxxv, Mitt. i. 1-9. Cf. Vincent, *Rev. Bibl.* 1922, p. 376; 1927, p. 414; 1929, p. 110; also Thomsen, *Reallex*. s.v.

Beth-Anath. Jud. i 33 [J].
Var. *LXX Baitheneth, Baithanach. EGN.* T³ (No. 111) *B-t'n-t*; S. (No. 23) *B't-n-t*; R² *B-y-t'n-t.*

Loc. The context merely indicates the territory of Naphtali (northern and eastern Galilee). The list of R² associates it with Tyre, in a descriptive reference, 'the city on the Mt. of Beth-Anath named Kerpe[t].' *Onom.* would place it at Batanea, 5 miles from Caesarea, clearly in error.

Ident. Possibly the deserted Bronze Age mound in upper Galilee called Tell el Khurbeh (Pl. LXI), at the south foot of the Jebel Marun, overlooking the Wady Farah. Called El Kurbeh in Adam Smith's Maps (p. 102, n. 2). See further p. 244, Fig. 5, and p. 279. [G. 1928, P. *LIA*.]

Beth-Aven. Jos. vii 2 [J], I Sam. xiii 5; xiv 23.
Var. *LXX Baithel, Bethaun.*

Loc. Close to Ai, and west of Michmash. *Onom.* locates it between Ai and Bethel over against Michmash, and adds that 'some think it is Bethel' (see *LXX* var.). Further refs. in Hosea (iv 15, v 8, x 5), Amos (v 5) where it is identified with Bethel. The refs. in Sam. prove its separate identity. Cf. Cooke's note on Jos. vii 2.

Bibl. Cooke, *Josh.* p. 53 n. 2. Cf. Albr. *JPOS*. iii 114.

Beth-Barah. Jud. vii 24 [J]. Var. *LXX Baithera.*

Loc. A crossing-place, or ford, on or near the Jordan, south of the valley of Jezreel, and commanded from the mountains of Ephraim. Not otherwise known.

Ident. Possibly Abu Sidra (p. 320), where there is a small ancient mound, but quite uncertain, as there are several fords which would suit the context.

Bibl. Cooke, *Judg.* p. 89, note 24.

Bethel. Beitin. Jos. vii 2 [J], xvi 2 [J]. Jud. i 23 [J].
Var. *LXX Baithel.*

Loc. Definite indications are that it lay west of Ai (Jos. vii 2 [J]), and south of Shiloh (Jud. xxi 19). *Onom.* locates it 12 miles from Jerusalem, to the right of the road to Neapolis (Nablus, Shechem) between Bethaven and Ai.

Ident. The modern village of Beitin satisfies all the indications.

Descr. The site is a dip in a spur of the hills on the eastern border of the plateau; it is supplied with water by a perennial spring (see p. 225 and Pl. L). That the old city of the Bronze Age occupied much the same spot (Pl. IV) was made clear in 1927 when Dr. Albright, then Director of the American School of Oriental Research, sank a trench into the ground to a depth of twenty feet, at a spot on the west side of the village near an old building which proved to stand on mediaeval foundations. The top of the shaft was already ten feet below the general level surface of the site. The results showed a normal sequence of deposits of increasing age proportioned to the depth, in which all the familiar epochs were represented from Mediaeval Arab down to the Early Bronze Age. E.I.A. i (1200-900) was found at the third metre of depth, and L.B.A. (1600-1200?) at the fourth metre. The shaft proved to have probed the city just inside its ancient wall, which was found to be standing at a height of more than 12 feet. It pertained to Late Bronze Age, restored partly, it may be, in E.I.A. A mass of debris 9 or 10 feet thick represented the period 1700-1400 B.C.; and the excavator records his view that 'there was a destruction of the city before comb-facing had passed out of use, that is, not later than the fifteenth century B.C., before the end of L.B.A.i.

Bibl. Albr. *Bul. ASOR.* Feb. 1928, p. 29; *ZATW.* 1929, p. 1.

Beth-Horon (the Lower). Jos. x 10 [J]. Var. *LXX Horonin, Baithoron.*

Loc. The *Cont.* indicates a position westward from Gibeon, upon one of the natural routes towards the plain. *Onom.* placed it 11 m. from Jerusalem.

Ident. Mod. Beit Ur el Tahta (Pl. LI), on an old road from Jerusalem by El Jib towards Jaffa.

Descr. The site occupies a broad, low, isolated hill overlooking the road down the ridge upon which it is placed. It is scarped, particularly on its northern face, by numerous rocky terraces suitable for defensive works, and traces of strong walls are visible. L.B.A. pottery may be picked up all around the site (G. 1928, P. *L.I.A.*); but it is not possible to define the precise area of the city of that age, which must, however, have been important and covered at least 8 acres, possibly 10 acres, of surface (see further, p. 168).

Bethshean. Jos. xvii 11 [J]. 1 Sam. xxxi 10.
Var. *LXX Baithsan.* *EGN.* T^3 (No. 110) *B-t-š-y-r*; A (Kn. 289) *Bit-sa-a-ni.*

Loc. *Cont.* associates B. with Dor, Megiddo, Ibleam and Taanach; I Sam. xxxi places it near Mt. Gilboa and not far west of Jordan (night-raid of the men of Jabesh Gilead). In Jerome's day it had been known for some centuries as Scythopolis.

Ident. The mound of Tell Husn (Pl. LII), immediately to the N.W. of the modern village of Beisan.

DESCR. Bethshean occupied the crest of Tell Husn, a prominent mound which commands the junction of the Valley of Jezreel with the Jordan rift, and stands upon the south bank of the Nahr Jalud, overlooking the modern village of Beisan (p. 71). The necropolis of L.B.A. and E.I.A. is found on a low limestone ridge, on the opposite side of the river, distant only two hundred yards from the Tell (Pl. LIII). Previous to excavation the mound and tell rose about 200 feet above the surrounding area, which is covered with the remains of Roman Scythopolis. The original length of the habitable rock surface of the mound is estimated at about 900 feet, with half the width. The total depth of occupation-debris is not yet ascertained, but the excavations have already removed 30 feet from the top: a preliminary sounding down the course of an ancient well worked down 40 feet, without passing through the Middle Bronze Age strata (*M.J.* 29, 44), though the origins of the mound have been traced back to E.B.A. (*M.J.* 22, p. 40 f.).

EXCVNS. on behalf of the Univ. Museum of Pennsylvania, commenced by Dr. Clarence Fisher in 1922, continued for four seasons under Mr. Alan Rowe, and still in progress under Mr. G. M. Fitzgerald, have traced the history and growth of the city from the mediaeval monastery upon its surface down to the historical layers of the XVIIIth and XIXth Dynasties of Egypt. Reports on the progress of work and its results have appeared periodically in the *Mus. Journ.* of Philadelphia, from which the following summary of the city's chief phases is derived.

Period of Thutmose III (*c.* 1500-1450 B.C.). The city walls of this period were in many places double, enclosing small rooms, with a total thickness of about 16 ft. (Cf. the double walls of Jericho at this time, pp. 131-2.) Two temples have been uncovered: one for Mekal, the god of Beisan, and one for his female counterpart, Ashtoreth. A Canaanite massebah and a stela with an Egyptian representation of the god were found close together in the sanctuary (*M.J.* 28, 147). Cult objects included clay models of bread-cakes and representations of Ashtoreth; while traces of a serpent-cult make their appearance at this time, to become more numerous later (*M.J.* 28, 159). In plan the temples formed a complex of rooms with elaborate arrangements for sacrifice and the dressing of the carcases. Outside the wall, but probably belonging to the door of a temple, was found a carved panel on which a lion, possibly representing the death and pestilence god, Nergal, is being driven away by a guardian dog (*M.J.* 29, 44-48). Several Syro-Hittite cylinder-seals found in this level (*PEF, QS*, April 29) presumably reflect the contemporary overlordship of N. Syria by the Mitannian Hittites.

Period of Amenhotep III (*c.* 1400-1375 B.C.). The city-walls of this level have not been discovered, but the foundations of a migdol have come to light: it was built of large sun-dried bricks on a foundation of undressed stones, with flanking towers some 35 feet in height, and was generally reminiscent of the gates of Carchemish and other Hittite towns (*M.J.* 29, 53). Cf. also the north gate of Shechem (p. 250). Close by was the residence of the Egpytian commandant, with kitchen and large granary: an Egyptian army standard was among the finds. A building near may have been used as a stable, and was large enough for 10 horses; and a pottery model of a two-horse chariot was found in the migdol. The residence, and some streets of a slightly earlier period, showed traces of a drainage system with drain-pipes recalling those at Knossos. Some of these streets were found in good preservation, with about six feet of side-walls standing; these were built of mud-brick, some on low stone foundations, and there were observed examples of barrel-vaulting in brick. At this time there appears to have been only one temple. While Egyptian objects predominate, there was observed a notable influx of other foreign influences in this period, seen, for instance, in some Babylonian cylinder-seals; in imports from the Aegean world, and Cyprus, chiefly pottery and cult-objects (*QS*. 28, 77), and noticeably a number of Hittite traces, p. 107 (*M.J.* 29, 63). These include the plan of the migdol itself; a small bronze, like a Teshub-figure, found within the migdol; a bronze axe-head in the temple of this level (*M.J.*, M 27, 17); and also a seal with Hittite design and motives (*M.J.* J 27, 160). A second dagger, less certainly of Hittite type, had previously been found in the Inner Sanctuary of the South Temple of Thutmose III (*Q.S.* 28, 76).

Period of Ramses II (B.C. 1290-1225). The city was re-fortified with strong double walls, those of Seti I being dug away to lay the new foundations. A gateway uncovered on the west side proved to have been defended by flanking towers of brick. The two temples were rebuilt. Some clay 'breadcakes' of this and Seti I level were found to have been marked in Egyptian writing with the words 'daily offering.' Other cult-objects included figures of serpents, doves, and deities of the Cypriote-Aegean type. Aegean influence strengthened when Ramses II, reconquering the town after a temporary loss, left Mediterranean mercenaries, possibly Sherdens (Fig. 8, p. 279, and p. 331), as a garrison under an Egyptian governor. Burials of these foreign soldiers (*M.J.* 22, p. 42; *Q.S.* 27, 75) were accompanied by a mixture of purely Mediterranean and Egyptian objects: these mercenaries, it is inferred, apparently amalgamated with the Philistines on their arrival. Aegean influence was thus strong in the Early Iron Age city, while the temples as built by Ramses II continued in use. Inscribed monuments include stelae with Egyptian records of Seti I and Ramses II (pp. 73, 235, 271), in addition to a life-sized seated statue of Ramses III (*Pal. Mus.* 1923). In the opinion of the excavators, the Egyptian fortress appears to have remained in continuous occupation, except for the Hittite interlude (p. 107) in the Amarna period (*c.* 1360 B.C.) from the reign of Thutmose III to that of Ramses III.

BIBL. *Excvns.*: *Museum Journal* (Philadelphia), 1922, 32-45; 1923, 5-7; 1925, 307-313; 1926, 295-304; 1927, 9-47, 411-441; 1928, 145-169; 1929, 37-98. *PEF, QS.* 1927, 67-84; 148-9; 1928, 73-90, 110; 1929, 78-94. Cf. further Dhorme in *Rev. Bibl.* 1908, 518; 1909, 381; 1927, p. 62. Abel, *ibid.* 1912, 409; Vincent, *ibid.* 1928 (p. 123); See also pp. 71, 106-8; Pl. LIII.

(i) **Beth-Shemesh** (North). Jud. i 33 (Jos. xix 38 [P])

Var. *LXX Bethsamus* (Jud. i 33), *Thesamys* (Jos. xix 38).

Loc. From the *Cont.* 'Naphtali drave not out the inhabitants of Beth-shemesh nor of Beth Anath.' Beth-Shemesh sppears as a strong place in the territory allocated to Naphtali, *i.e.* Eastern Galilee. There is no basis for identifying it with the place of the same name in the Vale of Sorek, at 'Ain Shems, described below (Beth-Shemesh, South). The name suggests that it was the site of a shrine with a solar cult; and in the present incomplete state of knowledge of Upper Galilee it seems most likely to be identical with Kadesh (Pl. LXI), where the traces of a solar cult may be seen among the ruins of later times (see p. 244 and n. 2; also pp. 102, 280). This place was captured by assault by Seti I (Fig. 4, p. 243), and soon after became the headquarters of the tribe of Naphtali (Jud. iv 6 [E]). Though the Tell is prominent, and shows plentiful evidence of occupation in the Bronze Age, it is not of great extent; so that the city, if confined to the Tell, would hardly be more than five acres in extent, and contemporary Egyptian pictures confirm these indications.

(ii) **Beth-Shemesh** (South). Jos. xv 10 [P]. I Sam. vi 9. II Chron. xxviii 18.

Var. *LXX City of the Sun* [cf. Mt. Heres, Jud. i 35 [J]]. *EGN.* A (Reading Doubtful).

Loc. The border of Judah [P] went down to Bethshemesh and passed by Timnah. Other contexts indicate a site in the low country of Judah, associated with Timnah (II Chron. xxviii 18), not far from the Philistine cities (especially Ekron, I Sam. vi), and near Kiriath-jearim. *Onom.* located it 9 m. on the way from Eleutheropolis towards Nicopolis.

Ident. 'Ain Shems, an ancient site in the vale of Sorek (Plan No. 3, and Pl. LXXIII). Though Beth-Shemesh is not mentioned by name in the early documents, it claims consideration as one of the strong places of Shephelah, especially as it would seem from its strategic situation to have been involved in the route of the Amorites described in Jos. x 10 [J], and more particularly in the later struggles with the Philistines (cf. Jud. xiii 25 [J] ff.). The site has been partly excavated, and the interest of the results is greatly enhanced by the exceptionally clear evidence of Mediterranean contact and Philistine occupation.

Excvns. The area enclosed by fortifications is roughly oval in form, about 220 yards in length and 170 yards across, with an area of approximately seven acres. Excavations were first undertaken in 1911 and 1912 for the P.E.F. by Dr. Duncan Mackenzie, and the results were published in two special 'Annals' for those years. More recently the work has been resumed by Dr. E. Grant (*PEF, QS.* 1929, pp. 201 ff.), and as his archaeological results amplify greatly those previously obtained, and his conclusions seem to differ on matters of interpretation affecting the era of this volume (L.B.A. and E.I.A.i), the publication of this new material must be awaited before any final opinion can be formed. Already as regards the earlier work there was apparently some divergence between the Rev. Père Vincent, the leading authority of the day on Palestinian archaeology (*Rev. Bibl.* 1929, p. 110 ff.) and the excavator himself. The former held that after a very remote period of occupation, evidenced by the presence of Neolithic pottery, the city was enclosed in M.B.A.i; and that this, a brief period, was brought to an end about 1800 B.C., possibly by the Hyksos invasions. In M.B.A.ii the culture was similar, and the city was destroyed about 1600 B.C., probably by the Egyptian conquerors

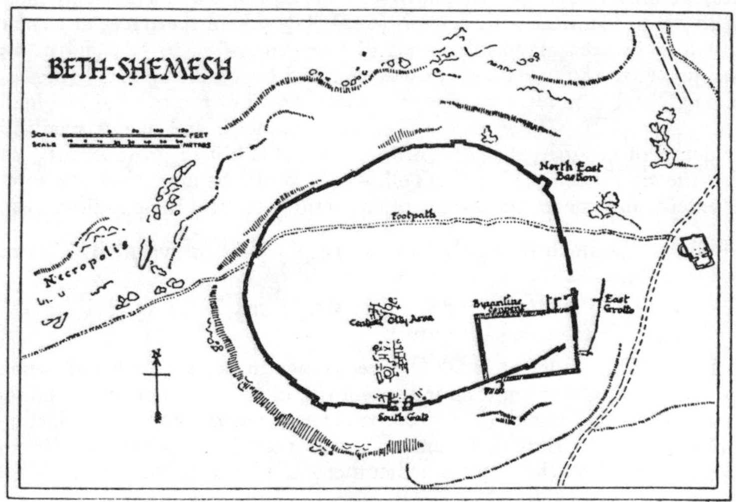

Plan No. 3. The mound of 'Ain-Shems; site of Beth-Shemesh.

of the early XVIIIth Dynasty. Then in L.B.A.i arose a period of brilliant civilization, enriched by much imported Mykenaean ware. A 'high place,' and evidence of an Astarte cult with Egyptian attributes and serpents (as at Beisan), pertained to L.B.A.ii; and seemingly the place was again destroyed about 1200 B.C. In the opening of E.I.A.i the city was of a poorer type (cf. Debîr); but the 'high place' was replaced by a built temple similar to one at Shechem; and later the city revived and lasted until the Exile. Dr. MacKenzie came to the conclusion that the Canaanite city of L.B.A.i was first fortified about 1500 B.C.; that this marked the best building period, distinguished by the importation of Mykenaean and Cypriote wares, and that it was destroyed about 1400 B.C. According to this interpretation there next apparently ensued a gap (cf. again Debîr, and note the absence of the name in the early text of Joshua). But following a period in which the absence of imported products is noteworthy, the Philistine occupation became well marked by the appearance of plentiful Philistine wares, and a simultaneous Egyptian influence. This phase terminated, doubtfully, about 1100 B.C. In E.I.A. the Hebrew city was unwalled : the Philistine influence gave way to a native Canaanite with an Israelite infiltration ; and the place was destroyed possibly by Sennacherib, about 700 B.C. As between these two opinions concerning the general evolution of culture in L.B.A., the radical divergence appears to be a matter of chronological detail. In general, modern results elsewhere show that while Cypriote-Phoenician infiltration may be discerned before 1400 B.C., that date marks the starting-point for the importation of purely Mykenaean products. It is to be expected that the new materials will contain more conclusive evidence on the point. Meanwhile the possible gap after 1400 B.C. and the fresh influx of Egyptian influence at the same time that Philistine wares make their appearance, are two significant details. (Cf. also Debir).

BIBL. *PEF. Annual I*, 1911. *PEF*, *QS*. 1929, 201 ; 1930, 133-4, 174-5. *Rev. Bib.* 1929, 110-112. Cf. further Kn. 290 and Weber, p. 1343 ; Burch. *Fremdw.* 855.

Beth-Shittah. Jud. vii 22 [E]. VAR. *LXX Bethsedta, Bethseed, Basetta.*

LOC. The context indicates a position on the Midianites' line of flight towards the fords of the middle Jordan from the valley of Jezreel (p. 320, Map p. 322), in the direction of 'Zererah.' The latter is perhaps the same as Zeredah (I Kings xi 26), and generally identified with Zarethan *q.v.* (Josh iii 16 [JE]). Cf. Cooke, *Judges*, p. 88. Not identified.

Bezek. Jud. i 5 [J]. VAR. *LXX Bezek.*

LOC. *Cont.* suggests southerly position (see pp. 207, 208), but no such site is known. *Onom.* locates two neighbouring villages of the name, 6 miles from Nablus on the way to Beisan : this should be the Bezek of I Sam. xi 8, modern Ibzek, not that of the context.

Bochim. Jud. ii 1 [J]. VAR. *LXX* (*place of*) weeping.

LOC. The name is not necessarily that of a place. The *Cont.* indicates a site either between Gilgal and Bethel, or between Gilgal and Shiloh, in the latter event possibly in the Wady Samieh. See p. 251. Cf. Cooke, *Judges*, p. 23 n. 1.

Chephirah. Jos. ix 17. VAR. *LXX Kapheira.*

LOC. Associated in *Cont.* with Gibeon, Beeroth and Kiriath-jearim as a Hivite city. *Onom.* merely locates it 'near Gibeon in Benjamin.'

IDENT. Name survives in that of KH. KEFIREH, 5 miles west of Gibeon. This site occupies a bold position on a spur of the plateau (Pl. XXXVI) in the fork between two steep valleys ; and commanded the approaches towards Gibeon from the west. The Tell itself rises characteristically in a series of ascending terraces, facilitating the defence of the city upon its crest. This must have been rather small, perhaps 5 or 6 acres in area. Pottery of the Late Bronze Age has been collected from the site (G. 1928, *P*.LIA.). See further p. 166 and Pl. LXXI.

Debir. Kiriath-sepher (City of Letters). Jos. xv. 15 [J].

Var. *LXX Dabeir. EGN. Beth-t-p-r, Pap. Anast.* i 19 (p. 24).

Loc. A site in the southern hill-country, and in communication with Hebron, is indicated by the *Cont.*

Ident. Tell Beit Mirsim. The general reasons for identifying this place with Kiriath Sepher or Debir have been discussed on pp. 210 and 214: no other known site satisfies so closely the topographical or historical conditions. Site and situation are described on p. 211.

Excvns. Work being still in progress, no final report or plan is available for study, while the interpretation of results tends naturally to be modified by the technical details of successive discoveries. None the less, the city's development is clear in outline. The site was occupied in the Early Bronze Age before 2000 b.c. by a timber-built settlement (Level F). Later in M.B.A.i about 1900 b.c. (Level E) it was fortified with a massive wall some ten feet thick. The pottery found was comparable with that of Egypt under Dyns. XII, XIII. Then in the latter half of the M.B.A. (*c.* 1800 b.c.), which here and elsewhere marks the great period of Canaanite works, a new town arose (Level D), with an area of about 9 acres. Its walls were solidly constructed of the characteristic ' polygonal ' masonry, varying in thickness from 10 to 13 feet, and near the west gateway additional protection was afforded by a glacis (cf. Jerusalem, Jericho, Shechem). This city contained a large and well-built palace, the plan of which showed a number of store-rooms grouped around an open court. Ivory, ebony and alabaster objects, and inlaid furniture betoken a prosperous epoch. The presence of scarabs of the Hyksos type and of the early XVIIIth Dyn. of Egypt, associated with some Cypro-Phoenician pottery, well indicates the period of occupation for this city of Level D, while the complete absence of Mykenaean wares points to a date of destruction before 1400 b.c. Indeed, the excavator, while expressing the view that the period of abandonment may have fallen in the fifteenth century b.c. (*ZATW*. p. 7), inclines to the opinion that it fell in the previous century, as early as 1550 b.c., and possibly a little earlier (*c.* 1570 b.c.), when the Hyksos were expelled from Egypt. He also finds that the city then lay deserted for some time, perhaps a century, and was probably not reoccupied until after the time of Thutmose III, *i.e.* after the middle of the fifteenth century b.c., though the L.B.A. stratum on the site is represented by an average thickness of more than six feet.

The next reconstruction of the city (Level C) shows indications of relative poverty when compared with D. The houses were poorly built, and separated by open spaces containing grain pits, suggesting a diminished population. None the less, the size of the city was maintained; the old fortifications were restored, and the East Gate was entirely rebuilt. ' The destruction of the city (at Level C) was accompanied by a terrific conflagration, and by the complete demolition of the fortifications.' The date of this event, though doubtful, falls within the period of L.B.ii (1400-1200 b.c.), and pending further information, depends upon that of the

Kh. el Kefireh stands upon a spur of the plateau between two branches of the Wady Kotneh, and the village of Kutanneh lies at the foot of its southern slope.

CHEPHIRAH.

The crown of Kh. el Kefireh as seen from the E.

See also p. 166.

reconstruction of the city (Level B) which arose at once upon and among its ashes. The city at Level B was of much the same extent as its predecessor, but was not so well built. Its walls were only about six feet thick, on the average, while 'the glacis was formed by a series of rounded bastions built of much smaller stones. The masonry of the gate was also relatively inferior in all respects, and it presents a new type with indirect ingress, comparable with the Turkish gates of Jerusalem.' (*Bull. ASOR.* Oct. 1926, pp. 4-5.) The archaeological evidence enabled the excavator to distinguish three periods in the life-history of this city (*ZATW.* pp. 8, 9).

i. A period of 50 to 100 years characterised by decadent Late Bronze Age pottery and by a conspicuous absence of Cypro-Phoenician wares. (Cf. Ashkelon, Beth-Shemesh, Gerar.)

ii. A long period of characteristically E.I.A.i pottery, with an abundance of Philistine vases and Egyptian influences maintained.

iii. A short period of transition to E.I.A.ii.

These three periods should represent respectively three historical epochs in Bible history, namely (i) the destruction and reoccupation of the city by the Israelite-Kenite allies under Othniel. (ii) The coming of the Philistines, who seemingly entered the city without trace of hostilities. (iii) A subsequent period of Israelite occupation, interrupted, it may be believed, by the inroads of the Pharaoh Shishak (Sheshank) about 912 B.C.

In the apparent absence of materials supplying fixed dates, the excavator arrives at the probable epoch of the destruction of city C and the beginnings of city B by calculation from the date of the Philistine occupation, which he places at 1150 B.C. To this the addition of 75 to cover the pre-Philistine period (i) gives the approximate date 1225 B.C., which he regards as 'precisely the age of the Israelite irruption' (*Bull.* 23, p. 4). In view, however, of the new evidence (p. 310) as to Philistine settlements on the frontiers of Egypt before the reign of Ramses III, and of Prof. Petrie's discoveries of Philistine burials at Tell Fara in confirmation of the record (p. 285), the Philistine occupation may have commenced *c.* 1225 B.C.; so that the beginning of the destruction of city C and the occupation of city B may be ascribed with equal probability on these premises to 1325 B.C., a date which falls within the career of Othniel as determined by Biblical chronology. Presumably the actual date lies within the century 1325-1225 B.C., but it must clearly be determined by independent archaeological considerations before it can be treated as a historical landmark. This comment does not gainsay the learned excavator's studied conclusion that the pre-Philistine stratum of level B represents the occupation of the city by the Israelite-Kenite allies. 'We can therefore date the fall of city C about the same time as the latest possible date for the invasion of Canaan by the Israelites, and, in view of the total change in the character of the fortifications, as well as in the culture of the following period, we may confidently ascribe the burning of city C to the incoming men of Judah' (*Bul. ASOR.* Oct., 1928, p. 8). The narrowing down of the date, by further discovery and observation, may thus throw light upon the still open question as to the individuality of 'Caleb' and 'Othniel,' frequently regarded in these contexts as clan-names (see pp. 217-8). Briefly summarised, these four periods, levels B-E, in Tell Beit Mirsim represent in round figures a fairly continuous occupation throughout 1000 years and comprise marked culture phases.

City B.	L.B.A.ii and E.I.A.i,	*c.* 1300 B.C.– 900 B.C.
„ C.	L.B.A.,	*c.* 1450 B.C.–1300 B.C.
„ D.	M.B.A.ii,	*c.* 1800 B.C.–1550 B.C.
„ E.	M.B.A.i,	*c.* 2000 B.C.–1800 B.C.

BIBL. *Zeit. Alttest. Wiss.* N.F. 6, 1929, i, p. 1-16. *Bul. ASOR.* Oct. 1926, pp. 2 ff.; Oct. 1928, pp. 1 ff.; *PEF, QS.* 1927, p. 223; 1929, p. 111. *Rev. Bibl.* 1927, 409-13; 1929, 103-107.

Dor. Jos. xvii 11 [J]. Judg. i 27 [J].
VAR. *LXX Dor, Nafethdor. EGN. D-r (Papy. Golen.)*

LOC. Associated with the line of fortresses Bethshean, Taanach, Megiddo (see Map 13, p. 188). Egyptian sources show it to have been a port, frequented by Eg. ships, though at the time (*c.* 1110 B.C.) in the hands of Thekels (p. 329). Placed by *Onom.* at Dor Nafeth, 9 m. north from Caesarea.

IDENT. Provisionally with the classical DORA upon the coast just north of the village of TANTURAH; DOR in the story of Wen-Amon (B, *AR.* iv 567); but subject to the reservations indicated on p. 232, n. 6.

EXCNS. made during the years 1923-4 for the Br. Sch. of Arch., under the supervision of the writer and Mr. Phythian-Adams, determined the outline of the site and of its history. The results are published in the *Bulletin*, Nos. 4, 6, 7, of the *BSAJ.*, including a historical introduction in No. 4 (by Phythian-Adams), Plans, pp. 64-6; photographs, pp. 36, 70; and a study of the Iron Age pottery (by Mr. G. M. Fitzgerald), pp. 80 ff. The most ancient site is disclosed as a detached Tell upon the sea-front, some 300 yards in length, and 200 yards across, having thus an area of about 9 acres. The extreme point of land in the S.W. of the site juts into the sea; the position was adopted in the Middle Ages as a signalling post, and there may still be seen the remains of a strong building called El Burj. Judging from its height, this spot may mark the place of a more ancient acropolis or migdol. To-day a small bay is found just to the south, and beyond that a reef gives shelter to small craft visiting Tanturah; but the form of the coast has changed, and it seems probable that the harbour visited by Wen-Amon (p. 329) lay to the north, where opposite the extreme end of the ancient occupation area may be seen the remains of a mole leading out to the weathered rocks beyond. Owing to the size and elaborate masoned buildings of the Hellenistic city, it was not found practicable to determine the exact outline and nature of the earlier remains; but it was shown that the place was inhabited in L.B.A., when the culture was of the characteristic Canaanite type, and that it was probably surrounded at that time by a defensive wall, of which rough foundations and sections of the masonry were brought to light. A layer of ashes and debris separated the Bronze Age stratum from that of E.I.A., when the introduction of a fresh culture, including pottery which shows Philistine affinities, but at the same time marked differences of detail, corresponded to the probable occupation of the place in the twelfth century B.C. by the Thekels, or Zakkala, whose coming with the Philistines is recorded in the annals of Ramses III. While the identity of the site with the Egyptian Dor and classical Dora is well established, there remains much to be explained before its identity with the Canaanite Dor can be accepted with full confidence. In contrast with Ascalon and Gaza, the place possessed a natural harbour, and its fortunes were linked primarily with the sea; but the Canaanite Dor appears in the Biblical contexts only as one of a chain of inland fortresses along the S.W. frontier of Esdraelon, cut off from the coast by the ridge of barren hills that terminates in Mt. Carmel (cf. p. 89 f.).

BIBL. *Bul. BSAJ.* Nos. 4, 6, 7, 1924-7.

Eglon. Jos. x 3 [J].
VAR. *LXX Ailam, Eglom* (Jos. x 3, 5), *Odollam*. *EGN.* T³ (No. 89, doubtful) *Hykrym*.

LOC. One of the five Amorite cities leagued under Jerusalem against Gibeon; the text associates it frequently with Lachish, one of the great cities of the Shephelah. *Onom.* placed it 12 m. west from Eleutheropolis (Beit Jibrin).

IDENT. of Eglon with TELL EL HESY (as proposed by Dr. Albright, *Bul. ASOR.* Oct. 1924) is strongly indicated, (*a*) by the reference in *Onom.* (*Klos.* p. 85, quoted above); (*b*) by the local survival of the name Ajlan in a ruin 2 miles away; (*c*) by the discovery on the site of a tablet of the Amarna period from Zimrida (of Lachish), with which city Eglon is associated in the *Cont.* of Josh. x 3; (*d*) by the archaeological considerations. The suggested identity of Tell el Hesy with Lachish (*q.v.*) is not supported by evidence, and cannot be sustained.

DESCR. Tell el Hesy occupies an important position, near the border of the Philistine plain, on the high road from Gaza to Jerusalem, and in control of the valley (the Wady el Hesy) leading down from the Shephelah. The Tell rises from the south side of the valley to a height of 100 feet, about 60 feet being composed of occupation-debris. The mound, properly speaking, measures only about 200 feet each way, with a superficial area of less than one acre; but it stands in the N.E. of a more extensive enclosure about three-quarters of a mile across, which also showed signs of habitation.

EXCVNS. made first by Prof. Petrie, then by Dr. Bliss for the *PEF.* in 1890-92, have traced the occupation of the site from M.B.A., when it was already fortified, through numerous phases of destruction and reconstruction. During the late Bronze Age several successive cities occupied the site: the Second City, being the first to be associated with typical

L.B.A. pottery, may have arisen in the sixteenth century B.C. A Third City quickly followed, being dated to about 1450 B.C., the epoch of Thutmose III. In this Egyptian influence was strong, as seen in scarabs of the XVIIIth Dynasty and other objects. The site, some 300 feet each way, was now strongly defended after the Egyptian fashion with a wall of sun-dried bricks, nearly 29 feet in thickness. This city contained the cuneiform tablet mentioning Zimrida (of Lachish) of the Amarna letters.

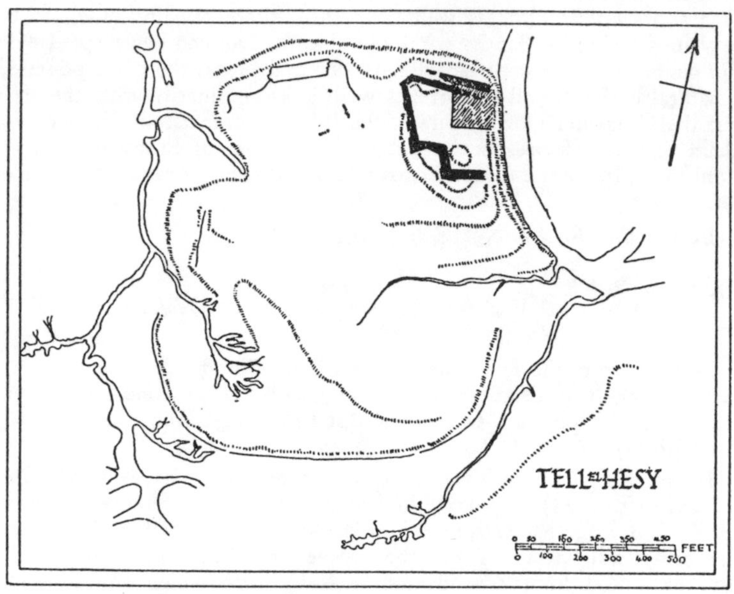

Plan No. 4. Plan of Tell el Hesy, probable site of Eglon.

Soon after that period (1375 B.C.) it was sacked and destroyed, and became covered by a layer of ashes, coming not, however, from its burning, but from the use of the deserted site by alkali burners or furnace workers. A Fourth City of very similar culture soon rose, 1350-1200 B.C., in which Egyptian influence (scarabs, charms, etc.) persisted. Some of its buildings appeared to have been destroyed by an enemy; and its upper layers contained the first iron objects found.

The first Iron Age City was less well defended, lacking the usual wall along the steep north side. This also was destroyed by war, but a new one was speedily built from its remains. Later cities carried the history of the site down to about 300 B.C., when it was deserted.

BIBL. Bliss, *Mound of Many Cities*, esp. pp. 51-89. Petrie, *Tell el Hesy* (Lachish), 1891. Albr. *Bul. ASOR.* 1924 (Oct.) *PEF. Fifty Years' Work*, p. 106.

Endor. Jos. xvii 11 [J]. *LXX* omits in this passage.

Loc. The *Cont.* associates it with cities on the S.W. border of Esdraelon: but it is possible that the name is misplaced in this passage, being omitted in *LXX* and Jud. I 27. The En-dor of I Sam. xxviii 7 is near Mt. Tabor: *Onom.* placed it near Nain, not far from Esdraelon, where it survives to-day in name, and Tell Ajjul may mark the site. See p. 93.

Eshtaol. Jud. xiii 25 [J].
VAR. *LXX Astaol, Esthaol, Ethael.*

Loc. Assoc. with Zorah and the Danites; in the neighbourhood of Beth-shemesh (cf. Ir-shemesh and Mt. Heres) and Aijalon (cf. Judg. i 35). *Cont.* also groups it with Timnah and the Vale of Sorek. *Onom.* placed it 12 m. N.E. from Eleutheropolis (Beit Jibrin).

IDENT. Probably Eshua, a modest site still partly occupied by a modern village (see Pl. LXIX and Map 19, p. 335). Pottery of the site dates from E.I.A.i, *c.* 1200 B.C. (G. 1928, P, *LIA.*). See further pp. 334 f.

Gaash. Jos. xxiv 30 [E]. VAR. *LXX Gaas, Galaad.*

Loc. The *Cont.* indicates a location in Mt. Ephraim, south of Timnath-serah. A similar name is said to survive in the form Nebi Gais, just south of Tibneh (*Syria*, vii. 19 n.). Not identified.

Gaza. Jud. vi 4 [JE].
VAR. *LXX Gaza. EGN.* T[3] (B. *AR.* ii 417) *G-d-t.* A *Ḥa-za-ti* (Kn. 289); *Azzati* (Kn. 296). R[2] (*Pap. Anas.* I 27) *Ḳ-d-t.*

Loc. In the extreme S.W. of Palestine, near the Egyptian frontier, a position which made it a centre of Egyptian imperial authority in the country. In the *Cont.* of Jud. vi 4, one of the Philistine garrison cities (p. 336).

DESCR. The important modern town of GHAZA (Engl. GAZA) still occupies the mound whereon according to continuous tradition (cf. Steph. Byz. s.v. *Gaza*) and recent investigation stood the ancient city. Though proportionately not very high, the site is extensive, being in places fully three-quarters of a mile across; its surface is well covered with houses or private property, so that research has been limited for the most part to its scarps (see Pl. LXX). Peters in *Nippur*, 1897 (p. 350), the present writer in 1920 (*PEF, QS.*), Petrie in 1927 (*QS.* p. 56), have called attention to the visible traces of stout brick ramparts of Egyptian style on the northern side, the last estimating their height at 27 feet.

EXCVNS. Soundings scientifically made in available spaces for the P.E.F. by Mr. Phythian-Adams in 1923 (*QS.* pp. 11, 18) made it clear, from finds of Cypro-Phoenician wares of L.B.A.i, that the city was in occupation previous to 1400 B.C.; but that the Bronze Age city proper was to be sought nearer the heart of the mound. On the other hand, there was relatively abundant trace of Philistine occupation from 1200 B.C., and various other epochs could be discerned in the life-history of the site.

A number of superimposed brick walls were examined and classified; of these the lowest, together with a somewhat slender glacis, were also attributable to the Philistine period. As at Ascalon, the city expanded with the successive epochs, and its earlier history lies buried in the depths of accumulated debris representing centuries of occupation.

BIBL. *PEF, QS.* 1923, pp. 11, 18. See further Thomsen, *Reallex. Bibl.*

Gezer. Jos. xvi 3, 10 [J].
VAR. *LXX Gazer. EGN.* T[3] (No. 104) *K-d-r*; T[4] *K'-d'-* (B. *AR.* ii 821); A. *Gaz-ri* (Kn. 253, 254, 287, 292, 299, 300); *Ga-az-ri* (Kn. 290, 298). M *K'-d'-r'* (B. *AR.* iii 617).

Loc. The *Conts.* cited mention Gezer as a Canaanite city on the border of the children of Joseph, beyond Beth-horon. Later sources, and A., associate it politically with Lachish (Jos. x 33 [D], xii 11, 12 [D]).

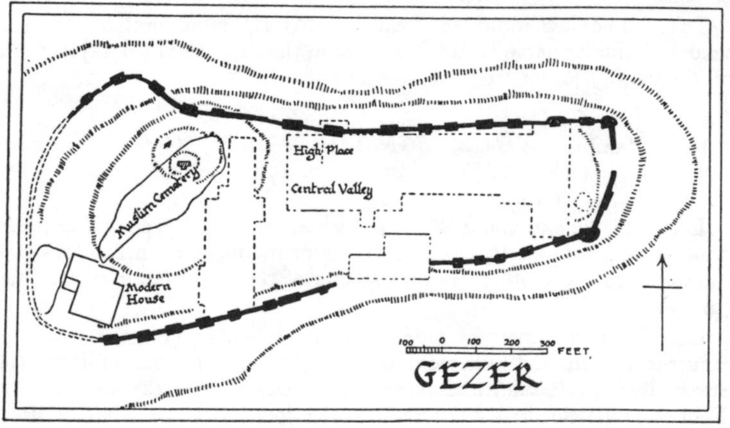

Plan No. 5. The fortifications of Gezer, Tell Jezer (P.E.F.).

Its position is further defined as on the Philistine border, near Ashdod (I Macc. xiv 34). Stated by *Onom.* to be 4 m. from *Nicopolis* (Emmaus), being known as Gazara; the name survived in Crusaders' times as Gisart, and in Arabic as Tell Jezer. The place itself, however, was lost sight of, but recovered in 1871 through the clue of an Arabic literary reference.

IDENT. The mound of TELL JEZER, a prominent and partly natural knoll in the N.E. of the Philistine plain, on the edge of the Shephelah, 11 m. from Beth-horon, a strategic position which commanded both the high-road from Gaza to the north (p. 84) and the main lines of communication between Jerusalem and the coast at Jaffa (Map 5). The identification was confirmed by M. Clermont Ganneau's discovery in the vicinity of some bilingual Greek and Hebrew inscriptions referring to Gezer by name. A special feature of the site is its subterranean water passage. (Cf. Ibleam.)

Excvns. were made on the site of Tell Jezer by the P.E.F. under the direction of Prof. R. A. Stewart Macalister during the four years 1902-5, and again during three years 1907-9; and the results have been published in three monumental volumes. These make use of a special system of classification based upon Egyptian periods, well adapted to the elucidation of the local discoveries, but differing from that based upon the broad periods of Canaanite and Palestinian culture now in familiar use: its outlines may be appreciated from the following schedule, which shows in round dates the links and overlapping between the chief phases of the two systems:

1. Pre-Semitic: Pre-Canaanite, *i.e.*	Before 2500.	Latest Stone Age.	
2. First Semitic: to end of XIIth Dynasty	2500–1800	E.B.A.	2500–2000
		M.B.A.	2000–1600
3. Second Semitic: to end of XVIIIth Dynasty	1800–1400	L.B.A.	1600–1200
4. Third Semitic: to Hebrew Monarchy	1400–1000	E.I.A.i	1200–900
5. Fourth Semitic: to end of Hebrew Monarchy	1000–500	E.I.A.ii	900–600

The place was occupied before the Bronze Age by pre-Semitic troglodytes small of stature, who cremated their dead, and placed the remains in their caves with provisions and foodstuffs. Pottery was handmade and implements were of flint. Animals domesticated included the sheep, goat, cow and pig, while the presence of grindstones implies the cultivation of cereals.

In the M.B.A. the settlement was surrounded by a stone wall, ten or eleven feet thick, constructed in characteristic fashion (cf. Jericho, Shechem) of large irregular stones, the joints being packed with small stones. Two towers of rude rubble were faced with sun-dried bricks. Eleven scarabs of the XIIth Dyn. and Hyksos period, and other objects, indicate thus early an Egyptian contact. Burial was by inhumation, in caves; accompanied as in Egypt by a supply of foodstuffs and other objects.

In the latter half of the Late Bronze Age (Third Semitic period) the city defences were stronger, in this respect marking an exception (cf. Beeroth, Jericho, Hazor). The protective walls were now 14 feet thick, supported by no less than 30 towers, both external and internal, masonry being rough and covered with plaster (cf. Beeroth). Missiles of stone indicate some form of catapult at this age, and flint arrow-heads remained in use (cf. Jericho). A strongly walled castle, presumably the chief's residence, was erected at this time, and with occasional restoration lasted for centuries notwithstanding the various political and cultural changes. Egyptian influence and trade continued strongly in evidence, including scarabs of the XVIIIth and XIXth Dyns., amulets of various Egn. types, alabaster vessels, beads, etc. The majority of these pertained to the reign of Amenhotep III, while even that of Akhenaton was well represented (vol. i p. 136; ii. p. 100). Pottery, as throughout this part of Canaan, showed marked Aegean and Cypriote affinities, the latter as usual less marked than in L.B.A.i (cf. Askalon, Beth-shemesh, S).

Philistine wares made their appearance as elsewhere in E.I.A.i, *i.e.* the end of the Third Semitic period (vol. i, pp. 289 ff.). Of this epoch, a group of masoned tombs, unlike any others of the site, contained ornaments and other objects of gold, silver and alabaster, reflecting the art of Cyprus in sub-Mykenaean times (*L.M.* iii *b*), and may be attributed to the actual presence of Aegean intruders (whether Philistines, Thekels or other sea-raiders) from the N.E. Mediterranean (cf. pp. 292, 309). Before the end of E.I.A.i the King's palace fell into partial ruin and neglect, suggesting the cessation of local government, though no trace was observed of any general destruction or conflagration.

In religion the worship of Astarte prevailed during historic times, superseding the more primitive cults indicated by the high places, standing monoliths, and child burials. Here also Egyptian influence was visible in the cult objects, notably certain 'Hathor-Ashtoreth' plaques, and the figurines of other divinities. Indeed, the outstanding feature in the archaeology of Gezer is to be seen in the clear and continuous evidence of its Egyptian relations.

Bibl. Macalister, *Excav. of Gezer*, 1912, espl. Vol. i, pp. 244 ff., 289 ff.; Vol. ii, pp. 307 ff., 411 ff.; and the Plans, Vol. iii, Pls. IV, V. Cf. our Plan No. 5, which is derived from the same source. See further T. R. Père Vincent, *Canaan*, esply. pp. 79 ff., 208 ff., 298 ff. *Rev. Bibl.* 1914, pp. 293 f., 504 f. For the Philistine pottery types, cf. Miss G. Levy's Corpus, in *Pal. Mus. Bul.* No. 4, Pl. II.

Gibeah of Benjamin. Jud. xix 13 [EJ].

Var. *LXX Gabaa. EGN.* T³ (No. 114, doubtful) *Ḳ-b'-w*.

Loc. The *Cont.* of Jud. xix 13 [JE] and xx 10 [P] suggests that Gibeah lay to the S. of Ramah and S.W. of Geba, not far from Bethel (xx 26 [J]). Later contexts confirm and supplement these indications. Thus the watchmen of Saul (I Sam. xiv 16) were able to see the multitudes of the Philistines melting away towards the west of Michmas. Next Asa, King of Judah, caused the stones and timbers of Ramah to be carried away to build Giba (probably in this case Gibeah of Benjamin) and Mizpah (I Kings xv 22). Isaiah's description (x 29) of the Assyrian march on Jerusalem names Gibeah between Ramah and Anathoth; and there are other references in Josephus and Jerome pointing towards the location of Gibeah of Benjamin and Saul on Tell el Ful (p. 160, Pl. XXXIII, Map 11), which uniquely fulfils the topographical indications, and has been found on excavation to satisfy also the archaeological conditions.

Excvns. on Tell el Ful were made for the A.S.O.R. in 1922 under the direction of Dr. Albright; summaries of the results appeared in the *Bulletins* of that Institution, Nos. 7 ff.; and a fully illustrated report was published in the *Annual*, No. 4 (1924). The area proved to contain the remains of a village and a strong fortress upon the summit of the hill (Pl. XXXIII). The foundation of both was attributed on the archaeological findings to the closing phase of L.B.A. (the thirteenth century B.C.), its history belonging essentially to E.I.A., a conclusion in seeming accordance with the fact that the place is not mentioned in the early sources before the closing chapter of the Book of Judges. The fortress was found to be a solid structure built in typical fashion of roughly shaped stones with small stones as packing in the interstices. As seen in its final plan it presents a complex of compact chambers enclosed by relatively thick walls, the whole supported by an outer glacis. But this was the result of several periods of reconstruction. The earliest building, found below a layer of ashes, had two stories; and its burning is assigned to near the end of the twelfth century B.C. The second fortress was more elaborate, and carefully constructed. It does not seem to have been a tower (or migdol) as were its successors. Its outer wall varied from 6½ feet to 7½ feet in thickness; and it would seem that access to the building was gained through the first storey by means of a corridor, from which a massive staircase communicated with the ground floor, where there were found also the traces of an inner door. This fortress building was attributed by the excavator to the age of Saul, in the eleventh century B.C. The surrounding glacis, which obscures its outer plan, pertained to a still later epoch.

Bibl. *Ann. ASOR.* No. 4, pp. 3 ff., with illustrations on pp. 56-59, and archaeological records, plans, etc., pp. 77-89. Cf. *PEF. Mem.* iii, pp. 158 f. Guerin, *Palestine*, i, p. 188. Vincent, *Rev. Bibl.* xxxii, 1923, pp. 426 f.

Gibeon. Jos. ix 3 [E], x 9 [J]. Var. *LXX Gabaon.*

Loc. Chief of the four Hivite cities; and 'as one of the royal cities.' The *Cont.* indicates a position on the highlands above Gilgal (Jos. x 7) in contact with Jerusalem (Jos. x 3-5), and with access to the Valley of Aijalon and the coast-plain *via* Beth-horon (Jos. x 10). This route was followed later by a Roman road between Jaffa and Jerusalem, upon which it is stated (Josephus, *Wars*, II, xix, i) that Gibeon stood. See further pp. 162-5. (The position suggested by the *Onomasticon* corresponds with no ancient site.)

Ident. The extensive terraced mound partly occupied by the modern village of El Jib (Pl. XXXIV) stands upon the road mentioned, which is still traceable, 5 m. from Jerusalem (Maps 5, 11, 12), and in all other respects well satisfies the indications. No trace of fortification remains, but potsherds of L.B.A. and E.I.A.i have been found on the site.

Bibl. Albright, *Ann. ASOR.* 4. 1922-3, 90 ff.; also *JPOS.* No. iii. 1923, pp. 111-2. Alt. *P.J.* 1927, p. 22, n. 3. *Palast. Jahrb.* 1926, pp. 11 ff. Jirku, *Wo Lag Gibeon? JPOS.* No. viii, 1928, pp. 187 f.

Gilgal. Jos. iv 19 [JE]. VAR. *LXX Galgal.*

Loc. West bank of Jordan, between Jericho and the river; 'in the east border of Jericho.'

IDENT. Presumably JILJULIEH, on the plain between Jericho and the Jordan, where name survives, and the site seems to be represented by a series of small sandy mounds (pp. 138-9).

Harosheth, *of the Gentiles.* Jud. iv 2 [E2].

VAR. *LXX Areisoth, Aseiroth.*

Loc. The *Cont.* of Judg. iv v indicates a position on the N. side of the

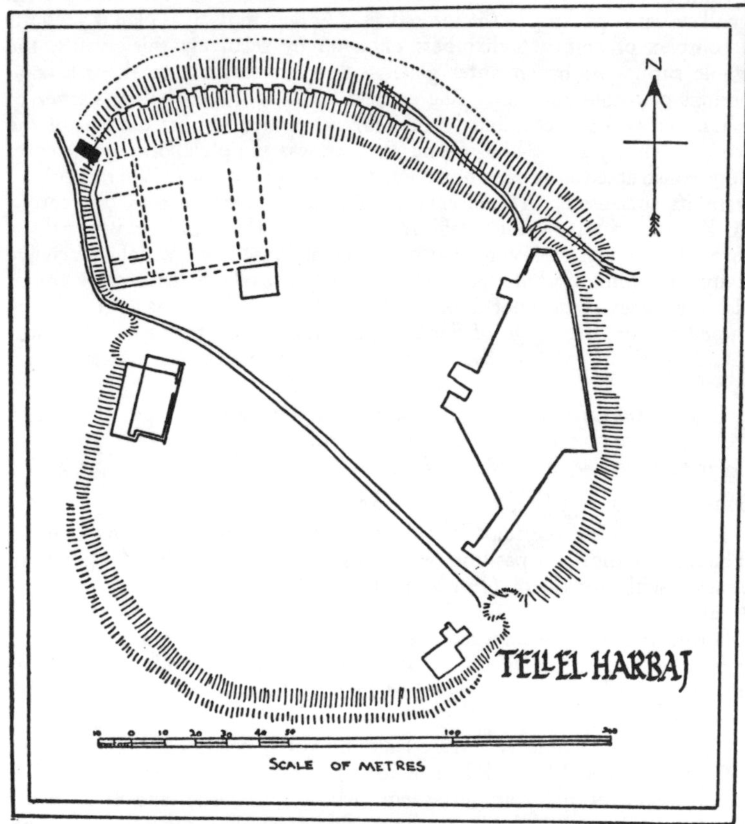

Plan No. 6. Tell el Harbaj ; probable site of Harosheth.
(From *BSAJ. Bull.* No. 2, Pl. III.)

R. Kishon where the latter is deep, and in ready communication with Hazor. Such a position is found at TELL EL HARBAJ, in the S.E. corner of the plain of Acre, commanding the entrance to Esdraelon from the W. (See Maps, pp. 97 and 299.) Local survival of the name *Harithiyeh* lends support to this identification. (See further p. 296.) The Tell is low, not rising more than 50 feet above the plain (Pl. LXIII); its form is roughly oval, with a length of about 700 feet and width 600 feet, giving a habitable surface area of about 6 acres. See the Plan No. 6 (from *BSAJ. Bul.* No. 2, Pl. 111). The summit is fairly level, though occupied on the N.W. end by the ruins of an Arab castle, and on the E. and S.E. by a decaying Arab village. There is a supply of fresh water; and a small tributary of the Kishon partly enfolds the site, which by neglect has become surrounded by swamps.

EXCVNS. Soundings were made in the slopes and surface of TELL EL HARBAJ by the writer for the B.S.A.J. in 1922, and a small area (shown in the N.W. area on the Plan), together with some cave tombs, was examined by Phythian-Adams in 1923; details of results being published in *Bulletins* 2 and 4 of that School for 1922-4. The tombs (*Bul.* 4, Pl. IV) showed that habitation of the vicinity commenced possibly even before the beginning of the Bronze Age, in the earliest phase of which, however, began the occupation of the mound itself. The M.B.A., exceptionally, was not represented in the strata examined; but in the L.B.A. the town was fortified with an enclosing wall of stone. Connected with this were found two buildings, the one of stone attributed to the fourteenth century, the other, of large sun-dried bricks, ascribed to the thirteenth century B.C. With the latter were associated fragments of Mykenaean pottery. The E.I.A. also was marked by two superposed layers of buildings, the lower one, associated with Philistine wares, Astarte plaques, and a terra-cotta bull's head, belonging to the twelfth century, and the uppermost to the end of E.I.A.ii.

BIBL. *Bul. BSAJ.* Nos. II, IV, pp. 12, 46.

Hazor. Jos. xi 1 [J].
VAR. *LXX Asor. EGN.* T[3] (No. 32) *Hḏr*; A (Kn. 148, 227, 228, 288; L.AO. 7094) *ḫa-zu-ra*; *Pap. Anast.* I. 21, 7, *Ḥ-ḏ-r.*

LOC. The Biblical *Conts.* and Egyptian lists point generally towards some strategic position in the vicinity of Kadesh in northern Canaan. The Egn. allusion in *Pap. Anast.* I (*Ed.* Gard. I. 22) associates Hazor with a river, the latter apparently flowing N. and S., hence the Upper Jordan. A ref. in I Maccabees xi 67 shows further that it lay in a plain dominated by mountains. Consequently it must be sought in the plains of the Huleh Basin (Pl. XVII), not, as often surmised, upon the plateau.

IDENT. The Tell and camp-area of EL KEDAH, 4 miles W. from the foot of the Huleh lake and the Jordan, at the junction of the main roads, satisfies all the conditions. It was discovered by the writer in 1926, and described in the *Annals of Archaeology* of the University of Liverpool (*L.AA.*), Vol. xiv, pp. 35 ff. See further pp. 183 f. and Pl. XVIII, XLIII.

Excvns. Extensive soundings were made upon the site in 1928 by the writer, under the patronage of Sir Charles Marston. The archaeological

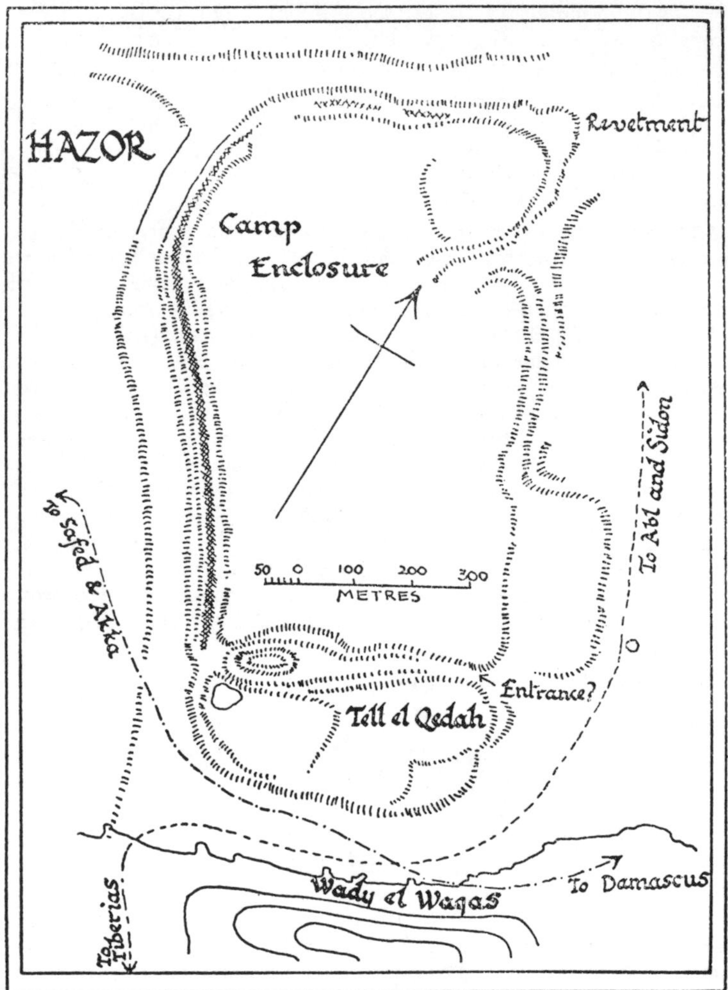

Plan No. 7. Hazor, Camp and City: El Kedah.

details are not yet published, but the broad results are embodied in this volume (pp. 184-5). As the name Hazor implies, the camp-area is a special feature (see the Plan, No. 7). This proved to be nearly 1000 yards long and from 500 to 600 yards in width: it occupied a natural platform partly protected by nature, and surrounded by a stupendous artificial rampart of beaten earth, some 60 feet in height (Pl. XLIV and LXXII). Two entrances seem to have pointed eastward, giving access to the plain, and on this side an advanced terrace provided a suitable park for chariots. During M.B.A. occupation of this area was shown to have been fairly intensive and of a permanent character (with stone-built houses); but in L.B.A. there appears to have been only a surface occupation, in tents or huts, which was brought to a close by a general conflagration. Some 2500 fragments of pottery from the surface deposits were examined, and while L.B.A.i was well represented, both by Cypro-Phoenician and local fabrics, no Mykenaen specimens were found. The latest single dateable specimen ranges down to the Tell el Amarna period (found at Beisan in that stratum); but as a whole and in round terms, the complete absence of Mykenaean specimens, as at Jericho, suggests a date of destruction about 1400 B.C. (See p. 106 and p. 146, n. 1.)

The southern end of the area was closed by a great mound, TELL EL KEDAH, whereon evidently stood the city proper of Hazor. This proved to have been encircled in M.B.A. by a stone rampart (Pl. XLIX), repaired during L.B.A., but there were traces of much earlier fortifications in the slopes of the Tell (Pl. LXXII). Layers of burning were traced in the interior, associated with Cypriote pottery (L.B.A.i), but the occupation seems to have continued, less intensively, until towards the end of L.B.A.ii. Thereafter ensued a considerable gap in which specimens of E.I.A.i were conspicuously absent; but in E.I.A.ii the city sprang again to life, with traces of Solomonian work, including stamped bricks, and a building supported by a row of square stone monoliths, possibly a stable (cf. Megiddo). On the west end of the Tell stood a palatial building or temple, the origin of which could not be determined; but it seems to have been in use in E.I.A.ii, and to have lasted on until Hellenistic times: it was separated from the rest of the hill by a deep ditch, which produced on excavation nothing but loose earth.

BIBL. *L.AA.* xiv. pp. 35 ff.

Hebron: KIRIATH-ARBA. Jos. x 3 [J].
VAR. *LXX Chebron*. *EGN.* ? T[3] (No. 105) *R-b-t*; A *Ru-bu-te*.

LOC. Continuous tradition locates Hebron in or near the modern town of that name, called in Arabic EL KHALIL, which lies at the road centre of the southern highlands (Map, p. 76). The megalithic work on the hill of El Rumeidah which rises to the west, and the Deir El Arba'in, may indeed preserve a vestige of the most ancient site and name. The general question of its IDENT. is discussed on p. 209 (see also p. 170). With Hebron are associated the Anakim, whose three chieftains Caleb is said to have driven out (p. 209; Jos. xv 14 [J]). The *LXX* refers more definitely to Kiriath Arba as 'the mother (city) of the Anak.' It is therefore of interest to note that certain documents, dating from before 2000 B.C., include among other Palestinian chieftains a group of three collectively called by a name I-y'n-q. Cf. Dussaud, *Syria*, viii. 1927, p. 218.

Bibl. *PEF. Mem.* iii. 305, 333. *Rev. Bibl.* 1920, 525 ff. *Syria*, viii. 216.

Helbah. Jud. i 31 [J]. Var. *LXX Chebda.*

Loc. Possibly merely a variant of Ahlab in the same verse; and the same as Mahalab (*LXX Leb*) of Jos. xix 29 [E], which is apparently the *Mahalleba* which later surrendered to Sennacherib, evidently in the plain of Acre, but not identified (p. 241).

Heshbon. Jud. xi 19 [E], 26 [? JE]. Var. *LXX Hesebon.*

Loc. In Trans-Jordania. At the close of Israel's desert wandering, Heshbon was the headquarters of Sihon, King of the Amorites (Jud. xi 19), and lay to the north of the R. Arnon (*ibid.* v 18); p. 332. The *Cont.* of Judg. xi 22 shows that it lay between the R. Arnon (Wady Mojib, p. 69) and the R. Jabbok (Zerka). Exactly placed by *Onom.* ‘ In the hills opposite Jericho, 20 m. from the Jordan.’

Ident. In the position indicated, Tell Hesban preserves the name and satisfies the conditions. This is a large mound (Pl. LXVIII) partly under cultivation, so that without excavation it is not possible to determine the outline of the city, nor to affirm that it was walled. None the less, the traces of occupation in M.B.A. and L.B.A. are plentiful all over its slopes, and the superficial potsherds bear a marked resemblance to the local types of Jericho, which is just visible from its summit, low down in the Rift. In the vicinity are other, smaller, Bronze Age sites, doubtless its dependencies. Cf. ‘ Heshbon and her towns,’ *loc. cit.* 26 [E].

Hormah : Zephath. Jud. i 17 [J]. Var. *LXX Sephek, Sepher.*

Loc. Apparently on the edge of the southern highlands, in the region of Arad. It was attacked according to Num. xxi 3 [JE] by the Israelites during their early passage round the S. of Canaan, and later destroyed by Judah and Simeon; p. 216. As Hormah, it appears on later city-lists (Jos. xv 30 [P], xix 4 [P]) between Bethul or Bethuel and Ziklag, but there is no clear indication as to its position.

Bibl. *PEF, QS.* 1871, 33. *Bul. ASOR.* Oct. 1924, pp. 6-7. *JPOS.* iv. 155-6.

Ibleam. Jos. xvii 11 [J]. Judg. i 27 [J]. *LXX Ieblam.*
Var. *Bileam* (I Chron. vi 70). *LXX Iemblaan* or *Iblaam.*
EGN. T^3 (No. 43) *Y-b-l-m.* *Onom.* ? *Abelmea.*

Loc. The variant readings of I Chr. vi 70 identify Ibleam with Bileam; and make it probable that the Belmen or Belmaim of the Bk. of Judith (iv 4; vii 3) refers to the same place. The *Conts.* show that it was one of the frontier fortresses of Esdraelon, with Taanach and Megiddo, *q.v.*; and that it stood by the ascent of Gur (I Kings ix 27) from the ‘ garden house ’ (probably at Jenin, En Gannim), otherwise described as one of the ascents of the hill country of Samaria (Bk. of Judith, *loc. cit.*). These indications are satisfied by a location in the Wady Bilameh, which leads up from Jenin towards Dothan, and preserves the name.

Excavations at the foot of the Acropolis, El Kedah, disclosed a stone wall or revetment of the Early Bronze Age.

HAZOR.

The inner slopes of the acropolis opposite the camp area. In the back ground the Hueh Lake and plateau of Bashan.

See also p. 184.

DESCR. Bronze Age remains are found upon a hill, once KH. BELAMEH, now EL BURJ (upon one end of which is the Moslem shrine of Sheikh Mansar), immediately above the spring called 'AIN BILAMEH, and dominating the Wady of that name from the west. Its position is further marked by the meeting of two old roads, not quite 2 miles to the S. of Jenin. The top of the hill is relatively large in area, and covered with Roman and Crusaders' ruins, so that without excavation the outline of the ancient Ibleam cannot be defined. The site is naturally defended on three sides by steep ravines, and well suited for a Canaanite strong place. The general indications are supplemented by a rock-cut passage descending from the city to the spring (as at Gezer and Jerusalem), restored and arched over in Gothic style seemingly by the Crusaders.

BIBL. Phythian-Adams, *PEF, QS*. 1922, p. 142 f. Cf. also Conder, *ibid*. 1877, p. 182; Macalister, *ibid*. 1907, p. 129. *PEF. Mem*. ii, p. 47.

Jabesh-Gilead. Jud. xxi 8 [J]. VAR. *LXX Iabeis Galaad*.

LOC. In Trans-Jordania; and, as its name shows, in Gilead, *i.e.* between the Zerka and the Yarmuk. This *Cont*. gives no further indication, but later references (I Sam. xi; xxxi 11) indicate a site east of Jordan, but more than a day and night march from Beth-shean. *Onom*. placed it across the Jordan, 6 miles from Pella (Kh. Fahil, Map, p. 72), on the slope of the plateau on the way to Jerash; and in this direction the Wady Yabis, entering Jordan from Gilead, 10 m. below Bethshean, seems to preserve the name. Tell Husn, upon the plateau S.E. of Irbid, is the most impressive Bronze Age site of the area as a whole, and may be reached by way of the Wady Yabis; but this site may be that of Ramoth Gilead, and would seem too far from the Jordan for Jabesh-Gilead, which remains unidentified.

BIBL. *PEF, QS*. 1876, p. 176.

Jahaz. Jud. xi 20 [JE]. *LXX Iasa*.

LOC. In Trans-Jordania, towards the south. From the *Cont*. it would appear to have been near the S. border of 'Sihon, King of the Amorites,' perhaps not far N. of the Arnon. It was near Kedemoth, became a Levitical city in Reuben (I Chron. vi 78), was fortified by the King of Israel, and captured according to the Moabite Stone by Mesha, King of Moab, who refers to it seemingly as near Dibon. *Onom*. gives no clear indication, but seems also to connect it with Dibon. Site uncertain.

Jarmuth. Jos. x 3 [J].
VAR. *LXX Ierimuth*. *EGN*. ? M.K. (*Syria*, viii 224). *I-y'm(w)t*.

LOC. From the *Cont*. Jarmuth was one of the cities allied with Jerusalem, Hebron and Lachish. Elsewhere (Jos. xv 35 [P], Neh. xi 29, 30) it is associated with Lachish, Adullam, Socoh, and Azekah. The place of similar name (Yarimuta), known to the Egyptians from early times, lay probably in the north (cf. Jarmuth of Issachar, Jos. xxi 29 [P]). *Onom.* (Kl. pp. 106-7) mentions two villages similarly named, one 4 m. from Eleutheropolis (Beit Jibrin) towards Eshtaol, the other (Jermucha) 10 m. from the same point towards Jerusalem : the latter is the accepted site.

IDENT. KH. YARMUK (Pl. XXXIX) occupies a strong position on a hill-top near the Wady Sunt, overlooking Tell Zakariya and the coastal plain (Pl. XLII). Upon the slopes there may be seen a winding ramp as for chariots; on the summit the traces of defensive masonry surround a terraced area of about 6-8 acres, potsherds indicate occupation in Late Bronze Age. See further pp. 171-2.

BIBL. *PEF. Mem.* iii, 128; Guérin, *Judée*, II, 272; Weber, p. 1153; *Syria*, viii, 224.

Jericho. Jos. ii 1 [J]. *LXX Jericho.*

IDENT. KOM EL SULTAN, near El Riha, modern Jericho. The location, identification and general description of ancient Jericho have been discussed in full. Cf. Map, p. 126, pp. 130 ff., and Plates XXIII, XXVI.

EXCVNS. Researches were carried out on the Kom el Sultan by the writer in 1930 under the patronage of Sir Charles Marston. The general results are described in this volume so far as they elucidate the narrative. See especially pp. 145 f., and Pl. XXVII; and a report on the technical issues is published in *PEF, QS.* 1930, pp. 123 ff., with Plates 1-10. The work is still in progress (Feb. 1931), but the following conclusions have been established. The original site was shown by a deep and continuous section to have been occupied long before the Bronze Age by a people using floors and receptacles of beaten and stuccoed earth, and whose weapons were of flint, somewhat crudely fashioned in the mesolithic style. At this time the mound was only half its present height.

In E.B.A. the characteristic pottery wares made their appearance (cf. *Bull.* No. 3 of the *Pal. Mus.*, Pl. I-IV); and at the same time the flint culture underwent a pronounced development, illustrated by nicely fashioned barbed arrow-heads of 'neolithic' style. In M.B.A.i the top of the mound was enclosed by a stout wall of brick slabs roughly jointed, which had a thickness of about 5 yards: its course may be partly traced upon the plan (No. 8), underlying the inner (L.B.A.) brick wall upon the surface (No. 5 in the legend), all along the western side, but extending further towards the north, and turning eastward behind the later glacis: towards the north its return on the east side has been found (Sq. E 8 in the Plan), crossing and underlying the later wall. The occupation debris of this period proved to be about three feet in depth.

In M.B.A.ii the city underwent a great expansion, and the whole area of the mound was enclosed by a solid stone revetment, about 21 feet high, which descended below ground level and was further protected by an outer fosse. Upon this rampart rose a defensive parapet of brick, and the level of occupation was raised considerably in the interior. The debris of occupation formed a layer all over the area, varying from 6 feet on the

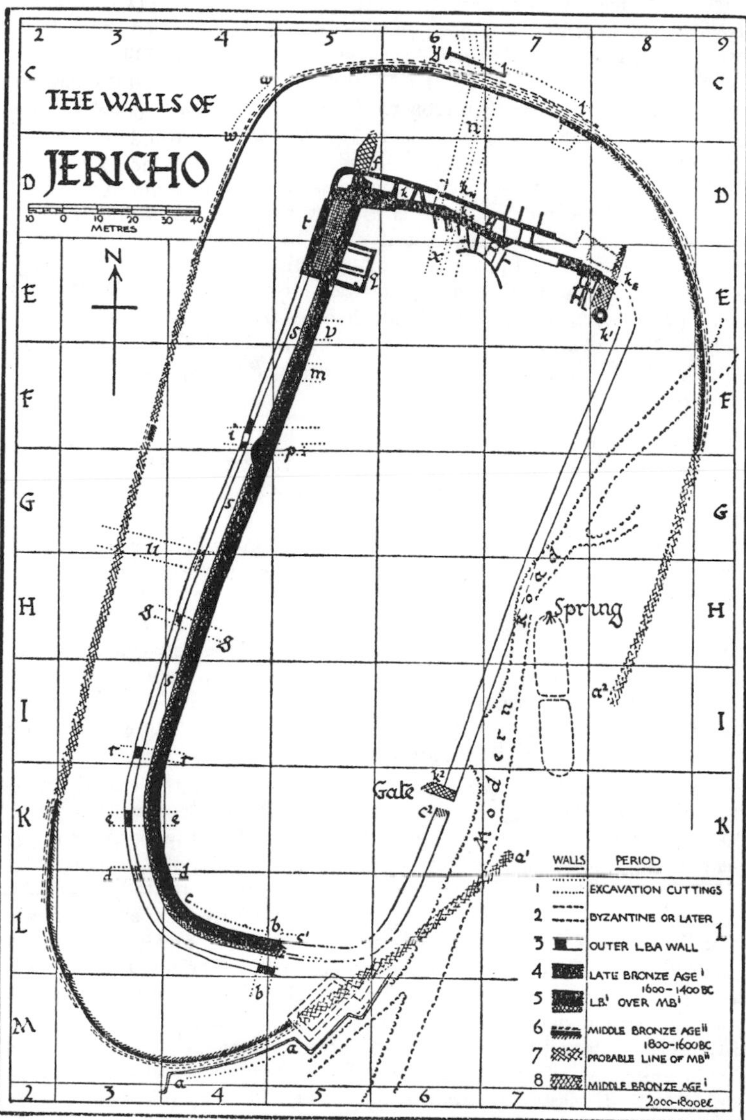

Plan No. 8. Jericho, Kom El Sultan, Site Plan, 1930.

surface to 3 feet on the slopes. This city was destroyed, like its predecessor, by fire. In L.B.A.i the smaller outline around the summit of the mound was re-fortified, the new wall, 12 feet thick, following the line of the M.B.A.i fortification around the S. and W.; with the additional protection on the outside of a screen wall 6 feet thick, at a distance of about 5 yards hence at the top of the slope. Houses of this period in the vicinity of the Tower (Sq. E 5) contained Cypro-Phoenician potsherds, and were destroyed by fire while in occupation, grain being found stored in bins in the corners of the rooms. The date of destruction is estimated from the complete absence of Mykenaean deposits in the occupation layers and other details at about 1400 B.C. For later history, see further p. 147.

BIBL. Sellin and Watzinger, *Jericho*, 1913. T. R. Père Vincent, *Rev. Bibl.* 1913, pp. 450 ff. Watzinger, *ZDMG.* 1926, 'Zur Chronologie der Schichten von Jericho,' pp. 131 ff. G. *PEF, QS.* 1930, pp. 123 f., with Plates I-X. See further Thomsen, *Reallexikon*, pp. 153-157, with Bibl.

Jerusalem. Jos. x 1 [J].
VAR. *LXX Ierousalem. EGN.* M.K. (*Syria*, viii 229-30) *'w-s-'m-m* or *W-r-w-š-l-m*; A (Kn. 287, 289, 290) *U-ru-sa-lim.*

LOC. and IDENT. The position of Jerusalem is determined by continuous tradition and almost uninterrupted occupation through 4000 years, from E.B.A. until to-day. The Jebusite city of L.B.A., which figures in this narrative, occupied the narrow plateau of MT. OPHEL, to the S.E. of the city (Pl. XXXVIII), upon the ridge between the Valley of Hinnom (Wady el Nar) and the old Tyropoeon valley, now filled, with its northern limit marked by the depression named the Zedek valley. See Plan No. 9; also pp. 169 f. Its width averaged about 40 yards, and its surface contained approximately 11 or 12 acres.

EXCVNS. on an extensive scale have been made for the P.E.F. in the central part of the area, commenced by Prof. Macalister, assisted by the Rev. Garrow Duncan, and continued by Dr. J. W. Crowfoot, during the years 1926-28. At the southern end, above the pools of Siloam also, Dr. Weill, on behalf of the Baron Ed. de Rothschild, made considerable clearances about the same time, and traced the city rampart on the E. These researches leave no doubt as to the situation and growth of the Jebusite city. Occupation of the site began in or before E.B.A. The first line of defence on the exposed site to the N. was formed by a deep rock-cut trench, dating from about 2000 B.C. Among the potsherds of M.B.A. were found two bearing the impressions of early seals, the one of a Babylonian cylinder, and the other of two Egyptian scarabs of the XIIth and XIIIth Dynasties (*c.* 2000 B.C.). The defences, relatively poor in the early part of the period, were greatly developed later by the construction of an additional wall of large stones, 15 to 20 feet thick, the space between the ramparts apparently being kept clear as a measure of defence. Similar features have been observed at Tell el Nasbeh, Gezer and Jericho.

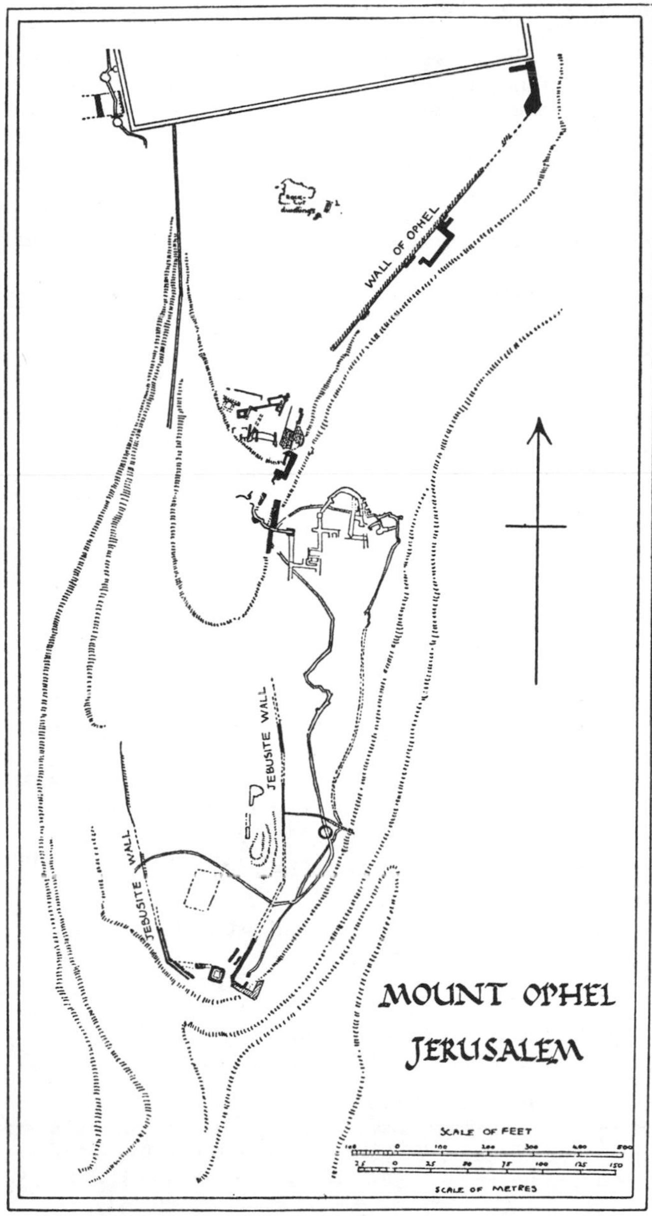

Plan No. 9. Site of Jebusite Jerusalem on Mt. Ophel.

Strong walls were also built upon the E. and W. side of the ridge (see the Plan). That on the E. side is particularly massive, having a thickness towards the base of perhaps 40 feet, and it still stands about 27 feet in height. Hereabouts was probably a water gate, and a rock-hewn shaft communicated with the water supply now captured in the well at the foot of the scarp (cf. Gezer and Ibleam). On the W. the city wall followed a wide rock shelf below the general level of the ridge, and was some 27 feet thick. On this side was another gateway, about 12 feet wide, defended by flanking towers. The interior of the area proved to have been largely denuded, but the excavators succeeded in bringing to light interesting remains of later historical epochs.

BIBL. *PEF*, *QS*. 1923 f.; also *Annual*, IV. 1923-5 (especially pp. 15, 33, 73, 174, 178 ff.), and *ibid*. V. pp. 17-19. Weill, *Rev. des Études Juives*, 1926, pp. 103 f.

Jogbehah. Jud. viii 11 [E]. VAR. *LXX Iegebal*.

LOC. In Trans-Jordania, between the Jordan and the nomad resorts (to-day the Upper Zerka), p. 321. According to Numbers xxxii 36, it lay in the territory of Gad, and was a fenced city with a built sheepfold (a feature of the country). These general indications point to the region between Amman and the Zerka, where El Jubeilhat seems to preserve the name (Map, p. 322). Possibly it may be found in the ruins called Kh. Ajbehat, but archaeological evidence is wanting.

Karkor. Jud. viii 10 [E]. VAR. *LXX Karkar*.

LOC. In Trans-Jordania: from the *Cont*. a nomad's retreat in the wastes to the E., and on the desert route towards the land of Midian in the S.

IDENT. A place of the same name, pronounced KARKAR, well known to desert peoples to-day, lies far up the Wady Sirḥan (pp. 321 f. and Map 17), a day's journey beyond Kasr el Azrak, and 150 miles S.E. of the fords of the Jordan by El Damieh. The identification is due to the explorations of Musil, and the writer is indebted to H.H. the Emir Abdallah and his staff for further information.

BIBL. Musil, *Northern Hegaz*, pp. 283 f.; also *Arabia Deserta*, pp. 495.

Kedesh. Jud. iv 11 [E]. VAR. *LXX Kedes*.

LOC. A position within range of the battlefield 'by the waters of Megiddo,' p. 298, where Heber, the Kenite from the south, had pitched his tent. Its IDENT. is probable with TELL ABU KUDEIS (Pl. LXV), a small mound on the edge of Esdraelon between Taanak and Megiddo which shows trace of habitation in L.B.A. The position is marked by a circle on the map, p. 299. See further p. 301.

Kedesh-Naphtali. Jud. iv 6 [E].
VAR. *LXX Kades*. *EGN*. T[3] (No. 1) *K-d-š-w*. A (Kn. 151) *Ki-id-ši*; (162) *Ki-id-ša*, (189) *gi-id-ši*, (197) *gi-iz-za*; (54, 174, 175, 176) *Ki-in-za*. S. (B. *AR*. iii 141) *k-d-š*.

Loc. In the part of Galilee allotted to Naphtali. Associated (in II Kings xv 29) with Abel-beth-Maacah, Janoah and Hazor (Map, p. 195), and hence in eastern Upper Galilee. An Egyptian representation (Fig. 4, p. 243) shows it to have been a hill fortress, contrasting in this respect with Kadesh in the Orontes.

Ident. Tell Kades, on the plateau of Upper Galilee (Pl. LXI), 7 m. N.N.W. of Hazor; a Bronze Age site (p. 244) where to-day may be seen the remains of a Roman sun-temple. This Kedesh is not mentioned in either Book until after the settlement of Naphtali had been effected, but as the name implies the presence of a shrine, it possibly marks the site of the northern Beth-shemesh ('House of the Sun'), which Naphtali failed to occupy (Jud. i 33 [J]) before the Pharaohs had reduced Kadesh (pp. 244, 280).

Bibl. B. *AR.* iii. § 140, note *a*. *PEF. Mem.* i. p. 227. Cf. *Bul. ASOR.* Oct. 1925, p. 12.

Kiriath-Jearim. Jos. ix 17 (?), Jud. xviii 12 [J].
Var. *LXX Kariathiareim.*

Loc. From the *Cont.* one of the Hivite cities in touch with Gibeon, *q.v.* (Map, p. 164), close to a halting-place of the Danites between the Vale of Sorek and Mount Ephraim (see Mahaneh-Dan). Placed by *Onom.* 9 miles from Jerusalem towards Diospolis (Lydda).

Ident. The mound of Der el Azar (Pl. XXXVII), above *Kiryat el Enab*, a Bronze Age site (P. *LIA.*). For Descr., see p. 166. Maps, pp. 76, 164, 171.

Kitron (Kattath). Jud. i 30 [J]. Var. *LXX Kedron, Kattath.*

Loc. *Cont.* merely indicates a position in the territory of Zebulun. The site cannot be identified: Tell Qurdaneh, in the southern plain of Acre, suggested by Albright, seems to preserve the same name.

Bibl. Albr. *Cont. Hist. Geog. Pal.* p. 26. *Bul. BSAJ.* 1922, p. 10, with Map.

Lachish. Jos. x 3 [J].
Var. *LXX Lachis. EGN.* T^3 (*Petersburg Pap.* 116 A.Z. 2) *Ra-ki-ša*; A (Kn. 287, 288) *la-ki-si*, (335) *la-ki-ši*, (328, 329) *la-ki-ša*.

Loc. Associated in the *Cont.* with Jerusalem, Hebron, Jarmuth and Eglon. Elsewhere (Jos. xv 39 [P]) it is placed in the lowland with Eglon and Makkedah. Gezer appears, in Jos. x 33 [D], as a friendly neighbour: *A.* also associates it with Gezer. As early as T^3 it sent envoys to Egypt. It was fortified by Jeroboam (II Chron. xi 9), besieged by Sennacherib (II Kings xviii 17) and by Nebuchadnezzar (Jer. xxxv 7). In Roman times it was still known as Lakeis; and as such *Onom.* (pp. 130-1) placed it 6 full miles from Eleutheropolis on the road towards Daroma. See Map, p. 67 and p. 173.

IDENT. The great mound of TELL EL DUWEIR (Pl. XXXIX) exactly suits the indications as to the position and importance of Lachish. This identification was proposed by Dr. Albright, and an examination of the site with him convinced the writer of its probability. For further discussion and description, see pp. 172-4. Tell el Hesy marks more probably the site of Eglon, *q.v.*; its identity with Lachish was already regarded as doubtful by excavator Dr. Bliss (*PEF. Fifty Years' Work*, p. 106).

BIBL. Guérin, *Judée*, ii. 299-303. *PEF, QS.* 1878, 20. Petrie, *Tell el Hesy*, p. 18. Bliss, *A Mound of Many Cities*, p. 139. *JPOS.* ii. p. 130. *OLZ.* xvii. 1914, 202-3. Albright, *Zeits. f. d. Alttest. Wiss.* vi. i. p. 3.

Laish. LESHEM. Jos. xix 47 [J]; Jud. xviii 7, 28 [JE].
VAR. *LXX Laisa, Lesem. EGN.* T[3] (No. 31), *R-w-s* (? *Luz*).

LOC. 'In the valley that lieth by Beth-rehob,' within the sphere of Sidon, but far from that city. As 'Dan' it became the proverbial north extremity of Israel. Josephus (*Ant.* V iii, 1) placed it 'near the springs of the lesser Jordan,' and the *Onom.* seems to indicate the same position, where the names Nahr Leddan, Tell el Kadi (Kadi, like Dan, meaning 'judge') point to a traditional association with that mound.

IDENT. TELL EL KADI, below Banias in the N.E. of the Huleh Basin (Pl. LVI). For further description see pp. 103, 247.

BIBL. Jos. *Ant.* V iii, 1. *PEF. Mem.* i. pp. 139 *et seq. Bul. ASOR.* Oct. 1925, p. 13.

Libnah. Jos. x 29 [D].
VAR. *LXX Lebmna, Lebna. EGN.* T[3] (No. 10) *L-b-n.*

LOC. Though not mentioned in the Early Sources, this site is included owing to the peculiar interest of its position and archaeology. It lay in the Shephelah; the *Cont.* cited mentions it between Makkedah and Lachish; and it appears again after Makkedah in Jos. xv 42 [P]. Sennacherib besieged it (II Kings xix 8, Isa. xxxvii 8) after the capture of Lachish and before moving on Jerusalem. *Onom.* located it 'in the neighbourhood of Eleutheropolis.' Its name (=white) connects it with the Crusaders' fortress of Blanche Garde, on *Tell el Safi* (the shining mound), noticeable for its vivid white limestone scarps (Pl. LXXIII). This is a natural fortress, at point where the Vale of Elah debouches into Philistine plain. The mound is crescent-shaped, its sides in places being partly sheer cliffs, the lofty south end forming an acropolis. See Plan No. 10. At its greatest extent the city, as delimited by rampart and cliffs, had a length of 400 yards, with a breadth of about 200 yards; but doubtless in the Bronze Age it would occupy a smaller area.

EXCVNS. made for the P.E.F. in 1899, by Dr. Bliss and Prof. Macalister, showed that the occupation of the site dated from the beginning of the Late Bronze Age, *c.* 1600. During the Late Bronze Age it was apparently an intensively occupied but unwalled site, a fact which seems to

LIBNAH.
Tell el Safi viewed from the north.

BETH-SHEMESH.
The mound of ‘Ain-Shems, seen from the north.

See p. 367.

account for its apparent lack of strategic interest in the old narrative; though Mycenaean pottery, Egyptian scarabs, charms, etc. (the latter in an unstratified rubbish-heap), show that it shared in the culture relations

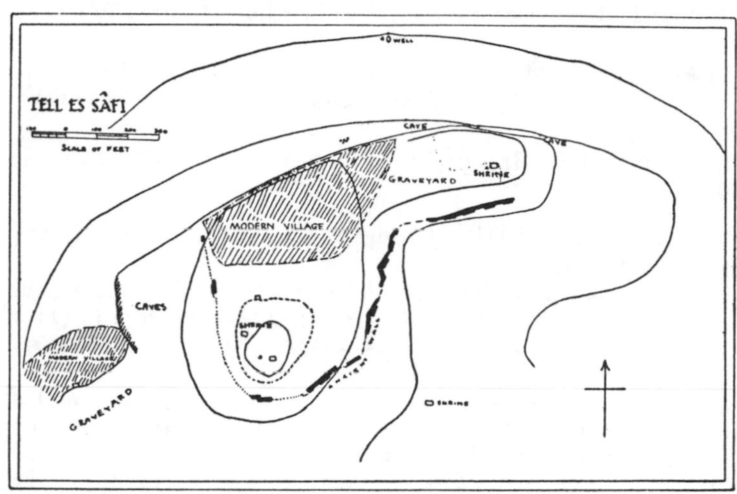

Plan No. 10. Plan of Tell el Sâfi, probable site of Libnah.

of the period (cf. Askalon, Beth-shemesh, Gezer). The massive city walls were not built till the Iron Age; and the site was deserted after the Seleucid period until the time of the Crusades.

Bibl. *PEF. Mem.* III. 259, and *Excav. in Pal.* p. 28, with the Plan, Pl. 7.

Madon. Jos. xi 1 [J].
Var. *LXX Maron.* ? *EGN.* T³ (No. 20) *M-d-n.*

Loc. Associated with Hazor, as one of the Canaanitish allies, but not mentioned elsewhere. Possibly the name a textual corruption for Maron, the reading of the *LXX*. For the argument, see p. 189; cf. further under 'Merom.'

Mahaneh-Dan. Jud. xiii 25 [J].
Var. *LXX. the camp of Dan. EGN.* (?) A (Kn. 292) *Ma-na-ḫa-te.*

Loc. Between Zorah and Eshtaol (Jud. xiii 25); near Kiriath-Jearim (Jud. xviii 12). Cf. Pl. LXIX and p. 335 and Map 19. Accepting the emendation Manahath-Dan for Mahaneh-Dan (Cook in *C.A.H.* ii. 314 n.), it may be equated with Manahate, a town or fortress prepared by the loyalist Addu-dani for the reception of the Pharaoh's troops (Kn. 292).

Makkedah. Jos. x 10, 16 [J].

VAR. *LXX Makeda. EGN.* T^3 (No. 30) *M-k-t.*

Loc. From the *Cont.*, westward from Beth-horon and with a large cave at hand. *Onom.* placed it 8 m. from Beit Jibrin (*contra solis ortum :* Jerome), a dubious record.

IDENT. Possibly MOGHAR (Pl. XL), out in the coastal plain (Map, p. 171), where Bronze Age sherds and caves help to satisfy the conditions. See further, p. 181.

BIBL. *PEF, QS.* 1871, 91. *Mem.* ii. 413. *Bul. ASOR.* Oct. 1924, p. 9.

Megiddo. Jos. xvii 11 [J]. (I Kings iv 12 ; ix 15 ; II Kings ix 27 ; xxiii 29.)

VAR. *LXX Mageddo. EGN.* T^3 (No. 2) *M-k-t-y.* A (Kn. 242, 234) *Ma-gid-da* ; (243) *ma-ki-da* ; (244) *ma-gi-id-da* ; (244, 245) *ma-kid-da* ; R^2 *M-k-t* (*Pap. Anas.* I. 23.2).

Loc. An impregnable position on the northern boundary of the territory originally allocated to Manasseh ; p. 231. Associated frequently in *Cont.* with Taanach and Ibleam, and evidently the central point of the Canaanite frontier, along the S.W. of Esdraelon. See Map, p. 188. The Egn. *Cont.* of T^3 (see p. 90 and Map 5) shows that it commanded the entrance into the plain by the Wady Arah. Mediaeval writers identified it with the Roman station Legio, the name of which survives in the position indicated in the form El Lejjum.

IDENT. Assuredly TELL EL MUTESELLIM (Pl. XX), an ancient site which satisfies all the indications ; a bold mound, strategically placed, and well supplied with springs. The walled enclosure, as determined by excavations in 1903-5, covered about 15 acres (*c.* 320 × 240 m.), an almost unrivalled area.

EXCVNS. on the site were begun by the German Palestine Society in 1903. The earliest settlement, as described by Schumacher (*op. cit. inf.* p. 11), dates from the Stone Age ; and E.B.A. pottery (2500-2000 B.C.) was found later (1925) in some of the extra-mural burials on E. slope. The town of M.B.A., the Second Level, was well fortified, the walls being of brick on stone foundations with glacis and buttresses (pp. 23-6). To this level was attributed, doubtfully (p. 192), a vaulted tomb, which produced scarabs of *c.* 2000 (p. 15). The Third Level (L.B.A., E.I.A.) produced an iron object (p. 74), also Graeco-Phoenician and Cypriote wares ; but apparently little indicating Egyptian influence. The Fourth Level, which ended with a conflagration, was marked by a fine city-gate on the south (pp. 77-80) and a Mykenaean sherd from the N. fort (p. 84). In the Burnt-layer were many definitely Egyptian or Egyptianising objects (including scarabs with name of *Men-kheper-re* (presumably late imitations).

In 1924 excavations were resumed by Dr. Clarence Fisher for the University of Chicago, under the patronage of Mr. J. D. Rockefeller, and are still in progress. Early results included some extra-mural burials (*Armageddon*, pp. 41-3). Tomb 2 had been used as dwelling as late as E. or M.B.A.; then, *c.* 1300, cleared to be used as burial-place. *Tomb* 3, of the same date, as shown by plan and pottery, contained a small bronze image of Hittite warrior (or warrior-god), with shield and upraised axe.

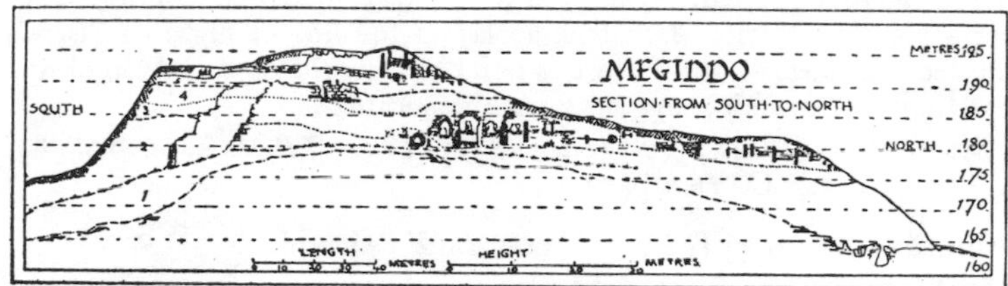

Plan No. 11. Section of Tell el Mutesellim: the site of Megiddo.

The accompanying pottery included Cypriote 'milk-bowls' with 'wish-bone' handles and ladder decoration (presumably *c.* 1450 B.C.). *Tomb* 51 (p. 45), belonging also to L.B.A.i, lay outside a heavy wall, possibly one of the enclosing walls of the city; but the chronological relation of tomb and wall was not determined. Adjacent tombs (p. 47) produced pottery of the E.B.A. 2500; also good pottery, ivory objects and a fine series of scarabs of Hyksos date (Fig. 26). More recent discoveries, under Mr. P. L. O. Guy, include the fortifications and other features of the Solomonian period (cf. I Kings ix 15), including capacious stables (*ibid. c.* 19), in which the stalls were divided and the roofs supported by stone monoliths, as at Hazor. The depth of deposits on the Tell is great, and some time may elapse before the L.B.A. stratum comes to light.

BIBL. Schumacher and Steuernagel, *Tell el Mutesellim*. Fisher, *Excavation of Armageddon*. Cf. *Biblica*, July 1926. *PEF, QS*. 1926, p. 210.

Merom, WATERS OF. Jos. xi 5 [J].
VAR. *LXX Maron*. *EGN*. T³ (No. 12) *M-r-m*.

LOC. The point of concentration for the Canaanitish allies who responded to the call of Hazor, hence presumably not far from the convergence of roads leading towards Hazor and Achshaph, and also towards Sidon, whither some of the defeated Canaanites fled. See p. 190 and Map, p. 195.

IDENT. Probably a spot near Bint Um el Jebeil, the natural road-centre of Upper Galilee, below the JEBEL MARUN, where numerous and copious wells exist. The name MARUN, reproducing Maron of the *LXX*. appears repeatedly in the neighbourhood. Later tradition, reflected possibly in the form *Merom* of the Massoretic text, seems to have leaned towards identification with modern *Meiron* (Map, p. 195), at the foot of which is found also a copious spring. This site lies 7 miles only S. of Jebel Marun, and is linked equally with roads E., N. and S., but it does not satisfy so readily in other details the indications of the narrative. See p. 195.

Meroz. Jud. v 23 [E]. Var. *LXX Meroz ; Mazor.*

Loc. There can be no certain explanation of this name, which occurs only in the passage cited. It may, however, be conjectured from the *Cont.* that a place or district of that name lay in the line of flight of Sisera's defeated charioteers : and from this point of view the modern 'Ain el Roz near Lejjun (Megiddo) suggests a possible location.

Bibl. *PEF, QS.* 1875, p. 32 ; 1883, p. 125. *JPOS.* ii. pp. 79, 284. B. *Jud.* p. 151. C. *Jud.* p. 65.

Minnith. Jud. xi 33 [? E]. Var. *LXX Semoeith.*

Loc. In southern Trans-Jordania ; associated in the *Cont.* with Aroer and Abel-cheramim (*q.v.*). The limit of Jephthah's pursuit of the Ammonites. Ezekiel (xxvii 17) mentions 'wheat of Minnith.' *Onom.* suggests 'a village Mannith, 4 m. from Heshbon on the way to Philadelphia' ; but the site remains unknown.

Misrephoth-Maim. Jos. xi 8 [J]. Var. *LXX Maseron.*

Loc. From the *Cont.* it would appear to have lain on the line of flight of one of the defeated Canaanite contingents, presumably that from Achshaph, since later tradition (Jos. xiii 6 [D]) associates it with the Zidonians.

Ident. Possibly Kh. el Mesherifeh (Pl. XLVII), between Tyre and Akka. The similarity of name and the presence of hot springs suggested by the biblical name, favour the identification. The site dates from the Bronze Age, and satisfies the topographical indications. Cf. Map, p. 195. For Descr., see further p. 190 f.

Bibl. Cooke, *Joshua*, p. 103.

Mizpeh, Valley of. Jos. xi 8b [J].
Var. *LXX Massepha, Plain of Massoch.*

Loc. Eastward from the scene of the battle at the Waters of Merom in Upper Galilee ; hence in the Huleh area (p. 195). The name Mizpeh, meaning 'watch-tower,' indicates a conspicuous height.

Ident. Possibly Kala't el Subeibeh (Pl. XLVI), which looks down over the N.E. of the Huleh basin from above Banias, the valley being that of the Nahr Banias, one of the sources of the Jordan. See further p. 191 and Pl. LVI.

Nahalol. Jud. i 30 [J]. Var. *LXX Naalol.*

Loc. Mentioned in *Cont.* as lying within the territory originally allotted to Zebulun. *Onom.* gave it as *Neila,* a village near *Batanea.* The indications are vague; it is usually identified with the ancient site of Malul (p. 240), which overlooks Esdraelon from the north. But see Albright, *Cont. Hist. Geog. Pal.* 26-7, who suggests that it may be Tell el Nahl in the S. plain of Acre, and that Kitron of the same *Cont.*, *q.v.*, may be Tell Qardaneh.

Nobah. Jud. viii 11 [E]. VAR. *LXX Nabai.*

Loc. In Trans-Jordania, apparently between Succoth (Tell Deir Allah) and Jogbehah, *q.v.*; being grouped in the *Cont.* with the latter and with the favoured centre of the tent-dwellers farther east. According to Num. xxxii 42, it was originally called Kenath. Presumably not far from Jubeilhat, W. of the Upper Zerka, N.W. from Amman; but the site is unknown.

Ophrah. Jud. vi 11 [J]. VAR. *LXX Ephratha.*

Loc. In Manasseh; apparently between Shechem and the Midianites' camp in Jezreel (Jud. vi 33-35, viii 31). The position of modern SILEH, more fully SILET EL DHAHR (Pl. LXVII), which has a good water-supply and occupies seemingly an Iron Age site, suits the situation; but the identity can only be regarded as provisional (pp. 319, 327) pending a more exhaustive exploration of the area.

BIBL. *ZDPV.* xxxiii (1910), p. 105.

Penuel. Jud. viii 8, 9 [E]. VAR. *LXX Phanouel.*

Loc. In Trans-Jordania, upwards and eastwards from Succoth (Tell Deir Allah, Map, p. 322), hence presumably upon the plateau. Site uncertain. See p. 321.

BIBL. *PEF, QS.* 1878, p. 81; 1888, p. 197; 1927, pp. 89, 189; 1928, p. 28. Cf. Müller, *Asien*, p. 168.

Ramah. Jud. iv 5 (?); xix 13 [E]. VAR. *LXX Rama.*

Loc. From the *Cont.*, in Benjamin, N. of Jerusalem and close to Gibeah; also associated with Bethel. *Onom.* placed it 5 m. N. of Jerusalem, 'over against' Bethel.

IDENT. The modern village of EL RAM seems to occupy the site. It lies 5 m. to the N. of Jerusalem, just E. of the highroad towards Ramallah and the north.

Rehob. Jud. i 31 [J].

VAR. *LXX Ereo.* *EGN.* T[3] (No. 87) *R-ḥ-b*; (*Taanak Letters, No.* 2) *Ra-ḥa-bi*; R[2] (*Pap. Anas.* I. 22-7) *R-ḥ-b.*

Loc. In Asher, in the neighbourhood of Achzib and Acco, hence in the Plain of Acre. To be distinguished from a place of the same name near Bethshean (? Tell el Sarem, p. 72), to which some of the Egyptian references may allude.

IDENT. Possibly TELL BERWEH (Pl. XIV), an imposing and well-watered Bronze Age site 7 m. inland from Acco, commanding the two routes from the plateau, by the Wady Shagour and the Wady Shaib. The Tell rises nearly 100 feet above the plain: its surface now covers only 3 or 4 acres, being roughly triangular in form and sloping away towards the west. Pottery from the site (*LIA.*) represents M.B.A., L.B.A.ii, E.I.A., as well as Hellenistic and Roman times.

BIBL. Cf. Dussaud, *Syria*, viii. 223. Sellin, *Tell Ta'anak*, p. 115. Albright, *Cont. Hist. Geog. Pal.* pp. 27-8.

Seirah. Jud. iii 26 [JE]. VAR. *LXX Setirotha, Seeirotha.*

LOC. On Ehud's route from the neighbourhood of Jericho to Mt. Ephraim. The only clue as to the choice of routes (pp. 135, 251) is the mention in the *Cont.* of 'the quarries,' which may conceivably be those mentioned by the name Shebarim in Josh. vii 5 [J], p. 152. The position of Seirah is unknown. The name recalls distantly that of *Selom*, the *LXX* rendering of Shiloh, *Selo* of the *Onom.*, but the Gk. variants do not support the identity.

Shaalbim. Jud. i 35 [J]. VAR. *LXX Thalabin.*

LOC. In the original allotment of Dan in the Shephelah associated in this *Cont.* and in Jos. xix 41, 42 [P] with Aijalon; in Jos. xix 41 with Zorah, Eshtaol and Ir-shemesh; and in I Kings iv 9 with Makaz and Beth-shemesh. Jerome places it in between Aijalon and Nicopolis (Emmaus). Its IDENT. is uncertain. Extensive ruins are visible at Selbit, 2 m. N. of Emmaus, a situation which might suit the indications.

BIBL. *PEF. Mem.* iii. 157. Vigouroux, *Dict. Bibl.*

Shebarim. Jos. vii 5 [J] (the quarries). *LXX* omits this name.

LOC. The *Cont.* indicates a position near Ai, on a route towards Jericho. The only ancient workings in the locality known to the writer are to be seen near KH. EL HAI, 1½ m. S. of Ai, on the road to Jericho *via* Mukhmas, p. 152.

Shechem. Jos. xxiv 1 [E]; Judg. ix 1, 49 [E].
VAR. *LXX Suchem*; *Sikimon. EGN.* M.K. *S-k-m-m*; A (Kn. 289) *Ša-ak-mi*; R[2] (*Pap. Anas.* I. 21.5) *S-k-m.*

LOC. The chief city of the central highlands, now represented by Nablus (Pl. V). The general position is fixed by continuous tradition. In the fourth century A.D. it was identified by Eusebius in the *Onom.* with Neaspoleis (Neapolis), from which the modern town derives its name. It lay between Mts. Ebal and Gerezim. In the era of Joshua (p. 249) the fortified city stood on its ancient site near the S.E. entrance to this valley, at BALATA (Pl. LVII), where later, in the age of Abimelech (p. 327), rose the tower of Shechem (Judg. ix 49 [E]).

EXCVNS. at BALATA, commenced in 1914 by Prof. E. Sellin, have shown that the occupation of the site began in E.B.A., and that the city was founded and fortified in M.B.A.i, soon after 2000 B.C. Its great Cyclopean walls, comparable with those of Tell Nasbeh and Jericho, had a circuit of about 800 yards, enclosing a roughly circular area of 11 or 12 acres, one of the largest fenced cities of the country. A gateway-reconstruction on the N. shows N. Syrian or possibly Hittite influence (*ZDPV*. 26, p. 235). A palace adjoined this gateway and a 'temple' lay near by, in the *temenos* of which was found a Hyksos scarab. Scarabs of early XVIII Dynasty and other Egyptian objects were found in a house containing tablets (Z. p. 319), on one of which appears the possibly Hittite name *Birassenasil* (Z. p. 326). Houses of M.B.A. were found to have been destroyed by fire (Z. 27, 209). The L.B.A. was represented by characteristic pottery, including numerous painted and imported fabrics and a large scarab (Z. 308). More recently (1929-30) excavations have been continued by Dr. Welter, disclosing the pyramidal foundations of a tower, crowned by a chamber, 85 by 68 feet, with walls 16 feet in thickness, flanked by two towers. See further p. 249.

Bibl. Sellin, *Zeits. Deut. Pal., Ver.* 1926, pp. 229-236, 304-327; 1927, pp. 205-210; 1928, pp. 119-122. Cf. Vincent in *Rev. Bibl.* 1927, pp. 419-425. *PEF, QS*. 1929, pp. 2, 118.

Shiloh. Jud. xviii 31 [E]; xxi 19 (?). Var. *LXX Selom*.

Loc. In Jud. xxi 19 [P] it is stated that Shiloh lay 'on the north of Bethel on the east side of the highway that goeth up from Bethel to Shechem, and on the south of Lebonah.' *Onom*. also located it at Selo in Efraim, 9 m. from Neapolis.

Ident. The site called Kh. Seilun (Pl. L) in the position indicated seems to satisfy the conditions. It occupies a low hill in a passage through higher ground by which it is almost enclosed.

Excvns. zealously conducted during 1926-8 by Dr. Aage Schmidt, under expert assistance, have traced the first occupation of the site to M.B.A. There were found no structural remains of L.B.A., the era of Joshua, corresponding with the impression conveyed by the narrative that Israel still dwelt in tents throughout this period. In E.I.A., however, the area was enclosed by a city wall. See further p. 251.

Bibl. *PEF. Mem.* ii. 367-70. *PEF, QS*. 1927, 85, 157, 202 *et seqq. Rev. Bibl.* 1927, 418-9. *Bul. ASOR*. Oct. 1929, p. 4. Cf. B. *AR*. iv. 131. *Rec. des Trav.* xxi. 37-8.

Shimron. Jos. xi 1 [J].
Var. *LXX Sumoōn*. *EGN*. T³ (No. 35) *S-m-n*. A (Kn. 224, 225) *Šamḫuna*.

Loc. In northern Palestine; one of the cities allied with Hazor in the battle by the Waters of Merom.

Ident. The variants admit of two philological possibilities; (*a*) Semuniyeh in Lower Galilee, west of Nazareth, a site which, however, to judge by its superficial indications, seems to have been abandoned during L.B.A.i, before the period of the narrative; and the situation cannot be reconciled with the strategy of the campaign. See p. 187. (*b*) Summaka, to the east of L. Huleh, a name which can be traced back through the classical *Samachonitis* to the *Sam-ḫu-na* of the Amarna period. This proposal alone suits the topography of the context, but there is no archaeological information. See further, p. 189.

Shittim. Jos. xi 1 [E]. VAR. *LXX Sattein.*

LOC. In Trans-Jordania: the same as Abel Shittim (Num. xxxiii 49 [P]); on the E. bank of Jordan, opposite Jericho.

IDENT. Josephus (*Antiq.* IV viii 1, V i 1) locates a place Abila, 7 miles back from Jordan in this neighbourhood, which seems to correspond with KH. KUFREIN, a Bronze Age site, with a broad camping ground and a good water supply. See further pp. 125-7.

Succoth. Jud. viii 5 [E]. VAR. *LXX Socchoth.*

LOC. In Trans-Jordania, not far E. from the fords of Jordan near El Damieh, p. 320.

IDENT. TELL DEIR-ALLAH (Map No. 17), or perhaps more particularly TELL EL EKSAS in the immediate vicinity. Both are Bronze Age sites, and the latter name is the exact Arabic equivalent of the Hebrew *Succot*. See further p. 321.

BIBL. Abel, *Rev. Bibl.* 1910, p. 555 f. Albright, *Bul. ASOR,* 1929, p. 13 f.

Taanach. TAANAK. Jos. xvii 11 [J]; Jud. v 19.
VAR. *LXX Tanach, Thanak, Thanaak. EGN.* T[3] (No. 42) *T-n-k*; A (Kn. 248) *Ta-aḫ-nu-ka.*

LOC. One of the Canaanitish frontier fortresses of Esdraelon. Assoc. with Ibleam and Megiddo, *q.v.*

IDENT. The imposing mound called TELL TA'ANUK (Pl. LXVI), which retains the ancient name and satisfies all the topographical and archaeological indications of the various Biblical and Egyptian contexts. It stands between the sites of Ibleam and Megiddo, guarding a pass into Esdraelon. See the Maps, pp. 90, 188 and 195.

EXCVNS. made on TELL TA'ANUK (also called TELL TA'ANEK) by Prof. Ernst Sellin in 1900, though not providing materials for a final explanation of the stratigraphy of the mound, none the less give an insight into its general character, and testify to its ancient origins. In the M.B.A. it shared in the general culture of Canaan; and in L.B.A.i its occupation was in full activity, while its historical relations with Egypt are illustrated by numerous scarabs and other objects. To this period, to judge by the absence of Cypro-Phoenician objects, belong twelve cuneiform tablets. They were found in a plundered palace of *Istar-wasur*, presumably the local dynast. The next phase was not clearly distinguished, but the discoveries point to a normal sequence of periods corresponding to the unexplained depths of the various strata. Traces of the characteristic culture of L.B.A.ii and

E.I.A. ii are clear, but a scientific re-investigation of the site would seem to be indispensable before full appreciation can be given to the historical

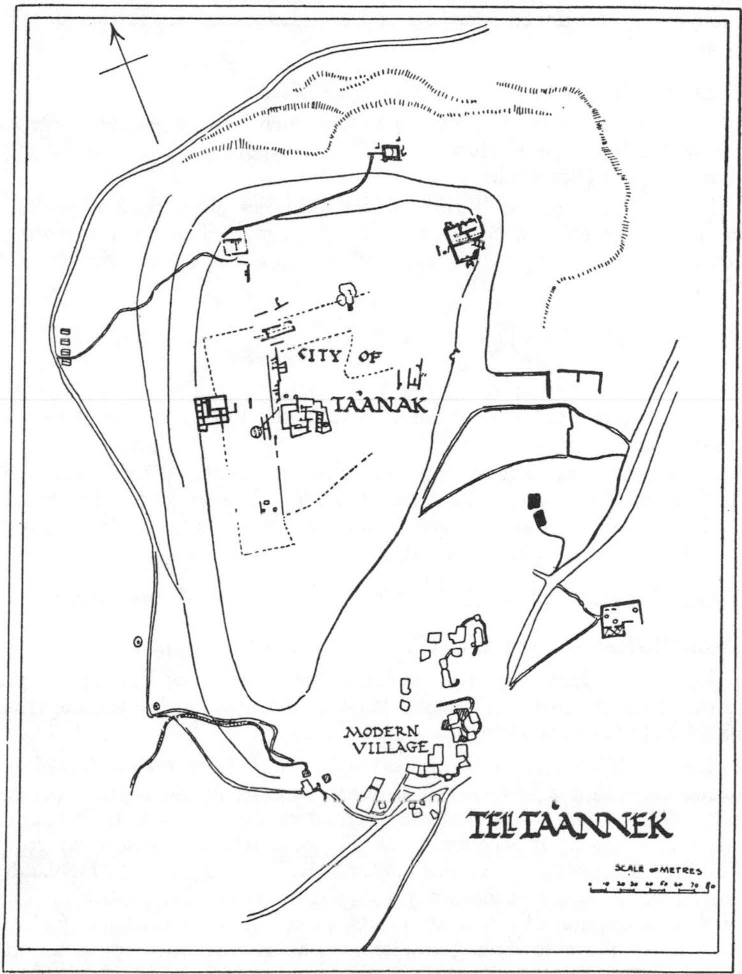

Plan No. 12. Site plan of Taanak, after Sellin and Schumacher.

aspect of the abundant and important materials uncovered at that time, when Palestinian archaeology was still in its infancy.

Bibl. Sellin, *Tell Ta'anek* (Vienna), 1904, especially ff. 40, 49, 102, 112 f. Albright, *JPOS*. ii. 1922, p. 132. Barton, *Arch. and the Bible* (Phil. 1927), p. 105.

Tabbath. Jud. vii 22 [J]. VAR. *LXX Tabath.*

LOC. The *Cont.* indicates a site near Abel-meholah (*q.v.*), on the Midianites' flight from Jezreel, hence presumably in the mid-Jordan valley. Not mentioned elsewhere and not identified. See further p. 318, n. 4.

Thebez. Jud. ix 50 [E]. VAR. *LXX Thebes.*

LOC. In the vicinity of Shechem; not mentioned elsewhere. *Onom.* placed it at a village Thebes, 13 m. from Neapolis (Nablus), on the way to Scythopolis (Bethshean).

IDENT. Probably at TUBAS, which occupies an important position between Shechem and Bethshean. Map, p. 79. The modern town is large, and apparently more than covers the ancient site. See further p. 327.

Timnah. Jud. xiv 1 [J].
VAR. *AV. Timnath. LXX Thamnatha.*

LOC. Viewed from Zorah (*q.v.*), the standpoint of the *Cont.*, Timnah lay further down the Vale of Sorek towards the Philistine territory in the coastal plain.

IDENT. The name survives at KH. TIBNEH, suitably placed some 4 m. S.W. from Zorah across the Vale of Sorek, Map, p. 335. The site is ancient, and shows traces of fortifications, while potsherds relate its history to E.I.A., the period of the narrative. See further p. 336.

Timnath-Serah. Jos. xxiv 30 [E]. VAR. *LXX Thamnasarach.*

Timnath-Heres. Jud. ii 9 [E]. VAR. *LXX Thamnathares.*

LOC. The *Conts.* place the site 'in the hill country of Ephraim on the north of the mountain of Gaash,' itself unidentified, unless the lingering name Nebi-Gais marks the place (see Gaash).

IDENT. The familiar theoretical location at Kefr Harris (based on Samaritan tradition of doubtful antiquity) has no archaeological foundation. The variants show that the essential part of the name is Timnath; and *Onom.* placed it accordingly at Thamna, which evidently lay from Eusebius' account in the extreme S.W. of Mt. Ephraim upon the highlands, within the territory theoretically assigned to Dan (*Kl.* p. 100). The further description of Thamna (p. 96) placed it at the confines of Diospolis, on a route towards Jerusalem. The identification, proposed by Guérin, with KHIRBET TIBNAH, which overlooks the coastal plain from the western border of the highlands, 17 miles as the crow flies from Shechem and from Jerusalem, seems to satisfy all the indications. The site is marked by a true Tell, which bears trace of occupation in the Late Bronze Age (the period of Joshua) as well as E.I.A., that of the town itself going back to Hellenistic times. According to Eusebius and Jerome, the tomb of Joshua was still shown there in the fifth century A.D. In this connexion the *LXX* adds that 'they put with him into the tomb in which they buried him, the knives of stone . . . and there they are to this day.'

Bibl. *PEF. Mem.* ii. 322. Guérin, *Samarie*, ii. 84-104. Albright, *Bul. ASOR.* Oct. 1923, p. 4. Cooke, *Jos.* pp. 187, 222; *Jud.* p. 27.

Zaanannim. Jud. iv 11 [? E].

Loc. Near Kedesh, a site located at Tell Abu Kudeis in the plain of Esdraelon, possibly the Kedesh of Issachar mentioned in I Chr. vi 22. A position near Kedesh Naphtali, as sometimes suggested, is irreconcilable with the tactics of the battle by the Waters of Megiddo (p. 301) notwithstanding the later text of Josh. xix 33 [P]. This reference to Zaanannim in the *cont.* (Jud. iv 11) may possibly be also a late insertion derived from the same source.

Zarethan. Jos. iii 16 [JE]. Var. *LXX Kariathiarim.*

Loc. In the Jordan valley below the mouth of the valley of Jezreel, between the ford of El Damieh and Beisan. Cf. I Kings iv 12. In I Kings vii 46 it is associated with Succoth (Tell Deir Allah), 'in the plain of Jordan.' The site is not identified. See also Zeredah.

Bibl. *PEF. Mem.* ii. 99. *JPOS.* 1925, 33 n. Cooke, *Jos.* pp. 23-4.

Zererah. Jud. vii 22 [J]. Var. *LXX Garagatha.*

Loc. In the mid-Jordan valley, between Beisan and El Damieh (Map, p. 72). Associated with Beth-Shittah and Abel-Meholah, on the way from the valley of Jezreel towards Succoth.

Ident. A comparison of the record in II Chr. iv 17 with that of I Kings vii 46 shows that Zeredah is a variant reading of Zarethan (*q.v.*), and Zererah, otherwise unknown, but in the same region, would appear to be another version of the same name. Cf. p. 328, n. 4, and for the full Bible text see p. 40. Cf. Cooke, *Jos.* p. 88.

Zidon. Jos. xi 8 [J]. Judg. i 31 [J]. Judg. xvii 7, 28 [J].

Var. *LXX Sidon. EGN.* A (Kn. 92) *ṣi-du-na*; (Kn. 75, 85, 101, 114, 144, 146, 147, 148, 149, 151, 152, 154, 155) *zi-du-na*; R^2 (*Pap. Anas.* I. 20, 8) *D-d-n*; R^2 (*Wen-Amon.* B. *AR.* 574) *D-d-n.*

Loc. At the extreme northern border of the territory allotted to Asher, who failed to drive out the inhabitants. It held close relations with Hazor (p. 183), and on the decline of this old Canaanitish centre in E.I.A. it would appear to have established a measure of authority in the north (Jud. xvii 28).

Ident. Sidon on the Phoenician coast.

Zorah. Jud. xiii 25 [J].
VAR. *LXX Saraa, Saral.* (The Egyptian name, A, *Ṣa-ar-ḳa* (Kn. 273) is a doubtful rendering.)

LOC. Near Eshtaol (*q.v.*) in the original Danite territory, p. 229.

IDENT. The Tell of modern SURAH, which crowns a ridge to the north of Beth-shemesh and the Vale of Sorek (Map, p. 335). Not excavated, but dated by potsherds to the close of the Bronze Age, with well-defined traces of occupation in E.I.A. See further p. 335.

POSTSCRIPT

FURTHER investigations at **Jericho** in the Spring of 1931 disclose the possible effects of earthquake shock affecting particularly the western wall, but not affecting the northern and southern walls. The eastern wall is entirely destroyed. These observations indicate tremors east and west across the Rift, as was apparently the case in the earthquakes of 1927-8.

INDEX

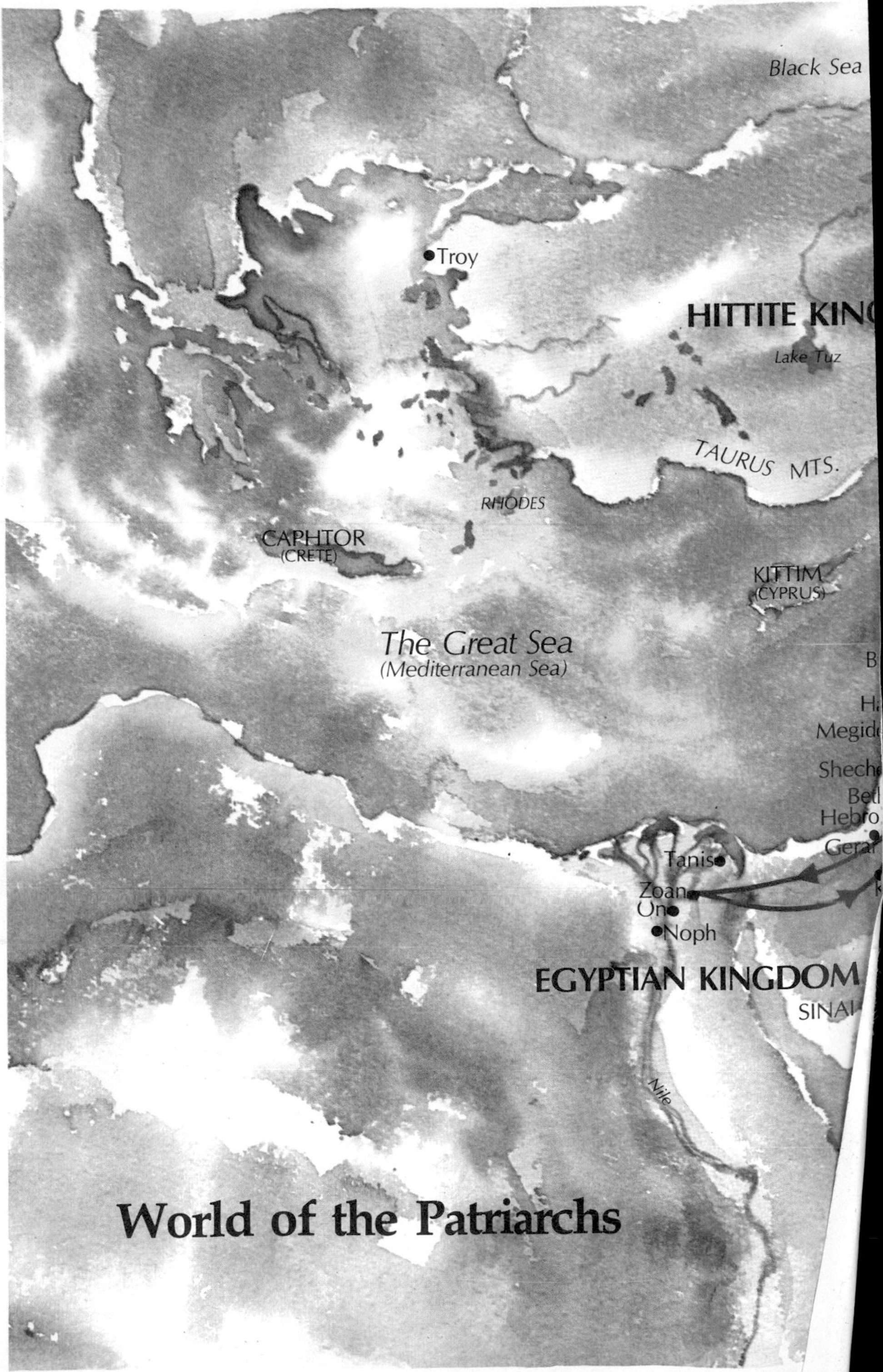

Black Sea

Troy

HITTITE KIN

Lake Tuz

TAURUS MTS.

RHODES

CAPHTOR
(CRETE)

KITTIM
(CYPRUS)

The Great Sea
(Mediterranean Sea)

Megid

Shech

Hebro

Gera

Tanis

Zoan

On

Noph

EGYPTIAN KINGDOM

SINAI

Nile

World of the Patriarchs

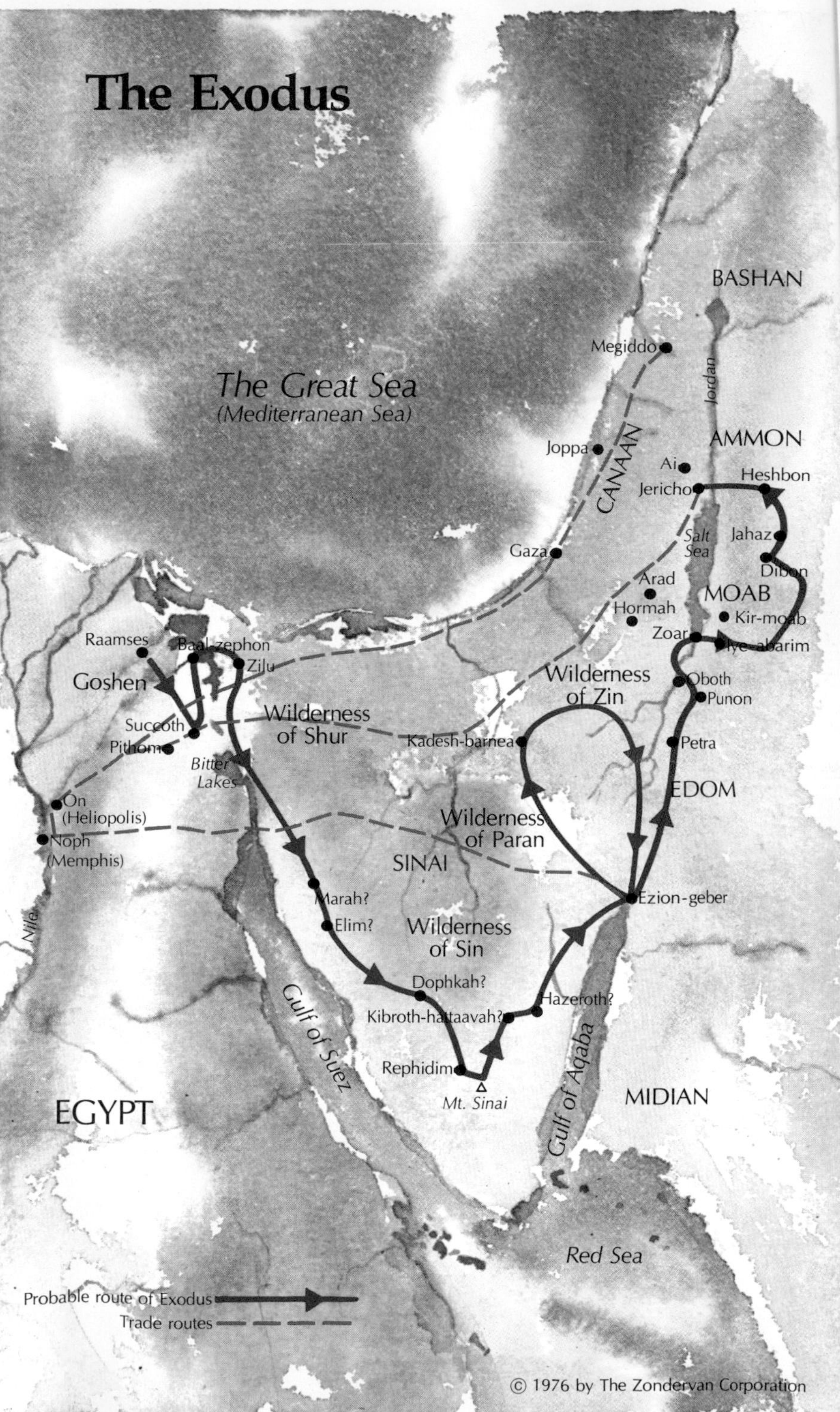
The Exodus
The Great Sea
(Mediterranean Sea)
BASHAN
Megiddo
Jordan
AMMON
Joppa
CANAAN
Ai
Heshbon
Jericho
Salt Sea
Jahaz
Gaza
Dibon
Arad
MOAB
Hormah
Kir-moab
Zoar
Iye-abarim
Raamses
Baal-zephon
Zilu
Goshen
Wilderness of Zin
Oboth
Punon
Wilderness of Shur
Succoth
Kadesh-barnea
Petra
Pithom
Bitter Lakes
EDOM
On (Heliopolis)
Wilderness of Paran
Noph (Memphis)
SINAI
Marah?
Ezion-geber
Nile
Elim?
Wilderness of Sin
Dophkah?
Gulf of Suez
Hazeroth?
Kibroth-hattaavah?
Rephidim
Gulf of Aqaba
Mt. Sinai
MIDIAN
EGYPT
Red Sea
Probable route of Exodus
Trade routes

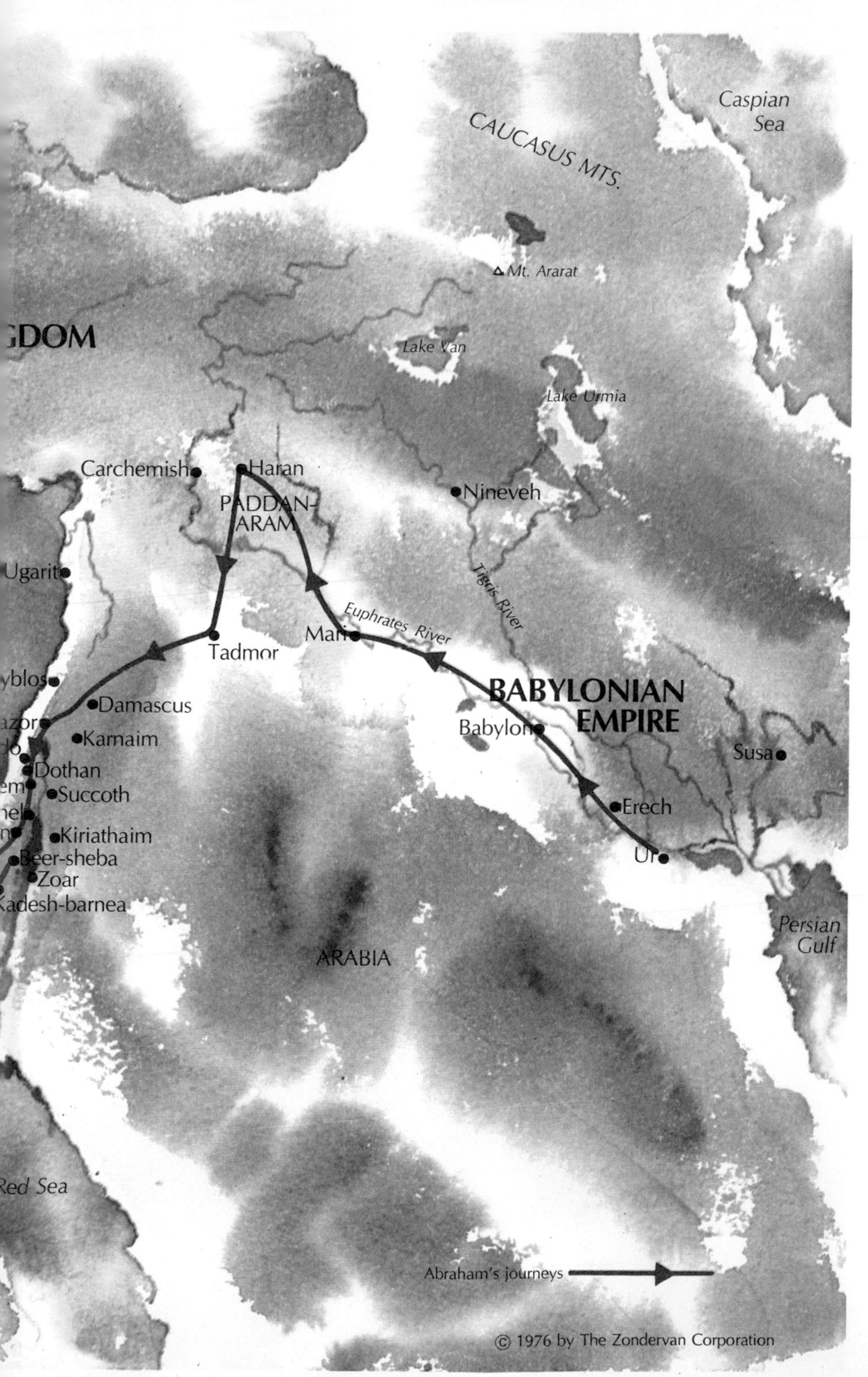
Caspian Sea
CAUCASUS MTS.
Mt. Ararat
Lake Van
Lake Urmia
Carchemish
Haran
PADDAN-ARAM
Nineveh
Ugarit
Tigris River
Euphrates River
Mari
Tadmor
BABYLONIAN EMPIRE
Babylon
Damascus
Karnaim
Dothan
Succoth
Kiriathaim
Beer-sheba
Zoar
Susa
Erech
Ur
Persian Gulf
ARABIA
Red Sea
Abraham's journeys
© 1976 by The Zondervan Corporation

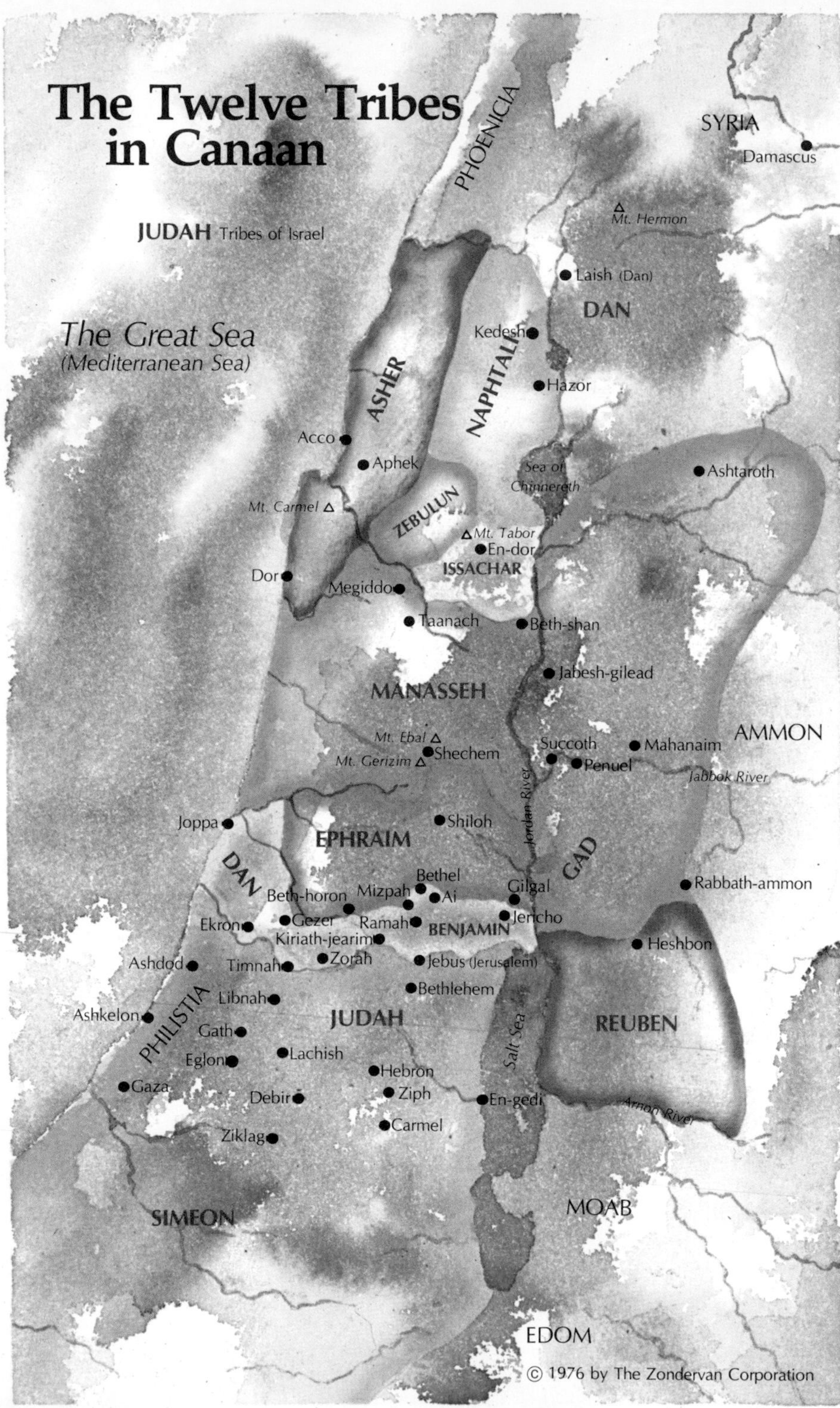

The Twelve Tribes in Canaan
JUDAH Tribes of Israel
The Great Sea
(Mediterranean Sea)
PHOENICIA
SYRIA
Damascus
Mt. Hermon
Laish (Dan)
DAN
Kedesh
NAPHTALI
ASHER
Hazor
Acco
Aphek
Sea of Chinnereth
Ashtaroth
Mt. Carmel
ZEBULUN
Mt. Tabor
En-dor
ISSACHAR
Dor
Megiddo
Taanach
Beth-shan
Jabesh-gilead
MANASSEH
Mt. Ebal
Mt. Gerizim
Shechem
Succoth
Penuel
Mahanaim
AMMON
Jabbok River
Joppa
Shiloh
EPHRAIM
Jordan River
GAD
DAN
Bethel
Mizpah
Ai
Gilgal
Beth-horon
Rabbath-ammon
Ekron
Gezer
Ramah
BENJAMIN
Jericho
Kiriath-jearim
Heshbon
Ashdod
Timnah
Zorah
Jebus (Jerusalem)
Bethlehem
Libnah
PHILISTIA
Ashkelon
JUDAH
Gath
Salt Sea
REUBEN
Lachish
Eglon
Hebron
Gaza
Debir
Ziph
En-gedi
Arnon River
Carmel
Ziklag
SIMEON
MOAB
EDOM
© 1976 by The Zondervan Corporation

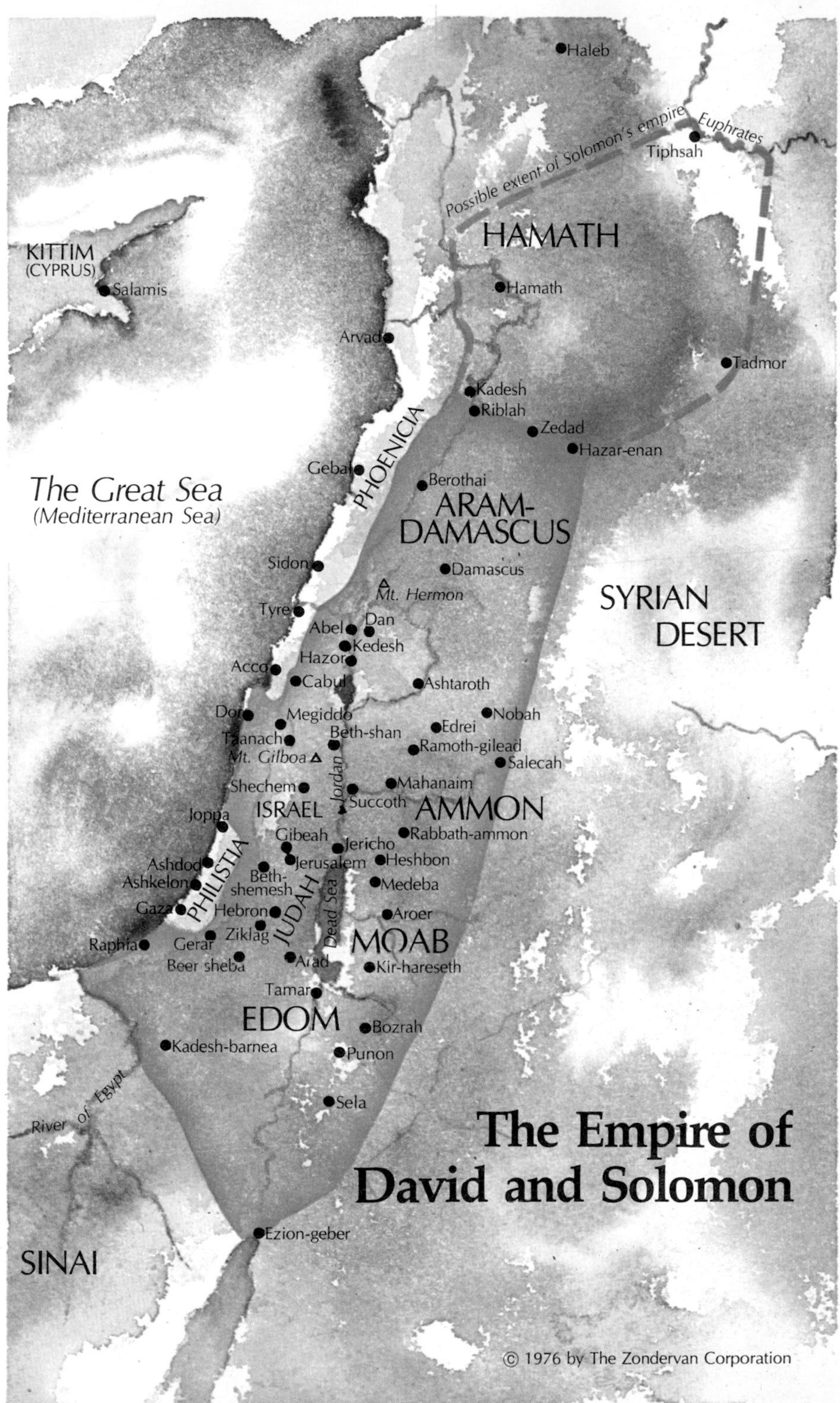

The Empire of David and Solomon

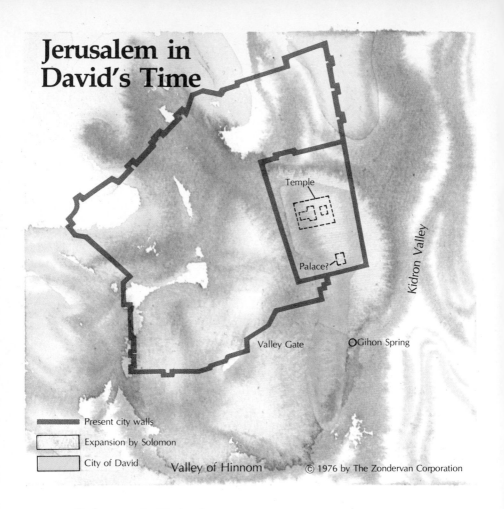

Jerusalem in David's Time

Temple
Palace?
Kidron Valley
Valley Gate
Gihon Spring
Present city walls
Expansion by Solomon
City of David
Valley of Hinnom

Solomon's Temple

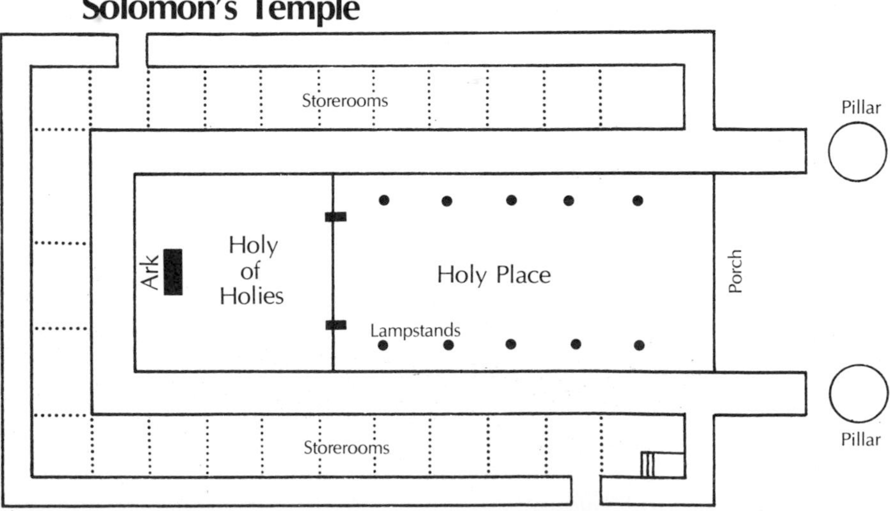

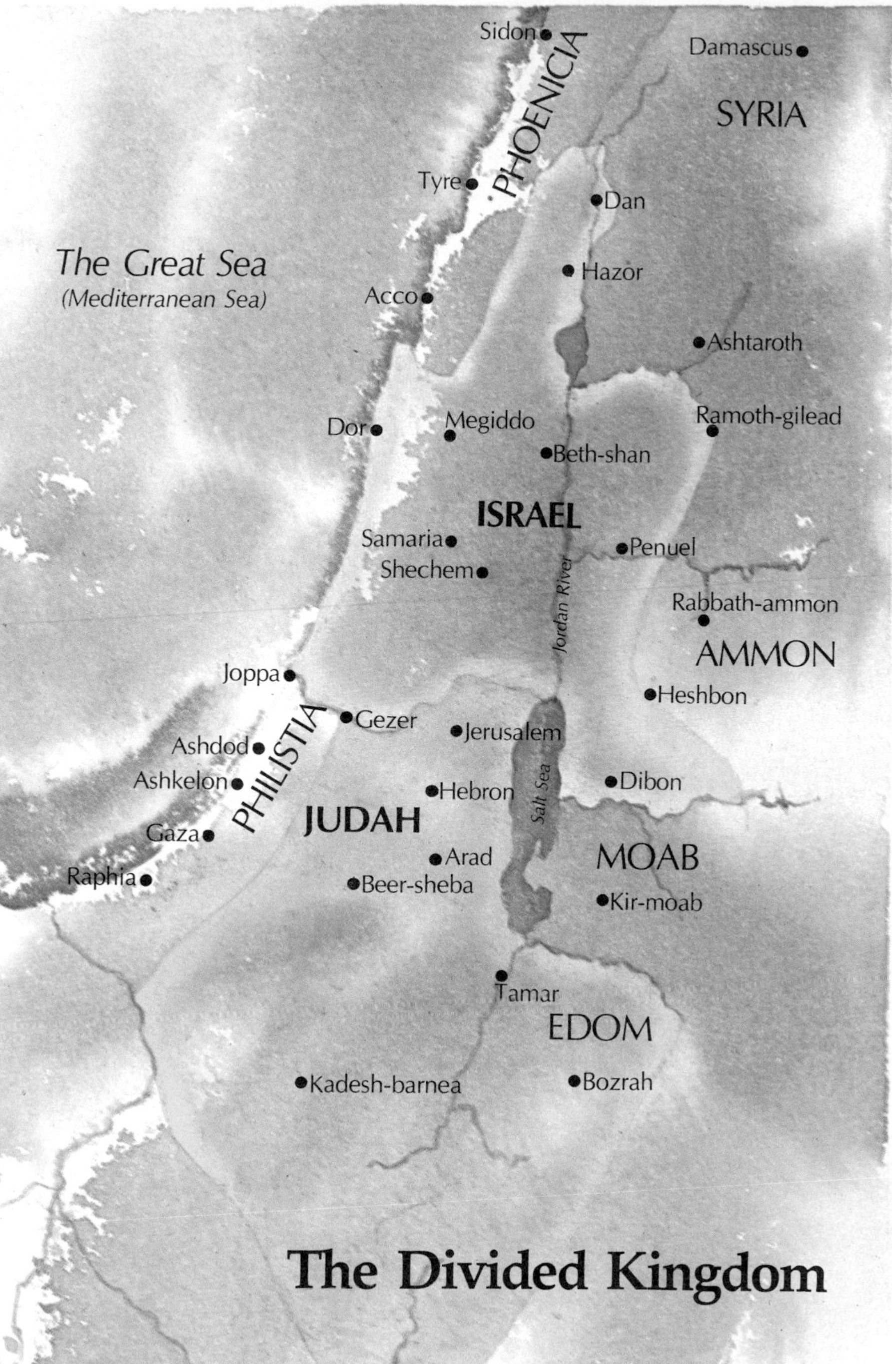
Sidon
PHOENICIA
Damascus
SYRIA
Tyre
Dan
The Great Sea
(Mediterranean Sea)
Hazor
Acco
Ashtaroth
Dor
Megiddo
Ramoth-gilead
Beth-shan
ISRAEL
Samaria
Penuel
Shechem
Jordan River
Rabbath-ammon
AMMON
Joppa
Heshbon
Gezer
Jerusalem
PHILISTIA
Ashdod
Salt Sea
Ashkelon
Hebron
Dibon
JUDAH
Gaza
MOAB
Arad
Raphia
Beer-sheba
Kir-moab
Tamar
EDOM
Kadesh-barnea
Bozrah
The Divided Kingdom
© 1976 by The Zondervan Corporation

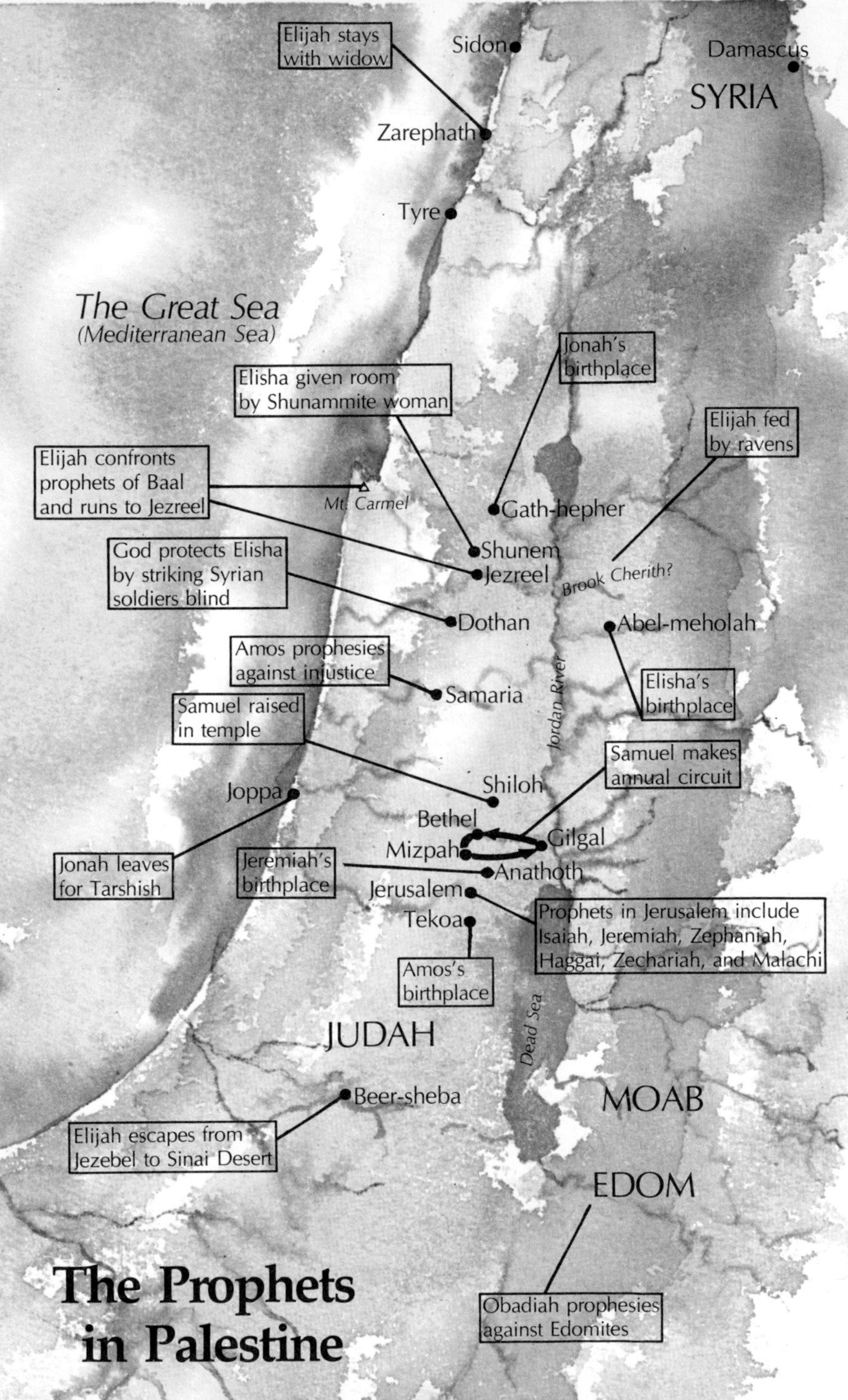

Elijah stays with widow
Sidon
Damascus
SYRIA
Zarephath
Tyre
The Great Sea
(Mediterranean Sea)
Jonah's birthplace
Elisha given room by Shunammite woman
Elijah fed by ravens
Elijah confronts prophets of Baal and runs to Jezreel
Mt. Carmel
Gath-hepher
God protects Elisha by striking Syrian soldiers blind
Shunem
Jezreel
Brook Cherith?
Dothan
Abel-meholah
Amos prophesies against injustice
Samaria
Jordan River
Elisha's birthplace
Samuel raised in temple
Samuel makes annual circuit
Joppa
Shiloh
Bethel
Gilgal
Mizpah
Jonah leaves for Tarshish
Jeremiah's birthplace
Anathoth
Jerusalem
Prophets in Jerusalem include Isaiah, Jeremiah, Zephaniah, Haggai, Zechariah, and Malachi
Tekoa
Amos's birthplace
JUDAH
Dead Sea
MOAB
Beer-sheba
Elijah escapes from Jezebel to Sinai Desert
EDOM
The Prophets in Palestine
Obadiah prophesies against Edomites

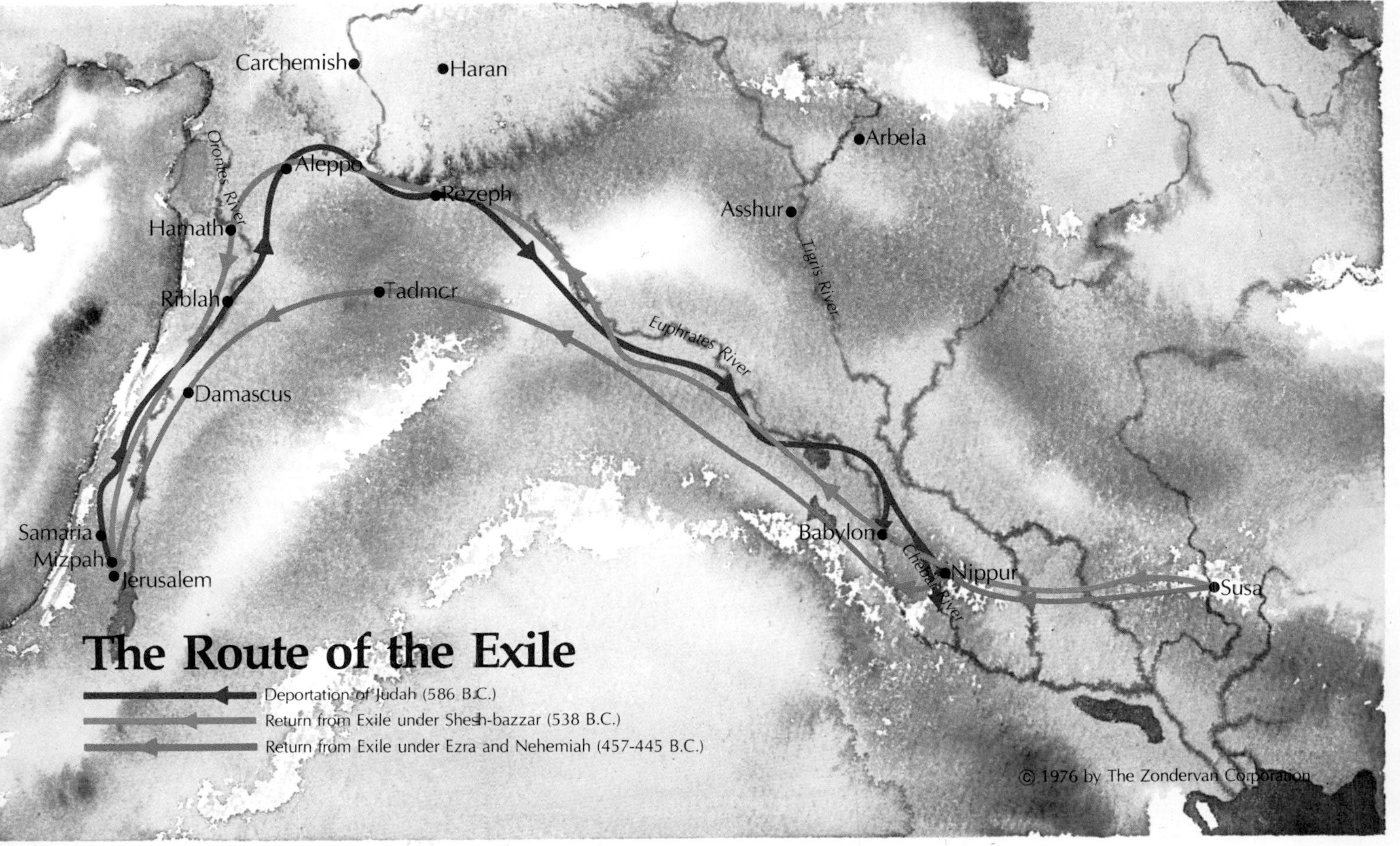

The Route of the Exile
Deportation of Judah (586 B.C.)
Return from Exile under Shesh-bazzar (538 B.C.)
Return from Exile under Ezra and Nehemiah (457-445 B.C.)
Carchemish
Haran
Arbela
Aleppo
Rezeph
Asshur
Tigris River
Orontes River
Hamath
Riblah
Tadmcr
Euphrates River
Damascus
Samaria
Mizpah
Jerusalem
Babylon
Chebar River
Nippur
Susa
© 1976 by The Zondervan Corporation

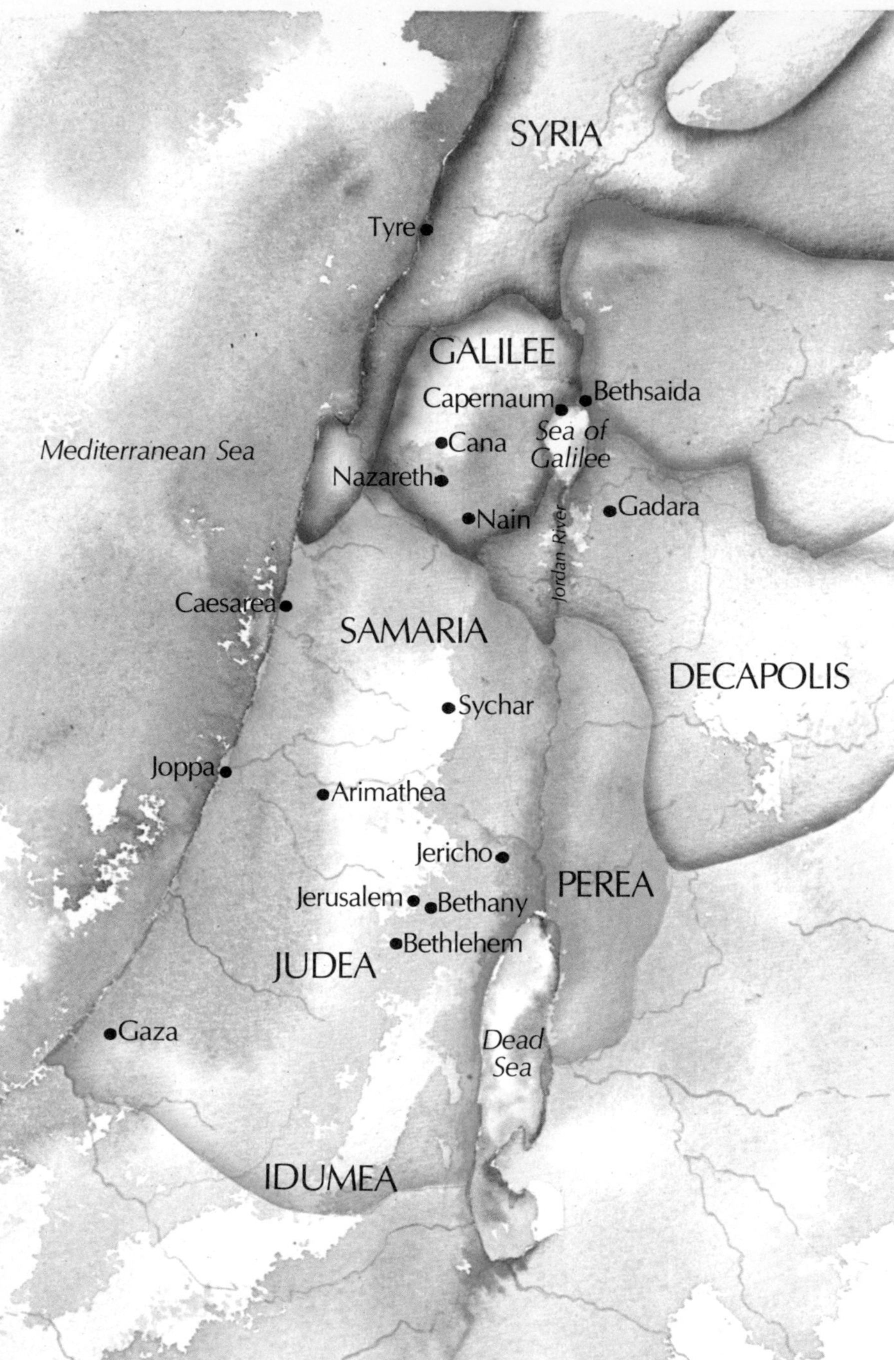
SYRIA
Tyre
GALILEE
Capernaum
Bethsaida
Sea of Galilee
Cana
Mediterranean Sea
Nazareth
Nain
Gadara
Jordan River
Caesarea
SAMARIA
DECAPOLIS
Sychar
Joppa
Arimathea
Jericho
PEREA
Jerusalem
Bethany
Bethlehem
JUDEA
Gaza
Dead Sea
IDUMEA

Palestine in Jesus' Time

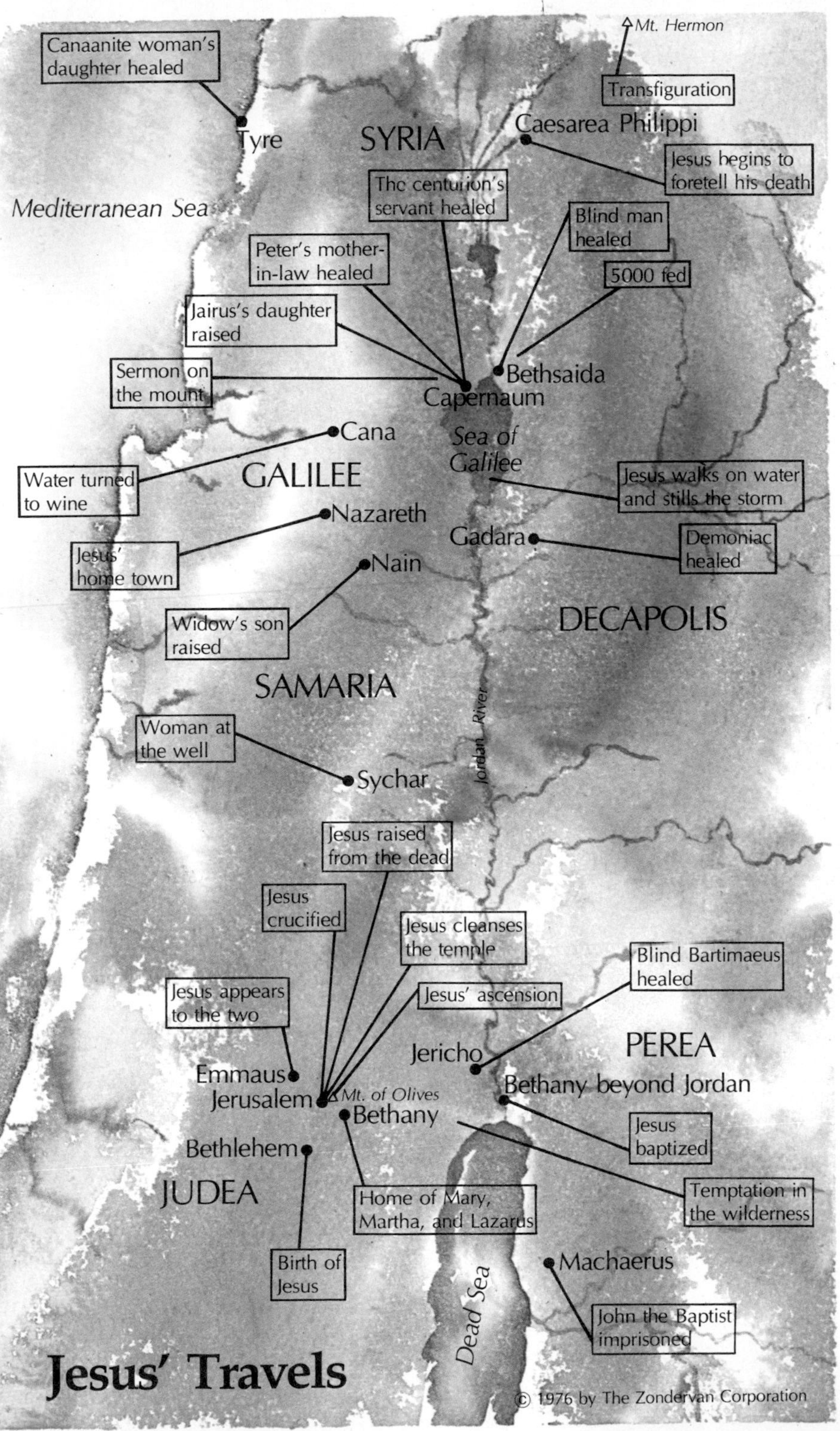
Mt. Hermon
Transfiguration
Canaanite woman's daughter healed
Tyre
SYRIA
Caesarea Philippi
Jesus begins to foretell his death
Mediterranean Sea
The centurion's servant healed
Blind man healed
Peter's mother-in-law healed
5000 fed
Jairus's daughter raised
Sermon on the mount
Bethsaida
Capernaum
Cana
Sea of Galilee
Water turned to wine
GALILEE
Jesus walks on water and stills the storm
Nazareth
Gadara
Demoniac healed
Jesus' home town
Nain
DECAPOLIS
Widow's son raised
SAMARIA
Jordan River
Woman at the well
Sychar
Jesus raised from the dead
Jesus crucified
Jesus cleanses the temple
Blind Bartimaeus healed
Jesus' ascension
Jesus appears to the two
PEREA
Jericho
Emmaus
Jerusalem
Mt. of Olives
Bethany beyond Jordan
Bethany
Jesus baptized
Bethlehem
JUDEA
Temptation in the wilderness
Home of Mary, Martha, and Lazarus
Machaerus
Birth of Jesus
Dead Sea
John the Baptist imprisoned
Jesus' Travels
© 1976 by The Zondervan Corporation

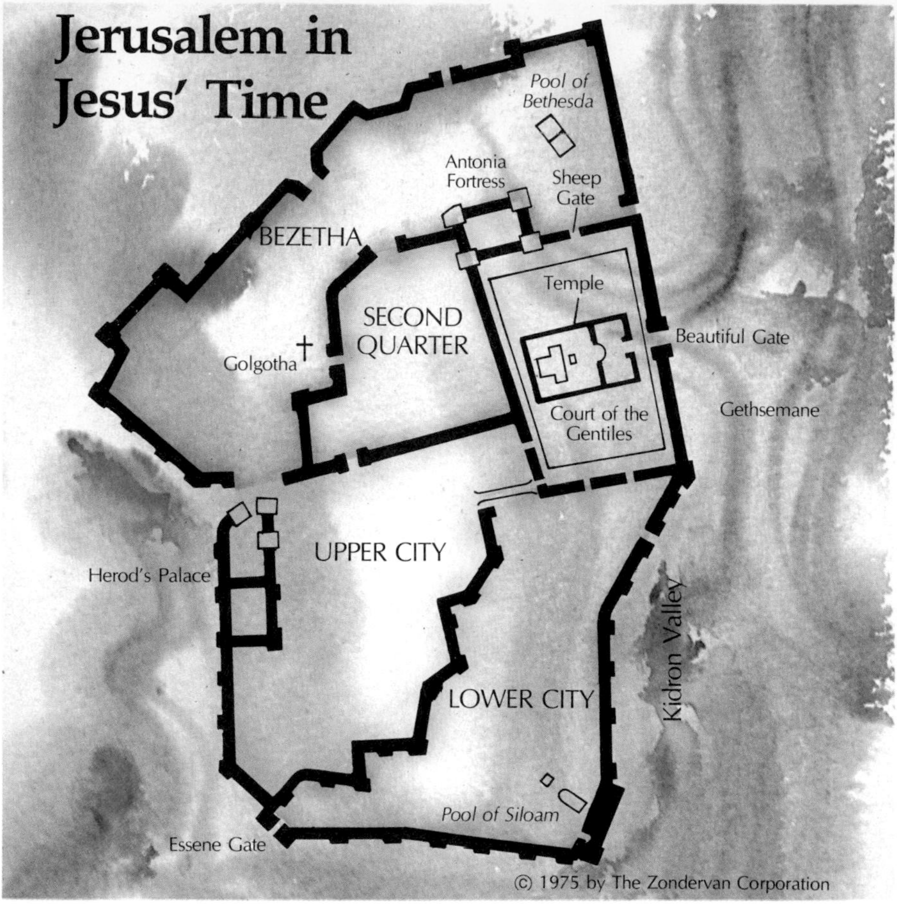

Jerusalem in
Jesus' Time
Pool of
Bethesda
Antonia
Fortress
Sheep
Gate
BEZETHA
Temple
SECOND
QUARTER
Beautiful Gate
Golgotha
Court of the
Gentiles
Gethsemane
UPPER CITY
Herod's Palace
Kidron Valley
LOWER CITY
Pool of Siloam
Essene Gate
© 1975 by The Zondervan Corporation

Herod's Temple
Antonia
Fortress
Priest's
Court
Balustrade
Royal Porch
Court
of the
Gentiles
Altar
Court
of Israel
Court
of the
Gentiles
Women's
Court
Solomon's
Porch
© 1976 by The Zondervan Corporation

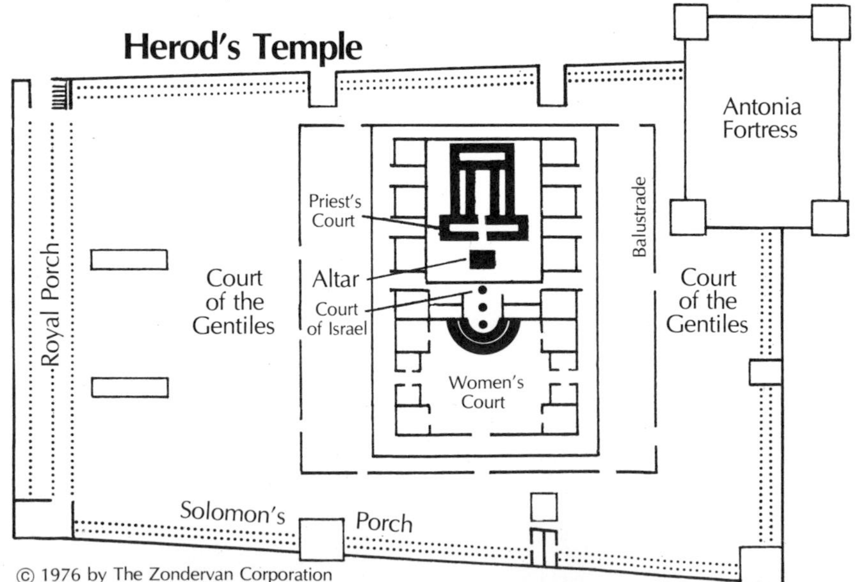

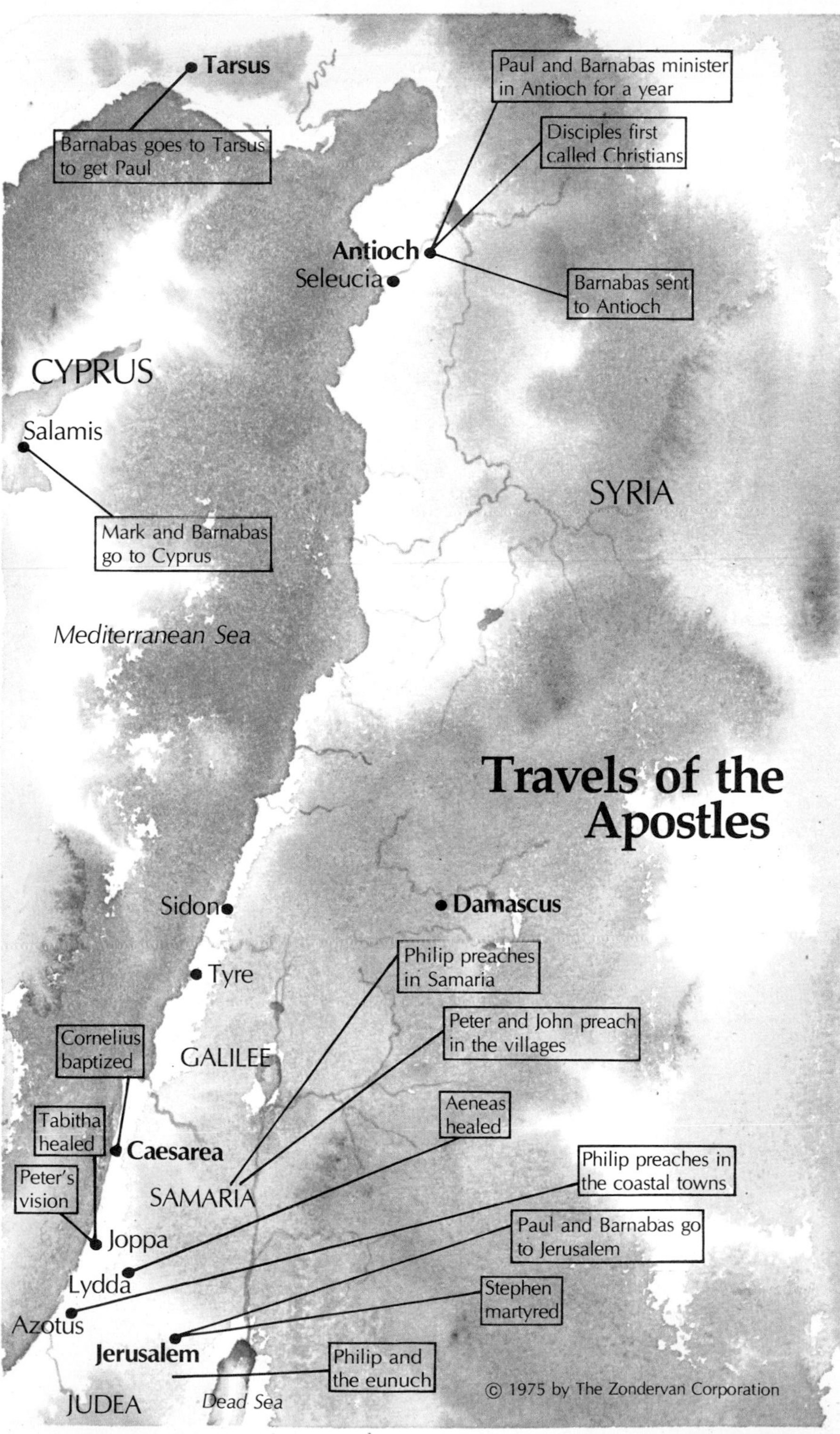
Tarsus
Paul and Barnabas minister in Antioch for a year
Disciples first called Christians
Barnabas goes to Tarsus to get Paul
Antioch
Seleucia
Barnabas sent to Antioch
CYPRUS
Salamis
SYRIA
Mark and Barnabas go to Cyprus
Mediterranean Sea
Travels of the Apostles
Sidon
Damascus
Philip preaches in Samaria
Tyre
Peter and John preach in the villages
Cornelius baptized
GALILEE
Aeneas healed
Tabitha healed
Caesarea
Philip preaches in the coastal towns
Peter's vision
SAMARIA
Paul and Barnabas go to Jerusalem
Joppa
Lydda
Stephen martyred
Azotus
Jerusalem
Philip and the eunuch
© 1975 by The Zondervan Corporation
JUDEA
Dead Sea

Rome
Three Taverns
Forum of Appius
Puteoli
MACEDONIA
Philippi
Thessalonica
Berea
Appolonia
Rhegium
ACHAIA
Corinth
Cenchrea
Athens
Syracuse
MALTA
Phoenix

Paul's Missionary Journeys

Paul's first missionary journey
Paul's second missionary journey
Paul's third missionary journey
Paul's journey to Rome

Black Sea
THRACE
Mysia
GALATIA
CAPPADOCIA
Troas
Mitylene
ASIA
Lydia
Phrygia
Antioch
CHIOS
Ephesus
Colosse
Iconium
Lystra
Miletus
Perga
Derbe
Attalia
Antioch
COS
Cnidus
Patara
Myra
Seleucia
RHODES
CYPRUS
Salamis
Paphos
Sidon
Mediterranean Sea
Tyre
Ptolemais
Caesarea
Jerusalem
Judea
EGYPT

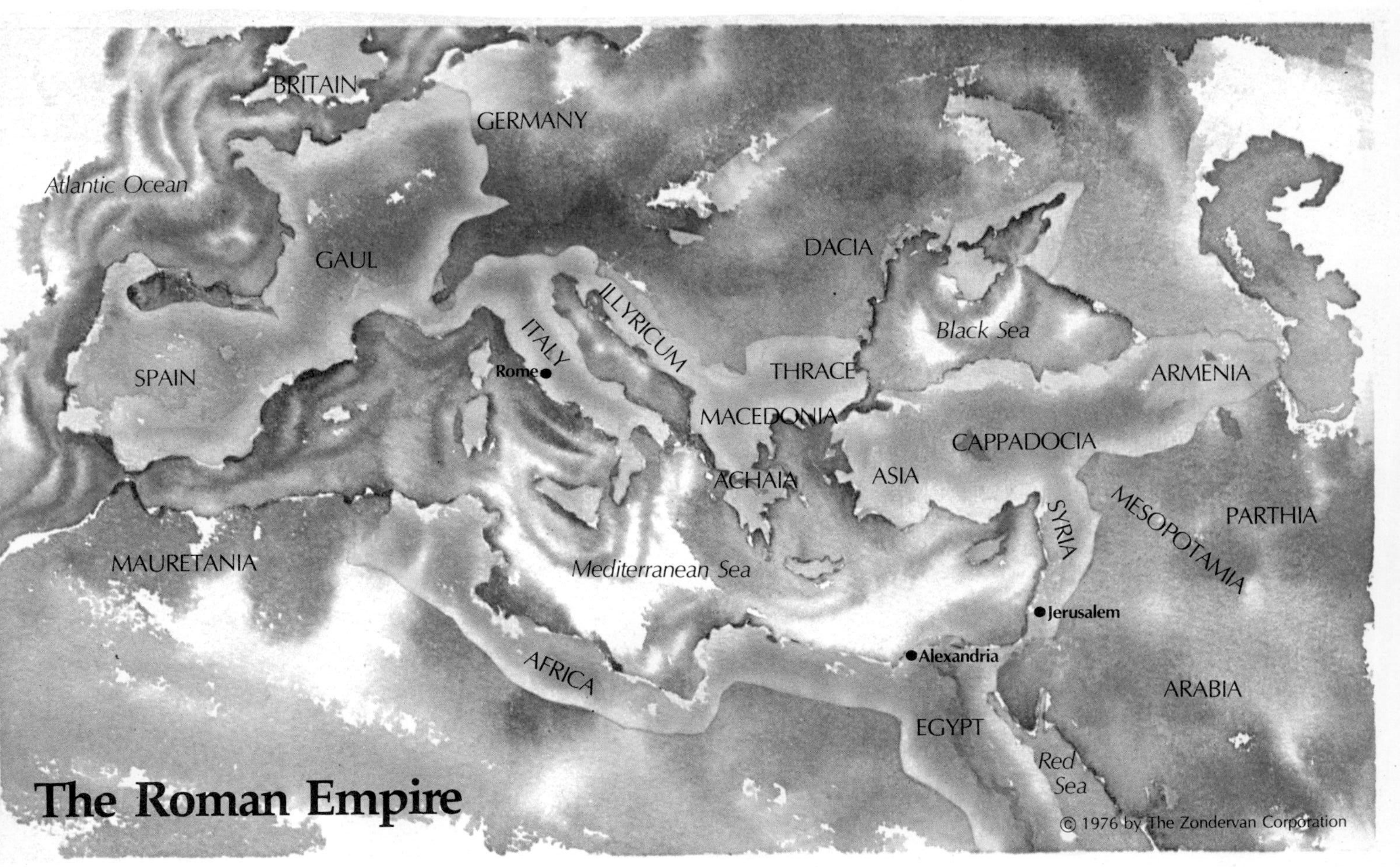
The Roman Empire
BRITAIN
GERMANY
Atlantic Ocean
GAUL
DACIA
ILLYRICUM
ITALY
Black Sea
Rome
SPAIN
THRACE
ARMENIA
MACEDONIA
CAPPADOCIA
ACHAIA
ASIA
SYRIA
MESOPOTAMIA
PARTHIA
MAURETANIA
Mediterranean Sea
Jerusalem
Alexandria
AFRICA
ARABIA
EGYPT
Red Sea
© 1976 by The Zondervan Corporation

9014